I WAS SUPERBLUE

HAPPY HOLIDAYS - THE ESSENTIAL GUIDE TO
THE HOLIDAY OF A LIFETIME, EVERYTIME

WRITTEN BY: SUPERBLUE

ILLUSTRATIONS BY: BOB COOKE

ISBN: 1453801197
ISBN-13: 9781453801192

Library of Congress Control Number: 2010913164
CreateSpace, North Charleston, SC

"As far back as I can remember all I ever wanted to do was entertain"

At the age of five my mum lost me in Tottenham recreational park. After quite some time of panic she heard my voice coming from the open air theatre. The whole family rushed over to find me on stage in a talent competition, singing both male and female parts of the sixties record-

ONE MORE DANCE by ESTHER & ABI OFARIM
(C. Carter) -Philips 329 008 JF
Oh you know the one.....**begins with:**
Darling, go home, your husband is ill
Is he ill, let 'em give him a pill
Oh come, my dear Franz
Just one more dance

and ends .....

I said, the will's to be read
Oh no no, my dear Franz
This is no time to dance
I must go weep for my poor old man

(Check it out on You Tube)

Yes there was this tiny little figure in a grey pullover with the collar of his bestest shirt sticking out from under it like a pair of broken wings, grey knee-length shorts, socks that should have been knee-length but were down around his ankles as usual (Only my nobly knees would have been visible otherwise) and little brown sandals. A bit frump-ish even for 1962 I know, but we had family over from Ireland so I had to look my best, even if they were second best. Well we weren't a very well off family you see and often things were from second hand stores in those days. You just had to make do with what there was so soon after the Second World War. It wasn't a bundle of laughs going to school dressed as a Japanese general I can tell you. Seriously though my mum worked tirelessly against all the odds, which is a whole other story, to ensure I did have decent clothes and we always ate healthily because of her selflessness. So I was clean and smart for my relatives and of course her little soldier gladly wore whatever made her happy. As it turned out on that beautiful hot sunny summer's day I was to look smart for more than just visiting family....I was up on stage in front of a couple of hundred people. I had heard the music ringing out from that fascinating auditorium, of course at the time to me it was just a nice big shiny place where people were having fun, and I had wandered off and gotten up there all by myself. I obviously knew the song from the radio and thought that singing both parts would be a good way of being part of that fun. Such was my innocent excitement that no one thought to ask if I actually had an adult with me and unfortunately I finished the song to thunderous applause...unfortunately? Well that did mean that I had to come down off of the stage where my mum was now waiting...oops! Her face didn't look as happy as all the other peoples, in fact she looked decidedly cross with me. What had I done? I had just sang a song and made people laugh what on earth could be wrong with that? Little does a five year old realise the trauma that a little lost boy puts his mother through. But just as I approached her to ask her what the matter was, little realising how close I was to a 'damped good talking to' to say the least, the nice man who had been talking to me on the microphone on stage came over and said "here you are son here's your prize" and handed me a bag of sweets and a certificate. Turning to my mum with a massive smile on his chubby red face he cheerfully commented "you've got a natural there Missus, he belongs up there" These words certainly had an effect because she grabbed me up in her arms and squeezed me almost to death while, with tears in her eyes, she told me she was very proud of me which in turn made the other ladies in the family group cry too. Of course it had had a profound effect on me too because while I now know he was the compere for that summer show which included the talent show that I had apparently just won? All I knew at the time was that this bubbly real life Hi-De-Hi Ted Bovis type character was extremely happy being up there, he made my mum happy saying I should be up there and everyone in the entire place seemed to be happy with me up there doing my little song and comedy routine. Looking back on it all though I think even at that young and tender age I knew.................... Entertainment here I come.

IT HAD STARTED!

CHAPTER ONE

SO WHO WAS SUPER BLUE?

My best childhood memories are of holidays at Butlins Holiday Camps, watching the Red Coats having so much fun and making thousands upon thousands of people happy. I dreamed of the day when I would wear that jacket so much that it hurt. At the age of fifteen and a half however I joined the RAF my second love being flying and planes. I had been talked into getting a proper job, little realising this was to be the catalyst propelling me right back where I wanted to be. I was very soon running the NAFFI entertainment, Radio station and disco at RAF Wyton in Huntingdon, DJ'ing on radio Wyton 522, and compere in the 'Skyways' club where the main hall was massive. Having a fabulous fully equipped theatre stage it was here, in those very early days, that I was lucky enough to be the compere introducing bands like Shawaddywaddy and Mud onto that stage. Every week hundreds of young ladies were brought by coach from places such as Cambridge, St Neots, Biggleswade and Sandy to the Thursday and Saturday night Discos where I was the DJ. My partners in crime were 'Bogie' Night and 'Noddy' Edmonds both as mad as March hares and between us we got up to some of the most unbelievable and funny stunts.

On one occasion for example we almost burnt the armoury down! Honestly you would not believe it but it was during the execution of one of our grand entries for a squadron party in that unusual venue. There we were dressed as characters from the TV programme 'The Goodies' and had worked out a little dramatic piece to announce our arrival. Noddy entered first as a space monster, Bogie followed a few seconds later as a police officer to apprehend the creature and I followed moments later dressed as one of the players from the film 'Rollerball' to assist? Well it all made sense at the time!!!

But as often happened with our madcap ideas the well planned theory did not exactly translate in practice. On this occasion it all started to go wrong when Noddy fell over because of his costume, Bogie stopped and bent over to help him up just as I came flying in.........only to discover that the metal studded motorbike boots I had borrowed from Bogie (four sizes too big to make me look menacing) meant I could not actually stop on the wooden ramp that led into the room, particularly at the speed I had entered to create this stunning effect. The result was at first very comedic as I flew past my comrades in arms with a look of bewilderment on my face unsurprisingly met with howls of laughter from them as I crashed into a row of trestle tables lovingly laid out by the Flight Lieutenant's wife. Tables laden with all manner of wonderful food and drink, including an enormous punch bowl containing a rich red concoction colourfully festooned with floating fruits. This dutifully took flight decorating the room and all that stood within 100 yards of that particular culinary display, including the Flight Lieutenants wife, as if they were living examples of a Pimms, well it was a fancy dress party!

What was that? Oh how did we nearly burn down the armoury? Oh yes! Well it was their own fault really, firstly for inviting us in the first place, you have to remember this was the disco loving free spirited 70's and we certainly lived up to the free spirited bit so were invited to many a function to liven things up and get the party started. It was a bit like inviting Freddie Star onto your TV chat show, you knew his antics would guarantee you great viewing figures but it was that same lovable clowning around that made things so unpredictable and could cost you your showbiz career.

And to be very honest I think the fatal flaw in this specific set up was when someone decided it would be a good idea to decorate the room from ceiling to floor in old parachutes and then have lit candles on every table, including the little row that had now become my personal landing strip. Unbelievably the room they had chosen to hold a party in and then beautify it with such an explosive design was right next door to the armoury. No need for alarm however my friends because after much panic and mayhem the fire was eventually extinguished to everyone's relief. There still remained the little matter of a large group of fancy dressed party goers with no party to go to. This clearly was an unacceptable situation so as usual we came up with a cunning plan. The three of us set off and liberated the portable disco unit from the NAFFI club and set up in the rather less adorned surroundings of a large empty building somewhere on the airfield and a good time was had by all until the early hours.

I sometimes wonder if we had actually held the first rave without realising it at the time?

As wonderful as this was after five years I still yearned to fulfil my dream of being a Red Coat so a couple of my buddies and I took leave and went to Butlins. You can imagine how upset I was when to my horror this was turned into a nightmare. It seemed like the security just wanted to have a fight with us wherever we went and the Red Coats didn't seem to be having much fun either so nor did the campers (that's what we used to call guests you know). Maybe I had grown out of it? Maybe it was just a kid's dream?

However not being one to give up on such a quest I spent the next two leaves checking out Warners and Pontins respectively. Thankfully they were just like I had remembered holiday camps to be and in particular the entertainments teams. Everybody was enjoying fun and games with things to do all day with great evening entertainment too. The coat's shows being the highlight of the week because, as they had done their jobs properly, it was *your* entertainments team performing. Working so hard for such long hours, they were there when you went to breakfast and still going when you said goodnight as you left for bed. Fantastic!

I left the RAF and auditioned for the big three, Pontins, Warners and Butlins (having returned to Butlins with a friend and happily found that things were back as they should be. It must have been just a glitch). However while the others were great I had decided that the company that would be right for me at that time was Pontins. The auditions were being held at the Empire Ballroom, Leicester Square. I turned up with my fully completed application book and I do mean book. It was pages long full of questions which you had to tick an answer to, such as Do you sing? Can you tap dance? Any ballroom experience? What about magic? Do you have an act? Have you ever been a fire-eater? Had ballet classes? Then there were the sports questions football? Golf? Tennis? Bowls? Swimming? Archery? Shooting? Well in my naivety I had ticked the lot and then I ticked the box for General Bluecoat (you could be a Bluecoat entertainer or general Bluecoat in those days). There were four tables one in each corner of the dance floor with a person sat behind each of them. One after another hopeful youngsters went and sat in front of them trying to sell themselves to get one of the few coveted vacancies of Bluecoat. I watched as a few left with beaming smiles while most were despondent some even rushing out in tears. I was particularly glad that I had ticked general Bluecoat now, as I admired those that had tried for Bluecoat Entertainer, as they were required to get on the stage in this mammoth Mecca of showbiz and perform something. I remember thinking how clever I had been as I would have died on my bum in front of hundreds of prospective future stars. Eventually my name was called and I was directed to a pretty lady with a very warm friendly smile sat at one of the tables. She began by asking me about my age, after all I was twenty one, most people have done a couple of seasons by then and most have even left to get on with ordinary lives or become successful elsewhere in the entertainment industry. I explained about the RAF and totally embellished how good an entertainer I had been (I never did know when to stop) She then went onto question me about the application book and quickly realised I had no idea about almost anything I had ticked. Luckily, although I didn't realise it at the time, she was laughing at the answers I was giving as I tried to dig myself out of an ever increasing hole. Eventually she asked if I could actually do anything at all, not thinking about it, I just blurted out "I am a good comedian". She asked about my singing and I lied and said I was having lessons. The lady asked how the lessons were coming on so I said "I am still a good comedian". Clever ah? Well I thought so until to my horror she then said "go on then" pointing to the stage.

Gulp! "Go on then what? I ticked the general Bluecoat box" desperately trying to back pedal.

"You also ticked every other box in the application so let's see what you can do"

As I walked across the massive dance floor knowing that hundreds of pairs of eyes were watching me just as I had watched all those before me I was sure this would be the longest walk of my life, I was however wrong. I clambered onto the stage absolutely pooing myself as the room sank into a deathly silence I approached the mic. My mind went to jelly along with my legs and I blurted out two of the worst gags ever. Not knowing what else to do I clambered back off the stage and began to make my way back to the table. Now that *was* the longest walk of my life and to the sound of my own footsteps. I sat down again and the lady exasperatedly said "well?" "I'll book the lessons" I cheekily replied. This made her laugh again and also the lady on the next table who had apparently been intrigued as to why her friend was laughing so much at an unfunny comedian. Astonishingly she had seen something in that 21 year old that would change his life forever. I was later to be told "you were just a natural there was something about you that meant you were always going to be a great "Bluecoat".

That lovely lady was Pam Knight and on the other table was the fabulous Bridie Reid.

They were the head of entertainments at Pontins back then preceding the legendary Jan and Jim Kennedy who I also had the pleasure of working for. Strange to think that they are the reason I am writing this book today. I did get an offer of a job from all three companies but went to Pontins where I began a wonderful journey of entertainment, starting with that brilliant company before venturing abroad, returning to run the entertainment at centres in the UK via agents. Finally I paid the ladies back for having confidence in that young nobody and became a cabaret act in my own right (and yes it was stand up comedy). A career that has thus far spanned some thirty years, oh there might just be another book in there somewhere. Having worked alongside the likes of Shane Ritchie, Goz, Gary Wilmot, Larry Grason, Bob Monkhouse and sports stars such as Dennis Taylor, David Wilkie, Cliff Wilson, Duncan Goodhew, Ray Reardon, British Wresters and many more there are a good few humorous anecdotes not to mention great stories about my personal exploits that I could tell.

So why am I telling you about this terrible start?

Why would I want to advertise my uselessness at that time?

Why share the humiliating fact that I had little or no knowledge of what a *holiday camp entertainer* was supposed to do?

Why make it public knowledge that I had no real act to talk of?

Why mention that I just got away with it when all I had was the gift of the gab and a cheeky smile?

And why is the book called *I was Superblue,*

Well that's quite simple really, how can I ask you guests and holidaymakers to trust what I am going to be telling you in this book if you don't know me, where I came from, what my background is, how I got started and what gives me the right to be advising anyone in the first place?

Also how could I instill a confidence into aspiring youngsters and encourage them to believe that they, can not only make it onto a holiday centre entertainments team but, can be the best there is and even become a great Entertainments Manager.

Now while there will be budding stars reading this to enhance their chances of employment within in the industry, it is with you the holidaymaker, the guest, the paying customer, in mind that I will be writing this book so you will know what standard of entertainment I consider those already in the industry should be providing you in return for your hard earned money.

However my unflatteringly awful start can only serve to inspire anyone that really wants to be a holiday camp entertainer or go for any kind of job for that matter. The fact is I had ambition, a longing to be that holiday camp entertainer it's actually not humiliating if you don't know the intricacies of the job so long as you are willing to put the effort in and learn. It doesn't matter that I didn't have an act, remember the camps were my apprenticeship. Did I just get away with the gift of the gab and a cheeky smile? No the reality is that god kindly gave me the most important attribute any holiday camp 'coat' must have, a happy, friendly and outgoing personality.

Superblue? Well as it turned out I was rather a good bluecoat after all. I was exceedingly fortunate that at my first camp I was under the Entertainments Manager Richard Walsh, Richard taught me so much about the art and yes there is an art to successful holiday camp entertainments. It was during this first season that I created a character called 'Superblue'. I spent the whole day, every day, wearing yellow tights, weird coloured swimming trunks and a blue t-shirt with Superblue written on it all under my uniform and carrying a bag with a cape and a silly bird mask everywhere. At various times, Donkey Derby for example, Richard would get the kids to call for Superblue and I would have to go off find somewhere quiet to change very quickly and pop up as **Superblue.** It was so successful that the next season Pontins had a Superblue drawing and colouring competition at all their camps.

Was I a great holiday camp entertainer now? - No but I was learning from the best!

WHAT HAPPENED?

Luckily I was to build a successful career out of those humble beginnings becoming an Entertainments Manager at Pontins in a short space of time. I reluctantly left that wonderful company after five years, having worked at many of their camps and even being used as a 'trouble-shooter' for them during this time. However I needed to expand my knowledge of working abroad and so managed entertainment at holiday centres such as the famous Club Tropicana in Majorca (I could write a whole other book with this season alone taking up a few chapters). My reputation as Entertainments Manager was now such that I became highly sort after by entertainment agents back in the UK commanding, what was at that time, a fairly large salary. This meant I was to spend several very happy years being employed by holiday companies wanting to make significant profits by keeping their guests on the centre that season and returning the next. While all this was going on a parallel career was taking shape and more and more I was to supplement my earnings as a stand up comedian. I am therefore fortunate to have firsthand knowledge of the workings of holiday centre entertainment and the expectations of the guest, including as a child, the standard of entertainment that the entertainments team should be aiming to give them and the professional manner in which the Entertainments Manager must ensure it is carried out and finally as a visiting cabaret knowing the pleasure of performing at a centre with a good team because the audience is already happy as well as the pain of working a room at an unhappy camp.

SO WHY WRITE THIS BOOK?

Over the past few years I have been known to comment on the declining standards and values of entertainment and entertainers at holiday centres. Usually however I just annoy my mates by winging on about it for a while and then forgetting it until next time. That is until now! Due to the recuperation of a family member following an operation I spent two weeks at a centre owned by a holiday company that is a household name. I am sad to say I was absolutely appalled by the entertainment programme, team and particularly the Manager. Speaking to the team at this centre I was to discover that these young people were arriving at this and many other centres with virtually no training whatsoever. I had seen for myself that the Entertainments Manager at this centre was next to useless but have generally found the standard to be dropping at others as have family and friends I have consulted. The assistant Entertainments Manager was the only one with any experience and consequently had to work her heart out day and night to keep an entertainments programme of sorts running (although it truly was dreadful). She was quite magnificent in fact and tried to fit in words of advice and training where she could. As I was leaving a new Entertainments Manager arrived so at least the company agreed with my analysis of the situation. A situation which means that: People joining some entertainment teams these days are not being trained to any kind of standard because the entertainers already there haven't been trained. So when new people arrive they are never going to have the benefit of learning from experienced Entertainments Managers or colleagues and so the vicious circle goes on. The result is that experience and knowledge is haemorrhaging from the trade and is not being replaced.

I complained so bitterly about the atrocious state of the entertainment and entertainments team it drove my family and friends mad. So much so that more than one of them snapped at me to stop complaining and do something about it.

What could I do? I couldn't train everyone myself could I? Could I?

Even if I could do that I couldn't let every guest at every centre know if the entertainment they are receiving is the quality and standard they should rightly expect and in fact should absolutely be demanding now could I? Well......possibly.........maybe.... What if I were to write a book? A sort of informative yet entertaining read for guests and entertainers incorporating the sort of advice I would put in a manual with interesting anecdotes that impart knowledge and the basic tools needed. Knowledge that you the guest will be armed with next time you go on holiday to your favourite destination or somewhere completely new. Well I did write such a book with insights into the workings of holiday entertainment and that of the 'coat' and in particular the exploits of **Superblue**.

I have to tell you though that I thought about calling this........
'The book that they didn't want you to read'

Why? Well I have approached a number of companies and directors within those companies with the idea of 'Superblue', my thoughts on such things as training and even sent them excerpts from the book. I received a variety of reactions from polite "we don't think it's for us" to people such as those in a very highly established entertainment company saying that they would look into it and get back to me, after many exchanges by email in which they seemed interested, but I'm afraid to say they never did. I think it fair to mention Mr Andy Edge here, famous for his decisive and positive action as a Holiday company director following his appearance on 'Undercover Boss', because he did indeed like what he read and passed the package I had sent him onto one of those companies who put entertainment and teams into UK holiday centres among others.

But the worst in my opinion was the absolute ignorance of the now ex-owner of Pontins to even have the common decency to acknowledge receipt of the many letters, emails and copies from the manuscript I sent him, even though his P.A. kindly informed me he had received them. I wasn't going to name and shame but thought better of it so there you have it. I was genuinely upset when my dear beloved Pontins went into liquidation following that. I only hope the company can be saved for the sake of all those campers yet to enjoy the thrill of a fab Pontins holiday. As I update this paragraph to the book ready for publication I currently await a response from the new Pontins owner, however it is now the 10th of August 2011 and still no word so we will see what happens? I still wish Pontins well and would love to go onto www.SUPERBLUE HAPPY HOLIDAYS.com and start to read great guest reviews again.

So I will let **_you_** decide if they and others really did **not** want you to have firsthand knowledge of what I honestly believe you should be getting for your money and indeed how they should be employing the right people and training them to provide you with first class holiday entertainment....AT NO EXTRA COST!

I thought to myself that if they are not going to take any interest in what I believe would be improvements to their guest's holiday enjoyment then I should arm those very guests with that knowledge. Those guests, your good self included of course, will be in a very desirable position should you wish to make a complaint to the Entertainments Manager (not that a lot of them seem to know much about entertainment these days) or even the camp manager (I explain why I still call them camps in a little while).

So here it is! - Your very own personal fun filled book packed with information to guide you through, but through what I hear you ask?

Well as a **_guest_** you will know exactly what those involved in the holiday entertainment business should be providing you with and the standard of entertainment you must demand for your money!

As for those of you who are reading this or have already read 'Tales of Superblue' and are in holiday entertainment or management you will, now, be only too well aware of what I have told your guests about it.

Such as an entertainments team must:

- Be professional and keep their guests happy and entertained at all times in all weathers
- Know the basic principles and etiquette to ensure they are a successful entertainer or manager
- Be able to construct and run a variety of entertainment programmes
- Organise and devise all types of competitions
- Script, choreograph and perform shows and cabarets
- Compere confidently
- Know the art of stage management
- Know about relevant laws and where to look them up
- Be aware of health and safety

For those wishing to enter the trade I explain:

- How to become a holiday centre entertainer
- How to choose which company to work for
- How to progress from the camps to be a cabaret act or even a star

WHO WAS THIS BOOK WRITTEN FOR?

Well this book is strictly for you, the holiday centre or hotel guest.

However it has become apparent to me that that it could be of great importance to a variety of people for differing reasons.

For example:

You lovely Guests, Campers, Holidaymakers, Tourists (i.e. The Paying Public)
Why will you all have a copy? For nostalgic reading to remind you of how good it used to be? To make sure the entertainers are giving you the professional package that you deserve on holiday? To know the rules of competitions and things such as bingo?

Of course all of the above will be good reasons for you having your own copy so sit back relax and enjoy the book, the book that I '**DO**' want you to read. Because while I do lay bare what you should be getting from your entertainments team and indeed holiday company I also tell a tale or two along the way that I hope will result in you wearing a grin from ear to ear.

I would be very grateful if you would bear in mind one little thing when you have finished reading however............

And that is a *good* holiday camp entertainer is worth their weight in gold, a *great* one is priceless! So please don't forget to look after them, they work long, hectic, energetic sometimes stressful hours. Please be kind, helpful, caring and appreciative. After all they are mostly young people just doing their best to make you happy. Of course that does not mean you should not complain if they are not very good and at least trying their hardest to be even better.

Also:

Those who want to become a holiday centre entertainer

As a guide in the first instance of course, but also informing prospective employers they have read it will be a valuable enhancement to their prospects of getting the job.

Entertainers already employed at centres

Will find this an excellent reference book and be aware of what is expected of them by management and of course their guests.

Entertainments Managers

Not only as a personal guide but will ensure they are aware of what their teams now know and expect from them. Not to mention what you now know and will be demanding.

Holiday centre owners and general managers

Should always have a copy in order that they are fully aware of the extent, calibre and variety of professional programme an Entertainments Manager and team should be providing for their guests. Happy guests remain on site spending their money at the bars, restaurants, takeaways and shops etc.

CHAPTER ONE 'A'

A NEW BEGINNING?

It's one of life's big questions

If you could start it all again would you?

Something that I must admit I had struggled with, in fact had a battle raging inside of me when it came to rewriting the beginning of I was Superblue!

Should I start it over, as if I was writing it for the first time that day?

When the actual truth is I began writing it three and a half years ago.

Should I deceive you right from the outset?

What sort of person would that make me?

What sort of relationship could I expect us to have?

How could I ask you to trust me when I tell you this is what you should be expecting, nay demanding from your entertainment team?

And...........

Why did it take so long to even contemplate a new beginning?

Well truth be told about six months after starting 'I was Superblue' for the first time I went to an adult only holiday centre only to discover that the quality of service, shows, general attitude and lack of enthusiasm of the entertainments team was no better than my previous experience which I had already documented in those early chapters, in other words part of the 'original beginning'. But I found this experience even more unforgivable because that team didn't even have to consider the intricacies of family entertainment. They just had to please adults who, over many years had become primed with the knowledge of what to expect at a holiday camp. Shortly after that I visited another couple of family sites and just began to resign myself to the fact that this was 'just how it is now', this is what entertainment teams are these days, this is the standard that the British holidaymaker has come to expect and is 'putting up with'. This poor quality of entertainment and so called holiday fun is what we have ended up dishing out after years of holiday centre owners and management devaluing our entertainment teams was here to stay.

Dejected and downhearted I stopped writing.

What would be the point?

If parts of the industry have decided that under-trained, unenthusiastic and unprofessional people with 'let's just make do' attitudes are the standard of 'coat' they are happy to represent them........

Who am I to fight against that? Who am I to attempt to instil hope and pride into newcomers to the trade? Who am I to try and re-ignite the fire and passion in those already in the business? Who am I to be informing guests that they rightly ought to be expecting a higher standard of quality from their holiday entertainment team and by geepers should be demanding it too? Who am I to be telling anybody about this wonderful way of life that some have been lucky enough to embark upon and what they jolly well owe their guests in return? Who? Superblue I suppose?

Does that make me special?

No not at all but crucially I am still full of the passion, the fire and enthusiasm that I had when I set out as Superblue and am in the enviable position of having firsthand knowledge of the trade from all its aspects, from desperately wanting to be a 'coat', loving being that 'coat', the rigors of an Entertainments Manager to that of a visiting cabaret artiste and of course as a guest.

So did I rewrite the beginning? No! 'Chapter one' is where it all began three a half years ago so to preserve my integrity and cling on to your trust it proudly remains 'Chapter one'.

So what is this then? This, my friend is quite simply the tale of the reawakening of that passion in me, the desire to impart this knowledge onto you and the inspiration to complete this book which is now especially for you the paying guest, holidaymaker, tourist and camper. It's the reason for pulling out those dusty pieces of paper containing eighteen chapters already penned all that time ago. The motivation to rewrite these chapters with a new flare, hope and invigoration, the impetus to write the remaining chapters in the honest belief that this is now, so, worth it and can actually make a difference. So what is it that has caused this eruption of enthusiastic exuberance? What could have made such an impact on me that I went out bought a tatty old note pad and started furiously writing with a head full of happiness and a heart bursting with exhilaration? The Caribbean that's what!

The Caribbean?

Yes or to be more precise the entertainment teams where I was staying at the time. (Known as animation teams as they are in a number of places around the world, for example as the Entertainments Manager at Club Tropicana, Majorca my title became Animation Chef)

The people running these animation teams have taken the entertainment blueprint and ethos from British holiday camps of thirty years ago and masterfully brought them into the 21st century with style, vigour, professionalism, passion, colour, razzamatazz, flare, excitement, boundless energy and above all a SMILE!!! It was the most fabulous reminder of how it could be done.....NO! let me rephrase that!! It was a brilliant 'in my face wakeup call'. This **_is_** how it **_should_** be done.

It is like stepping back in time to my first day as a Blue Coat (more about that later in the book though) these marvellous people entertain their guests non-stop day and night. They are constantly happy while nothing is too much trouble and all that they do is carried out with a sense of effortless fun and cheerfulness. The evening shows are sophisticated, superbly choreographed, stage managed, costumed and performed. These are preceded by a fun competition each evening that really does harp back to yesteryear in its basic make up, well for us Brits anyway. Because not only were we loving it they were thrilling American, Canadian, German, Dutch and so many other guests from around the world to whom it all appeared to be a somewhat novel concept. However their mastery at working this multi-cultural, multi-linguistic, multi-aged audience is indeed thrilling to behold.

Is this the only area of the world where this kind of entertainment still exists? Of course not, there are companies in Europe that have caught on to the fact that quality entertainment and customer service means repeat customers as well as an increasing custom base as new 'paying' guests arrive all the time. Brought there by the most powerful medium of all..................Word of mouth!!!

Take 'Magic Life' for instance, it is not so long ago that I performed and stayed at one of their resorts in Bulgaria. The experience was so good that I have told literally hundreds of people about the company since then. If just 1% of those people tried a 'Magic Life' holiday and having had the same experience told another hundred people and just 1% of them tried a 'Magi.......Well you get the idea.

No the Caribbean resorts are not the only ones doing it but they are particularly good at it! And whilst on the face of it they may appear to be playing catch up on the 'fun competition' front as far as customer service and quality holiday centre entertainment are concerned they are most definitely streets ahead on anything I have seen in the UK of late.

So you can see why I felt the need 'the need for speed' oh sorry wrong film, I did try to write something clever and fitting here but my intellect and sense of irony let me down on this occasion so I thought I would just slip in a little ditty, a quotation on writing to get me out of trouble so.....

"Write a wise saying and your name will live forever" by anonymous.

Now that's a true quotation and no one does actually know who wrote it...irony or what? I'm not sure that did in fact help me out of a tight spot though. Oh well back to the plot....and all joking aside you can see why I absolutely needed to start writing again can't you? It just completely blew me away and reinforced why I had picked my pen up in the first place. Why I felt it so important to write a book that told paying guests, old and new, what they have every right to expect from their holiday entertainment not just abroad but also right here in the UK. A book that may even inspire newcomers to the business and teach them what it means to be part of a great entertainments team. Remind and at times educate holiday companies that good quality entertainment is not an extra cost but actually an essential element to continued profits. So I began writing again, writing a book, writing a positive book, writing........**'I was Superblue'**

I say this is a positive book and it is most definitely that! It positively highlights how excellent entertainment can so easily be achieved. Of course it would not be fair to suggest that all UK holiday centres are neglecting this very important aspect of their business, indeed I have in the past few months attended the Warner hotel at Sinah Warren and it was run very well with the resident Entertainments being fab. However the bad experience at an adult centre I mentioned previously is owned by that same company so as you can see it can vary from centre to centre, hotel to hotel or park to park etc, even within the same chain. If you are a guest at a well run holiday centre or hotel you will be only too well aware of how good it is and appreciate it even more after reading this book. You will, however, be armed with the fact that the management of these centres, parks, resorts, villages and hotels will now be only too well aware that you and every other guest is judging them on these standards. They won't be able to relax and rest on their laurels until they are providing the quality entertainment that you will be demanding from now on. On the other hand they can bask in the knowledge that you fully recognise how hard they are working to deliver this when they do get it right.

To be very fair, following a letter from me recently, Warners were absolutely brilliant in returning the entertainment at one of their centres back to its former magnificence. Head office went to the trouble of informing me that they took what I had to say very seriously and were looking into the situation. I was then called by the Entertainments Manager from that centre and we went over each of the points I had raised regarding their entertainment one by one. They responded by employing an entertainments team specifically for that centre, as they had split one between two, as well as bringing back a key member of the team, while bolstering up their daytime team and programme and even changed the times the resident band played in the evenings.

This is some of the greatest customer service I have ever witnessed, for which they must be hugely congratulated.

It does of course also tend to prove that I do actually know what I am talking about and you can trust what I have to say, after all..........**They did**

So this new beginning is especially for you my friend, now that the fire has been rekindled within me. So let me continue to invoke my passion for great quality entertainment to inform you of, what I believe, you should be getting and indeed demanding for you money.

CHAPTER TWO

WHAT IS A HOLIDAY CAMP?

Well to be fair Camp is an old fashioned term now. When we were kids and indeed when I started out we went to Holiday Camps. However in the early eighties the corporate image was all important and companies desperately tried to steer away from that old Hi-Di-Hi stereotype of holiday, where campers would be more than happy to be woken at some unearthly hour by a youthful over exuberant Red, Blue or Green Coat announcing over a really loud scratched record via the 'Tannoy' system that breakfast was ready. Oh and yes that was another thing that had to go 'Campers' in those days that's what we would call the guests, the client, the customer or the holiday maker. In fact at that time I worked for a company, as did many of my friends in others, that banned the Entertainers from using the words Camp or Camper and Hi-Di-Hi was a definite no no! I for one have very fond memories of growing up dying for my one week a year holiday when I would be woken for another day of magical fun with the Red Coats at Butlins. The mad enthusiasm of "Good morning campers", scratchy record and the pounding of feet as people rushed along the chalet lines to the toilet block for a quick wash before going to breakfast were all an integral part of the thrill, and the day hadn't even started yet. Of course things have to change and we all have to move with the times and so these days the modern holiday camps are called Holiday Parks, Centres, Villages, Sites, Resorts, Clubs and even Hotels. But I can tell you right here and now, that no matter what the title of the venue you are going to be staying at, the principles of professional holiday entertainment should be the same and what I am going to reveal to you in this book is exactly what budding entertainers should be taught to ensure that they shine in any coloured 'coat' at any camp. The basic fact is that us guests still want to have fun, still want quality entertainment, still want value for money and above all still want our entertainments team providing it (More about that later).

Throughout the book I will use a variety of terms such as centre, park, resort, hotel or village just to keep everybody happy. You just change the title to whichever one you like best. I mentioned chalet lines just then didn't I, well believe it or not even the biggest camps had rows of chalets or little huts some two stories high one on top of another and, although some still do, these didn't even have a toilet never mind a bath or shower. You had to gather up your towel, washing and shaving kit etc and head off to the toilet block. If you were lucky you would have one about half way down the line from you so not too far to run especially if it was cold or raining. You could have been a little unlucky and it seemed miles away or really unlucky and it was right outside your chalet. Why was that unlucky? Remember I said not even a toilet? That's an awful lot of people constantly frowing back and forth by your chalet. Imagine the end of the night when copious amounts of alcohol had been consumed, it was sometimes as busy, noisy and at times as rowdy as the club house, ballroom or towards the end of that era even the disco, oh yes it's not as long ago as you may think.

The accommodation for the most part these days is generally very good with a wide variety of choice. Some centres are all chalets while others are all caravans or even hotels or hotel style buildings with apartments. The number of parks that offer a mixture of these styles has been on the increase for some years and is a trend that looks set to stay. They are of course now all en-suite with many having excellent self catering and audio visual entertainment facilities as standard. In comparison there are very few touring caravan or camping (I mean with tents) sites that offer substantial entertainment in the package.

The way we take holidays has changed over the years also and has meant companies now offer more than just the traditional one or two week summer holidays. With most centres being open year round guests can take weekend or mid-week breaks enjoy specialist events and stay on a full board, half board or self catering basis. Full and half board being much better for the entertainments team as you will see later.

Another major difference in the way some holiday centres operate is the ownership principle. Instead of relying on guests returning year after year and the constant advertising for new clientele some companies have adopted a new strategy. They actually employ sales teams to sell the ownership of a chalets or caravans on the site. The owner then pays ground rent and is entitled to certain extras and priorities and of course will attend that centre on a regular basis, some spending every weekend at their camp. It is possible to make a profit as an owner by renting your caravan or chalet out to others or at the very least make it pay for itself (More about owners in a later chapter). But as an owner you should be one of the people most interested in the quality of entertainment being first rate. The reason for this is simple, even if you don't use the facilities as much you still want to be able to entice the best customers at a decent price when letting your caravan or chalet out. You need repeat custom and good word of mouth sales to be sure of this. I promise you anyone staying at a camp such as the one I will be telling you about soon would definitely be spreading the word about booking a holiday there....and trust me they won't be words you'd like to hear.

A manager of a site should be seriously concerned if owners aren't coming out and using the onsite facilities. It means, amongst other things, they're probably not up to scratch, interesting or updated enough, shows aren't changed infrequently and the staff are unfriendly. But what they definitely are doing is..............LOSING THEM MONEY!!!

Holiday camps work and they work well because they offer a lot of different things to a lot of different people but generally the main things are value for money, fun and laughter for all ages, entertainment provided on site **free of charge**, parents relax in the knowledge that the children are having a great time in safety, there is rarely any real trouble with good security being present in the main and you know when you come to think of it they have quite simply become a great British institution.

It is important to remember the vital secret ingredient however, and that is that a good number of us guests want to get up let our hair down have fun making fools of ourselves while the rests want to watch us do it. I tell entertainers to always bear this in mind and they won't go far wrong.

The size and style of centres can differ greatly each having its own personality although some are part of a large corporate franchise all will retain some individual character and you will have favourites for different reasons.

Most will consist of all or a combination of a family bar or ballroom for family entertainment, children's club, theatre, cinema, an adult room which speaks for itself, swimming pool, aqua fun pool, games rooms and a sports field all of which are part of the entertainers world and we will cover in later chapters. Even hotels or hotel style centres will have a semblance of these facilities.

The facilities can depend of the size of the company, i.e. Butlins has great theatres, nightclubs, kids clubs and fairgrounds amongst other things in large centres, Pontins offers a number of different holidays to suite different families during the day and generally have at least a ballroom and adult show-bar at each village while Warners are adult only resorts and hotels but like the others they offer entertainment during the day and evening. There are of course many others Haven, British Holidays, Bourne Leisure, Parkdene (some former Weststar holidays) Holiday Parks, Hoseasons, Potters, Park Resorts etc etc.

You must not forget however that there are many lovely independent camps too. I spent some of my favourite seasons at a number of these. They can of course suffer from not having the financial backing of the large companies but on the other hand the guests that go to them are, in my experience, happy with the facilities and enjoy the less formatted style that many offer and stay loyal to that park returning time and time again. It can be a very liberating experience for the entertainer also, in particular the Entertainments Manager. Without a head office always breathing down their neck and in some cases constantly pushing them to make more and more money at the expense of providing good entertainment, indeed at times their creative talents and resourcefulness are tested to the limit with the budget they have to work to. Oh fond memories indeed. For example Romney Sands in Romney, funny enough, and Whitecliff Bay on the Isle of Wight are two of those where I was happy and really enjoyed being the Entertainments Manager. Both had very different centre management styles, Romney had a lovely lady, Ex Pontins, camp manager who really knew her stuff and was very approachable which in turn made for a friendly happy team, and not just the entertainments. It was excellent having an ex Pontins lady in charge, a manager that understood what the running of the entertainment team entailed, what was required by the manager to run that team and how hard that very small team of wonderful people worked. I say wonderful and that's not overstating the point. It was one of the smallest teams, if not the smallest, that I ever had to run an entertainments programme with, having been requested by an agent to take on this post to see what could be done with it. Having such a small team meant that choosing the right few would be key, to its success, if indeed it was going be a success.

That small group of individuals came together as a team worked their socks off for me and well and truly pulled off something very special that year. I was so proud of them. Whitecliff was a family owned and run camp and I do mean family run. There was the grandfather of us all. He was just a superb man in his seventies then and that was back in the 90's, but what a man, a fabulous man. He was nobody's fool and knew what was going on everywhere all of the time. He was there first thing in the morning and many a time at the end of the day too. His son was second in command and he was a more robust gentleman to say the least. But we had a good working relationship once I put on my first show with my new team at his camp. So much so that he invited the mayor to pay a special visit for a performance. This was a significant thing for someone to do on the Isle of Wight and I was immensely humbled by the gesture. But because it was their camp, their, business and their livelihood they watched every single penny so as the Entertainments Manager I really had to prove my worth every single step of the way every single day. This, however, is where you really do learn to appreciate how the cost of entertainment has to be balanced with the amount of custom that it generates for the business. It shows why the men and women whose job it is to abstract as much profit as they can from every aspect of that business need to be convinced that you are indeed keeping the optimum number of their guests in the venues and spending at all times. It can be difficult to persuade private holiday camp owners to invest enough in your department to allow you to do this so I advise any prospective Entertainment Managers to make sure they are aware of what is being offered in any contract they are thinking of taking on at one of these centres. I particularly tell them that if they're not happy with the deal and crucially the support offered, try to renegotiate to begin with but be prepared to turn down an unrealistic offer if they have to. It can be very arduous attempting to shake off a bad reputation and could affect their prospects for some time. Most significantly I remind them that it is their guests that's, you and me, that will suffer while still paying through the nose for our holiday.

If you are holidaying abroad of course there are obvious differences, the weather for a start, water sports, beaches, all inclusive basis and very likely all male or female groups but believe me if your entertainments team sticks to the basics, and I will be letting you in on those secrets in this book, they will win over the most difficult of guests (yes you've met them haven't you), conquer the most challenging and at times stressful of situations. I know I have done it!

Club Tropicana in Majorca for instance was to become quite a challenge in so many ways. An ex Pontinental camp it had both elements of management style described above. There was the owner who retained 55% share in the camp no matter whom else was involved and he did run this place with military proficiency. Many of the staff were family members from all over Spain but one word from this man and everyone jumped and I do mean everyone. In fact the only question you asked was "how high?" I make him sound like a real big ogre, don't I? Well to be fair that's far from the truth he was a short man for a start, but there was nothing demure about his ability and definitely not his presence. You certainly knew when he was in your vicinity and commanded respect from us all by his professionalism, work ethics, knowledge and humility as opposed to demanding it because he was the owner. He did take me for a very early morning stroll once where we inspected the site together before anyone else was up and about. Except for one lone barman who, he had instructed to open the pool bar on conclusion of our evaluation of the beautiful whitewashed camp. I have to confess that the theme tune from the godfather was running through my mind at times as I wondered why I had been ordered to be up so early and was wandering around this peacefully silent resort with the man himself. I was to be pleasantly surprised however because as we sat at the deserted pool bar sipping espresso he calmly dropped into the conversation that he was very happy with the way things were going in the entertainment department and that I was to receive a mid-season bonus, and a pretty penny it was too. Just by way of proving the point re his professionalism and love for that marvellous resort and his unswerving desire that his guests should have nothing but the very best at all times, I take great pleasure in recounting the absolutely true tale of the night we had a rain storm from the Sahara. Apparently not as uncommon as you might think, these storms carry grains of sand in each droplet. Well, Senior Domingo not being content that our guests would understand why their lovely whitewashed bungalows where a yucky yellowish brown colour when they woke in the morning got all the staff out of bed in the middle of the night, including me and my pal Nick, and we set about repainting the entire place. We whitewashed every chalet, the main building and outbuildings. Surprisingly we managed to finish the whole lot before a single guest surfaced from slumber so when they did emerge into the glorious Majorcan early morning sunlight all they saw was the same gleaming white walls that were there when they went to bed. Nothing to shout about, no big shakes, just a magnificent example of customer service….fantastic!! I learnt so much about this aspect of our trade from being part of the management team there. I did say both styles of management though didn't I and indeed there was. You see they also had a lovely lady manageress and guess what……………yes indeedy she was ex Pontins to boot. It was very reassuring having her at the helm, in reality they did sort of run it together although he owned it and his word was final however she was so well respected by him and without a doubt the rest of us managers and department heads that little was ever decided without her endorsement. We will discuss agents towards the end of the book but it may be just as well to point out here that it was while working at this holiday centre an agent attempted to ride rough-shot over myself, other entertainment staff and, unfortunately for him, the camp owner. Because having acted in, what was deemed, an inappropriate manner in this regard he was required to leave the centre, having arrived unannounced in the first place, never to set foot in it again. So you budding entertainers please do bear this in mind when you get to read that chapter. There are agents and then there are agents! I said at the beginning of this paragraph that it was to prove challenging in so many ways and this was of course one of them. Others were just part and parcel of the natural learning curve of taking up a post abroad. Multinational guests meant employing multinational entertainments staff. The language barrier to overcome, the cultural differences of the various nationalities and their varied expectations were just a few of the aspects that needed to be mastered as this was my first foray into this uncharted world. Thankfully I was to emerge at the end of a very long season with dignity and yet another unexpected bonus payment from that charismatic and charming man, Senior Domingo.

TRUE FRIENDS

You never know when you are going to meet good people in this world but I can guarantee that on this journey I definitely came across some weird and wonderful characters. It was during a couple of these seemingly more difficult of situations that I was extremely fortunate to have met my two best lifelong friends.

At Romney Sands the incomparable Phil Hallam, who I had previously met when we both worked for Pontins …can you see a pattern forming here? Well anyway Phil was the bars manager running the pub and entertainment venue connected to the centre and he firstly became a great working partner helping me to put a variety of entertainment packages together for our guests at that holiday centre. He was always there for me no matter what, any little problem I needed solving he would come up with some game plan or other even for my maddest of plans and somehow with his energetic enthusiasm, logical mind and out and out boundless energy and love of life we would bring that plan to life. He never failed to support me in any show or cabaret, running his venue with supreme professionalism with knowledge and understanding of the needs of an Entertainments Manager and an entertainments team. But it was in my private life that I was to enjoy the company of this most extraordinary friend that season. You see though all the long hours, hard and sometimes stressful work we became the best of fiends getting up to some fantastic antics. We have some absolutely hysterical stories from our time there including the incident when I caused a full scale nuclear alert only to discover the beautifully greenish blue fluorescent water you could see for miles along our bit of coast, with the power-station sitting on the horizon, was in fact not escaping nuclear waste but millions of tiny jelly fish that had just been born. Or the day I kept winning at Folkestone races after horses seemed to keep talking to me in the paddock or Phil's brilliant charity walk with Ian Botham. My surprise birthday party with just about every cabaret, band, coat and staff member from the area not to mention my family, secretly hidden away for the day, in attendance will always be a very special piece of nostalgia for me and I will never cease to be amazed at that particular illustration of his power to make things happen. My ungainly charity swim from the Isle of Wight to the mainland after a boast that I could beat my lifeguards when I was slightly inebriated and so many other escapades were what made life so much fun, it was a pleasure, a sense of ease, being at that and other venues like it......Oh the memories! Phil was then, has been ever since and will always be one of my inspirations to get up and do things in life. He never fails to make a success of anything he takes on and does it all with a great sense of humour and panache. He has remained in the industry becoming one of the most respected and sought after leisure entertainment managers in the country. I also owe Phil a great deal in so many ways over the years for which I thank him from the bottom of my heart.

It is here that I must publicly acknowledge another very special man, a man that was thankfully to become my other lifelong friend a man whose talent, determination, tenacity, strength of character, sense of humour and incredible loyal friendship saw me through some difficult times at Club Tropicana. Nick 'Spike' Botterill a brilliant musician joined me out there to be resident pianist in the lounge bar but became my right hand man. He did not have to do this it was certainly never in his contract to do anything but play in that bar, which he did to magnificent nightly acclaim. But Nick being Nick just took any challenge in his stride and when all of my staff went down with a mystery bug one day and I was about to cancel that evenings show he stepped up to the plate and said let's see if we couldn't do something. I of course initially thought it a bonkers idea but I will be ever indebted to my friend, as we did put a show on that night a show comprising of just the two of us and a friend who was visiting from England who I should point out was not an entertainer but was game and gave it a very good shot. We grabbed a couple of 'volunteers' from the other departments to work the sound and lights and……did we get away with it? No!

No?

No – You guests know when someone has done something special to at least try for you…..get away with it…..no they loved it!

They really appreciated it, the effort that had gone into it and the fact that we were all outside of our respective comfort zones for much of the time but we still did it for them.

Indebted? Oh yes indeed I was, that man pulled me up by the scruff of my neck that day and said "we don't give up that easily, were not ill, there's a show inside of us somewhere so let's get on and go for it" I learned a lot about myself that season from that brilliant friend a now well renowned composer, producer, band leader and solo artiste. Whilst he started playing the organ at Westminster Abbey as a young boy as a man he has performed music all over the world including jazz to an audience of 20 million, yes that's right, 20 million in a live concert that was broadcast all across Russia. We too continue to be the best of friends up to this very day and he remains one of my greatest inspirations in life.

It probably won't come as any surprise that Phil and Nick, who I love like brothers, are two of the very special people that this book is dedicated to, but I talk about them here to illustrate to future entertainers that no matter the type of centre you end up in during your career in holiday entertainment there is always something to take away from it. Whether that's a steep learning curve, a gentle reminder about customer service, the value of entertainment to generate profits (not at the expense of quality entertainment for your guests) and where you fit in to the bigger picture or great memories of fun and finding lifelong friendships.

It is such a pity that Romney Sands holiday village proves many points in this book, for you see a year ago I visited it only to find the so called entertainments team where absolutely abysmal. Oh well perhaps it is better now. Why not go to www.SUPERBLUE HAPPY HOLIDAYS.com and see what others say or you be the one to tell other guests what you think of it now.

How many people go to holiday centres?

Well there are no exact figures but here are some that you will find quite staggering.

I have taken a smattering of companies with centres, villages, camps, parks, resorts of varying size and given them, what I believe to be, a conservative number of guests that may be at their venues **at any one time**.

So in no particular order here is a small sample of what's out there:

Pontins – 5 centres	18,000
Butlins – 3 resorts 1 hotel	12,000
Warners – 13 locations	28,000
Potters – 250 bungalows and hotel	2,000
Haven Holidays- 34 parks	75,000
Park Resorts – 35 parks	80,000
Centre Parks – 4 locations	6,000
Searles Holiday Resort	3,000
Parkdean – 20 parks	40,000
South Devon Holidays – 3 Villages	9,000
Hoeseasons – numerous venues	68,000
Cinque Ports Holidays – 22 parks	45,000
Hotels (The Burstin for example)	10,000

Total: **372,000** guests **at any one time.**

Amazing ah! And remember this is a conservative figure of only those companies mentioned, you will know of many others of course including the independents we spoke of, so, as you can see the number of guests shown is clearly just the tip of the iceberg.

Add to that the fact that it was officially announced that at least *4 million extra* people had chosen to spend their holidays at home here in the UK just a couple of summers ago and that trend was set to stay for some time to come. Even more so since the economic downturn the British Airways strikes and weather turmoil, such as the Icelandic volcano, and you find yourself a member of an extremely powerful customer base worth absolutely millions upon millions of pounds to these companies.

What does a holiday camp mean to an entertainer?

Well that greatly depends on what they want out of the experience and that's the one thing that they will all have in common, it will be the experience of a lifetime. In fact some of them will want just that, they will do it for a season or two to get some life experience, most of them being young when they apply. It is without doubt one of the best ways of gaining the confidence and skills to deal with people from all walks of life in a variety of situations, just as they are embarking on the employment and adult social ladder. Of course some of them may be dreaming of stardom and there is no denying that the camps can and have been a superb training ground and stepping stone onto greater things. After all many well known celebrities today have roots firmly stuck in the camps where they began and openly admit that their rise to stardom was at least enhanced, if not directly because of their holiday camp apprenticeship. Then there will be those like me growing up going to camps all their young life longing to do just one thing and that's all that matters to them at this moment in time, putting the jacket on and walking out among the guests for the very first time as a Redcoat, Bluecoat, Greencoat, Funstar, a *holiday camp entertainer,* the dream come true. What the future holds for them after that? Who cares it's all they want and need right now. For those that succeed, and they can with this book, there is a vast array of career opportunities within the industry if that's where they decide their long term future lies. What will a holiday camp mean to them? Well something different to everyone in the end analysis but they will all share the fact that they were one of the few, they were a 'coat' and only 'coats' (whatever the colour) will know what a camp means to them, the fun, the laughter, the tears, the long long hours, the shows, the camaraderie, the drinking, two or more of your girlfriends or boyfriends turning up the same week, the heartache of saying goodbye, the joy of saying hello again, the glorious feeling of making others happy and the overwhelming sense of pride and achievement that you made it. *You were a 'coat'!*

How do they know which company or camp is the right one for them?

This is important because as a guest you want your entertainers to be happy or how can they possibly expect to make you happy and give you 100% which is what you have paid for after all. I therefore espouse that there are a few ways to try and ensure that they end up at the best place with the best company offering the best prospects for them which in turn will mean they will have the best of times which translates to great times for you as a guest. But don't worry I will cover this in a later chapter.

But now to the all important question of:................

What does a holiday camp mean to you the guest?

It's the middle of winter, pouring with rain and a car is parked on a quiet seaside road the young man inside is sitting with the window open so his view won't be obscured by the droplets on the glass. As you walk past you notice that he has tears streaming down his face as he silently observes what is taking place just the other side of a wire fence. What could be so heart wrenching to make him drive so many miles to this very spot just to witness an event that would invoke such a reaction? Butlins Clacton that's what, my sanctuary for one week of the year every year for so many years of my childhood was being torn down before my very eyes. I can't put into words the feelings that were running through me that cold rainy day in 1985. The pain of seeing the palace of my dreams, being bulldozed, the ecstasy of all those wonderful memories from toddler to teenager coming flooding back, the realisation that not one single camper will ever again set foot into Butlins Clacton and experience the magical world that had existed since 1938. Well it was all those emotions and so many more and was I alone? Of course not! others were there some sat in their cars many braving the elements to get a greater sense of the moment, which I must admit I eventually succumbed to and found myself standing with them dripping wet but not noticing how soaked I was getting, just the sound of the big ball and chain as it swung crashing into those hallowed walls time and time again. Those walls that must have had the essence of almost forty years of laughter imbedded into them, mine included. The colourful fun murals of the various venues, ballroom, show-bar, theatre and disco etc were exposed as the exterior gave way under the bombardment each one stirring yet even more fond reminiscences. The quiet empty space where the magnificent free fairground used to be seemed particularly poignant and desolate for someone who had played out so many childhood fantasies on the rides when growing up, fighter pilot, spaceman, racing driver, paratrooper and so many more. As I left that place on that sad day and drove thinking about what I had just gone through I vowed that I would never forget what a holiday camp can mean to a person..........

And I never have!

That's why I ask the entertainers among you to never underestimate the power of happiness that your camp or hotel can bring to people's lives............and that you are the guardian of childhood memories. Heavy? Maybe but this is what a holiday camp truly can mean to a guest and particularly a child or someone who has been going there since they were a child. So for as long as you are lucky enough to be an entertainer at a centre, you need to remember this fact, and make sure you create some of the best times of your guest's lives.

As a guest you have the absolute right to demand that your entertainments team are at least striving to invoke such magic.

How are you to know how good your entertainers should be? What type of person should you insist upon when entrusting them to delivering those dreams? What calibre of team should a centre or company be investing your hard earned cash on?

Well please allow me to tell you in the following chapters.............

CHAPTER THREE

WHAT IS A HOLIDAY CAMP ENTERTAINER?

Don't be daft that's obvious I can hear you shouting. It's someone who entertains at a holiday camp, centre, park, village, club or hotel. Well of course you're right but let's have a closer look and see if it is that simple a definition shall we?

Firstly you will have noticed that I used the term 'coat' in previous chapters and probably wondered why and that's a fair enough question. The term 'coat' was once upon a time the generic title for all of us holiday camp entertainers. For instance you might be asked "where did you work this summer?" "I was a 'coat' at Pontins" That meant you had spent the season as a Bluecoat. In those days just about all British holiday camps had a coloured jacket that their entertainers wore. The big three of course had Red, Green and Blue and the 'coats' were as famous as the companies themselves.

Many 'coats' have gone onto become very famous for example Des O'Conner was originally a Butlins Redcoat and more recently my old mate Shane Richie started as a Pontins Bluecoat and there is nothing stopping today's entertainers becoming the next big name on this list.

Oh and while we're on the subject of 'coats' and what to call them I must just point out that in 1991 whilst at Romney Sands Holiday Village as Entertainments Manager I gave birth to the title 'FUNSTARS' for my entertainments teams. I noted a couple of years back that Haven had dropped the well known 'Haven Mates' for their teams and replaced it with my 'FUNSTARS'. Well I suppose imitation is the finest form of flattery so to be copied by such a major company must be seen as an endorsement and testament to my creativity and professionalism which have clearly been noted over the years within the trade (I'm sure it's just a coincidence, but it made me feel good anyway).

Once again I will be democratic and use a smattering of the terms 'coat', entertainer etc and as always you just choose the one you like best.

OK so they can sing and dance or they are a budding comedian when they turn up at a holiday centre. What are they going to do all day until show time? Lounge by the pool? Sunbath on the nearby beach? Have a round of golf maybe? Go for a few beers with the gang?

If they were a budding holiday centre entertainer and liked the sound of that and thought it a vaguely realistic picture of what they might be expected to do as a 'coat', dream on! They will be in for the mother of all wake-up calls. The reality is most of them will be working long and I do mean long hours six days a week before they ever set foot on stage in the evening. They will have done everything from keep fit to calling bingo, leading a sedate ramble before running a sports day, referee the snooker and darts tournaments prior to hosting the junior fancy dress competition then stage a race day on film including working out all the betting odds and winnings just in time to dress up and be that nasty but stupid captain blood so the kids can chase them and throw him into the pool. Of course it could also be raining so imagine all that and having to pack in even more for a wet weather programme in order to deliver you a quality days entertainment.

That's all in a day's work for a 'coat' and if it's not, you guests are not getting your money's worth by a long shot. You see the term 'entertainment' in this context encompasses an array of talents and job titles some of which have obvious roles i.e. Life Guard and sports organiser (if you are at a large centre otherwise who do you think is organising the sport? Yep just add it to the list). Most teams however are dependent on the 'coat' mastering a multitude of competencies in order to run all of the above and more throughout the day to 'entertain' their guests.

Ah but here comes the evening the time they have been waiting for, surely their chance to shine, up on stage performing that routine they have worked so long and hard to perfect. Well maybe sometime during the evening one evening they will get to be part of the show or even have their own spot. But not yet, there is still a lot more that the holiday centre entertainer has to do before that small event takes place. I say small event, and I of all people know it's anything but small to them, but believe me in the day to day running of a good entertainments programme their stage performance is the cherry on the icing on the cake. Don't get despondent for them though because *it is* worth the wait and you guests will love them for it, you see when you have a good team of 'coats' you will know how hard they have worked for you all day every day and you will even forgive a few little faux pas along the way.

The variety of tasks that they have to master does indeed carry on into the evening programme but for 'coats' it should on the whole be an enjoyable mixture of strutting their funky stuff, gaining experience such as speaking on a microphone and audience control, learning new aspects of the trade and most importantly mingling with their guests.

These will differ from centre to centre but the mainstay of evening entertainments programmes will include bingo, fun competitions, party dances, disco, raffles etc and the early evening junior programme including their own competitions and cabaret. Add to that the fact that you should expect them to dance with as many of you as they can throughout the evening as well as taking care of visiting cabarets for whom they will be required to cover a variety of roles. Then there's the stage management that needs to be carried out in all venues, while some of them will be learning the intricacies of running the adult show bar and as if that's not enough who's going to do the late night disco? I think by now you are probably beginning to get the picture.

Yes there is a lot to do but don't panic if you are that budding entertainer you can take it all step by step in this book alongside your prospective guests so they should expect nothing less than the very best from you in the future.

It all reminds me of one young bluecoat during his first few days at a sister Pontins village. His manager called and asked me to go and see him as the 'coat' was driving him to distraction. He explained that this young man was very pleasant and talented but he could not understand why he was quite simply disobeying him. The manager told me that he had tried to get the young man to mingle more than he did but he just completely ignored these instructions. My fellow Entertainments Manager now exasperated by the situation called the wayward 'coat' to his office and put in the plainest of words "I have told you enough times now, this evening I want you to get out there and mingle". The young 'coat' looked a little worried by this and so it seemed the message may have finally sunk in and all would be fine. However that evening I observed that, while he got up and danced to everything there was to dance to he then kept returning and sitting at the same table each time to the frustration of my colleague. I said I would have a quick word and see if that makes any difference. I met the dancing 'coat' in the manager's office and was soon to clear up the mystery of his insubordination. I said "you clearly have a lot of potential to be a good bluecoat and seem to be a confident and nice person.

So why will you just not do the one thing being asked of you….and mingle?" He looked at me very sheepishly and replied "I don't know how to mingle, I know the slosh, night fever, the jitterbug and most of the other dances but…..the mingle?" Needless to say all was explained and he did indeed turn out to be a very good 'coat'.

TEAMWORK RULES OK

The other good news is that they won't be doing this all alone they will be part of a team. In a few large centres some of the jobs such as stage manager, DJ, sports organiser are specialised and that's all they do. That doesn't mean they can't or won't join with other fun events or shows as they often do and can be very good at it. Of course other coats can always learn from them so that when they go to a smaller centre they are well armed with knowledge that others may not have. This is particularly important if they intend to become an Entertainments Manager.

The makeup of an entertainments team will vary dramatically from village to village, camp to camp, club to club and so on. It will depend on the size, whether company or privately owned, financial status and most importantly the company or owners understanding that a good entertainments team keeps guests on site and makes them money in a myriad of ways. As opposed to seeing entertainment as an extra cost and cutting it, which I am sad to say is what I have witnessed recently.

Most teams will be headed by an Entertainments Manager and assistant (more about them later). The main body of the team will be made up of a number of 'coats' (dependant on the factors mentioned above) some of whom will have a range of raw talents i.e. singing, dancing etc but, whilst it is important to have these talents at your disposal, as I have clearly outlined talent alone just isn't enough. There should be some, who I call, personality people. These are those who may not have a particular stage talent but who, if they have chosen the right people, are worth their weight I gold. Working their socks off they tend to be with their guests all day and evening, for the most important reason of all, because they want to be! They are generally keen to learn and take part in the shows etc and in my experience guests just love them for it, so much so that they usually even get the biggest round of applause. One such person was the incorrigible Billy Brown at my first ever, centre for Pontins. He was the original 'Peggy' for years he wanted to be a bluecoat but alas was to look on from the sidelines as he was employed as kitchen porter and not taken seriously at all. Until the fabulous Richard Walsh arrived, this Entertainments Manager spotted the potential in this character that spent every moment of his spare time with the guests. Richard gave him a shot at wearing the famous jacket and was repaid by a 'coat' that worked non-stop and that every guest absolutely loved. This is a group of people I do believe some companies have forgotten about in the pursuit of having just talent on site and in my humble opinion not **all** those with the talent have the enthusiasm for guests or the tasks I have highlighted above. And to be perfectly honest the standard of *some* of the talent I have witnessed of late does leave a little to be desired. I for one would much rather see a mixture of 'coats' and get caught up in their good old fashioned enthusiasm. What's that? Bias? Me? Well yes I suppose so having started out as a General Bluecoat myself but dare I be so cheeky and say "I rest my case".

An extremely important part of any team is the children's entertainment. Traditionally known as the Uncle and Aunty this definition has now disappeared at many sites. No matter what title they use for their children's team all 'coats', and in particular the management, must be aware of their enormous worth. The correct recruitment of this marvellously talented, patience of a saint group of individuals is paramount. The hiring of someone to 'make do' or 'just to get by' or worse 'to save money' would be disastrous. If the children's entertainments is not up to scratch you have unhappy children, unhappy children means unhappy parents, unhappy parents means grief for the Entertainments team and trust me once you have a camp going into a downward spiral of this kind it's very hard to stop it and a whole village of unhappy guests will be their worst nightmare come true. Believe me I have seen it happen and it is horrible. The whole team should do what they can to support the children's entertainment at all times. It's in all their best interests, trust me!

The life guards and sports organisers have historically come under the auspices of the Entertainments Manager therefore are part of the team. I have noticed however that at some parks, and in the big centres in particular, this has changed. Not everywhere though so I will mention them here but also see the chapter on 'working abroad'. You may, however, be pleasantly surprised at the amount of lifeguards and sports organisers that will join in with the rest of the fun stuff that the 'coats' get up to and of course they will be invaluable when running sporting events, swimming gala's and associated lessons etc so everyone should ensure they are made to feel like part of a team and not left out of anything.

At Little Canada and Whitecliff Bay, for example, lifeguards took part in the shows. One of them, actually reaching the televised heats of New Faces where the ladies on the panel completely fell in love with him, moving him on to great things.

I have touched on DJ's and as I said the large centres may well employ people for that specific role but for the most part members of the team take it in turns to run the disco consul for a variety of reasons not least of all the late night disco sessions......... obviously.

What about your Entertainments team if you are on holiday abroad? Well I do cover this in more detail later but the basic difference is obviously language. Doesn't get more obvious than that does it really? Your British entertainers may be lucky enough to work to an all British audience and not have to alter their routine much if at all. Don't mistake all English speaking with all British. You see it doesn't matter what colour, creed, religion height, shape or sex a British person is we have a particular brilliant sense of humour and we love to be entertained and entertain (as I mentioned earlier half want to do it while the other half want to watch them do it). As opposed to trying to run an entertainments programme for a mixture of countries who can speak English. Of course all of the guests from these fab nations also want great entertainment but there are subtle differences in what we all find humorous for instance. But it's generally the timing of events that you will notice if you are part of a mixed audience. For example I was Entertainments Manager at Club Tropicana in Majorca. We had Spanish, Italian, French, German, Belgian, Swedish and British guests. This had formally been a Club Pontinental and so the British guests wanted and expected the holiday camp environment, but abroad with sand, sun and sea, which was in fact our remit. Most guests from the other countries did enjoy this concept once they got used to the idea and joined in the fun and indeed taught me a thing or two about entertaining a multi-national audience. Of course it helped that I could speak all of those languages. What? Oh you know me too well already, yes of course I am fibbing. I got by on broken working Spanish but after that I needed one of my two Belgian translators with me at all times. These lovely ladies left school, as do most Belgium's, speaking about five languages each. So everything I said would be repeated by them five times, this kills comedy and bingo takes hours. It meant having a smattering of people from various countries in the entertainments team or as they are known abroad the animation team. This again was a further testing of my multilingual expertise as there was many a morning when I needed to let one of them know that I was not impressed with something they had done the previous evening. I would say to my translator "tell him that it was a bad thing and I would be grateful if it did not happen again" or words to that effect. She would translate this in the appropriate language and the reply by the transgressor, who would normally be very animated. (Perhaps that's why they are called an animation teams?)

Anyway the reply would be something like…

"@@@@@$$$$$$$$!!!!!&&&&****@?!"£$%^&*()   LE   BON   DELAGRUG @@@@@**********$$$$$ SPRAKEN ZE STUPID ******&&&&%%%%$$$$$ EL SUPERBLUE DE FOOL!!!!! ET TOO BRUTA@@@@@ SHOVE IT *******" ending with a gesture or two.

Me "What did he say?"
Translator "oh he said he's sorry"
Good to know you're in control isn't it!
But for the most part these were very happy days and I did learn a lot from both entertainers and guests. Your entertainers just have to be prepared to adapt if they find themselves in this situation. I did have a number of British 'coats' with me and adapt we did.

One of the team was not a 'coat' but a brilliant pianist who has gone on to great things since, including wonderful works such as, beautifully composed instrumental albums, live recordings of his jazz concerts, composing the tune that accompanied the Swedish Tsunami disaster appeal as well as producing records and albums for other artists. There is at least one chapter in that other book on that one season alone and in particular our escapades, a couple of which I do share with you in this one though. I am glad to say that we have remained the best of friends and he was one of the best men at my wedding a short while ago and one of the people this book is dedicated to.

Whether they are a 'coat' here or abroad the basics are the same and they can carry what they learn from 'I was Superblue' anywhere because it's a one size fits all manual for them as well as an informative guide for you. They just have to adapt it to suit the park, centre, village, camp, hotel, club or even country that they are working in therefore once again there is no excuse for them not supplying you with anything but superb professional entertainment every time, no matter where and when you are on your holiday.

I will talk about the Entertainment Managers role soon but let me give you a little bit of an insight that stems from my experience of situations that have arisen at centres over the years bearing in mind I have done more than a little troubleshooting in my time. The manager's job may look very easy and a good manager will make it look effortless but believe me they are in fact constantly working like the proverbial swan as you will see in the next chapter. The point I am making here is that within a team there is quite often someone who thinks they can do better. I have to say that in my experience they are generally a particular type of person but that's not important here. What is of vital importance however is your reaction to that person. They typically begin by slagging the manager off behind their back to both carefully picked members of the entertainments team and guests. This has a terrible affect normally splitting the team in two and in its worst form can cause a nasty atmosphere among the guests. The reality is that these people rarely have the experience or capability to take on the role and inevitably end up being sacked, but not before creating absolute havoc at the camp. The best advice I can give you is not to side with this person and tell them you won't. I also give other coats the same advice otherwise they may find themselves being fired too. I believe it is normally best for coats to stay loyal to the manager if they are doing a good job and treating them well. These are important issues of course and I realise that if they are not doing a good job the coats are in an awkward situation, you will be complaining to them, they will not be learning the trade as they should be and it can be a thoroughly un-enjoyable experience. If this happens and the manager is approachable the coat should try to talk to them one to one and explain what is occurring. If they have tried this and things have not improved or the person is unapproachable they may find it prudent to subtly raise issues at the daily meetings being careful not to directly confront or argue with the manager. Once they have tried all of this and things are still bad they may want to consider approaching the Camp Manager or the Entertainments Executive or similar at head office. But these actions should always be taken as a last resort of course and I would suggest they do this as an individual so as not to appear to be ganging up. Why tell you this? Well the reality is, as in the centre I was talking about earlier, you guests will invariably be the ones who ultimately ensure a bad Entertainments Manager is removed from the post. On the other hand my advice is contrary to that above if the 'coats' are being treated in any way other than professionally, respectfully and without bias, prejudice or bullying in any of its forms. If any of these do exist they must deal with injustices at an early stage. You know life really is too short to be unhappy and particularly in what should be such a joyous time in theirs. Importantly, however, not passing on any of their unhappiness or team problems to their guests is imperative so you should never be aware that anything is amiss. You are on holiday having paid good money to escape the workplace and other grief.

Just one of the fabulous entertainments teams I had the pleasure of working with and managing over many years. It shows that a team at a smaller centre need not be massive. But they absolutely have to be as happy and as wonderfully friendly and hard working as these lovely people were. They did all happen to have a talent too but you know my feelings about personality first and this magical team had that in abundance.

TAKING CARE OF THE TEAM

I must touch on something here which is really for Entertainment Managers to address in the first instance but feel that it is important that you all to know and be aware of. I realise that I have highlighted a great number of things that a holiday centre entertainer needs to be able to do and the fact that they will be covering a plethora of activities during any one day or evening. But always remember they are employed as part of the entertainments team and NOT as a dogsbody for jobs that no one else will or can do. The skills I have mentioned are legitimate for an entertainments team to be asked to perform. Unfortunately however it has been known for owners or camp managers to treat a team as a spare workforce and that's not on. Don't let it happen to your team, after all you have paid for them to be exclusively for your entertaining pleasure. Should they be used for anything else, unless in an emergency......I would complain bitterly!!!

An extreme instance of where this happened was when Pontins requested that I take up the post of Entertainments Manager at Brean Sands one Christmas in the mid 80's. They were having serious problems with the centre manager and wanted a strong person in there to take on what promised to be an arduous time to say the least. So much so that I was actually furnished with the personal phone numbers of, not only the entertainments executive but of Trevor Hemmings the managing director himself. Their fears proved to be well founded from the very start with the centre manager making all kinds of unwarranted demands but the big crunch was to come on Christmas Day itself. Although 'Brean' is a self catering holiday village they had sold two complete sittings of Christmas dinner which took in just about the entire guest list. The worst part of this situation, so far, was that the chef had only been informed of one sitting so the centre had overbooked by double the figures he had planned to cater for. However while the poor chef struggled with this problem things were about to take a drastic turn for the worst. Because in his delusional world the general manager had decided that he did not need to take on any extra staff to serve the meals at said sittings as he would simply get the bluecoats to do it!!!

To make matters worse this proposal was not put to me until the middle of that very morning. What was I to do? I of course told him in no uncertain terms that this was unacceptable and indeed would not be taking place so he had better find staff from somewhere because it wasn't going to be my bluecoats. With this he threatened to have me ejected from the site and he would take charge of the team in any case. He attempted to enlist the help of the head of security to do the ejecting but he also informed him that that was unacceptable and most certainly 'press ganging' fellow managers was not in his job description.

So you can see the plight we found ourselves in, dealing with a completely unreasonable general manager, a chef with a few hundred meals to dish out, how he managed that I will never know but bravo to him and his staff for that one, a full entertainments programme to run including an after lunch Christmas show and no waiting staff to serve guests who were just about to be informed that they cannot all have Christmas dinner at the time planned because of the almighty mess caused by this man.

I phoned the numbers I had been given for the first time during that Xmas break, which I was very proud of considering all that I had put up with up to this point already. I explained the dire situation that we, the whole centre that is, were in. I can only imagine the frantic panicking that went on behind the scenes over the next hour or so before I eventually received a call from the very top asking if it was at all possible that the team could help out in the company's hour of need.

I put this proposition to my team of bluecoats who magnificently rose to the challenge. Not for the stupid general manager, not for the entertainment executive, not for Trevor Hemmings even, though the latter two were very good employers it has to be said, and certainly not for the money. No the only reason they said they would attempt to pull this minor miracle off was for the guests, so their Christmas would not to be completely ruined and for no other reason whatsoever.

That team of 'coats' made me so proud to be part of this great industry of ours that day. Our motto 'the show must go on' was brilliantly and bravely carried forward through one of the most difficult days I have ever experienced. Not only did those 'coats' have to inform guests as they arrived that some would in fact not be seated until a second sitting which would be two hours away but had to face the anger of those guests as we tried to explain that we were trying to be as fair as possible and serve those with children or elderly members in their party. As you can imagine this was by no means an exact science, particularly at such short notice, but we somehow got past that hurdle.

Now what was I going to do with those waiting for the second sitting?

We hastily reworked the Christmas show and split the entertainments team in half one half serving at each sitting. This meant that the other half, far from having a break, continued to entertain the guests not eating at that time. The show was a mish-mash of the talents available while the others served at each sitting but again we somehow came through on this one too. We ran what was effectively an 'off the cuff' number of events after that until we came back on track with the original programme.

If I live to be a million, I will never know how they pulled it off that day!

Those 'coats' were exhausted, run off their feet doing a job that was completely foreign to them. Not stopping for over six hours, running themselves into the ground serving hundreds of Christmas starters, dinners, sweets, coffee and biscuits for one half of that time and putting a show together and performing it as well as running this add-hock programme that I was throwing at them as we went along the other half. They were quite simply amazing nothing short of heroic!!!

Yes the guests were up in arms at the beginning of it all, and they had every right to be. But by the end of that marathon session they gave the bluecoats a thunderous standing ovation which seemed to last for hours. They had done it for the guests and the guests knew it and thanked them in the way all performers would love to be thanked. We saw the rest of the Christmas out in relative peace as someone arrived from head office to sort out the general manager who had now locked himself in his chalet refusing to come out. He was in fact still there as we all left to return home and await our next adventure at Easter.

I hope the members of that incredible team such as Linda Brown and Stan Abbott to name but two are reading this with immense pride because even after all these years I think of you all with immeasurable humility and incalculable gratitude as indeed I guarantee those guests, the entertainment executive of the day and Trevor Hemmings himself do and thank you.

Trevor Hemmings, did indeed show his gratitude over the incident, a great example of how to treat people by one of the richest men in the industry.

I doubt very much that this situation would ever occur again at a major holiday centre and as I say it is an extreme example however you should be aware of such practices and not allow them to take place. I am not a union activist, backstage lawyer or anything like that and I would always advocate assisting a colleague from any department where they can, particularly in an emergency, but you should never find yourself in circumstances, where your entertainments team are doing other jobs just because it saves the management money. They will have quite enough to do if they are running a decent entertainments programme as it is. You have paid your hard earned cash and have chosen that centre normally because of what it promises to deliver. So you now have the right to expect them to deliver a first rate entertainments programme with staff dedicated to that goal. Please trust me when I say you have a very strong voice when it comes to such matters.

SO THAT IS A HOLIDAY CAMP ENTERTAINER.

Well now that I have scared the pants off you and made you worried about the life of any budding 'coats' with all that stuff above let me reassure you that if they enter the trade with the right frame of mind always willing to learn and follow the simple tips and lessons they can read at the same time as you in this book they will:
- Have the time of their life
- Enjoy the challenge
- Love entertaining
- Get immense pleasure from the whole experience
- Be ready to adapt to any situation
- Stand out from the crowd
- Enhance their chance of being employed in the first place
- Carry wonderful memories which will stay with them for the rest of their life

What all of this means to you, of course, is that they should be transferring all of this positive happiness and joy onto you giving you and your family the holiday of a lifetime... *every time*.

CHAPTER FOUR

THE ENTERTAINMENTS MANAGER

He that would govern others, first should be the master of himself
Philip Massinger 1583 – 1640

Another little gem of wisdom I impart to budding entertainers is......Enjoy your days as a 'coat' and don't rush to become the Entertainments Manager. I say this as someone who loved his time in the role but as many before me didn't realise the enormity of the responsibility that came with it until I took the job on.

But as a guest just what should you expect from your Entertainments Manager? After all they are the one entrusted with ensuring you get that all important professional quality holiday entertainment package. Are the companies employing the right calibre of people to deliver this? Well read on and judge for yourself because this is what you should be getting.

In many respects the Entertainments Manager has the most difficult job on the entire centre. They are answerable to just about everyone, the camp management, owners, entertainments team, and of course most importantly their guests. The responsibilities that this post brings with it are great and hugely varied. In short there is no other job like it in the world.

I said I loved the job and trust me if you get it right it is definitely one of the most rewarding and satisfying in the world too.

Getting it right is the trick of course and everything in this book applies to the Entertainments Manager as much as to the 'coats', in fact more so, as he or she will be responsible for implementing, upholding and delivering the quality programmes, professionalism and downright entertaining fun that I am telling you to demand from them and their team.

The first thing to be said is that they must have spent time learning their trade, it takes time to become a good Entertainments Manager and in my experience the best have been 'coats' for some time doing just that. I have seen, too many times now, people employed as Entertainments Managers for all the wrong reasons and it all ends in tears. I used one particular park as a perfect example and while this was admittedly a couple of years ago now I am sad to say I have not witnessed anything at some centres to make me believe things are any better today. As always you can let each other know what you are finding out there, by placing your **<u>Good or Bad</u>** holiday experiences onto the website www.SUPERBLUE HAPPY HOLIDAYS.com

The example I used? Oh yes well the Entertainments Manager was a young girl who could sing a bit but clearly had absolutely no idea about running entertainments at a holiday camp. She had so little impact on the guests that no one even knew who she was. Her 'coats' were untrained, undisciplined, scruffy and unpunctual while basically being used as sales people for the camp shop. The programme was diabolical to start with made even worse, if that's possible, by the fact that even that leant heavily towards selling products from, not only the shop but, lessons for this or that or rides on things in the pool all carrying an extra cost to the guest. I felt desperately sorry for the young team as their enthusiasm waned under the stress and total lack of direction, training or leadership. It was the last two weeks in June so the main summer season hadn't started yet but the centre was still very busy. The world cup was on so one of the bars was showing almost nonstop football at times but even this became a massive sales drive to the extent that guests were seriously getting miffed at the fact that every time they saw a member of the entertainments team they were trying to sell them something. Two days before my departure I was informed that she was being sacked and an experienced manager was being brought in from another site. I met the new Entertainments Manager when she arrived and joined her as she watched, in horror, at what was being dished up to the guests as an excuse for an evening entertainments programme. It was at least satisfying to know that my perceptions had been correct and that I wasn't being harshly overcritical by comparing the manager, team and programme with my own exacting high standards.

The point being that if the wrong person is employed as the Entertainments Manager everyone suffers. The guests, the company, the owners, the camp management, the entertainments team, the rest of the staff at the centre cop the fallout and the Entertainments Manager themselves eventually looses out by being sacked and now carrying a bad reputation. Remember also that the company had brought in an experienced manager from another site. What will the impact be to that camp? Do they have a good replacement? Has someone there been dumped in a position they don't want to be in because they are not ready to be a manager yet, no matter how good a coat they may be? Are the guests, team and management at one centre, being taken care of at the expense of all those at another? And if you're with a small company or at an independent camp who are you going to replace the wrongly employed Entertainments Manager with?

Daunting isn't it? Well yes it is but if they learn their trade, look after their team and guests as they should they can carve out a great career for themselves and deliver the quality entertainment you have paid for.

So what does the Entertainments Manager do? Well you will have read the myriad of things a 'coat' is expected to cover in the last chapter. Guess what....the Manager has even more to contemplate. Obviously they will need to make sure the 'coats' are doing what they are supposed to be doing when they are supposed to be doing it, not to mention not doing what they shouldn't be when they shouldn't be doing it? Oh you know what I mean. They really do need to be in total control of their team, the guests and all of the entertainment venues. Ensure the programme runs smoothly and most crucially make sure it runs on time. Choosing the right person for each task or event, without bias or favouritism is a must but they should remember to let less experienced 'coats' learn from the others shadowing them before having a go themselves. The choice of their assistant is of paramount significance, they absolutely need to know, without a shadow of a doubt, that when they're not present that person is providing them with solid and loyal backing while taking care of business.

Daily meetings are essential to maintain the cohesive structure of the programme and discipline. Posting their team for the day's events they can ensure their appearance is up to the required standard inform them of any transgressions that they wish to address while remembering that it is vital to boost the 'coats' confidence, congratulate and thank the team whenever possible. They can also take this opportunity to monitor health and welfare issues and allow grievances to be aired. They will find that, to some extent, they become a Mother of Father figure to many young 'coats' setting out on their first experience of working away from home. This can be strange and sometimes stressful especially if they're not that old themselves. They must always watch for mid season blues and make sure that they have someone, normally another member of the management team, that they can talk to and who will be looking out for their welfare (more about this in the chapter on health and safety).

They should hold regular training sessions as these are essential to keep things professional, up to date and fresh for their guests.

Remember they are the Entertainments Manager and the team should be looking to them for support and guidance, by far the best way to provide this is to lead by example. They can accomplish this by generally conducting themselves in a manner that follows the rules of etiquette as well as the obvious basics that I will cover next, always being immaculately turned out for instance. After all how can they ask the team to achieve a high standard if they are attaining less than that themselves?

Their job starts much earlier than all of that however they may even be required to take an active role in the hiring of the entertainments team. If this is the case I hope they have remembered my little tips in the last chapter as they really will have helped to select a good team. Another thing they should have tried to achieve is picking a team who they think not only compliment each other's talents but who might get on with one another, not an exact science I know but I have found going with your instincts is a good rule.......... they are usually right, and haven't forgotten my personality people.

One of their most important responsibilities needs to be completed at the outset of their appointment, the entertainments programme! These will vary from centre to centre and even week to week for special events etc. Fear not we've got it all covered in a later chapter and of course in 'Tales of Superblue'. Leading on from that the shows are down to them too, they take a bit of putting together but guess what, I help them out there too. I will mention something here though that is peculiar to the Entertainment Manager's role. They may find that sometimes they will have to supply costumes and or props for shows. I have had to do this at private camps but the upside is once you have them they are yours and you are even more employable than before. Generally though even the smallest company these days has some sort of budget for this. They should not be scrimping at the large centres at all but something to bear in mind and as a guest there is always fun to be had if you feel like helping out in this department should the occasion arise.

I talked about them ensuring they can confide in at least one other member of the management team but the reality is that as soon as they arrive at a site they should set out to meet and befriend, at the very least, the following fellow managers. The bars manager will often be their closest ally as many events are run in tandem with the bar opening times, promotions and sponsorships etc. They, as well as the bars manager, will be judged on the bar takings at many resorts with even outdoor events requiring a bar to be established for that period of time so a good working relationship is vital for all concerned. The catering manager is another obvious friend in the making and pretty much for the same reasons with catering being a particular special feature in some of the themed days or weeks and for little niceties such as supplying a birthday cake for a guest or children's parties and functions etc. Both of these colleagues will support them if approached in the right manner and of course they will repay this in the pivotal role of Entertainments Manager by promoting their fine fare. The maintenance manager and his crew may not seem likely people to mention here but never underestimate the mystic powers of the maintenance man. He who can transform an empty stage into a cabin on a cruise liner or a scene from cats, what am I on about? Well the amount of centres I have worked at where the maintenance man was a master craftsman, all be it just as a hobby at times, was incredible. The Entertainments Manager has to make sure they find out what theirs can do and more importantly would like to do. They can transform a good show or event into a brilliant one or of course they could just have the bulbs or fuses needed to keep them going in an emergency. The arcade manager is another you're probably scratching your head at but again I have found that, electronically, they can quite often get you out of a fix at the most awkward of times. They nearly always have the change we want to run bingo, horseracing on film or other wet weather activity. They will also clear the pool tables or bowling alley etc and make them free of payment for competitions. The best rule of thumb of course is that the Entertainments Manager should try to get on with all of the management and staff at their camp always thank them publicly for their part in any event or show and privately over a beer or similar doesn't hurt either. Entertainment Managers must always remember to approach a fellow manager if one of their staff wants to take part in a show or help backstage or with the spotlight etc. Its only good manners and not doing so can cause serious rifts between departments.

I will be covering the art of the compere later, but specific to the Entertainments Manager are the welcome and farewell 'line ups'. As simple as these are they are also the first words, a full camp of, guests will hear the Entertainments Manager speak and will set the tone for the week. They should treat this as any other professional performance and be imaginative about what they will say to introduce each of their team and other managers on the centre. They must always rehearse it and make the others rehearse it too especially if they are going to add a little visual or verbal comedy into it. The farewell line up is notorious for falling out with people. It is imperative that they ensure they mention everyone even if they are not present. They have all worked very hard for the guests and if you had been a 'coat' yourself you will know how important that applause is on the last night. They should never limit this to their own team and be sure to thank all other staff and department heads. Again at some parks they like the managers to join the 'line up' so the same rules as the welcome apply including insisting they rehears it. The village manager will thank them for it when *they* look good.

Another subject I will go into in depth is gaming. It is something that the 'coats' should know about but imperative that the Entertainments Manager understands and knows what scams to look for. Anything involving money Bingo, Horseracing on film, raffles or hoy etc, are all areas where the unscrupulous 'coat' could attempt to make a fast buck. They must know the rules of any and all events involving cash and institute practices that are open and transparent to the guests showing the amount of money taken and the amount of money to be paid out or the equivalent prizes etc. Remember taking money is not a perk it is theft!

You probably read the paragraph about the person who always thinks they can do better than the Entertainments Manager, in the last chapter, with mixed feelings. Well if they're a good manager they will be pleased that I advised the 'coats' to be loyal and support them as indeed I did in 'Tales of Superblue'. If the bit about prejudice and bullying worried them, best the management take a long hard look at them because they are certainly not someone they should have employed to be your Entertainments Manager.

There are of course obvious things that you should look for in your Entertainments Manager in order to ensure that they are the right person providing you with the entertainments team and programme you deserve and should rightly demand.
Such as they;

Are always professional

Remain approachable

Support, encourage, train, guide and protect their team

Lead by example

Give their guests the best possible entertainments programme

Run that programme on time

Put on great shows

Constantly control their venues

I am going to finish however by letting you in on a secret that is the ultimate piece of advice I give Entertainments Managers and that is: *They should take at least one* **whole** *day off a week and either lock themselves away or get away from the centre altogether.*

As long as they don't do either of these they will *never* have a proper day off. There will always be something someone wants to know, do or say.

Trust me they will need this day to revitalise themselves, give their brain a rest and have some personal space. They will be all the better for it, better for the team and you. If they have chosen the right assistant this is where it really pays dividends.

As a guest you can help by talking your Entertainments Manager into taking that day off and respecting this private time. Because as you can see they do have a lot on their plate and after all the more rested they are the better your entertainment should be!

Visit SUPERBLUE HAPPY HOLIDAYS.com the home of honest holiday reviews

CHAPTER FIVE

THE BASICS

While I have shown them how to perform their duties and complete specific tasks in the book 'Tales of Superblue' there are, as in any profession, a set of basic principles that are the foundation on which to build upon. All 'coats' should know and understand the reasoning behind each of these and their importance. While some will seem obvious I will still cover them in this chapter because, as you will have gathered by now, most aspects of this trade are actually more in depth than they first appear.

Here for your delectation are the 'basics' I have passed on to them and are absolutely fundamental to the service you should expect from your 'coats' at any venue you stay at.

A 'COAT' MUST ALWAYS WEAR A SMILE

The first and most important basic rule is actually very simple, or is it?

Well the rule is that a 'coat' must always wear a smile.

Simple?

When was the last time you smiled? This morning? An hour ago? Yesterday?

Can you remember when?

Why did you smile?

Did someone give you something nice?

Was it while trying to impress someone?

Were you reading something amusing?

Or have I just reminded you of that time and now your smiling again at the thought of it?

The chances are the last time you smiled was when someone made you smile, sounds obvious doesn't it? But think about it for a moment, when have you actually set out to smile at someone? See what I mean it's not so straight forward after all is it? In fact to smile is at the very heart of what being a 'coat' is all about. Their role in life is to make their guests happy and the simplest way to begin this process is by making them smile and the easiest way to do this is to smile at them. Humans can't help but respond to a smile with a smile. Anyone who has seen my stand up comedy act will know my closing line and how it relates to this fact. Why are you making such a big deal of it I hear you ask? How difficult can it be to smile at people? 'Coats' don't have to smile at everyone anyway if they smile at half or even a quarter of the guests it will spread wont it? Your right I am making a big deal of what seems such a little instruction and the reason for this is as simple as that instruction. Try leaving where you are today for half an hour and while you are out just smile at every person you meet or walk past. You will soon realise that it's not as easy as you may have thought. You may even get some strange reactions because, sadly, we are not used to people smiling at us anymore but hopefully you will receive some nice smiles in return. Luckily for 'coats' at holiday centres you guests will be hoping they will be smiling all day. Now that you have conducted that little experiment just imagine a 'coat' waking up with a hangover or just tired from the long hours worked that week they leave their chalet and walk past a hand-full of guests looking like death warmed up and *no smile*. Imagine how they have just started those guests day, those guest's day on holiday, those guest's day at that 'coats' centre, those guest's day that they have worked so hard to pay for. Imagine what they are going to say to the next guests they talk to, imagine how co-operative they are *not* going to be when they turn up at the competitions that 'coat' is running that day, imagine how much they *aren't* going to join in with the party dances and fun games in the evening when that 'coat' asks them to and imagine how much applause that 'coat' is *not* going to get for their performance in the shows. Dramatic? Think so? Yes their smile to half the people could spread ,it is infectious after all,but so could their tired hungover face. If they are really unlucky and those guests were on their way to the centre manager to complain about something guess what they are going to add to the list now!!!. On the other hand had the 'coat' just smiled at them they may have calmed somewhat and be less angry when they speak to the camp commandant er I mean manager and even praise the entertainments team because of it. And even though they had a complaint about something else imagine how that 'coat' just turned around all those things I mentioned above and how they, their family and other guests they talk to will be treating that 'coat' for the rest of the day. You see one smile from a 'coat' can make your day, defuse a situation before it even begins, make you feel noticed and valued as a guest at their resort and then ....*YOU* **smile**.

THEY SHOULD PUT THAT SMILE ON BEFORE LEAVING THEIR CHALET

As a 'coat' I would be up and dressed and ready to walk out of my chalet door but as I reached for the handle a beaming smile from ear to ear would spread across my face. I would repeat this ritual each and every time I came from a guest free area, such as the office or back stage etc and into the public domain. Your coats should be doing exactly the same for you today.

'COATS' MUST BE IMMACULATELY TURNED OUT

I am sure you don't really need me to go into too much depth for the second Basic rule. It really does speak for itself for the most part but we will just have a little look at it anyway shall we. I can still remember the fantastic feeling of pride and walking ten feet tall the first time I left my chalet crossing the camp to the main building wearing my brand new gleaming white Shirt, Trousers, shoes and socks while Sporting the Pontins Bluecoat with the bright yellow 'P' on the pocket and shining blue and yellow striped tie. I sincerely hope some of you reading this will get the chance to experience that wonderful once in a lifetime moment there really is nothing to touch it if you want it bad enough. Yes I know it was all brand new stuff but you will remember I had arrived as a twenty one year old having recently spent five years in the Royal Air Force where cleanliness and smartness had been instilled into me. This meant that not only was I clean and smart for that first small step for mankind one giant leap for Superblue, sorry getting carried away again (and many think I should have been long ago), but I continued to present myself in an immaculate fashion throughout my career and still do to this day. I was exceptionally lucky one evening when Bob Monkhouse watched me perform a comedy routine at Pontins Blackpool after which he kindly requested that I be allowed to be compere for his cabaret spot .. I was to spend some of my most memorable times during my Pontins days backstage in his dressing room with him and his lovely wife, as she sat there knitting he imparted pearls of wisdom to me, there's that other book again. However I am going to share one of those jewels with you here and now. He said always dress to go on stage, no matter where or how big or small, as if you were going to meet the Queen.

He said if you're dressed to that standard you are ready to meet anyone, you will feel great and confident and this will come across to the audience and you never know one day, that might mean you actually will meet Her Royal Highness. I know it's a bit of name dropping but if the guvnor of comedy could be kind enough to pass it onto a humble bluecoat like me then the least I can do, is to do justice to the great mans memory by passing it onto you.

I went out and bought my first 'hand-made' stage suit from 'Pauls' of London. I was just starting out so didn't have much money but this was where many of the stars went for their suits and costumes etc. I told him I was working at Pontins but was hoping to be a comedian. He asked me to tell him some jokes and must have seen something he liked because he made me the most wonderful suit, a little jacket cut to a taper at the waist, slightly flared cuffs with silk on the lapels and down the trouser seams. It looked a lot better than I am making it sound. The material was left over cuts from a major star's touring stage-show, it did cost me a few bob, but not as much as it probably should have I expect, he was a very kind man. The point is that I felt like a million dollars in it and walked on stage every time feeling like I may well be a star.

Could I have met Her Majesty the Queen in it?...................Oh yes!

The fact is that your 'coats' are on a stage, the world is a stage and we are merely players on it, what? Oh don't moan I thought it would make me look cleverer than what I am. Seriously though remember they are representing their company, camp, team and themselves each time they are in uniform. There is nothing shoddier than a scruffy unkempt or worse, dirty 'coat'. If they look good they will feel good as a wise man once said...oh I know but it's true. You know yourself when you're getting ready to go out on the town you scrub up well, splash on the smellies, a dash of war paint and slip into the best outfit you can find. You don't run round all day building up a sweat, dashing about from place to place, going to the gym, socialising in hot crowded places, playing with a load of your families and friends kids, getting covered in all sorts of gung for the amusement of people and then dance the night away nonstop putting the same clothes on the next day and the day after that to do it all over again do you? No of course not, so why then have I seen so many 'coats' doing just that? Think about it, they should have pride in themselves, if necessary do what I used to do and buy an extra uniform or at least parts of it, i.e. shirts, blouses, trousers, skirts etc. I always had a fresh clean uniform ready to change into. I know it's not easy but if they plan properly they can manage it. I always found the person running the camp launderette a good friend to make right at the outset they have saved my bacon on more than a few occasions I can tell you. I never forget to say thank you with their favourite tipple or a nice box of chocolates etc it really was worth every penny.

They should never neglect their footwear either always keep their trainers clean and fresh, whiten when appropriate and polish their evening shoes.....every evening.

SMELLY?

Well they should be big and ugly enough by now to know to wash their bits and keep themselves clean and fresh at all times. The last thing you, as a guest, would want is someone with body odour or bad breath at your table. I tell the 'coats' one important thing at this point and ask them to please pay serious heed to, and that is that if one of their colleagues is suffering from one of the above problems *tell them!* Don't be worried about offending them because if they don't as sure as eggs is eggs one of the little cherubs will announce in front of a few thousand people while they are being interviewed on the mic for the best joke competition and yes I've seen that happen too. A colleague once told me that there was a cheesy pong when I took my shoes off so I bought some odour eaters, I'm not saying it was a bad smell but they ate my feet. Terrible joke isn't it? I was hoping to get better as the book went on, oh well there's a few chapters to go yet. But honestly personal hygiene is of paramount importance, to reiterate, they will be dashing about everywhere, dancing their socks off, running competitions, playing sport, rehearsing the shows in fact just about everything they do will mean the boys sweating and of course the ladies may perspire a little. I know that time is precious to a hard working 'coat' but they must make the time to do their ablutions properly. Make sure they get up early enough and leave a suitable gap between the day and evening events to cover this vitally important aspect of their day. It is for the good and comfort of you the guests of course but also for their well being and confidence.

I am sorry if I seem to be stating the ridiculously obvious to you at the moment but it is possible that not everyone will be bringing the same high standards with them when they arrive at a centre. Many will be working away from home for the first time and others may just begin to let them slip through the pressure of the hours etc. It is a subject that people are generally reticent about and so making it a difficult one to tackle. I figured if I make it an open forum topic here in the book it should be less of a taboo area and the team, in particular the Entertainments Manager can look after one another in this respect. They should also not be the least bit surprised if you complain should any of the above affect your holiday experience.

THE TEN MINUTE RULE

Never be late would be another obvious thing to say wouldn't it? Well it would but in fact a 'coat' should always be at least ten minutes early for any event. Ten minutes that's a bit excessive isn't it? On the face of it, it may seem so but as you travel through the book you will come to understand the importance of them not only being on time but being ready to run any event on time. Take daytime competitions for example, not only will they generally set the scene for it, possibly even clearing snooker or pool tables etc, they will also need to take the names of all those that turn up to take part in order to work out the byes. If they have not done this by the competition start time, as shown in the programme, they are not in control of the event and this in turn can cause problems even being the catalyst for things to turn nasty as I will explain in the chapter dedicated to competitions. Nothing they will do in the entertainments programme just starts on their arrival, everything from bingo to the lunchtime sing-a-long, from the swimming gala to man of the week, from mini golf to party dances needs to be set up. One of the most annoying things for a guest, and believe it or not something that generates a large amount of direct complaints and negative results on questionnaires, is a programme not running on time. It's a real pity because it is truly an easy rule to follow, they know what time they are due to start an event so just by making sure they are there ten minutes before that time, do what they have to do, start on time and be in control will allow their guests to enjoy whatever it is they have turned up to watch or take part in. There is no excuse for not doing this and it has always amazed me that some 'coats' actually seem to think they are getting away with something or putting one over on the Entertainments Manager if they don't bother with this rule. Well if this is their attitude it's only they that will suffer at the end of the day because, whilst they may get away with it a few times, one day they will have a lot of angry guests in their face because they messed up as I was alluding to above, and they will wish they had listened to me then. I guarantee this will only ever happen to them once, trust me starting all this grief because it's their fault for not being ready to begin on time is not something they will want to experience again. A good Entertainments Manager will be looking for the habitual offender also so they could even lose their job because of it. Is it worth it for the sake of ten minutes? If your 'coats' are not turning up early and ready to rock and roll at the advertised time....complain!

COMPETITION RULES

As we have already established 'coats' will be running all kinds of competitions during both the day and evening programme. We have discussed the basic rule of being on time and how they can lose control of the situation turning a fun event into a nightmare. Well there is a second basic rule that runs in tandem with this and that is they must know the rules to any competition or event they are involved in. As I was saying some situations can turn nasty and not knowing the rules will only exasperate the state of affairs and leave them wide open and very vulnerable to the interference by the guest that always thinks he or she knows better than them and tries to take over, trust me there's always one and they spoil it for the rest of you. If this happens where you are, make sure you flag it up to the Entertainments or Centre Managers because there is a training need here and once this all knowing guest takes over one event they will be there trying to do the same for them all...and you will end up hating them. That's not to say if you have good knowledge of a particular subject you can't offer to assist re the scoring etc. An intelligent coat will know exactly how to involve guests appropriately.

KNOWING THE PROGRAMME

A 'coat' should always carry a copy of the entertainments programme with them! That's about it really for this rule. Except to point out that they should always be able to answer a guest's query about any aspect of the entertainment for that or any other day, where and when is something taking place being the most frequently asked questions of course but there are many others they will need to know the answer to such as age limits etc. They should pay attention and make notes of any changes during the morning meeting and familiarise themselves with the cabarets that are to appear during your stay at the centre. If they don't know what a cabaret does or their suitability for certain age groups etc best they find out and have the answer as of now. Because I guarantee most of you reading this will be asking them at one time or another. If a 'coat' should find them-selves bereft of their copy of the programme and you ask them a question they don't readily know the answer to you should _NEVER_ hear the reply "I don't know" if you do....challenge them! In "Tales of Superblue" it's a golden rule that whatever phrase the 'coat' uses in this situation it must contain the words "I will find out for you" and then do just that. They must Never guess! Giving a guest the wrong information has obvious consequences but imagine how these can be magnified for instance if, by their false information, they have just caused you to miss the one thing you actually booked your holiday in order to enter, the talent competition for example with a free weekend at the final as a prize? The ramifications can be disastrous.....how unhappy are you? How much has this spoiled yours and your family's holiday? How much fuss are you going to make over this? Lots....and rightly so! It's their job to know in the first place but if for some reason they don't they need to quickly find out.....so you don't miss out.

THEY SHOULD ALWAYS CARRY A PEN AND PAPER

Guests make requests of us 'coats' anytime all of the time and that is what we are there for after all. So a 'coat' must be prepared and have a pen or pencil and something to write on with them at all times. It's so basic I nearly didn't bother to mention it at all, but then I remembered that now famous saying 'the questions only easy if you know the answer'. Well I guess that principle applies to the basic rules laid down for 'coats' in "Tales of Superblue" so I think it only fair that I pass them onto to you now. They are basic and simple to me having learnt from the best in the first place. However in some ways being taught even more valuable lessons when experiencing the consequences of not sticking to them. So as I was saying a 'coat' will never know when a guest will ask them to announce something special. A birthday, an anniversary, or engagement are the usual ones but the list is inexhaustible I was once asked to play D.I.V.OR.C.E by Billy Connolly because that guest was celebrating their 'decree nisi'. Whatever the request it is important to the person making it so for a 'coat' to forget or get it wrong is a massive no no.

'COATS' MUST MAKE TIME FOR ALL OF THEIR GUESTS

The importance of this one cannot be overstated so after long and hard deliberations I have decided that the only real way to bring home the magnitude of that import is to let you read exactly what I tell the 'coats' in "Tales of Superblue". This is of huge significance to you and your family's holiday happiness. Of course you should accept nothing short of absolute respect from any staff member at a centre but if your 'coats' are doing their job properly they will be spending a lot of time with you and can even influence the younger guest. I believe they should be doing what I write about here as a matter of course, making my thoughts in relation to this aspect no more than teaching a 'coat' to suck eggs.

But anyway the following are my exact words to them in that book:

If you have any prejudices at all being part of a holiday centre entertainments team is not the job for you and you should be made extremely unwelcome. You must enjoy being with people no matter their age, shape, size, colour, creed, disability or sexuality. Every person that arrives at your village wants to have a great holiday and they have the right to expect exactly that. All guests should receive the same treatment and attention with the only exception being when you have the opportunity and foresight to enhance a person's holiday experience such as considering a guests disability enabling them to take part in competitions or access to events etc. Of course all members of staff should adhere to this principle but being part of the entertainments team you are in the unique position of being with the guests for large amounts of the day and evening and in the privileged situation of being there because they want you to be. Whilst this is a lovely state of affairs for the 'coat' to find them-selves in, it has its own set of intricacies that you need to be aware of. It is all too easy to find a family that you get on particularly well with and sit with them all night while they ply you with drink but this of course would not be acceptable as you must spread yourself around as many guests as possible devoting equal amounts of attention to all taking particular care not to alienate any individual or group. What would be even worse however would be to impose yourself onto a family or group of people because you have 'fallen' for one of their number, although a perfectly human thing to do, this can cause a variety of problems. Obviously you are not sharing your time with other guests as we have already seen but those guests will be noting who you *are* spending all your time with and another one of my "I've seen it happen" moments is sure to occur. The least of your problems would be that other guests feel ignored by you constantly returning to the same table at the end of a dance, competition or show. The worst case scenarios, while equally hazardous, come from polarised stand points. Firstly the family themselves take exception to your constant presence or even to your intense interest in one of their party. This is a very awkward situation for them and can actually spoil the entire holiday for these guests. Secondly, and you can put money on this one, a member of that family and more often than not the very person who is the object of your desires wins a competition, bingo or raffle etc. I am sure you are already wincing at the thought of finding yourself in this predicament and that's while sitting comfortably reading the book. Imagine how you would be feeling with a whole ballroom of guests staring at you, knowing that the complaints are about to come flooding in to the management. You would not believe the ruckus something like this can cause, you are branded a cheat, families and guests openly argue (sometimes aggressively). And didn't you just know it was coming? Well I have seen it happen unfortunately more than once and it can spoil not only that event, day or evening but the entire week for everyone. The guests involved, and there can be quite a few by the time it's all over, of course have their holiday marred. You have managed to upset the person you had such amorous feelings for and will be facing the wrath of the Entertainments Manager, at the very least, if not the sack. Of course these are extreme examples I am telling you about and a decent Entertainments Manager should be watching for such behaviour and nip it in the bud in any case but they are real and have happened so bear them in mind. You are human and the fact that you have got the job should mean you are a sociable and likable person so the chances are you will find yourself in this situation from time to time. Remember be respectful of the families or groups right to enjoy a holiday without you hanging around 24/7. Declare your interest at the outset of any competition where they are an entrant and avoid taking part if you can particularly in the judging process. Make sure you are not involved in the drawing of raffle tickets or the checking of their bingo books etc. Always be discreet for both yours and the guest's sake. Guests take all this for granted and so they should it's your job to make sure they don't have a care in the world while they are in your hands *so don't let them down!*

OTHER BITS?

The other points I will highlight very quickly here again seem very obvious and self explanatory and I will be covering them, in greater detail in later chapters where they sit more decisively. They are worth a mention here though because if a 'coat' takes a single grain of sand and builds upon it they will be able to deliver you a fantastic holiday even if you're nowhere near the beach.

So I tell them to:

Stick to the rules of etiquette

Always strive to improve their part in everything

Never cheat their guests

Don't ask for applause for everything

THE BIGGEST RULE OF ALL

As usual it has been necessary to illustrate the downside of things covered in this chapter in order to emphasize the reasons for 'coats' doing them correctly in the first place. Don't get too hung up on those unpleasant consequences however because of "Tales of Superblue" they are now aware of their existence and are armed with the knowledge that prevents them getting into the situations in the first place.

All that is left for them to do is concentrate on fulfilling the BIGGEST rule of all............ *Enjoy them-self.*

Yes you did read that correctly you see these truly are the best days of their life so they need to relax. Now they have got the basics covered and I take them through all the other disciplines that they will need to be a great 'coat' in "Tales of Superblue" too. If they're not enjoying themselves there's no point in being there. When they are happy and having fun it comes across to you, the guests, and is contagious. All of the advice in the last few chapters is ultimately directed at this very point, so your 'coats just need to make sure they are in the right place doing the right thing being treated the right way and *ENJOY* giving **YOU** the holiday you have worked so hard to pay for and ***have every right to expect!!!***

Just so you know I also tell them to:

Always Smile

S - Smile

M - Make time for all of your guests

I - Immaculately dressed is the only option

L - Lateness is not acceptable be ten minutes early and know the programme

E - Enjoy yourself these are the best days of your life

WELL DEAR GUEST WHAT DO YOU THINK?

Have you always had service with a smile?

Are your coats always turned out immaculately?

Are they even clean and tidy?

What about on time?

Always knew what was on the programme and what cabarets were on?

No I thought not!

Well they absolutely should be delivering on all of these basic principals as a matter of course and you should be insisting upon it!

CHAPTER SIX

THE ENTERTAINMENTS PROGRAMME

I wonder how many of you dear holidaymakers are satisfied with the entertainments programmes that are, or indeed incredibly are not, organised and advertised for you these days?

I suspect the answer is not as many of you as there should be. Again a major reason for writing 'Tales of Superblue' was the appallingly poor excuse for an entertainment programme dished up at many centres I have been to over the past few years. As for any kind of decent advertising of a programme, or anything in that so called programme running at times that bear any resemblance to the times they should take place............. well the less said the better....er....actually no wait a minute that is completely wrong..... what am I talking about?

In fact the more you say, nay _shout_ about this terrible state of affairs the better!

How good an entertainments programme should you be getting? What should the Entertainments teams, Centre Managers and Holiday Companies be supplying you and your family with that would constitute an acceptable standard of entertainment programme? Well to be fair I must state here and now that it could depend on a number of things. The size of the centre, village, camp or park may determine the number of amenities and staff for instance. The time of year, particularly for junior programmes is a factor, that's not to say they should not run one at all. If they have taken your cash and booked in _any_ children they should be prepared to put something on for them. The location may mean that many guests attend because of the close proximity to great country or fell walks or mountain climbing or even, for example, one I stayed at recently that is on part of the coastline famous for surfing. These types of things do tend to take a number of guests off site during the day. There may be other subtle localised reasons that mean a full entertainments programme does not take place however having taken all of these things into consideration it is still my view that if you are at a holiday centre or hotel anywhere and have paid to be there....you have the right to expect some sort of activity to be arranged for you no matter how many others have gone out for the day.

It's also very short sighted of the management because all of the time you are not in the club house or ballroom they are losing revenue at the bars and cafes etc. Ah what about those lovely hot sunny days when we want to be outside? I hear you cry. Well of course we generally get so few of these in the UK that that is exactly where you should be and as you will see in the following pages a good Entertainments Manager will know how to ensure both you and the centre management are suitably taken care of in the open air on these rare days. You won't believe this but I actually wrote a chapter on precisely this subject in 'Tales of Superblue', I know your flabbergasted right?

OK then let's give you that all important information to make you all powerful in your quest for quality entertainment shall we. I know I keep repeating myself but................ **You have paid for it after all**

In fact I take this subject so seriously that the next 50+ pages are dedicated to it. Once you have read them you will know exactly what your anticipation should be from now on when booking a holiday. I pity the Entertainments Manager that fails to deliver and live up to those expectations.

They really do have no excuse .....

Why? Because once you have thumbed these pages you will know precisely the kind of programme I put together and know what standard I would expect if I booked into a holiday centre today. In fact not only will you merely be able to quote what you have learned from the book but you'll be able actually to write your own programme if you feel the need to complain. Now that would put the cat among the pigeons wouldn't it!

Yet again I have pondered how best to explain what it is that you should be demanding of your Entertainments Manager and Holiday Company in relation to this extremely important topic? After all it's at the very core of their business, the business that you have paid them for, the part of business that can mean the difference between you having the time of your life or the holiday from hell! So how should I approach this? Should I write some clever rhetoric about the awful excuses for programmes that I have encountered of late? Should I inform you of the good ones I am glad to say do still exist at some places? Now let me see decisions decisions oh what the heck. At the risk of giving away all my trade secrets I think you need to see exactly what I wrote for them in 'Tales of Superblue'. Imagine your one of them reading this chapter from now on and you will know exactly what to demand from now on. Please do also note the amount of hard work that goes into producing a good entertainments programme. Praise good Entertainments and Centre Managers as well as the team of 'coats'. It does go a long way if you write them up well in the obligatory questionnaire.

So here goes picture the scene your sat at home preparing for your first assignment as Entertainments Manager and you open 'Tales of Superblue' at the page on entertainment programmes and start to read..............

Never underestimate the importance of your entertainments programme. It is not something you can just chuck together and say "that will do them" then go down the pub. If you think it is please look for another job because you don't deserve to be in a position where thousands upon thousands of guests have saved their hard earned money and chosen to come to *your* camp to experience the holiday of a lifetime. You really must start to realise the enormity of your role as part of the entertainments team at a holiday centre by now and understand the concept of literally thousands of holidaymakers relying on *YOU* to make that dream come true. It is essentially the entertainment manager's responsibility to put the programme together before you even arrive at the centre. But you never know when you are going to be thrust into that role by design or default. Therefore this chapter is not only required reading for Entertainment Managers and an excellent reference for them on all types of programmes but a must read for all 'coats' and of course your guests. Remember a good programme keeps holidaymakers on site and spending their money instead of having to venture outside with their cash because your programme hasn't come up to scratch. This means that camp owners, managers and head offices will be perusing this chapter with particular interest. You have been warned!

I intend to help you understand the complexities that go into the planning of an entertainments programme, how to structure them so that the timing of each event is at the right time on the right day and is given the correct amount of duration in the programme. I will show you varied types of activities you should consider including in your programme to give your guests the widest possible choice throughout the day and evening. How to advertise your programme to maximise interest and attendance and how to cope with wet weather. We shall also have a look at giving it the friendly touch i.e. personalising your programme.

As I said your programme must be strong enough to keep your guests on site, that means making it fun packed and interesting for all the family. Not merely a list of things they can take part in at an extra cost. They have paid enough of their hard earned wages to come to your village now it's up to you to provide them with value for money. If you hit it right, and there's no reason not to, they will be enjoying themselves so much that they will spend whatever they have put aside as spending money at your park. Because you have kept them there the shops, bars, restaurant and take-aways etc all see an upsurge in takings. So you are making a vital contribution to the centres financial wellbeing by simply doing your job and giving your guests what they deserve.

Just to prove a point I will bore you once again with my dismay at the current state of affairs and say I think it's a pity the management of the centre I stayed at didn't have this book as an aide-memoir see what you think.

EXAMPLE OF A DAYS EVENTS FROM THAT PROGRAMME:
09.00am Learn to swim **£3**
09.00am Aqua Jets **£5** an hour **£3** for 30 mins (8 yrs+)

Not only are you starting the day by charging your guests extra money but putting two of these extra cost events on at the same time in the same place. This programme also did not offer a cost free alternative for adults or children during this period. In fact the adult daytime programme was non-existent.

THE NEXT EVENT THAT WAS:
09.30am Character Breakfast – 'Enjoy a full English breakfast'.

Two points here 1) Yet again using the children to make money by getting them to come and buy a full English breakfast and be in the company of the camps Characters. That means the parents inevitably will be pestered into being there and so even more meals sold. 2) Anyone that had swimming lessons or Aqua Jetted won't have time to join the characters so now you have upset children. They will have to choose between the lessons and Aqua Jets or breakfast, so not even an intelligent programme for making money or keeping the guests happy. If those having swimming lessons *could* have made it, you have to ask yourself what sort of value for money would they be getting.

There was a welcome meeting at 10.30am and at 11.00am activities for 1-4s and 5-11s. 12.00 noon was story time by a character (I heard a little boy complain to his Dad that the other character had told the same story yesterday this shows very bad organisation and control of the programme).

At 12.30pm I was pleased to see a period set aside for teenagers, but then I noticed:

1 pm Football lessons **£5,** so the very people likely to be attracted to the teenage activities now find themselves having to leave after half an hour and again paying a sizable extra.

The day was finished off with a character show at 2.30pm.

And that was about the gist of every day in the programme.

If you were an adult reading this programme when you first arrived at the centre what would you be thinking?

1) This is a rip off - so many extra costs?
2) There is absolutely nothing for me to do?

Well I can't talk for others of course but they were my first thoughts you will know what yours are now. Unfortunately it didn't stop there, the evening programme, apart from being an absolute shambles, was completely geared around making as much money from the guests as possible.

Two sets of cash bingo started the proceedings this was followed, would you believe, by prize bingo. Then according to the programme 7.45pm to 8.45pm was children's time (not that the programme bore any resemblance to the time any event took place). At 8.45 there was supposed to be a parade, one would imagine to signal the end of the children's time and the beginning of the adult entertainment. But no the very next item on the programme at 9pm, and this will astound you as it did me, a game using the bingo machine where the prizes were toys from the shop. They sold raffle tickets 1 to 90 as many times over as they could then simply called out the numbers as they came up on the bingo machine the last number called won the toys. Can you imagine how much money this could raise? Plus all the kids that lost now want something from the shop (of which by the way there were two and both situated in the entertainment venue, and there opening times? 6pm till late. Cynical? Maybe).

This should be prime time fun entertainment for you guests and you would like to think it got better after that wouldn't you? That surely must be the end of the moneymaking. After all the kids stuff is well and truly over now isn't it? Well it should have been but to my utter astonishment the entertainers would then hold a 'Party Dance' session. With the programme already in total disarray this meant that this did not begin until gone 10.30pm some nights. What made this even worse was the fact that the lights would be turned down and all the 'coats' would wear aluminous accessories from, yes you've guest it, the shop. Naturally all the children, who should have been discouraged from the dance-floor at this time of night, are now hitting their already well out of pocket parents for even more dosh so that they can buy these items and join in. Just imagine how you would be feeling by this time of night at this camp, I know how I felt!

Unfortunately the only actual entertainment during the week were so called visiting cabarets the like of which I have never witnessed before, they were dire with no band or live music at all (But more about that in the chapter on shows). Weekends were a little better in this respect 'only' as there was live musical cabarets brought in, but this would have been necessary to keep the caravan and chalet 'owners' happy.

When you look back at the day, what entertainment have the parents and other adults actually had? Next to none but the children are enjoying themselves aren't they? Yes but even going on the old adage 'keep the kids happy and the parents will be happy' is costing them extra money every part of the day, _every day_ of their holiday. People only have so much money to spend and what they spend in the shop they don't have to spend at the bar or in the restaurant etc so making them unhappy guests. What they do do however is tell friends, relatives, workmates and that includes people like you and me, how they feel about it and so a centre's short term profit could be its long term downfall.

I can only give you my personal response to such a programme and the reasons I would never put something like that together. That's not going to help you though is it, or is it? Well I figure if I present you with the problems as I see them and then furnish you with the tools to ensure you won't be caught out by those pitfalls you will be armed with everything you need to construct a good, value for money programme and be in a position to argue your corner should you receive pressure from the camp manager, head office or owners etc to do otherwise.

FUN PACKED AND INTERESTING FOR ALL THE FAMILY

A programme is like a jigsaw, you really must put a great deal of thought into when and where to place your events. Before you read any further try a little experiment, what? Oh go on humour me. Ok close this book now, go and make yourself a nice cup of tea or coffee, sit yourself down comfortably with a pen and paper. Give yourself fifteen minutes, no longer, and draft what you think would be a good days family entertainments programme. See you in about twenty minutes.

Oh your back, how did you get on with that little exercise? I hope you did it without cheating and having a sneaky peek at the next few pages. If you did you probably found it a little harder than you thought it might be. Well that's perfectly natural isn't it, because that's what we are here for today, to learn how to put that jigsaw together.

There are certain formats that have proven to be very popular over the years and I can assure you work very well and I will be showing you some examples of programmes that I have put together and utilised at a variety of centres for a range of special events and themed weeks as well as the all important summer season.

Fun packed I said and fun packed I meant. You need to be thinking about what you can cram into your daytime programme between breakfast and the evening meal. Even if you're not a full or half board centre your programme should generally start after the normal breakfast period and end in time for the guests to return to their accommodation, shower, change and have an evening meal. Some events such as keep fit or a ramble can take place before breakfast at some parks. One idea I have had lately is to add a dog walking session in the morning and evening into your programme if you are at a village that allows pets as these are now becoming increasingly popular particularly with owners sites. I have yet to see this ever growing section of the holiday market being catered for in this way. It puts a whole new slant on the ramble. I am surprised I am the first to think of it, or am I? Maybe not!

Cram it all in sounds a bit hectic doesn't it? Well of course you're right you can't just go squashing in one event after another. It has to be fun for a start and fun means different things to different people so make your day a varied one so there is something for everyone. Sounds difficult I know but don't panic we are going to go through it all. And remember what I told you earlier, half the people enjoy watching the other half taking part and you could conceivably have the majority of the camp all in one place at the same time doing just that. For instance out on the field for sports day, it's a knockout type fun or all manner of events such as donkey derby.

Interesting? Your probably saying well if they are doing something they think is fun then they must be finding it interesting mustn't they? Again you are right to a point but when you are devising your programme bear in mind that families or partners like to do certain things together, such as watching their children in the junior talent show. If you have put this on the same time as the gents snooker competition for example you're already spoiling Dads fun, as he now has a dilemma and will probably miss the snooker because he is interested in what his little darlings are doing and Mum would be none too pleased if he wasn't there too, while at the same time the children themselves *are* having fun. Get it? Oh it will all make sense soon.

Hopefully you now understand the importance of a great programme and are eager to give your guests the best you possibly can. Brilliant, but hold on a minute just what should you be considering before even putting pen to paper? A myriad of things is the honest answer but how about these few pointers for instance. The facilities you have to work with is an obvious factor, do you have a snooker room? If so how many tables does it have? Is the playing field suitable for a football matches or a sports day? is the swimming pool large enough for a gala and are there any health and safety issues? (I will cover health and safety in a later chapter). Do you have two or more indoor venues that will allow you to split the adult and family entertainment? How many staff do you have to run these events, and are they qualified to run them, keep fit being a good example. What sponsorship deals do you have to be wary of i.e. have the sponsors stipulated a particular time of day and or venue that their competition or fun event must take place in. Where will I put everyone if it turns out to be a wet day? What about visiting celebrities, these will have been booked via head office to perform at certain times on certain days and may include snooker, darts or football pros etc during the day and a variety of cabarets in the evening. What bands do you have, and do you have one for lunchtime sing-a-longs etc. Funding is an element that needs to be considered too e.g. do you have enough of a budget to purchase new equipment if needed? Can you afford prizes for all the competitions you want to run and so on?

Phew! A lot to think about huh? The list is literally exhaustive because every camp, village, centre, park or hotel has its own peculiarities. Basically there is no easy formula for this part of the process you just have to go and visit the place and see for yourself exactly where it is and what they have for you to run this particular programme. Follow this up by talking to head office or the owners of the camp to find out about the cabarets and sponsorships etc. Then and only then you can start to formulate the concept of your programme. ***NOW! The real work begins.***

You've visited your centre, found out when and where the cabarets will be and know all about the sponsored events so now you can put pen to paper. Where to start is the next question to answer, the beginning is always the cliché isn't it, but on this occasion I'm afraid there's no getting away from it. Day one, the day the guests arrive, this is conventionally a Saturday but the advent of split weeks and weekend breaks at some parks has meant you may well have two arrival days. If this is the case you will need to incorporate two welcome meetings or line ups depending on how you choose to execute yours. The next vital piece of information you will need to find out is do all the guests come just for the weekend going home allowing an entirely fresh audience to arrive for the midweek break or, as in most centres I know of, do the bulk of guests stay on for a week or two thereby overlapping these short breaks. You are most likely to find the latter is the norm and so will need to cater for the long term guest. They will not want to see the same thing over and over again. This includes the welcome so ensure you place the extra welcomes in a part of the programme that these guests will happily miss, for example between afternoon and evening bingo. This will also mean an even more complex working of the programme but so long as you have done your research you will be fine. Those that have come on short breaks will enjoy their few days with you if you have constructed your programme properly because every day will be fun packed, value for money and interesting. Never be bullied into changing your programme for a handful of guests or owners this will only upset the other guests and throw your whole, carefully planned programme into chaos. If *you* feel something is worth changing for a particular reason and can justify it then that's a decision for you to make. But make sure you plan any change very carefully so as not to cause that chaos I was talking about and the knock on affects that can produce. Above all advertise it in as many places as possible as many times as possible giving as much notice as possible.

In a while I will be showing you those examples I talked of earlier and they are probably the best way of giving you guidance when you come to create your own programme. Do remember though that is what they are, guidance. Nothing would flatter me more that to see one of my programmes being run at your village, the reality however is that many parks don't have the full range of facilities that an Entertainments Manager would wish for, while other centres are greatly improved some even with magnificent adventure amenities. So you will have to tailor yours to get the best out of it according to where you are. No I'm not going to cop out of it as easily as that, not when so much of your success rides on this. I will be going into the mechanics of putting together and running daytime and evening competitions in depth later so don't get bogged down with those worries now. We are concentrating on the structure and content of your programme at the moment and so back to day one. This may be a big 'change- over' day and a lot of managers like to give a bulk of the staff the day off because of it. Please do be mindful, however, of those guests we spoke about that are staying over for another week. To them it is just another day of their holiday and as such will be looking to be entertained and you will need enough 'coats' to greet the guests who are arriving. This is something I have noticed that a few centres don't bother with these days. You know some old sayings really do hold water and 'first impressions count' is definitely one of them. Get in early start making your guests laugh as soon as they arrive, whatever problems they may have booking in or after that they will remember the 'coats' were friendly and helpful right from the start.

So you have provided entertainment for your 'tweekers' what? Oh that's your 'two weekers', seen the new arrivals in with a smile and are ready for your first night. You will have a welcome line up in your evening programme. So remember what I teach you Entertainments Managers about this and keep it slick and swift. Make sure all the other things I have banged on about are happening too, everything running on time everyone immaculate etc etc. But as for putting it all together on paper it's just another evening so don't let the fact that it's the first one rattle you. While first impressions do count the guests should be just impressed with your Wednesday night programme as much as they are with your welcome Saturdays or farewell Friday party nights.

Just take each day as it comes write a rough skeleton outline putting in all the events you have no control over such as promotions, sponsored events, pro celebrities or cabarets etc. Make a list of all the amenities at your disposal that can be utilised for competitions i.e. mini golf, tennis or even such items as quad bikes and climbing walls etc.

Put these into columns and write male, female, teenage and junior next to them as appropriate. As you devise each day of your programme, delete male, female etc eventually crossing out the entire list. Bear in mind that you can run two adult events at the same time if you are sensible. For example Ladies Darts and Gents Snooker, this allows couples to choose that particular day to take part in events. They are normally held in the same part of the village. Keeping both entertained and can plan the rest of the day together maybe taking part in something else in the afternoon or even go on an organised excursion. While they are doing all that don't forget you have the junior and teenage events taking place, just bear in mind what I said about trying to match these up to keep everyone happy. It is important to remember the excursions also, if your centre is running these or has an agreement for discounts with a local coach company etc you can push the ones that you think are value for your guests and always send at least one 'coat' on them to keep up the holiday spirit and fun. This reminds your guests that you are providing their entertainment whilst advertising to other holidaymakers that your guests are having a great time. You never know they may just book to come to your holiday centre next year on the strength of it, well it all helps you know.

While you are penning your programme and are thinking of placing an event into a particular slot always take into account the following little tips:

1. Don't put two strong events or an array of small ones on at the same time this will unnecessarily spread your guests too thinly.

2. Make sure you will have enough staff to run the amount and size of events you are putting on at any one time.

3. Check that you have no clashing events (family sports day and junior talent for example).

4. Start competitions at a time that will ensure they don't run over into other events, meal times, the evening programme or as I have seen into the next day. Guests will leave, your competition will be a farce, your programme will be in disarray and you will be in a lot of bother.

5. Run compatible events alongside each other (i.e. 10am ladies pool – gent's darts – teenage table tennis – junior craft session).

6. Work around strong excursions, visiting cabarets and sponsored events.

7. Take into account any theme that you may be running that day and utilise events that fit in with it.

A good example would be Country and Western but with a little thought you can come up with items to enhance any theme.

How about these few suggestions for your Country and Western day:
Apache archery competition

Horse shoe pitching competition

Western film

Change the noddy train to the rawhide express

Line dancing

Your western show

Hunt the naughty outlaw who stole the sweets

Best dressed C & W chalet, caravan or table competition

Donkey Derby

Always have a wet weather alternative for each day as some days will be easier than others to cover. There will be days in your programme with a large amount of indoor activity and others where most events are outdoors (sports day for example). Don't forget to show in your printed programme where guests can go to find the 'Wet Weather Programme' should you need to invoke it.

Alternatively the sign of a great Entertainments Manager is one that has a hot weather programme up his or her sleeve. This is actually a very simple concept and yet I have rarely seen anyone put it into practice, hopefully this situation will be remedied by this book. The fact is that we do get some lovely days in the UK and your guests won't want to be stuck inside during them and you will lose them from the camp if you haven't got outdoor events that will keep them there. As with any of your programmes it takes a little imagination but it's not rocket science, use the facilities you have, redistribute your staff as appropriate and run activities that are compatible with the temperature. Importantly, advertise this in exactly the same way as a wet weather programme.

Liaison with the bars and catering managers is absolutely vital for themed, wet and hot weather programmes.

Special events such as the World Cup or the Olympics etc need particularly careful reworking of a programme so that your guests will be able to enjoy them. Obviously you will be planning it around the event but be mindful not to make the fundamental error of replacing the programme with it. Not everyone likes football or sports and those people have paid the same as everyone else and deserve to be entertained no matter what else is taking place, indeed they may have actually booked then to avoid the event, so ensure you have alternatives in place for them. It is also imperative that you make sure you have a comprehensive children's programme running throughout so that they are safe, occupied and happy leaving parents free to enjoy the event.

Let me just throw in an extra free tip here – Be very careful of taking sides in such events even if you see a great opportunity to use it for entertainment value.

THE CAMEROON INCIDENT

I recall it was a lovely warm sunny summer a perfect time to be at a holiday centre but around the country there was much more than the usual holiday excitement abound in the air, an exhilarated tension gripped the nation, a sense that this time yes this time we could do it, we could actually become champions of the world. Every English fan was pinning their hopes and dreams on this team bringing home the 1990 World Cup. As far as the eye could see there were union jacks, red and white shirts, hats, flags, scarf's, even entire buildings decked out with patriotic fervour. Every part of this great land and around the four corners of the world English fans adorned every inch of their domain in this regalia and sang rule Britannia at the tops of their voices.

Everywhere except, that is, in one little corner of the tiny little Isle of Wight!!!

One man stood out from the crowd, one man dared to be different, one man wore his colours with pride, one man set up a shrine of banners heralding his chosen team, one man proudly strutted around the holiday camp where he was the Entertainments Manager proclaiming his adoption of another magnificent team, one man defiantly flew in the face of the concept of following the crowd, one man endured public ridicule, yes one man, one

English man had decided to support..Cameroon.

Cameroon?

Well that's what you would have said prior to the start of that memorable tournament. And it certainly was to become a very unforgettable event for me.

I was indeed that man, that man that thought it would be a good hoot, a marvellous jape, a smashing wheeze, a great lark, a really good joke and just a downright bit of good clean fun to support a team other than the one most of my guests obviously would. I must not forget the other home countries here of course.

So I picked a team, a team that seemed to sit best with my idea of a fun squad to lend my support to, a team that would be lively and vibrant, a team that others would

---

warm to, a team that would ensure the whole scheme would result in a good laugh for all, a team that would not last too long in the competition!

So in the safe knowledge that I had covered all these angles I proudly announced my support for Cameroon. After all they had the fabulous 40 year old Roger Miller playing for them, what an inspiration, what a wonderful role model, what a nice person to hold up as a figurehead, to spearhead my flamboyant campaign.

I set out on my crusade of espousal for this little known football team by purchasing as much merchandise, as I could not that easy to find at the time I have to say, and festooned one corner of the ballroom in it and placed a golden throne (an old prop) on the spot. Attempting to elicit the assistance of a posse made up of other staff members on the camp I was soon to learn that my destiny would be to travel on this honourable journey of encouragement for the underdog single-handed, unaccompanied, by myself in a completely solitary fashion.....in fact totally alone, isolated from the rest of normal civilisation as we knew it back then. Yes I was supporting Cameroon!

No matter steadfast and undaunted I was on a mission and stuck resolutely to my course of action after all it would all get a good laugh wouldn't it? It's not like it was going to affect anything any of our teams were doing in the cup was it? I would only be able to string it out for a short time anyway because as lovely as the Cameroon squad was they wouldn't be in the competition for very long would they?

No

No?

No

So what happened?

What happened? What happened? I'll tell you what happened!

Cameroon qualified for the 1990 World Cup surpassing Nigeria and beating Tunisia in the final round playoff. In the final tournament Cameroon were drawn into group B with Argentina, Romania, and the Soviet Union. Cameroon shocked the world by defeating the current World Cup holders Argentina 1-0. Cameroon later defeated Romania 2-1 but then lost to the Soviet Union 4-0. However in the second round Cameroon defeated Colombia 2-1 with Roger Milla scoring the two goals in the extra time.

So in the quarter finals Cameroon faced England.

What?

England

England?

Yep

Oh no don't panic Superblue! Oh I am sure it'll be fine….wont it? Surely this will be a walkover for England……won't it?

I gingerly entered the ballroom that hot sunny afternoon, not that I needed the weather to make me perspire I was confronted by my worst nightmare. The place was heaving with English fans of course and they had decorated the remaining 3 quarters of the room in everything that said or stood for England. A deathly hush fell over the one thousand and something strong throng that were quite clearly awaiting my arrival, you could definitely have heard the proverbial pin drop as I looked into the corner of the room and……..OH NO! It was all still there, the golden throne along with my aggrandized Cameroon regalia … OH MY! What was I going to do now?

Run away and hide until it was all over?

That seemed the most logical course of action to me. But as I turned to head back out of the door my escape was blocked by a mass of red and white shirted guests who indicated that they would rather I stayed for this particular game and handed me my Cameroon shirt, hat, scarf and flag that I had somehow forgotten to wear or bring with me that fateful afternoon. But I should have realised I was never going to be let off the hook that easily. One of my colleagues had made certain that they found their way from my little flat at the top of the centre and into the hands of the guests. I never did find out who that was but I suspect it was my old buddy 'Pompeii' the bars manager, we did have some fun that season and I don't doubt he owed me a practical joke or two.

After they had helped me slip into in my brightly coloured Cameroon outfit I was paraded through the assembled guests and sat on my throne.

Of course at this point I was not at all nervous…

No?

No I was petrified!

What would the next couple of hours bring?

What on earth would happen if Cameroon actually did it again?

What if they became the most famous giant killers ever known?

The massive drop down screen suddenly became the focal point for everyone in the building as the game, the game I never dreamt in my wildest dreams would ever actually take place.....the game that had us all waiting with baited breath.....began!

It wasn't a dream, I was never to wake to find it was all a horrible nightmare, this was it..........................it really really really was England vs Cameroon in the world cup.

Yes One man stood out from the crowd, One man dared to be different, One man wore his colours with pride, one man set up a shrine of banners heralding his chosen team, One man proudly strutted around the holiday camp where he was the Entertainments Manager proclaiming his adoption of another magnificent team, One man defiantly flew in the face of the concept of following the crowd, One man endured public ridicule, yes One man, One English man decided to support.. Cameroon!!!

That One man,

That One extremely worried man,

That One man now sat on his throne in full view of a thousand plus English spectators,

What happened? What happened? I'll tell you what happened!

After 25 minutes England's David Platt scored for England.

In the second half however Cameroon came back with a 61st minute goal from a penalty taken by Kunde.

Then to my absolute horror Cameroon only went and took the lead with Ekeke scoring in the 65th minute.

Oh my goodness!!! (Or words to that effect)

Now how scared do you think I was?

How popular do you imagine I was at that moment?

One man,

One very lonely man,

One terrified man,

England however equalized in the 83rd minute with a penalty from Lineker.

And that lovely life saver of a man Gary Lineker made it 3-2 to England with a penalty in the 105th minute.

I was safe!

I had come through it all in one piece!

The boys had come through for me!

I was lifted onto the shoulders of my guests as the celebrations begun

And oh boy did we celebrate

A great party was had by all

BUT...

Cameroon had nearly created one of the greatest upsets in World Cup history.

Super Cameroon colours 1990

HOW TO ADVERTISE YOUR PROGRAMME TO MAXIMISE INTEREST AND ATTENDANCE

There is no point in going through all the blood sweat and tears of putting these programmes together if the guests either don't know or care what's on. Not knowing is obvious, you haven't advertised it properly. Not caring would be an absolute crime and mean that you have serious problems and you should probably be getting the sack. So if you get reports that the latter is happening do something about it and do it quickly. It can only be one of a number of things that have made your guests stop caring what's on, because believe me they arrived at your park wanting to know everything that you had to offer them. So lets have a look at those shall we, it could be that your programme is so bad that one event is as awful as the next or that the programme is ok but the events are so badly run that people don't want to attend them anymore or the timing of events bears no relation to the programme so there's no point in reading it, but in many respects the worst of all would be that you and or your entertainments team are sending out the vibe that you and or they don't care what's on, now that really would be a holiday camp sin and you *should* be sacked. You will have noticed that there is nothing in that lot that I have not covered already and we will be going into many of these points in more depth in the coming chapters so there truly is no excuse for any of these scenarios at your village. Again please do remember that managers and guests alike will be looking for you to come up to the high standards that this manual of guidance is setting out for you all so any lame excuse just won't wash.

MAKE SURE YOUR GUESTS KNOW WHAT'S ON AND WHEN AND WHERE IT TAKES PLACE

As with most things in this book this section starts with an obvious and fundamental statement of fact on which to build upon. This time it's 'Make sure your guests know what's on and when and where it takes place'. As I said obvious isn't it, but as with most things in this manual it is a little more complex when you look at it. The obvious way to advertise your programme is in a printed copy that the guests receive on their arrival at your resort. Make sure you have an input in the design of this as the programme must take centre stage throughout the booklet be easy to read and not swamped by adverts for the restaurant and shops etc. Note that I said booklet, I have seen many types of programme over the years. The latest park I stayed at had a folding piece of paper, you're ok I'm not going to go on about it again, but I have found the booklet to be the best format in which to present a good programme with a double page spread for each day encompassing the adult, teenage and junior agendas. Even though you have supplied a printed programme this is likely to be read and then left in the chalet or maybe there's not enough copies for the whole family to have one with them when they are dispersed on the variety of things you have laid on. So entertainment boards are a vital asset in getting your message across. They need to be placed in prominent locations around the centre such as entrances to venues the reception and shops etc. They should be easy to read and make them distinctive so they stand out. Ensure they carry all that day's events including themes and don't forget to advertise cabarets and shows. The cabarets and shows should always have a photograph to make the board more interesting and give a flavour of the fun the guests can expect when they come to watch them. Chase up agents or head office if photos are not being sent to you and updated regularly. On the subject of updating one of the biggest complaints a camp manager will get from the guests is the boards being out of date, and yes it is infuriating if you cross the centre to see what is on that evening before you go out for the day only to find yesterdays programme still on it. A very important rule you must stick to, and make sure it is done on your day off also, is 'The boards MUST be changed last thing at night'. When you are dishing out the postings for that day, at your morning meeting, designate at least one person whose last job will be to do exactly that. Should anyone let you down really impress upon them your displeasure over it so that they will pass this to the rest of the team. It is such a simple thing yet when it's not done it can cause great annoyance to the guests and earn you complaints that can so easily be avoided. These should be quickly changed when wet or hot weather programmes are to be instigated, particularly on short notice *but don't forget to change them back* if returning to the original programme or in any case before the evening one begins.

If you are lucky enough to have your own TV station as we did at Pontins make the very most of it. It is a fabulous way to get to your guests in their own accommodation, usually first thing in the morning and between the day and evening programmes and of course you can leave a copy of the programme running all day. It goes without saying you will make it fun and entertaining whilst remaining clean and tasteful. Take cameras out during the day and show highlights that evening or the next morning, guests love to see themselves on the screen and will also submit CD's or videos they have shot. Involve the guests where possible and always try to show something they will find amusing. Such as me having my hair permed and coloured for charity while at pontins, the whole camp got to see me with all that silver foil and various other bits and bobs sticking out everywhere from my head. Did I look good blonde and with a perm? Judge for yourself:

Ok you can stop laughing now I've had a lot worse than that, I dread to think about some of it now, but it made people smile so it was worth it. ***The donkey by the way was only a day old, ah!***

Anyway the TV is a fantastic tool if you have it, but as in anything else to do with your programme it is so important to be prepared and rehearsed, even though you want to make it look like your adlibbing and winging it, have all the information you need at hand and as always make sure it's on time every time. Never run it early, the only thing worse than sitting there waiting to see that mornings show that is running late is to sit there waiting to see that mornings show only to find you missed it because it was early. Guests, especially the children, really do look forward to tuning in to see their 'coats' larking about, delivering the programme and showing clips of themselves having fun but you will encounter massive complaints if you mess this one up.

Many villages, camps, parks, resorts and centres were originally built well away from any built up areas, such as on old military camps etc. The reason for this was twofold, firstly the land was cheep at that time and secondly the campers would have to stay on site and spend their money. It is particularly apt to note here that even though they had a captive audience with nowhere else to spend their money the owners of these early camps realised the importance of giving the campers value for money and a full entertainments programme, thereby ensuring their loyalty and constant re-booking to that camp. The days of people arriving at the camps by train and charabanc (coach to you and me) have long gone and of course most families now have a least one car. This has had the affect of transforming these centres, from out of the way places where guests had little choice but to remain, into perfect base camps to stay at while spending the days visiting beautiful parts of the country in which many of them are situated, ironically because of their isolated locations. This does of course pose you with a real dilemma, if they are going out during the day how are you going to let them know what's on. Well the first thing to emphasise here is to make sure your printed programme is clear and exciting when they arrive. They will of course still go out sightseeing during their stay but will choose the days best suited for them to remain on the centre to be entertained or take part in events. Don't do as I have seen and just give up saying there's no point in a daytime programme no-one comes. It's up to you to sell your daytimes as fun packed and interesting enough for people to at least take a look at. If you lose them after that, well your days aren't good enough and you need to revamp them. Don't rely on just the printed programme of course ensure your boards are changed so people can read them before leaving the venues to go to bed etc. Make sure you have really effective boards or banners on display as they leave the village for their day trips highlighting that evening's entertainment and don't forget to have the same pointing in the opposite direction for when they return. If you have a particular event to promote or are at a centre that is attracting a large amount of guests that do not attend the venues and just use it as a base camp, consider using flyers delivered to each caravan, chalet or room. Many centres offer a packed lunch facility to the guests providing you with a marvellous opportunity to reach them while they are off the park. Again by good working relationships with the catering manager you will be in a position to place a flyer or indeed a full programme into each pack for that day hopefully attracting them to the venues that evening and reminding them that they do have options to spend at least some days in the park and be entertained. The more you advertise what you have on for your guests the more they will be inclined to come and sample what you are offering. A lot of people who think it's not for them are pleasantly surprised once they experience the quality and variety of a good entertainments programme. So make it one you can be proud of and sell it like you believe in it, as indeed you should do.

I think it only fair to give credit where it's due and point out that there were some camps, my own Butlins Clacton for example, that were actually purpose built and given over to the military for use in wartime returning to their original use and bringing much needed laughter afterwards.

If you are lucky enough to have the wonderful 'guest traps' of full or half board catering don't you dare waste it. These are without doubt among the best times for an entertainments team to gel with its guests. Having a couple of 'coats' at the doors to greet guests at mealtimes is a practice lost at some centres, and that is a pity because communication is the key here. This is a time for not only pushing your programme for that day or evening, but for the guests to be able to talk to you without you having to rush off to run an event or be half occupied by a competition etc. You will discover a great deal about the mood of the park at that time and will be able to gage how you and your programme are being perceived and whether or not your guests are enjoying themselves. This gives you an almost unique insight and a chance to implement changes in a timely fashion thereby showing your professionalism and negating complaints. However on the lighter side of this important point the setting is perfect for even more fun with your guests. You can do anything from impose silly forfeits for being late or having a bad hair day at breakfast, best dressed table for themed days etc to the most outrageous costume for that evening. The possibilities are literally endless so think creatively and start the guest's day with fun and laughter, greet and get in amongst them, set their evening off in style and sell your programme to the max. The enjoyment that your entertainment brings at these times can be considerably enhanced by the introduction of friendly rivalry between the guests and the dishing out or indeed the taking away of house points. I know some of you are bemused by this but bear it in mind because it will all make sense when I cover this topic later. If you have staggered seating times, this is not a problem, all you will need to do is advertise the times between which you and your team will be in attendance and competitions and fun will take place, you will find people will make a beeline for the restaurant during that period. Liaison with the catering manager is a must to ensure the smooth running of any event and good staff relations as it's important to compliment and not impede the hard work that this vital department carries out. To sum up mealtimes are a brilliant time to interact with a large number of your guests but it's up to you to make this an event that they will enjoy and look forward to as well as telling others what they have missed thus becoming a self promoting fun experience. On this occasion I feel justified in repeating myself so: *don't you dare waste it.*

There is one more thing that I must nag you about in relation to programmes, I know I have said it before but it's worth saying again because it's so fundamental a point. The fact is every 'coat' should carry a copy of the programme with them at all times. They must be aware of any changes and be able to advise guests on such things as the names and suitability of the cabarets and shows for that day etc.

MAKE IT PERSONAL

Now that you have done all the hard work and put your puzzle together you can have an absolute field day writing your own programme. I must admit I always enjoy this part of the process being creative and silly adding my own personal touch that will make the guests smile and encourage them to come and meet the daft fool what wrote it. There is nothing worse than opening a programme to see what exciting events the entertainments team have in store for you only to discover a boring list of one mundane blurb after another. Spruce it up inject a bit of life and humour into it, the cornier the better if that's your personality or try to be intellectually funny if that's you. You just know I am the corny type don't you, oh well it works for me anyway. Some centres now have a bog standard pre arranged programme which is a shame because the guests can sense that and feel they are missing out and not getting the personal touch. If this is the case at your village flaunt your own personality on your boards and in flyers etc. There is of course an example coming up so I won't go into it too deeply here, after all it's supposed to be your personality that shines through not a copy of mine but just by taking bingo as an example you can quickly think of a number of phrases that take it from the mundane and give it a cheeky little life of its own, Clickety Duck eyes down and good luck for instance. Of course it's daft and silly but remember your guests are on holiday they want daft they want silly they want fun and laughter they want you to talk to them in your programme. They get all the seriousness they can handle the rest of the year, this is **holiday time**.

There are people who collect interesting programmes so try to get yours in that category. What about mine? I've got loads if that counts.

Well as I said I will include a sample of a programme using this style of personalisation and that will be coming up in just a minute. Just as a clear format to use as a template to build your own programmes upon.

Example of Adult Programme

For the sake of this example we will assume that the guests arrive on Saturday for a week
You will of course tailor your programme to the arrival day(s) and length of stay of your guests

We will keep the whole thing quite simple and generic and look at the sort of thing you might put together for a centre with one main venue plus a children's club. Once again you will be able to put more into your programme dependent on the makeup of your holiday camp and staff numbers

Don't forget to add ages to events such as junior, teenage and adult competitions quite often dictated by sponsors

There will also be your pro visiting sports stars that will need to be slotted in. These will include Wrestling, Snooker, Tennis, Football, Table Tennis and Darts etc

You will notice that I have placed some teenage competitions in the adult programme on this occasion but again dependent on all the usual factors it is likely they will have a complete programme of their own

We will call the 'coats' 'Supercoats' and our resident band 'Supergroup' for the purpose of this exercise

Saturday

10.00 am

If this is your second week come and have a nice cup of tea with your Supercoats in the café. We are always here to help so if you have any questions we are delighted to assist you. But it would be nice to see you for a good old fashioned gossip too!

If you have just arrived welcome to Camp Superblue please do come and say hello to your Supercoats who are looking forward to meeting you.

Don't forget the swimming pool and all of your sports facilities are also open.

12.00 noon

Your Supercoats are waiting for you in the bar for a couple of hours of fun.

2.30 pm

Come and let your cares drift away immerse yourself in the family matinee in the ballroom.

4.30 pm

Meet your Supercoats outside reception for a tour of the resort.

Evening

You are invited to join in our friendly house system here at Camp Superblue Holiday Resort and have heaps of fun wining points throughout your stay with us

Supers v Blues

(Even Chalet Numbers)   (Odd Chalet Numbers)

6.00 pm

Party Dance's and fun for all the family before the young ones are taken to the children's club for their very own special time.

6.30 pm

Welcome to your first session of bingo - books on sale now in the ballroom

7.00 pm

Clickety Duck eyes down and good luck.

7.45 pm

Who's Who? Meet the management and your talented team of Supercoats who are here to help you enjoy your holiday

8.00 pm

Time to take to the floor and enjoy the sounds of our fabulous band – Supergroup

9.00 pm

Team Chase Fun Competition – Lots of fun and the first of those important house points to be won by you adults!

9.30 pm

Supergroup take to the stage – Musical fun for all the family

10.00 pm

Good Night Children – your very own nighty night tunes. See you in the morning

WE RESPECTFULLY REMIND MUMS AND DADS THAT THE CHILDREN ARE NOT ALLOWED ON THE DANCE FLOOR AFTER 10PM UNLESS ACCOMPANIED BY AN ADULT...THANK YOU.

10.20 pm

Star Cabaret – We have the pleasure in introducing the first of our top class cabarets

11.00 pm

Back to Dancing with Supergroup – So come on shake rattle and roll

12.00 Midnight

Disco time - Until the wee small hours

Good night sleep well we have a busy day for you tomorrow.

***

Sunday

8.00 am

Good morning – the swimming pool is now open so get up and have a splashing time

10.00 am

Keep Fit – Come along and let us help you stay in shape

10.30 am

Party Dances – Come and learn the fun dances we will be doing in the evenings

11.00 am

Gents Darts Competition – Come on fellas three in a bed

11.00 am

Ladies Table Tennis Competition – No jumping over the net when you win now girls

11.00 am

Teenage Mini Golf Competition – Come on tiger!

12.00 noon

Sing-a- long and fun – Join your Supercoats - let your hair down over a drink but make sure it's your own

2.00 pm

Children's Competitions – Come to the ballroom and support your little ones

2.30 pm

Gents Table Tennis Competition – Who will be batman for the week?

2.30 pm

Ladies Darts Competition – Come on girls for the flights of your life

3.00 pm
Teenage Pool Competition – That's your cue for another get together

3.30 pm
Tea Dance in the **Ballroom** - Don't spill it now

4.30 pm
Hoy – Fun card game in the ballroom

Evening

6.00 pm
Music in the Ballroom – Let the young ones come and have a dance while you relax

6.30 pm
Bingo Books – On sale in ballroom

7.00 pm
Number Eight – Your too late the caller can't wait

7.45 pm
Junior Tarzan competition, in the ballroom - Who will be king of the jungle?

8.15 pm
Time to Trip The Light Fantastic - To the sounds of Supergroup

9.00 pm
Man of the Week Competition – 007 style can you handle it?

9.30 pm
Family Party dance time – Come and enjoy these easy fun dances

10.00 pm

Good Night Children – your very own nighty night tunes. See you in the morning

WE RESPECTFULLY REMIND MUMS AND DADS THAT THE CHILDREN ARE NOT ALLOWED ON THE DANCE FLOOR AFTER 10PM UNLESS ACCOMPANIED BY AN ADULT...THANK YOU.

10.10 pm

Supercoat Spectacular – Non-stop dazzling floor show

10.50 pm

Mid Evening Disco Time

11.05 pm

Time to take the floor again with Supergroup – Bring it back this time

12.00 Midnight

Disco here Disco's there – Boogie until the wee hours

Good night sleep well, if you think today's been busy wait and see what we have lined up for you tomorrow.

***

Monday

08.00 am

Good morning – The clear blue waters of the pool await you

10.00 am

Keep Fit – Still more to do so no trying to skive

10.00 am

Teenage Darts Competition - Come and chuck a few at the board

10.30 am

Party Dances – Come along and learn another one today

10.30 am

Adult Snooker Competition – It's in the pocket

11.00 am

Family Ramble – Meet in the ballroom for a trip full of fun and laughs. Build up a good appetite for lunch

11.00 am

Fun Quiz – In the ballroom for you lazy ones

12.00 noon

Sing-a-long fun – If you have managed to get through that busy morning come and sit down with a drink and lets get the atmosphere going again

2.00 pm

Mixed Mini Golf Competition – See you at the 19th for a well deserved drink

2.00 pm

Teenage Table Tennis Competition – Win a Ping Pong Gong

3.00 pm

Family Olympics – Join the Supercoats on the sports field – Lots of house points to be won and tons of fun to be had

4.30 pm

Dog Racing on Film – Come into the ballroom and watch the woof woofs do the running now – you can have a flutter on them too

Evening

6.00 pm

Junior Joke Telling Competition in the ballroom – then the young ones will be off to the club for their own time

6.30 pm

Bingo Books - on sale in ballroom

7.00 pm

Number One – The games begun and we're having fun

7.45 pm

Junior Princess Competition – In the ballroom

8.15 pm

Welcome Supergroup to start tonight's live music

9.00 pm

Perfect Couple Competition – How much does your partner put up with?

10.00 pm Good Night Children – your very own nighty night tunes. See you in the morning

WE RESPECTFULLY REMIND MUMS AND DADS THAT THE CHILDREN ARE NOT ALLOWED ON THE DANCE FLOOR AFTER 10PM UNLESS ACCOMPANIED BY AN ADULT...THANK YOU.

10.15 pm

International Cabaret Time – Star studded visiting entertainer

11.00 pm

Time To Stretch Your Legs Again With Supergroup – Followed by our very own disco sounds

What a great day, get some rest and we'll do it all again tomorrow. Good night sleep well.

***

Tuesday

08.00 am

Oceans blue – The pool is open for you

10.00 am

Keep Fit – You're looking better already

10.00

Teenage Tennis Competition – Hurry Murray!

10.30 am

Family Party Dances – You don't know them all yet you know!

11.00 am

Mixed Bowls Competition – No need to weight, get it? Weight! Oh please yourself

11.00 am

Fun quiz – in the ballroom

12.00 noon

Sing-a-Long Fun – Are we in tune today? We are, oh good

2.00 pm

Skittle Fun – Lots of fun in the ballroom and so many house points to won too

2.00 pm

Teenage Bowls – Try your hand out on the green

3.00 pm

Men's Volleyball – Game net and match on the sports field

3.00 pm

Ladies Water Polo – Without the hole

4.00 pm

Tea Dance – Come and have a Viennese Waltz with your Viennese Whirl

Evening

6.00 pm
Junior Disco Dancing Competition – Come and support the young ones as they strut their funky stuff

6.30 pm
Bingo Books – On sale

7.00 pm
Number Ten – Time to get your pen eyes down!

7.45 pm
Live music with our visiting band – Just because Supergroup are having a night off doesn't mean you can. Come on lets be having you up on those twinkle toes now

8.30 pm
Adult Disco Dancing Competition – Let's show them youngsters how to do it

9.30 pm
Party Dance Fun- Everyone up on that floor now

10.00 pm
Good Night Children – your very own nighty night tunes. See you in the morning

WE RESPECTFULLY REMIND MUMS AND DADS THAT THE CHILDREN ARE NOT ALLOWED ON THE DANCE FLOOR AFTER 10PM UNLESS ACCOMPANIED BY AN ADULT...THANK YOU.

10.15 pm
Ballroom Dancing Competition – There are 'Strictly' three categories, Ballroom, Latin and Jive. Let's see what the judges say about that

10.45 pm
Cabaret Time – Another wonderful act for your entertainment pleasure

11.30 pm
Our Visiting Band are back to take us through to **Disco Time**

*Get a good night's sleep we have so much more for
you to do tomorrow.*

***

Wednesday
Country And Western Day

08.00 am

Them there pesky Lifeguards – Are waiting for you down at the water hole

10.00 am

Keep Fit – Well I be Miss Daisy you sure are looking mighty fine, must be that there aerobics that is keeping your cheeks so rosy

10.00 am

Billy the Kid Teenage Horseshoe Throwing – On the sports field

10.30 am

Party Dance Fun – Doe se doe partners

11.00 am

Men's Water Polo – No no no for goodness sake get them horses out of the pool. I don't know....Cowboys!

11.00 am

Cowgirl Volleyball – Come on ladies knock that piece of hide over the net

12.00 noon

Sing-a-Long Fun – See you in the saloon for a hoe-down and a shot of red eye pardners

1.30 pm

Kentucky Derby Racing on Film – Which of those chaps will come past the winning post first? Get it chaps? That's what cowboy's wear you know, still not impressed huh? OK then why not just come have a flutter and spur them on. Spur them on...get it? Oh dear never mind see you there

3.00 pm

Donkey Derby - Saddle Up Cowboys and Girls – Ok you've seen it on film now it's your turn to hit that dirt trail. Mums and Dads you can be owners or just enjoy the brilliant family fun atmosphere on the sports field

4.30 pm

Cowboy and Cowgirl Mixed Horseshoe Throwing Competition – Oh ladies I expected it from the fellas but not you.....OK all of you take the shoes *off* the horses first this time!

<u>**Evening**</u>
<u>**Don't forget there will be a prize for the best dressed Country and Western table tonight**</u>

6.00 pm

Best Dressed Little Cowboy, Cowgirl or Indian Competition - In the ballroom

6.30 pm

Bingo Books – On sale

7.00 pm

Number Four - Wait no more – eyes down

7.45 pm

Supergroup Are Back – Giving you live music with both barrels tonight

8.30 pm

Best Dressed Country and Western Table Winners Announced
Followed by.......
Family Party Dance Fun – What about that barn dance? That's not bad dancing for a barn actually!

9.15 pm

Lady of the Week Competition – Calamity Jane style - No not a beauty contest just lots of fun!

10.00 pm

Good Night Children – your very own nighty night tunes. See you in the morning

WE RESPECTFULLY REMIND MUMS AND DADS THAT THE CHILDREN ARE NOT ALLOWED ON THE DANCE FLOOR AFTER 10PM UNLESS ACCOMPANIED BY AN ADULT…THANK YOU.

10.10 pm
Supercoats Country and Western Show – Clap your hands and stamp your feet

10.50 pm
Square Dance to Round CD's? – Short disco break

11.15 pm
Supergroup Have Been Rounded Up Again - Taking you through till disco time

Well night night pardners see you all at dawn.

Thursday
Today is Talent Competition day so make sure you plan yours around the rehearsals

Please Note!!!
Only those acts at the rehearsals will take part in tonight's competitions

08.00 Good Morning Lifeguards – Are you waiting to say hi to the guests? I thought so; open the pool doors because here they come!

10.00 am
Keep Fit – Only one more to go after this – then you can put it all back on again until next year
10.00 am
Teenage 5 a Side Football – On the sports field, boys and girls welcome to play. However there will be other activities going on too

10.30 am
Party Dance Fun – Your Last chance to learn from us this week

11.00 am
Fun Treasure Hunt – Meet in the ballroom

11.30 am
Gents Pool Competition – Give us a break lads

12.00 noon
Sing-a-long Fun
Including........

13.00 pm
Elegant Grandmother and Happy Granddad Competitions

2.30 pm
Ladies Pool Competition – Show em how it's done girls
2.30 pm
Teenage Volleyball – See you on the sports field

3.00 pm
Tea Dance – Last tango in Paris er I mean in the ballroom

4.00 pm
General Knowledge Quiz – Come along to the ballroom and see how good your knowledge of generals is. Only playing it's just me being daft again. See you there I have some real fun questions for you

4.30 pm
Talent Show Rehearsals – for all age groups.
PLEASE NOTE!!!If you want to enter tonight you must sign up in the ballroom at this time

<u>**Evening**</u>
<u>**Please Note!!!**</u>
<u>**If you wish to enter tonight's Talent Contests you must turn up**</u>
<u>**to rehearsals at 4.30pm**</u>

6.00 pm
Music and Fun in the Ballroom – Before the young ones disappear into their very own club

6.30 pm
Bingo Books – On sale

7.00 pm
Number Two, Someone will win, could it be You? – Eyes down

7.45 pm

Family Party Dances

(Contestants for the Junior and Teenage Talent Contests will be taken back stage by the Supercoats at this time also)

8.15 pm

Junior Talent Contest – My favourite competitions of the week begin right here I can't help but loving everyone for at least having a go!

Followed by......

Teenage Talent Contest – It's not easy to get up there you know so plenty of support please!

9.00 pm

More Party Dance Fun

(Contestants for the Adult Talent Contest will be taken backstage by the Supercoats at this time)

9.20 pm

Adult Talent Contest – We could discover the next big thing! Come on cheer them on!

10.00 pm

Good Night Children – your very own nighty night tunes. See you in the morning

WE RESPECTFULLY REMIND MUMS AND DADS THAT THE CHILDREN ARE NOT ALLOWED ON THE DANCE FLOOR AFTER 10PM UNLESS ACCOMPANIED BY AN ADULT...THANK YOU.

10.30 pm

Cabaret Time – Another fabulous visiting star act

11.15 pm

Dancing to the live sounds of Supergroup – who will leave you with one of your very own Supercoats on the decks for the disco into the small hours

---

We must have worn you out by now, but there's still tomorrows fun and games to come yet so you had better get some beauty sleep, goodnight.

***

Friday
Fancy Dress Day

08.00 am

Your Pool Awaits – Last time to 'wave' to the lifeguards

Please note the pool will be used for the Swimming Gala at 10.30 am today

10.00 am

Keep Fit – Come on it's the last time, you can do it

10.30 am

Family Fun Swimming Gala – See you poolside for a great family fun – super, splashing, great

12.00 noon

Sing-a-Long Fun Time – Last chance this week - Supercoats are in the bar for a singsong and a giggle or two

2.00 pm

Ladies and Gents Five a Side Football Tournament – Running them separately to find the male and female champs – we may just have a special men v women champ of champs game to finish with - keep it friendly though it's only a game

3.00 pm

Tea Dance – Last chance for a little spin around the dance floor

3.30 pm

Teenage Choice – Meet the Supercoats and choose an activity or do your favourite things all over again – it's your holiday

4.00 pm

Sports Quiz – In the ballroom – in keeping with today's sporting theme

Evening
Fancy Dress Night
Best Dressed Table to be awarded prize too
Last Chance to scoop those all important HOUSE POINTS!!!

6.00 pm
Prize Giving – Come and cheer all those fabulous competition winners as they collect their certificates and prizes – how did your house do?

6.30 pm
Bingo Books – On sale

7.00 pm
Number Five – the games alive – eyes down

7.45 pm
Junior Fancy Dress Competition – Can't wait to see what amazing costumes you have come up with this time

8.15 pm
Adult Fancy Dress Competition – Oh! did they really make you wear that? You're a good sport aren't you? (I knew I could get the sporting theme in there somewhere)

8.45 pm
Dancing - to the brilliant live music of your resident band **Supergroup**

9.15 pm
Supercoat Farewell Extravaganza – Another fast paced roller coaster ride of a show especially for you

10.00 pm
Good Night Children – your very own nighty night tunes. See you in the morning

---

WE RESPECTFULLY REMIND MUMS AND DADS THAT THE CHILDREN ARE NOT ALLOWED ON THE DANCE FLOOR AFTER 10PM UNLESS ACCOMPANIED BY AN ADULT...THANK YOU.

From here on in tonight is Party Night

10.20 pm
Hit that Dance Floor – Oo! Not so hard – feel that beat man with **Supergroup**

11.00 pm
Fun Dances – come join the Supercoats and boogie to that disco rhythm – but expect the unexpected – it is party time after all

11.45 pm
Supergroup – Back on stage to take us up to the witching hour and beyond

12.00 Midnight
Auld Lang Syne – We hope you have had a great time with us, have a safe journey home tomorrow and we look forward to seeing you all again very soon.
Bye for now from all the management and staff here at Camp Superblue.

***

Junior Programme

They will have to give the kids a fantastic time from now on because they are under the super-vision eyes and super-hearing ears of........

Superblue's Junior

Super Agents

Who can report back and find loads of stuff in their own section of Superblue happy Holidays .com

So I say to them

Don't forget to try and match events in your junior programme to those in the adult one so that parents can be with their children for certain activities and competitions

As you read this example compare it to the adult one above to see what I mean!!!

I will just show a sample programme here but as with the adult example above you will want to add to it in accordance with your facilities, staffing levels and expertise
For ease I will keep this one very straight forward and in plain language but don't forget the children will enjoy your play on words and the injection of your own personality into the one you write as much as the mums and dads – So have fun with it!

Example of Junior Programme

Hi mums and dads we are looking forward to a great fun week with the kids

Please note they can get their **free T-shirt and badges** in the junior club at **7.00 pm tonight**

We operate a three age group system for competitions etc

2 – 5 yrs   6 – 11 yrs   12 - 14 yrs

Saturday

8.00 am

Swimming pool is open

10.00 am

If this is your second week bring mum and dad for a nice chat with your Supercoats in the café.

If you have just arrived welcome to Camp Superblue please do come and say hello to your Supercoats who are looking forward to meeting you.

Don't forget the swimming pool and all of your sports facilities are also open.

12.00 noon

Your Supercoats are waiting for you in the ballroom for a couple of hours of arts and crafts fun.

2.30 pm

Come and join mum and dad for the family matinee in the ballroom.

4.00 pm

How about a trip on the supertrain

4.30 pm

Meet your Supercoats outside reception for a tour of the resort.

Evening

6.00 pm

Party Dance Fun – in the ballroom

7.00 pm

Welcome to your own club meet you very own Supercoats who will look after you this week. Get your **free t-shits and badges**- find out what **House** you are in.

Followed by fun games and competitions

7.45 pm

Who's Who? Your Supercoats will bring you back to the ballroom to meet the rest of your Supercoats who are here to help you enjoy your holiday

8.00 pm

Time to take to the floor - join mum and dad dancing to the sounds of our fabulous band – Supergroup

9.00 pm

Team Chase Fun Competition – Lots of fun watch the mums and dads make fools of themselves – very funny!

9.30 pm

Supergroup take to the stage – Musical fun for all the family

10.00 pm

Good Night Children – your very own nighty night tunes. See you in the morning

WE RESPECTFULLY REMIND MUMS AND DADS THAT THE CHILDREN ARE NOT ALLOWED ON THE DANCE FLOOR AFTER 10PM UNLESS ACCOMPANIED BY AN ADULT...THANK YOU.

Sunday

08.00 am
Swimming pool is open

09.00 am
Take a ride on the Supertrain

09.45 am
Megga life size drawing and colouring competition – in the club

10.30 am
Party Dances in the ballroom

11.30 am
Mini golf Competition

12.00 noon
Join mum and dad in the ballroom for lunchtime fun with the Supercoats

2.00 pm
Fun Competition time for all the boys and girls in the ballroom

4.30 pm
Scavenger hunt – meet in the ballroom

5.30 pm
Meet back in the ballroom for the scavenger hunt count up

Evening

6.00 pm
Dancing fun in the ballroom

6.30 pm

Magic Time in the club – visiting magical cabaret

Followed by fun and games before the Supercoats bring you back to the ballroom

7.45 pm

Junior Tarzan Competition

8.15 pm

Join mum and dad for dancing fun with Supergroup

9.00 pm

Watch the silly dads trying to be a secret agent

Followed by fun party dances

10.00 pm

Good Night Children – your very own nighty night tunes. See you in the morning

WE RESPECTFULLY REMIND MUMS AND DADS THAT THE CHILDREN ARE NOT ALLOWED

ON THE DANCE FLOOR AFTER 10PM UNLESS ACCOMPANIED BY AN ADULT...THANK YOU.

Monday

08.00 am

Swimming pool is open

09.00 am

Take a ride on the Supertrain

09.45 am

Trampoline fun – in the club

10.30 am

Party Dances in the ballroom

11.00 am

Join mum and dad for the family ramble

11.00 am

Make your own jigsaw fun – in the club- for those not going for a walk with mum and dad

12.00 noon

Join mum and dad in the ballroom for lunchtime fun with the Supercoats

1.30 pm

 Make a model Competition for all the boys and girls in the club

3.00 pm

Family Olympics – on the sports field

4.30 pm

Come and join mum and dad in the ballroom as they cheer for their favourite dog to win - we will have our own special face painting lessons there!

Evening

6.00 pm

Junior Joke Telling Contest in the ballroom

6.30 pm

More fun and games in the club with the Supercoats and they will bring you back to the ballroom

7.45 pm

Junior Princess Competition

8.15 pm

Join mum and dad for fun dancing with Supergroup

9.00 pm

Watch the mums and dads doing very daft things – they will make you laugh a lot! Followed by fun dances

10.00 pm

Good Night Children – your very own nighty night tunes. See you in the morning

WE RESPECTFULLY REMIND MUMS AND DADS THAT THE CHILDREN ARE NOT ALLOWED ON THE DANCE FLOOR AFTER 10PM UNLESS ACCOMPANIED BY AN ADULT...THANK YOU.

Tuesday

08.00 am

Swimming pool is open

09.00 am

Take a ride on the Supertrain

09.45 am

Junior table tennis competition - in the sports hall

If you don't want to play still come along anyway because you will be making your own Camp Superblue Scrapbook too! –then you can collect autographs and keep a diary of the week and win a prize too!

10.30 am

Party Dances in the ballroom

11.30 am

Rounders for all on the sports field

12.00 noon

Join mum and dad in the ballroom for lunchtime fun with the Supercoats

2.00 pm

Boys v Girls penalty taking and netball throwing Competition on the sports field

4.30 pm

Make a hat fun competition – in the club

Evening

6.00 pm

Junior Disco Dancing Competition in the ballroom

7.00 pm

Puppet Show Time in the club – visiting cabaret

Followed by make you own puppet which you can show mum and dad when the Supercoats bring you back to the ballroom

8.15 pm

Join mum and dad for dancing fun with Supergroup

8.30 pm

Support your mums and dads in their disco dancing competition

Followed by fun party dances

10.00 pm

Good Night Children – your very own nighty night tunes. See you in the morning

WE RESPECTFULLY REMIND MUMS AND DADS THAT THE CHILDREN ARE NOT ALLOWED ON THE DANCE FLOOR AFTER 10PM UNLESS ACCOMPANIED BY AN ADULT...THANK YOU.

***

Wednesday
Country and Western Day

08.00 am

Swimming pool is open

09.00 am

Take a ride on the Wild West Rawhide Supertrain Express

09.45 am

Cowboy, Cowgirl and Indian costume making – in the club

10.30 am

Party Dances in the ballroom

11.00 am

Junior Horseshoe Throwing, water pistol quick draw and sticky archery Competitions on the sports field

12.00 noon

Join mum and dad in the ballroom for lunchtime fun with the Supercoats

1.30 pm

Join mum and dad for while they horse around in the ballroom or come and watch Walt Disney's 'Pocahontas' in the club

3.00 pm

Donkey Derby - Saddle Up Cowboys and Girls – Ok you've seen it on film now it's your turn to hit that dirt trail. Mums and Dads you can be owners or just enjoy the brilliant family fun atmosphere on the sports field

4.30 pm

Paint your wagon – drawing and colouring competitions in the club

Evening
Don't forget there will be a prize for the best dressed Country and Western table tonight

6.00 pm

Time to wear those costumes we made earlier for the Best Dressed Little Cowboy, Cowgirl or Indian Competition in the ballroom

7.00 pm

Fun and games – in the club before the Supercoats bring you back to the ballroom in time for...

8.30 pm

Best Dressed Country and Western Table Winners Announced

Followed by.......

Family Party Dance Fun!

9.15 pm

This time you can laugh at mum being silly in the Lady of the week Competition

10.00 pm

Good Night Children – your very own nighty night tunes. See you in the morning

WE RESPECTFULLY REMIND MUMS AND DADS THAT THE CHILDREN ARE NOT ALLOWED ON THE DANCE FLOOR AFTER 10PM UNLESS ACCOMPANIED BY AN ADULT...THANK YOU.

***

Thursday
Today is Talent Competition day so mums and dads please make sure you plan yours around the rehearsals

Please Note!!!
Only those acts at the rehearsals will take part in tonight's competitions

08.00 am
Swimming pool is open

09.00 am
Take a ride on the Talent Express Factor Supertrain

09.45 am
Skittles Competition – in the club

10.30 am
Party Dances in the ballroom

11.00 am
Join mum and dad in the ballroom for a fun treasure hunt

11.30 am
Silly volley ball fun at the tennis courts – plus decorate the ball competition

12.00 noon
Join mum and dad in the ballroom for lunchtime fun with the Supercoats

2.00 pm
Nature Trail – come for a safari to see our wildlife and collect some creepy crawlies of your own – meet in the club

Mums and dads this could be a bit messy – you might not want your little cherubs to wear their Sunday best if you know what I mean!

(Please advise Supercoats of any allergies or phobias etc, ta very much)

4.30 pm

Talent Show Rehearsals – for all age groups.

PLEASE NOTE!!! If your young one wants to enter tonight they must sign up in the ballroom at this time

Evening

6.00 pm

Dancing fun in the ballroom

6.30 pm

Mad Circus Show in the club – Supercoats mayhem, balloons, gung and madness

Followed by fun and games before the Supercoats bring you back to the ballroom in time for…

7.45 pm

Contestants for the Junior and Teenage Talent Contests to go back stage

While the rest of us enjoy more party dance fun

8.15 pm

Junior Talent Contest

Followed by…

Teenage Talent Contest

Then back to dancing until…

9.20 pm

See if the mums and dads have the Extra Good Factor in their Talent Contest

Ok we will just have a few more fun party dances until....

10.00 pm

Good Night Children – your very own nighty night tunes. See you in the morning

WE RESPECTFULLY REMIND MUMS AND DADS THAT THE CHILDREN ARE NOT ALLOWED

ON THE DANCE FLOOR AFTER 10PM UNLESS ACCOMPANIED BY AN ADULT...THANK YOU.

Friday
Today is Fancy Dress Day

We will be making costumes at 2pm with those that want us too
But please make it a family thing if you prefer

And remember the best dressed table gets a great prize and valuable house points tonight too!!!

08.00 am
Swimming pool is open

09.00 am
Last chance to take a ride on the Supertrain

09.45 am
Best Dressed Pirate competition - in the club
Followed by…
Hunt Black Patch….The dastardly naughty pirate who has stolen all the sweets from the shop as well as all your prizes for tonight's prize giving
We must catch him and make him walk the plank into the pool
Where we will stay for the……

10.30 am
Family Swimming Gala – including toddler races in the paddling pool and silly inflatable fun for all ages

12.00 noon
Join mum and dad in the ballroom for the last lunchtime fun with the Supercoats

2.00 pm
Fancy Dress Making – If you're not doing this with mum and dad come and make a great costume for tonight's competition

---

If you are doing this with mum and dad come and have fun with different arts and craft stuff anyway

3.00 pm
Family Film in the club

4.30 pm
Last bit of Afternoon **fun and games with** the Supercoats this week in the club

Evening

6.00 pm
Prize Giving – Come and cheer all those fabulous competition winners as they collect their certificates and prizes – how did your house do?

6.30 pm
Visiting speciality cabaret in the club
Followed by fun and games before the Supercoats bring you back to the ballroom

7.45 pm
Junior Fancy Dress Competition

8.15 pm
I hope you helped mum and dad get ready for the Adult Fancy Dress Competition

8.45 pm
Join mum and dad for dancing fun with Supergroup

9.15 pm
Supercoat Farewell Extravaganza Show

10.00 pm
Good Night Children – your very own nighty night tunes. See you in the morning

Thank you for being such great fun people to be with this week
Don't forget to bring mum and dad back again really soon

WE RESPECTFULLY REMIND MUMS AND DADS THAT THE CHILDREN ARE NOT ALLOWED ON THE DANCE FLOOR AFTER 10PM UNLESS ACCOMPANIED BY AN ADULT...THANK YOU.

***

I did seriously consider adding a few more examples for you here but the more I thought about it the more it seemed a bit daft to be honest. The fact is that you now have all the basic tools at your disposal to conjure up a wonderfully interesting and imaginative programme of your own for any occasion.

Whether it be a one off 'Themed Day' to include best dressed chalets, tables, caravans etc or a complete 'Themed Weekend' or even a full 'Week' such as Country and Western, Elvis, Comedy, 70's, Rock and Roll, Brass Bands, Model Making, Baton Twirling, Ballroom Dancing, Snooker, Sequence or Disco Dancing. You just have to be creative and work around their specialist events adding a clever slant on the theme for your activities or shows etc. See Wednesday in my programme examples for some idea of what I am talking about!

Oh and yes I was a 'coat' or Entertainments Manager at holiday centres running all of those themes I just mentioned and many more besides!

Easter, Christmas and New Year; have traditionally been special times at holiday camps and some of my best memories are during these periods. But don't let the occasion daunt you. All the same rules apply as above just remember things like.....

The Easter Bunny - Easter Egg Hunt - Hot Cross Buns

Santa –Rudolph – Pantomimes – Presents - Carol Singers - Church Services - Christmas Dinner - And of course Mistletoe!

Old Lang Syne- Big Ben

I would be surprised if you weren't ahead of me for, at least, most of the time just then, but that's fine because it shows your thinking along the right lines now and so long as you treat these occasions with the due diligence, flare and respect they deserve you will be fine.

Wet Weather Programme

I go into this in great detail in a later chapter but apart from all that I say about it there it really is just a matter of common sense. Using the indoor events in that days programme as a platform to build upon and filling the rest of the day with fun activities for the whole family to enjoy;

Indoor fun sports day

Horse or dog racing on film

Arts and crafts

An extra 'coat' show

Fun competitions for all ages

Hoy type games

Films

Stage school for all ages (Which incidentally you can add to your ordinary programmes)

In door donkey derby (with toy horses big fun)

'Coat' cabarets (a good time to let individuals perform)

Skittles

Carpet Bowles

Quizzes

Casino time (non cash for prizes)

Oh the list is truly endless just use that good old imagination.

....

Well dear guest that's the advice and hopefully inspiration that I passed onto the Managers and Company Owners in 'Tales of Superblue'. I hope it helps you to judge whether or not you're getting value for money when it comes to your entertainments programme wherever you're on holiday from now on.

CHAPTER SEVEN

AN EFFECTIVE DAYTIME PROGRAMME

Ok I have banged on about the importance of your Entertainments Manager constructing a quality programme and of course it is vital that they get that right. Nonetheless now that they have mastered this, sometimes complex, aspect of the job it is time for them to run their masterpiece for your total enjoyment and pleasure. In this chapter we will take a look at the daytime bit and all that that entails and as you will have guessed by now there's probably a lot more to it than you first imagined. Equally by now though you will know that I am about to take you through it all step by step so providing you with the information I pass on to them in 'tales of Superblue' which offers them the tools and know-how to turn their cherished work into the slick, professional, safe, fun and grief free programme that you deserve. While a lot of this chapter is aimed at the standard of daytime programme your Entertainments Manager should be running for you it is equally important that all the 'coats' working at your holiday destination adhere to it too. It demonstrates what they should expect from their manager and what he or she will expect from the 'coat'. It also ensures they are aware of the reasoning behind why they are requested to do certain things while at the same time highlighting unfair tasks which may mean too much is being asked of them. Please cast your mind back to the beginning of the book where I talked of the hours a 'coat' may be required to work etc (although this is much better now due to European working directives etc).

However as always it would do those being paid to entertain you no harm to remember that not only, dear guest, are you thumbing these pages but also any astute camp managers, owners and head office staff will be too. Meaning you are all only too well aware of the high level of service both the Entertainments Manager and their 'coats' should be presenting you.

I tell them to
'Start the day right'

Trust me it will be all too obvious if they have not

The sun is rising poking his nose over the horizon, little children are waking their parents with eager anticipation dying to see what fun and games have been laid on for them today, mum and dad are even more anxious to find out what you have in store to keep their little angels occupied this holiday, couples are perusing the programme deciding which events to take part in, granny has noticed that the junior talent show is on so she can watch her grandchildren take part before she goes to the tea dance giving her time to have a nice little nap before bingo, teenagers have met new friends and can't wait to burst out on their own and have a taste of independence so for once they are up and out and ready to take part. In short the centre is buzzing with excitement and energy. What could possibly go wrong?

Anything basically, your Entertainments Manager has no way of knowing what the day has in store for them. I have seen the most perfect of days turn sour for the most ridiculous of reasons. The sad thing is they were almost all avoidable. There are usually two origins for an unhappy day, bad planning and worst of all bad attitude!

Bad planning is inexcusable: particularly now that I have laid everything out for them in 'Tales of Superblue', every chapter advising them on what to do when and where and even how to do it. This chapter of course is no exception and it starts with the Entertainments Manager, Their organisational skills, they're frame of mind and professionalism. Remember the buck really does stop with them.

I advise them to do as I did by beginning their daily routine by making sure they are up bright and early, no matter what happened the night before. Sort themselves out in plenty of time to allow them to turn their mind onto the matter in hand, 'today's programme'. They should do this in peace and quiet before venturing out from their accommodation so as to give it their fullest attention. The Entertainments Manager must run through the day's events and list what 'coats' are doing what for the day. Remember all I said about right people for right job while training others at same time etc. The worst thing they can be tempted to do is just leave it the same as the week before. I say this for a few reasons, one is, as soon as they start to become complaisant and lackadaisical they send that signal to the team of 'coats' and they're on that downward spiral we spoke of. Another is in the detail of planning the day, if they skip one part of it the rest is likely to come crashing around their ears. For example they have just dished out the order for the 'coats' to do what they did last week all is going well until they are surrounded by you and a group of guests who are livid because you have been waiting half an hour for the bowls competition to start. They suddenly remember the 'coat' that ran it last week is off today for an audition in London. Oh not too much of a problem though is it? They'll just get another 'coat' to run it instead won't they? Well now they are reminded by the other 'coats' that she was the only one who knows the rules of bowls. Not only that, the 'coats' already have their own activities to run, the same as last week! Imagine how angry you guests are getting now and it's only 10.30am it's going to be a long hard day for that Entertainments Manager, the team and most importantly you. Throwing a programme in disarray like this causes bedlam, as we discussed in a previous chapter. The unfortunate reality is that if this happens to them they will be in the front line not sitting comfortably reading 'Tales of Superblue' when they could have learnt to avoid it. The third reason follows on from that in a way, quite simply if they keep posting the same person to the same event or competition time after time

1) They will get bored with it and that will eventually show through to you the guests
2) No-one else has the opportunity of learning how to run that event or the rules of competitions etc.

Here is another major part of the preparation process, the importance of which I press home to them. One which as a guest you hopefully have never given a second thought to before, because you should only ever really know about it if it's not done correctly. The fact is that while they are giving consideration as to who is going to do what they must bear in mind the vast array of props that are needed for the day, sports equipment, captain bloods outfit and stolen treasure, outdoor sound system, face painting sets, projector for horse racing on film, costumes for the afternoon panto, judges marking sheets and boards, sheet music and words for the lunchtime sing-a-long etc etc etc and there will be three times as much to do if you are to enjoy a themed day. It is another one of those endless lists to be honest and in my experience a very, underestimated part of the morning routine but they pay it little heed at their peril. We have already seen how horribly wrong a day can go if a 'coat' fails to appear on time well the same scenario awaits if the Entertainments Manager has not planned to get their props and equipment to the right place by the right time, which as you will recall is enough time to ensure that the event is ready to run ten minutes before the advertised start time. A good Entertainments

Manager will rightly give this as much thought as the placement of their 'coats' because there are certain items that may need the technical or specialised knowledge of one of the 'coats' or it may quite simply be a heavy object that requires the 'coats' with greater strength to carry it. So obviously part of their postings process will need to take account of this forward logistical planning. In other words they need to make sure everyone has enough time to do what they are asking them to do without running them ragged.

If they have an event such as keep fit, a ramble or swimming lessons etc that takes place before their morning meeting the Entertainments Manager should make sure they have a failsafe in place so that they will be made aware straight away if a 'coat' has failed to turn up to run it. The only sure-fire way of knowing for certain that these things are running on time by the allocated 'coat' is to take an early morning stroll and check for themselves, well no one said it was an easy job did they. Alternatively if this is impractical for some reason, and it would need to be a good one, they can ask other staff members to assist. Take keep fit for example this normally takes place in the main venue and the café or coffee shop are generally open by then. All venues should be supplied with the Entertainment Managers mobile number so that as soon as guests start to ask why an event is not taking place as it should be, one of those staff members can immediately call and start the process of damage limitation in the guest's eyes. You would be surprised how forgiving people can be if a mistake is seen to be recognised by staff and steps are taken to rectify it without delay and of course a sincere apology goes a long way. However the Entertainments Managers should always turn up in person to make that apology and show that the faux pas was taken very seriously.

It's also a good idea if he or she has their day off noted at the venues and supplies their assistant's number for that day.

So they're up with the larks, gone over the days programme for postings and logistics, taken a nice early morning stroll checking the entertainment boards were changed last night and early events are running, welcomed the guests into breakfast, if on full or half board village, and all is well. Now it's time for the morning meeting with the entire team. We have already discussed the benefits of holding a meeting every morning so I won't go over old ground too much, suffice to mention they should check uniforms, cleanliness and watch for any health problems and act on any of these matters but of course sensitively and with respect for 'coats' and their privacy. I know I keep on about the ten minute rule too but it does no harm to sell its importance to their team every morning, leaving them in no doubt the magnitude they attach to it, enough said. The Entertainments Manager should then go through the programme step by step, boring as it may be the tenth time, believe me it's the only sure-fire way of knowing everyone they have posted is there and are aware of their duties for that day. This is also when the team will remind them that one of them is away for that audition or that things didn't run so smoothly last week because there was not enough time for some of them to set up the props required between two events. Thereby allowing the Manager to adjust the duties accordingly and saving them from the scenario above. I am always reminded of Hi-Di-Hi when I think of morning meetings it really was remarkably true to life in many ways. Their portrayal of the morning meeting was pretty much spot on with Mr Fairbrother dishing out news from Joe Maplin invoking a response from one member of the cast or another as to why it was ludicrous or unfair and wouldn't work or the posting of duties soliciting a bitchy comment about the person asked to do a particular task etc. Well of course that was all for comedic effect but in the real world an Entertainments Manager should take note of any comments of this nature. It may be that they are highlighting perfectly good grounds why attempting something would not work or that the pressures put upon them to get this thing done are indeed unfair. The bitchy comment may just be friendly team banter that goes both ways. They must judge it for themselves and listen to the 'coats' views but be aware of the beginnings of any dissent, unhappiness or bullying.

The 'coats' are all posted to their duties all the props for the day have been organised and are ready to be deployed to the right location at the right time so.....................**Let the festivities begin!**

THEMED DAYS

I love themed days there's so much fun to be had for both you the guest and the entertainments team not to mention the rest of the centre if it's done properly. I advocate that the whole day should start with the early-bird events and carry through breakfast with the best dressed table etc. Making sure my 'coats' would be in suitable costumes and not some half hearted attempt. You will encounter 'coats' that are so vein that dressing up is beneath them or believe it spoils their chances with the opposite sex. Tough! This is one of those occasions where I would say "if you don't like it you know what you can do there's always someone waiting to take your place" and there always is. I would always keep a wary eye on this one because this may not be the person I want on my team. Remember it is all about you the guests having fun so if dressing up and being silly helps to achieve this goal then that's what we will do. Anyway to be honest it is a basic part of holiday resort life isn't it and most of us love it which is one of the main reasons why you guests love it too. The other point is if we're not going to make an effort why should you guests and what sort of themed day would that be? Not very successful that's what! As we have seen your Entertainments Manager can, and should, devise a programme to take you right through the day encompassing events that fit the theme adding best dressed chalet, caravan or room etc but the Entertainments Manager and his or her team of 'coats' energy and enthusiasm will be the overriding factor that makes it a success.

VENUES

The Entertainments Manager should always make sure that all the venues they are going to need throughout that day are available and ready for use is another of those boringly unambiguous statements isn't it? Well it ought to be. But just as with everything else we have looked at thus far ignoring this most basic of actions can very quickly ruin your holiday experience.

They should always be one of the first people on site to be notified if urgent repairs or redecoration is to be carried out. All staff at all venues should be aware of and joining in with the themed day, just reiterating the importance of close liaison with other department managers. They must ensure that those in control of sporting venues such as the snooker room are aware that they are running a competition there. It is imperative that they know not to issue any equipment to guests after a certain time in order that the 'coat' has free tables on which to run that competition. Inspection of the sports field is a must so that they are happy it is ok regarding health and safety. Make certain the swimming pool and beach, if abroad, are properly staffed by the correct number of qualified lifeguards to cover normal swimming and any water features such as chutes etc. Check that there are enough of them to staff the venue for any extra event they may wish to run such as swimming gala, water polo, water volley ball etc. Test all equipment in the entertainment venues that are to be utilised for competitions, sing-a-long and so on. Always have their venues stocked up with the props they will need to be ready to swing into action should they encounter wet weather conditions. It is massively essential that venues for children and specialist activities like climbing walls or go karting are regularly examined and given the appropriate certification for their continued use. Although not instantly recognisable as something which might affect the running of the daily programme if not carried out could, in the best case scenario, render a venue unusable and in the worst case scenario, well that doesn't bare thinking about. I will go deeper into Health and Safety issues in a separate chapter.

If an Entertainments Manager has not started his or her day in this fashion you will quickly come to recognise it now. Yet again giving you the insight into what they should be doing to provide you with the best possible holiday entertainment your money can buy......no hang on just a mo.....I'm talking balderdash again.....of course that should read the best possible holiday entertainment *your money* has **ALREADY** bought!

You already know my views on your absolute right to expect nothing less.

Here's a little mnemonic I give the Entertainments Managers in that 'other book' it's one for you to remember and quote at them if they get it wrong....knowledge is power after all.

START YOUR DAY THE CHEAP WAY

Check all venues

Have failsafe for early-bird events

Ensure all props are ready to be deployed

Always have a morning meeting

Post your 'coats' wisely every day on the day

EXCURSIONS, RAMBLES AND OTHER OUTINGS

In mentioning these in passing previously I may have given rise to the idea that they are somehow a get-out clause for a lazy Entertainments Manager and their team. The reality in fact could not be further from the truth. There will be times when they will have scope to take advantage of a well subscribed excursion, for example on a smaller centre some of the team could catch up on rehearsals or even put new routines together etc. Don't imagine for one minute that getting their guests off site should mean an easy ride. Of course for a good Entertainments Manager that's the last thing they will want to do anyway. On the contrary these have always been wonderful opportunities for us to spend time with our guests while someone else takes the strain. We can generally relax in regard to having to organise the event once we are there and concentrate on enjoying being a 'fun' person in your midst. So why bother to go with you at all? Good question and the answer is twofold, firstly it serves to remind you that while you are having a great time away from the park it was your Entertainments Manager who arranged all this fun and that it is still very much part of the overall holiday experience provided by your centre. Secondly it is a very valuable advertising tool, you see us being in uniform performing and larking about as we 'coats' naturally would do, you other holidaymakers at that event or just out and about can't help but notice that guests at our centre are having a marvellous time and so may book with that centre or holiday company in the future. There are other concerns obviously such as the health and safety of our guests and in particular children. Some attractions insisting on 'x' number of 'coats' to accompany 'x' number of guests, again children are an understandable concern. We do cover health and safety later but a lot of things are common sense for example if they were organising a sea fishing trip they should never allow one single person to step aboard a vessel until they had completed checks into its and its captains pedigree. That it had enough lifejackets, life-rafts and a radio for basic survival and they must never take children without the appropriate adults on any such trip under any circumstances.

There is the matter of payment that I believe you have the right to know about here. After all if the Entertainments Manager or a 'coat' is pushing a particular trip you may want to ask why? Well it could and indeed should be that it's just a brill day out on the other hand if the rep or owner of a trip or attraction wants them to push it at the centre and there is **no** sitting agreement with the park management or owners, they could receive a payment for each guest that books. This is a matter for them and their company, park management or owners of course and I would not be so rude as to make any observations on the subject. However whilst this practice is probably less prevalent in this country, due to structured agreements between the tour operators and the holiday companies, I do ask all involved to please! please! please! *NEVER* put your interest in financial gains before the enjoyment of the guests. The only trips, excursions or attractions you should ever be sent on are ones that are value for money, interesting, safe and fun. They should not ignore little outings like rambles or a visit to the beach either. They don't take a great deal of organising yet can be packed full of hilarity and wackyness. You can have early morning strolls where one of the 'coats' tells a ghost or pirate story, you know what's coming of course, but it is still a great source of amusement when one or two of them jump out from behind a sand dune or old building in the old white sheets or cutlass's between their teeth. I know I have used the most basic ones as a demonstration but there really is a limitless pool of ideas to plunder not least of all the new ones that may still come from their own imagination or watching the latest film or video game etc. I must just tell you about one I was reminded of the other day when I bumped into a guest that had stayed at my favourite of all Pontins camps, Little Canada on the Isle of Wight. I was Entertainments Manager the year after Shane Ritchie had worked there and he and his team had set a high standard to follow which is always a nice position to be in so long as you are capable of rising to the challenge, which thankfully I was. Anyway as I was saying this guest reminded me of one little trick that had been played on the guests while he was there and which he particularly enjoyed. As with most things the concept was a simple one, they are on the Isle of Wight so why not get the guests out of bed for a ramble to where they could watch Queen Elizabeth the second (QE2) go by on her early morning sailing. Well the advertised start time was 6am from outside the Mounties Retreat Show-bar (Little Canada get it?) thinking a handful of guests might just turn up. 6am duly arrived and amazingly the tiny road outside the venue was packed with excited people all wrapped up warm and carrying videos, cameras and binoculars to get great shots and views of this wondrous spectacle as well as flags to wave as she majestically glides by. They all set off through the mist into the woods eventually emerging overlooking the Solent and the sea beyond, little did I realise that I would swim that stretch of water for charity while I was there but that's another story, It did look beautiful, calm and serene with the sun just beginning to rise in the distance but the team were not allowed to forget that the guests were all there, on a holiday morning, at that ridiculous early hour because they had sold this exciting event and as the bewitching hour drew ever nearer the fear amongst them was palpable as they began to wonder if in fact they had gone too far this time and had oversold it. Well it was too late now here were all the guests standing on a hill overlooking the shore in silence, straining their eyes and ears trying to be the first to hear or see the magnificent thing they had got up in the middle of the night for and all on their say so. Suddenly from out of the haze came the sound of a horn, every one gasped, one bright young lad noted it didn't sound very loud did it? Must be a long way off yet his dad explained; Then it happened! She appeared from around the headland, a little rowing boat with two sailors at the ores and a radiant Queen in all her finery sitting at the back. Apart from a crown and sceptre she also sported a football style horn which she gamely sounded off to warn other shipping of her presence. She was gracious enough to give the guests a right regal wave as they passed their position, the sailors grunting under the strain of transporting her majesty in such a manor through the sea. It had arrived, the moment of truth, judgment day, had the team gone too far on this one? Had they underestimated the guest's tolerance for having this trick played on them in order to amuse them? For a few seconds it seemed they had as the group stood there in a stunned silent daze, until one by one they realised the sailors were two of the team itself and the Queen? Well you can work that one out for yourselves. You can imagine the relief when the group erupted with laughter and the whole charade had been a complete success.

Imaginative, unexpected and simple means affective and that's a good motto to stick to when doing this type of thing. There are many other stunts that I got away with in a similar vein such as Cockle Shell Shooting with the intriguing instructions to bring your own stick, piece of string and bent pin. Most of us would in fact plan, advertise and execute such madcap spectacles for our guest's pleasure and enjoyment back then. We would of course share stories and keep each other stocked up with ideas. This is something that seems to be missing from many of the Entertainment Managers programmes these days.........pity.

The type of trip they can organise for you, dear guest, is limited only by where you are, which agency your camp or company has done a deal with if any, your age and ability and their own imagination. They can range from deep sea fishing to the circus or from a model village to a pearl factory from a donkey sanctuary to an air-show. While they will generally want to keep their guests on sight during the evenings in the UK, quite often abroad the opposite is expected so there they might be taking you to a top nightclub or show-bar or just on a pub crawl. Generally however if they are running the Entertainment at a holiday centre, wherever that may be, they will be there to ensure you remain on site spending your money in the bars and restaurants etc, which is fine of course so long as you are receiving the quality, value for money and comprehensive entertainments programme that warrants you remaining there and spending even more of your hard earned money. After all as I keep saying, only because it's a true and important point, you have already paid for it the second you booked with a centre or company that declares there is entertainment laid on for you.

VISITING ATTRACTIONS

You will recall I mentioned visiting attractions such as sports professionals and specialist cabarets. Well these are a big part of your daytime programme as you will generally put off other events or even going out for the day and stay on site to see one of your favourite sports personalities giving a demonstration or even get the chance to play them at whatever it may be. Your Entertainments Manager should never underestimate this facet of the programme and treat it as some sort of time filler for them and their 'coats'. They must treat every single one as a cabaret because that's what they are. They are giving a performance, an important performance for them and you guests and they warrant the same professional care and attention that should be afforded to the evening visiting cabarets. If your Entertainments Manager has started the day correctly of course they will already have posted the right amount of 'coats' to cover the event and all the props required will be there in plenty of time won't they? Won't they? Well this is one of those events that I would always attend myself, as an Entertainments Manager to make sure that all is well. Establish that the visiting cabaret or pro had all they needed when they needed it. If this is to be a regular attraction on my day off I would make a point of being there on their first visit out of courtesy and respect and set the standard I expected from my 'coats' for the rest of the season. The compering of these events is not to be taken lightly either and if they stick to the tips I have given them in 'Tales of Superblue', the very same trade secrets I let you into later, they won't go far wrong. But you will know when they do and indeed will probably be able to tell THEM why they did......good to be in the know isn't it?

Some visiting attractions need more attention than others of course and many of the pros just like to be introduced and then they take over only requiring the Entertainments Manager or 'coat' to be present for the round of applause at the end, Chester Barnes was one of these for example, others are more dependent on their involvement. This involvement takes many forms but as always the Entertainments Manager should make sure the right person is doing the right job, they'll need to compere, keep score on a number of sports, know the rules and generally assist. But must not forget this is a holiday camp and a lot of the cabarets and pros welcome a little more fun input indeed some will ask for it. This is great for the Entertainments Manager as it allows them to keep their 'coats' interacting with the guests while once again someone else takes the strain. The Entertainments Manager has to be very careful here though, taking part in their show or exhibition is one thing taking over is quite another, they need to keep a watchful eye on this one. Interaction is a good word to describe some of the things they and their 'coats' can get involved in to assist, for example they could stooge for them being the butt of the jokes, turning up in an inappropriate costume etc, I enjoy doing this with the snooker pros in particular as they seem to make the most of you in those situations. If you get the right pro you can lark about pretending you can't count as the darts scorer etc giving them an added dimension to their show. The busiest the Entertainments Manager is likely to be is when it comes to attractions and cabarets who are visiting the centre is during themed holidays. Let's stick to country and western for examples shall we, in just one day they could have to contend with the quick draw competition which is a self contained mini cabaret culminating in guests being able to take part in a gunfight scenario using a real colt and computer timing for the results, a wild west show on the sports field with a complete re-enactment of battle of little big horn, a countless number of bands constantly arriving needing to set up as others break down having finished their set, a myriad of speciality acts knife throwing and lassoing everything in sight, stunt horse riders plus much much more and all this is taking place during the day at as many venues as they have to stage them in. So now you begin to get the idea that visiting attractions are far from being a time filler and can actually be time consuming and labour intensive but please don't think that is a negative for us entertainers though, I promise it's all very much worth it in the end for the enjoyment of our guests. So make sure, wherever you are on holiday, your visiting attractions are being organised and run to this standard and giving you that enjoyment. All themed weeks, weekends or days will have their own particular speciality attractions and the Entertainments Manager will have to deal with these in isolation as and when the centre holds them. However they should make sure to contact those organising it well in advance so they are prepared and fully staffed to cope. Sounds like it can be a bit manic doesn't it? Well indeed it can be but if they just take it one step at a time they'll be fine and in my experience will have great fun with the events whether during themed or ordinary holidays and generally the pros and performers are interesting and nice people to meet. My absolute favourite of all is the professional wrestling, which can be a daytime or evening cabaret. I always refereed this and my 'coats' would second in each corner with a guest while another one or two would compere. When it comes to family entertainment you just can't beat it. You guests love it, the comedy bout where I got all sorts of things done to me usually incorporating my track suit bottoms coming down at some point and the audience, children and ladies mainly, going mad at the 'baddy', the serious ones where the action is concentrated between the wrestlers themselves and tag matches being a big crowd pleaser. People such as the great Brian Manelli, boss of one of the best English Wrestling Organisations and Phoenix Promotions with other great wrestlers like Dave Heinz, Mel Stuart, Tarantula, Billy Stock, the West's and Sanchez Brothers to name but a few over the years, being masters at the perfect way of entertaining at holiday camps in this fine art and make no mistake it really is an art if performed correctly. The agility of these big men, the impeccable comic timing, the injuries they regularly sustain, the hours upon hours of practice they put in, the setting up, breaking down and carrying of that great big heavy ring for every show. You would imagine them to be unapproachable hard nasty individuals wouldn't you? Not even close to it, they are some of the loveliest people I have ever had the pleasure of meeting and working with. But don't confuse that with soft, they are extremely hard and professional in the ring, they have to be to do the job they do and do it well and believe me that's the only way they would do it. But we are talking about the Entertainments Manager and 'coats' input here so they must treat these men and women with the respect they deserve and they will pay them back tenfold and their guests will thank them for it, trust me. In fact we'll end this where I began it and my advice here is quite simple, all entertainment staff should treat all attractions professionally and with respect they must be prepared for them and then *YOU* my friend will enjoy the variety they bring to your holiday.

PROFESSIONALLY RUN COMPETITIONS AND TOURNAMENTS

As with anything else I talk to you about in this book, daytime competitions and tournaments require a lot of forethought and planning. They take up a large portion of any day at your village and demand serious management and staging so much so that I have dedicated an entire chapter to the subject.

WET WEATHER

I think we have pretty much covered this aspect elsewhere but it would be remiss of me not to remind you of its importance in this chapter because it is so vitally important to your holiday happiness. In 'Tales of Superblue' I ask all Entertainments Managers to please, for their own sake make sure they have put a really good wet weather programme together and all the props are in place ready to swing into action at a moment's notice. I remind them that we talked about letting their guests know what's on and that's never more vital than when advertising their wet weather programme. I can hear a lot of you shouting at the page now saying what about the hot weather programme? And I am so glad you took that one on board because your right the same importance must be placed on both weather extremes if they are to be a great Entertainments Manager and keep your holiday dreams alive no matter the climate.

CERTIFICATES AND PRIZES

You've just spent the last three hours playing your best ever snooker and have won the tournament you're feeling on top of the world ready to do a lap of honour accept all the applause and adulation from the crowd when you lift that lovely trophy above your head. Imagine the dramatic anticlimax when the 'coat' running it just hands you a bit of paper uttering insincere words that mean no more than thanks for turning up. You look at the A4 photocopied sheet which purports to be a winner's certificate and wonder why you bothered in the first place. What sort of report do you think you are going to give the outside world of that holiday village now? This is such a basic and simple part of running an effective programme that I have been absolutely amazed to find that many holiday resorts are just missing the point of its importance. I have witnessed this very thing happening time and time again, 'coats' just handing out very sad looking, yes even photocopied, certificates at the end of a competition or tournament with little or no ceremony. Most people having left as they are knocked out means you are left with the winner and runner up so any presentation becomes a bit of a damp squid after all the effort you have put in. These are the sorts of little details that distinguish them as either a poor Entertainments Manager or a great one. You have put yourself out and entered the competition maybe even put off a day out to remain on site for it so the least they can do is give you the recognition for the loyalty and effort that you deserve. Instead of that damp squid presentation consisting of a bit of paper to a couple of people, they should make it a fully fledged razzmatazz event in its own right. There are two ways of doing this, either each evening or at the end of the week. I prefer the end of the week big prize giving where they also lead up to the overall winner of the house points competition (more about this later). Whenever they are going to do their presentation they must ensure the 'coats' get full details of winners and runners up at the end of the competition including ages where applicable and never let them say they will catch up with the guest later because they are in a rush or worse couldn't be bothered right then. Invariably this gets forgotten and come the prize giving the Entertainments Manager has to ask on the microphone for the winner and runner up to come forward without even knowing their names. This spoils your moment of glory yet again, so they might as well have given it to you at the time, and guess how ridiculous they will look having to do this in front of the whole resort. Also imagine how unhappy a sponsor of that event is going to be and you just know the day it happens is the day they have chosen to turn up to see how well the Entertainments Manager is promoting their product. They should also get the 'coats' to check that a person is not going home before the prize giving and if they are they must present them with their prize the evening before they leave. On the subject of prizes and certificates there is no logic in them scrimping or cutting corners in this department and a photocopy is absolutely inexcusable. Making sure whatever they are giving you is something worth winning is just plain common sense and good business acumen to be honest but as far as I am concerned the reason for getting it right is because it is a vital element of your overall holiday satisfaction. If you are at a corporate centre i.e. Pontins Warners, or Butlins etc they won't have much choice or, will they? If what they are being given is naff they have a duty to say so and tell head office that their guests are complaining. After all these are vital forms of advertising for the company. You should be going home proud to show off your victory at their holiday centre and you certainly won't if the certificate looks cheap and nasty and you can't if you haven't got a prize that means anything. If they are at a small or private camp and they have a say in the purchase of such items hopefully the Entertainments Manager will have thought about it. Got a good design on their certificates it's worth the extra few pence. They should ask themselves "would I put that on my wall?" if the answer is no – they ought to ditch it and get one that they and indeed you would. When it comes to prizes the same rules apply. Too often now I see people being given some poxy left over item from the camp shop or a load of cheap tat dished out to a child just so that others will want to get mum and dad to spend more cash on the same rubbish from the shop. Nothing to be proud of, nothing that advertises their centre or company, nothing that makes you want to talk about your holiday when you get home. A prize should be just that! So as you can see not spending a little extra on these is false economy therefore you should be getting prizes, good prizes. What is a good prize? Well a decent trophy always goes down well and of course covers all the above criteria re pride and advertising etc, again if you're at a large or corporate centre they should have a number of sponsors who will be supplying you with those decent prizes to promote their product, if not someone isn't doing their job properly. Again if you're not happy about what you are getting, especially if it's a cheap trick to make children want you to purchase even more junk from the shop, you should complain about this to your Centre and Entertainments Managers and if they don't listen inform head office. If you're at that small or private park, you should find the Entertainments Manager has, as I have advised them to in 'Tales of Superblue' gone out and found their own sponsors it's not difficult I promise you. They will be surprised how many large companies will invest in this kind of advertising because they are aware that their product is being associated with fun and good times and that sells.

Any company executive, centre manager and unquestionably Entertainments Manager that forgets to stage end of season *'FREE'* holiday finals is a fool, these are always extremely popular, you love them because you get a free holiday and are in the grand final, sponsors love them because they get really good exposure throughout the season and then take over the whole camp for that prestigious grand final, the camp management love it because while they have given away free holidays to the winners and possibly runners up they are accompanied by family and friends who all add up to a full camp spending their money. Why have I put this in the 'an effective daytime programme' section? It could sit comfortably in a few chapters of the book but I decided that this would be the appropriate place in the end because so much of your daytime programme will be made up of such competitions and tournaments, even the sports/ fun days can be sponsored. It's extremely important that your Entertainment Manager is aware of all aspects of this and does not waste this vast chunk of your participation in such events or squander an advertising potential for their sponsors. 'Coats' should be out there full of enthusiasm for the competition or event and showing exuberance about the prize to be won especially if it's being sponsored. Creating an atmosphere of friendly rivalry that all will want to join in with throughout the week leading to a spectacular prize giving that makes it all worthwhile.

LUNCHTIME FUN

I am afraid I am going to get back on my soapbox here because this is another of those parts of the programme that seems to have met its demise at many holiday resorts in recent years. I have to say that this astounds me because lunchtimes are a brilliant time for the entertainments team to get to know you, having a lot of you in one place at the same time, halfway during the day allows them to enforce the theme of fun and laughter you can expect whenever you attend one of their venues. It is also excellent for promoting the afternoon and evening programme, I would quite often line up people to play pivotal roles for events or enter competitions etc. Even more unbelievable is that park managements have chosen to ignore its disappearance and the massive revenue a good Entertainments Manager will generate by organising a well run and fun packed session. So what can your Entertainments Manager do to create this mini entertainment oasis at lunchtime? Well almost anything really if they put their mind to it but it has to be something that you, my dear guest, can't do at other times of the day or there is no incentive for you to turn up for this event in particular. Historically the reason for a lunchtime session was because of the licensing hours and the bars were not open all day so the Entertainments Managers were under pressure to attract guests inside for that two hour period when they were open to ensure it was a profitable venture. That was of course the view point of the Resort Management and understandably so but it had the desirable affects for the entertainments team that I spoke about above. As I write this I can almost hear Resort Managers saying "what's he on about now? The bars are open all day so we are making enough money" and the Entertainment Managers wondering why they should put on yet another event if their guests are going to the bar anyway. Well in the first instance I don't believe you are taking as much money, the bars at centres I have been to in the past few years are all but dead during the day. With no events taking place there is no incentive to make your way across the centre or stay there in the first place just to sit in a big quiet, often dark, empty venue. You might as well get a couple of cans of beer or a bottle of wine and sit and watch TV in your chalet or caravan etc, and that's exactly what people are doing. Even on wet weather days when they should have a captive audience to some degree you are just hiring a DVD and sitting it out in your accommodation, it really is a sad state of affairs that does not need to exist. Obviously you like to get in your car and go out sightseeing etc but that doesn't mean you are going to or even want to do it every day but if you aren't offered a worthwhile reason to stay you will at least go out for a nice pub lunch somewhere. If your Entertainments Manager is lucky enough to be on a full board centre they should have less trouble persuading you to join them in the bar before or after your meal, but again to my amazement I have known such venues to have absolutely nothing on at lunchtime what so ever, honestly the mind boggles. Should you find yourself at a park that is situated in an area of outstanding beauty or historical interest they will obviously have a harder time persuading you to remain on site so they will have to make lunchtimes a real event and possibly even only have one every other day or so but these centres are far and few between in the big scheme of things so most of them can easily enhance your empty open all day bars with a busy, fun packed lunchtime event. What sort of things am I talking about? Well the obvious one to me would be the sing-a-long and I don't mean karaoke (you can do this anytime and will probably find it on your programme in the evening at some bar already). A sing-a-long gets everyone going provided they remember to use the right mix of songs to cover all ages and use a band or at least live music of some sort for the backing otherwise your back to karaoke. They should get all the 'coats' to lead with a song or two even if they can't sing, such as the personality 'coats' like my friend Billy Brown that I told you about earlier, believe me it all adds to the fun and encourages you and your fellow guests to get up and keep it all going. It is important that they don't forget to have someone that can back the youngsters at least to some degree. A competition to compliment this is a good idea also, they can use one of the children's competitions here but must be careful not to use up all of these at lunchtimes leaving them nothing for the rest of the day or early evenings and of course making the already specialised role of the children's entertainers even more difficult, there are dozens of silly fun competitions for all the family they can pull out of the bag here anyway. Horse or dog racing on film are always very popular with holidaymakers and in my experience attract a significant number of you to a lunchtime session. Your Entertainments Manager should be a bit creative when staging something like this however and intersperse it with a bit of comedy or a song or two etc. I have just thrown two ideas into the pot to show you the sort of things that you should expect your Entertainments Manager to use to stage an event specifically for a lunchtime session, of course they are only simple ideas for them to work on and they will hopefully have many of their own to try out. The point is that this is a part of the day that they can exploit for themselves, their team and the camp management but more importantly they must use it to enhance your overall holiday experience and never forget that is their ultimate goal.

CHILDREN

Once again a subject that I don't wish to flog to death but one that warrants a mention when talking about any successful programme and in particular during the day as this is when any centre will have to cater for, potentially, a large number of children of varying ages for lengthy periods of time. In 'Tales of Superblue' I remind them that the children's programme is as important as the adults if not more so therefore this chapter is meant as an overall view of the day's events they should be providing for you all while on holiday at their centre. When it comes to children however they have added responsibilities so need to make sure they always put the children's safety and well being before absolutely anything else - no matter what.

CHAPTER EIGHT

AN EFFECTIVE EVENING PROGRAMME

As a guest this is very likely to be one of the main reasons that you will ever book a holiday at a particular centre or with a specific company. It is the one time of day that almost all of you will be saying to the entertainments team "right I am here, I am at your disposal, I am your audience.......Entertain Me!"

It is certainly the one part of the day that you should be guaranteed some sort of interaction with your Entertainments Manager and 'coats' and I don't mean them just giving it blah blah blah on the microphone either. I mean interaction, conversation, laughter, smiles, singing, dancing in fact I am talking about out-and-out pleasurable fun in their company. It is a sad indictment on the state of many of our holiday centres and companies today that you will probably be looking at this page right now and thinking "if only that were the truth" I know it's sad to say, at the very least, but it is the unpalatable reality of today's cost cutting, couldn't care less, untrained, unsupervised and ridiculously woefully employed 'so called' entertainment teams at a variety of centres that makes you feel that way. If on the other hand you can put your hand on your heart and say "oh yes Superblue that's exactly what I get, where I go on holiday" then that's fab and long may it continue and that centre and company deserve your custom and money. Because...... and yes I know I harp on about it......but today money is tighter than ever before so they, more so than ever, must justify taking yours.

I talk about untrained, couldn't care less and woefully employed entertainment staff and of course that is my opinion of numerous teams that I have come across lately. But you're probably sitting there wondering what else should I be getting? What class of evening entertainment should I rightfully expect? Well rather than just sitting here and banging away at my keyboard filling the next few pages by spouting off about it all and pontificating about what I think is wrong with those teams let me show you what I wrote in 'Tales of Superblue'. This is exactly what I would expect of myself as an Entertainments

Manager and from every 'coat' who was a member of my team. It is what I believe every Manager and 'coat' should be determined to achieve on your behalf as well as for their own professional pride. Just compare this to what you have received as an evening entertainments programme and from this day forth you will know if you're spending your pennies with the right company or at a centre worthy of your patronage. In order that you may be endowed with this power and for your delectation here is that excerpt from 'Tales of Superblue' for entertainers................................

I want you to close your eyes for a few moments - ok now that you have opened them again, I did actually want you to think about something in particular, so hang on a second before you close them again. Right now imagine that your backstage at the London Palladium there's a few minutes to go before the curtain rises and you've snuck into the wings and are taking a sneaky peak out at the auditorium. The audience are nearly all seated and there is an amazingly excited buzz of anticipation in the air, the lights go down and the band strikes up to play the overture, the last few stragglers rush to their seats eager not to miss a thing. As the curtains open, everyone sits to attention, eyes open wide as they take in the spectacle of the wondrous scenery before them, breaths held with expectant impatience at the thought of you walking onto that very stage and giving the performance of a lifetime as you take part in a spectacular show that will last for the next one and a half hours. Are you feeling it? Are you in the moment? What would you give to be stepping out onto that hallowed stage right now? Just about anything is the honest truth isn't it? But for most of you it's never going to happen is it, you're never going to have an audience sat there with baited breath, brimming with excitement at the thought of you entertaining them for the next one and a half hours and then once you step out onto the stage have them hanging onto your every word. It's not going to happen anywhere never mind the Palladium is it? No of course not - No? Well actually yes it will for any budding 'coats' reading this! And if they're already at a camp it already has, or at least it should have. You see there is no difference between looking out at the audience filling the Palladium psyching yourself up to give that magnificent performance and looking out from behind the curtain at your holiday village. The auditorium is filling up as guests take their seats, some will have been taking it in turns to sit there for hours saving the best front row tables, just so they can sample the evening's entertainment that you are about to provide. The excitement, the apprehension, the buzz of happiness in the air, people rushing their tea all trying to use the bathroom in the chalet or caravan before dashing over to the ballroom in time for your opening gambit, not wanting to miss a thing. They have paid good money for this, just as those at the Palladium have paid good money for their performance, and they have the right to expect a first class performance from you. In return however they are ready to give you all the applause and adulation you crave, and let's be honest there's nothing quite like that is there. Yes they are that audience! Your audience! So get out there and give them the performance of a lifetime!

Oh did I say there was no difference? Well actually I told a little porky "poetic licence you know".

The truth is there are three main differences:

1) One and a half hours
2) Performance night after night and
3) A few hundred people.

ONE AND A HALF HOURS

I've been there many times now, standing backstage waiting to go on and do a 45 minute stand up comedy routine. Feeling as sick as a parrot, stomach turning over, palms sweating profusely, heart thumping like a the bass on a sound system at the Notting Hill carnival and my brain screaming run away, run away. Like many other performers taking to stages all around the country about the same time that evening I overcome all that anxiety and mild stage fright and step out as the compere announces my name and the audience erupts with applause. Oh no not again! I really should have ran away, why do I never listen to myself? Why do I keep putting myself through this? I'm walking across to the microphone its seconds away from show-time, I'm out there all alone, no one to help me now, so what does my brain do? Only plays the nastiest trick of all that's what. It's gone to jelly I can't remember the opening word of the opening line of the opening gag. Somehow 45 minutes later there I am taking a bow ready to give them another ten minutes if they want it. The show at the Palladium lasts one and a half hours as do many other productions that night with all their performers going through the same or similar pre show nervousness. That's about 45 minutes for us cabaret acts, an hour and a half for those lovely show people and we view both of these feats with deference and respect don't we. Yes? Of course we do and rightly so. Those of us that aren't performing respect those that are and those that are will have enough respect for themselves and the audience not to be cocky or complacent, which is the surest way of messing up trust me, but they will indeed be worrying about delivering an outstanding performance during this period of time, that's 45 minutes to one and a half hours. You of all people must be thinking of course I respect them, it's a long time to keep an audience entertained and entertained so well and professionally that you leave them wanting more, and again you'd be absolutely correct. So stop for a moment and think, there you are backstage peering out from your curtain, the rooms buzzing and the audience is alive with anticipation as they wait for you to appear on stage and begin the evening entertainment. Let me just emphasise two points here, you and evening, that's all evening, in fact you are just about to embark on a mammoth six hours of entertaining, yes *six* hours and if it's your turn to do the late disco that could easily become a mighty *eight* hours. Suddenly 45 minutes or even one and a half hours pales into insignificance doesn't it? You have already done a days work and when most sane people are just settling down, putting their feet up to watch the telly, here you are setting out on your second shift of the day.

PERFORMANCE NIGHT AFTER NIGHT

At the Palladium the show will be repeated time after time, night after night and even cabaret artistes can go for a whole season or longer without changing much of their act. They can do this with reasonable confidence that each night they look from behind that curtain they will see a completely new audience with the excited buzz and anticipation of seeing the show for the first time. You on the other hand will look out from your curtain and see the same people filling the same seats night after night for the duration of their holiday, but here's the thing, they should still have that eagerness and excitement to see what you have in store for the next six hours. A totally new six hours worth of entertainment each and every day of their holiday, quite breathtaking when you think about it isn't it? Don't panic though you have seen my evening programme examples so you can use those as a basis to add your own ideas to and we will cover the finer points of translating that from the page to reality in this chapter.

A FEW HUNDRED PEOPLE

The Palladium, as beautiful an icon of entertainment that it is, only seats 2.286 people. Some of the holiday centres you will be working at will hold that amount and more in just one of their venues. Just imagine how many people you will have entertained in one week, one season, one year and eventually in your career. Staggering thought ah? All those thousands upon thousands of people that you made laugh, cry, sing, dance. All those people you made happy.

Now give yourself and the evening programme the deference and respect that you both deserve get out there and put on the performance of a lifetime.

WHAT'S THE DIFFERENCE BETWEEN RUNNING A DAYTIME AND EVENING PROGRAMME

Basically all the same rules apply when starting your evening as they did to your daytime programme. Remember **CHEAP**? Good, because you can stick to this ensuring you cover all aspects necessary for a successful evening.

Check all venues

Have failsafe for events that you cannot attend in person (i.e. just as in day programme ensure you or your deputy will be contacted if an event fails to start on time in another venue)

Ensure all props are ready to be deployed

Always have an evening meeting

Post your 'coats' wisely every evening on the evening

The next six hours however are like no other job on earth. You will need to meticulously plan each event and rehearse it until you get it down to a fine art. As I have emphasised previously, running your programme on time is of the utmost importance and never more so than in the evening. An event being a couple of minutes late starting or running over can throw your hole night into disarray, the knock on effect can mean you are hours out of sync by the end of the evening. Something you, your 'coats', visiting cabarets and bands won't want and guests won't tolerate. Please don't make the fatal mistake of getting it all down on paper and assuming it all fits together nicely, *try it out!*

You will need your 'coats' to work at various venues sometimes in isolation as well as in a team effort throughout the evening and they can't be expected to do this right off the bat. Just like any great performance, it needs to be rehearsed, it needs a run through. It's the only way you are ever going to know for sure you have enough of everything to make it work i.e. 'coats', space, equipment, props and costumes etc and of course most crucially *time!* If you have trained your 'coats' in everything from bingo to party dances or prize giving to fun competitions they will be prepared and confident meaning you and they will run the evening programme like a well oiled machine. If on the other hand you don't bother and try to 'wing it' the seconds will turn into minutes, the minutes will turn into…. Well you know all that by now. Seriously though would you even contemplate putting on a show without any rehearsal? Of course not! I can't even begin to imagine the shambling mess it would be, can you? No! Well then why would, you treat a six hour performance any differently, remember deference and respect. Obviously you only need to do this at the beginning of the season and then only as and when you make significant changes or new staff arrive.

EVENING MEETING

Now you have your fully trained team of 'coats' with their finely honed skills at the ready, I strongly advise holding a quick get together at the start of each evening. I say quick because you will have covered the bulk of issues in the morning meeting. Nevertheless things can crop up during the day that, require dealing with before you embark on the marathon that is the evening programme. For instance, you may have lost a 'coat' due to any number of reasons, sometimes meaning a complete rethink of a particular aspect of the programme, a show or even an entire venue according to how much was dependent on that person being part of your team that night. For example some 'coats' will be excellent at compering so it stands to reason that you would want them to be the mainstay on the microphone at one of your venues. Losing someone like this particularly at short notice can cause you major logistical problems. Because the evening needs to be run like a military operation, but by holding an evening get together you can set out your strategic plan and cater for any such occurrence. Just as in your morning meeting posting your 'coats' is vital, remember the right person doing the right job, but not forgetting to give others the chance to gain experience. When adhering to this rule however for the evening bear in mind the venue, some people just naturally flourish in certain surroundings or audience types some will excel in the family environment of the ballroom being equally happy dancing with your senior guests as they are with the kids. Others will not be so adept in this scenario but will relish the company and distinct entertainments of the adult bar. While everyone should at least experience all types of venues, and sometimes there will be no choice due to staff numbers etc, it just makes plain common sense that if someone is posted where they are most comfortable, you have a happy 'coat' and a happy 'coat' equals happy guests. *Never* use a posting as a punishment, all you are doing is making a 'coat' unhappy thereby punishing the guests and in the long run punishing yourself because unhappy guests complain! I have seen it done and in my opinion it's the sign of a very weak manager and let's face it a form of bullying. Evening postings have the added employment law, health & safety and just downright decent management of people aspects, in respect of the fact they can be working virtually nonstop, you must make sure your team all get adequate breaks throughout. This is something that you have to build in to your planning when you devise the programme and take into account when you do a run through etc. It is very important that 'coats' take their breaks at the times they have been allocated and for the length of time they have been allocated to ensure everyone is where they are supposed to be when they are supposed to be there. Otherwise you will quickly find yourself with a programme that is out of control because things are not running on time, yes I know I am nagging you but it is that serious a matter if you are to succeed. Put some thought into their break times and make sure you have the 'coats' you require on hand to run any event successfully. Of course it goes without saying you will need to work around any shows you are putting on. This is also the time to go through the evening programme and ensure all props and costumes etc are in place. Don't find yourself in the situation I have witnessed many times, where some or all of your 'coats' are legging it back to their chalets half way through the evening to get their costumes for a show when you need them to be in the ballroom with you, running a competition say. Although I call it a quick get together do still pay heed to the other items that we spoke about for the morning meeting, smartness, cleanliness, welfare etc etc.

You will have some 'coats' that will start at staggered times this is normally due to the fact that their day duties finish later than the others i.e. the late afternoon bingo session. Clearly it is unreasonable to expect them to be at the get together without having had a decent amount of downtime to unwind and get ready before throwing themselves into the hectic evening programme. Or when you have an adult venue that will run much later than the family room and you need 'coats' to start later to cover it and finish later. When this occurs make sure you give them a realistic time to come on duty and ensure it's at a juncture in the programme that will allow you to be free to meet with them and go through exactly the same items as you did with the main group earlier. Even if it's only one 'coat', remember a team is only as good as its weakest link, so if someone gets it wrong because you hadn't made the time to update them or ensure they had what they needed for the evening who is the weakest link, them or you?

EVENING MEAL TIMES

We covered this wonderful time of day for interaction between you and the guests in chapter six but it's so worth mentioning again. It is the perfect opportunity to get them interested, excited or even psyched up for the coming evenings events. It's the overture to your six hour performance it's the preview of your theme night or the advert for the next days. By all means do go back and take a glance at this subject to refresh your memory but this is such a unique occasion at camps, particularly in these days of increasing self catering and ownership sites, that I implore you to please take particular note of the very last five words of wisdom I bestowed upon you back there.......***don't you dare waste it.***

SIX HOUR PERFORMANCE

We've talked a lot about the six hour performance now but what in practical terms does this mean? Well for the Entertainments Manager it really does mean six hours constantly on the go both mentally and physically. Ensuring the team are doing the right thing at the right time as well as heading up the events on stage in at least one of the venues. As a 'coat' you should be looking to support the manager and your team in delivering a first class evening's entertainment for your guests. Be at that right place at that right time, take your breaks at the correct time and be back on duty, on time, ready to jump back into whatever role you have been posted to for that part of the evening and do all this with enthusiasm, vitality and wearing that all important smile. If you all play your part everything goes very smoothly and the evening actually flies by. The speed at which it all happens will surprise you the first time you work an evening like this, one minute you are arriving loaded up with costumes for your show and suddenly after what seems like no time whatsoever there you are sitting back stage happily exhausted at the end of it all. You should be happily exhausted because you will have put everything you have into it and that takes its toll but the buzz you should be getting from being out there entertaining your guests should never fail to put a smile on a 'coats' face at the end of a successful evening. I've said it before and I'll probably say it again, but there really is no other job like this one. Yes it is long hours but you get regular breaks and let's face it where else will you get paid to spend half the evening dancing and chatting with people and the other half being the centre of attention while making those same people happy?

There will of course be nights that you just don't feel up to it and we will discuss this in more depth in the chapter on health and safety. But as an Entertainments Manager you should be on the lookout for the tell tell signs and be approachable enough that your 'coats' feel comfortable letting you know when one of them feels like this. As for you 'coats', don't let it worry you unnecessarily, we all get mid-season blues at different times, just confide in your manager preferably or a friend if that's more comfortable for you and the time and space you need to recoup and recharge your batteries should be catered for. One of the things I used to do if I began to feel a bit ragged around the edges at times was take myself away somewhere quiet, usually on a beach at night, sit and think about how much I had wanted this job and how impossible it seemed that I would ever get it, then the overwhelming joy and pride I felt the first day I walked out in my Pontins Bluecoat. I recalled how many other people had been at the Empire Ballroom on the day I had auditioned and wondered how many hundreds of others I had beaten to get to wear that jacket. I wondered how fed up they might be feeling at that very moment because they have to get up at the crack of dawn to go to work every day in the same old factory, shop or office, that generally did the trick for me. That's not to make light of mental or physical exhaustion so please do look out for one another.

NO GAPS - NO DEAD STAGE

One of the secrets of a successful evening is to keep the whole thing flowing from one major event into another. This, as you will no doubt have surmised by now, is much easier said than done. But fear not for the human mind is thankfully a very forgiving organ and as long as there is something taking place that occupies its thoughts in a pleasant way it will take into consideration that there needs to be some pauses in the 'live' entertainment in order to facilitate the setting up of the stage for a show or cabaret and indeed it will know that the majority of 'coats' will have to leave the public arena of the venue in order to change and ready themselves for that performance. Obviously to run one major event into another without stopping for breath is an absurdity, however you can stage manage the entire evening so that it appears to the guests that that is exactly what you have managed to do. You can engineer it to give the overall impression that the whole night's entertainment was seamless. How is this possible I hear you cry, well stop crying now because, it's actually quite simple. Remember that proverbial swan we talked about at the beginning of the book? Brilliant! Because we welcome the majestic creature back again here, yes you will be running around like a headless chicken, blimey its turned into a wildlife book now, ok lets change that to your running around like a demented Basil Faulty, better? Ok well anyway there you are manically trying to get everything started on time, set the stage for competitions, shows, cabarets, prize giving and the such like, knowing most of your 'coats' will be diving backstage on mass at some point to get ready and you just don't have enough pairs of hands to do everything and what wouldn't you give to have the revolving stage at the palladium right now. That's the reality of the situation but just like our graceful royal bird you will keep all this wild paddling under the waterline and present the guests with an elegant image as you glide through the programme with an air of confidence and composure. The trick is to ensure that every time the guests hear or see you there is something significant about to take place and you are presenting it to them, time and time again, in a calm and professional manner. Surely they must have noticed the long silent gaps the empty stage and coatless dance floor? Ah well spotted, and of course you would be right if you were to allow any of those things to happen. So here's the real secret.....don't!

Remember that human mind? Don't give it gaps in the programme that will let it start to think about what you are up to, don't present it with a dead stage that suggests to it that you don't actually care about it and are being disrespectful by making it sit there without so much as a 'coat' on the dance floor to show you at least thought about entertaining it. Instead just like any good magician you need to pull off a wondrous illusion here, to be fair I've over egged it a bit there, but it is a kind of a slight of hand in that you are distracting their attention while setting them up for the big surprise ending. What I am getting at is that with a little forethought, imagination and planning you can actually have something going on all the time. For example if you want the dance floor to be kept clear for a short time while you prepare for a show or cabaret it's as simple as running a quiz which will only require one or two of your 'coats' who need not be in the opening number of the show. But if you are a small team don't forget willing staff from other departments or your lifeguards etc. There will always be someone that will want to be a part of it all and can assist with items such as this. Remember though this is part of your evening programme so make it much more than just another boring quiz, it needs to be upbeat, lively and fun. For example if it is a music quiz, use musical excerpts or even film, DVD and video clips, ensuring the music and questions are varied so that it is fun for all ages and have daft spot prizes or silly forfeits etc. It goes without saying you can and should spice up any fun quiz in this way you just have to put a little thought into it. But can you see how this, the simplest of simple ideas has subconsciously sent out the message to your guests *that you care*? Of course consciously all they have actually noticed is that you, the team, went from one event, party dances let's say, straight into another the quiz and will go straight from that one into a show or cabaret etc and all without a gap or a dreadful dead stage. Quizzes are by no means the only tool in your gap filling box of tricks I merely use these as an example to show you how easy it can be. You do in fact have an array of minor entertaining diversions at your disposal. Bear in mind that you do have competitions, both junior in the early evening and adult later on, to really keep your guests entertained during band breaks or leading up to a cabaret or show. Do however be mindful that in order to run some of these you will require a number of your 'coats' to assist so not always suitable directly before one of your own shows. You will also see, in a following chapter, that a properly run competition is actually a mini show in its own right. Party dances are always a great floor filler and can be run and fronted by one or two 'coats', again freeing up most of your team to get ready for a show or take breaks etc, we'll talk more about these later. You could in an emergency utilise the bingo machine for one of these slots, as you will recall I spoke about such use earlier in the book, which is why I say only in an emergency. For me this is a boring and lazy excuse for part of your evening entertainment, and on top of that, if you're charging for it too! Well as a guest I would feel cheated to say the least. The truth is there is a myriad of ways to fill your programme between shows, cabarets and bands. The only limitations are the nature of your venue, the size of the team you have to work with, your budget and of course most importantly of all………your own imagination.

Whatever you decide is right for you, your team, venue and guests make sure it is well organised and rehearsed. It needs to start immediately after one major event, a band set for example, and must end – *on time*- immediately before another major event is due to start, a cabaret for instance. The resulting reward for your extra care and attention to programme detail is that the guests are presented with that seamless night of entertainment you should all be aiming for. Don't lose sight of the fact that these are still part of that evening programme so approach them in that way ensuring they are as professionally run as the rest of the evening and just as much fun.

It really is one of the cardinal sins of holiday camp entertainment to ever have noticeable gaps in your evening programme. Where there is potential for this to happen you must use whatever 'coats' or other staff at your disposal wisely so that your guests are *never* sat looking at a dead stage or empty dance floor and *NEVER* in silence. If for some unavoidable reason you find yourself in a position where a short gap is necessary *always* announce that it is just that, and at the very least put some music on making sure these are for the shortest of times and that someone is back out front on stage as soon as is humanly possible.

VENUES (1 OR 2 ROOMS - BALLROOM/FAMILY ROOM – YOUNG GUESTS VENUE)

The number of venues that your establishment has will play a big part in determining the structure of your evening programme. For example if you only have the one room to work with you will have to fit in bingo, early evening junior events, all the cabarets and shows as well as the adult competitions.

In some ways this makes your life easier because you have all your guests in one place so you have all your 'coats' in one place. The converse of that is that you generally won't have as many 'coats' allocated to you as sites with two or more venues. This in turn means fewer 'coats' to run your day and evening programmes and fewer 'coats' to put on decent shows etc. You can immediately see that time management is again imperative, not least of all in respect of health and safety of your 'coats'.

Back to the upside though, you do have your entire audience in one room with you from the start to the end of the evening. It's not so difficult to work the early part of the evening because this will be family orientated and there should be something for everyone in that mix. Bingo is something in particular you will have to manage as it can be a nightmare if you have bored children making noise and running around everywhere. It is an absolute necessity that you provide them with something that will entertain them at least until bingo is over even if it's only cartoons, but I am sure you can be more imaginative than that. This is where a good children's uncle, aunty or entertainer is worth their weight in gold. Once bingo is out of the way you can get stuck into your programme proper with competitions, specialist cabarets, puppets for example, party dances and finally the march out all tailored towards the family audience. We'll discuss the march out later.

Once the march out has taken place you need to change step and swing into an adult orientated programme. This is not so simple with only one venue because you know that you will always have some children in the room and even though you will have announced that this is now 'adult time' you must be very respectful of this fact. The adult content of the evening in a single venue village *must* be such that it will not be offensive to those with children. This means for instance no foul language or overt sexual crudity. That's not to say you can't book good comedians or run competitions that may contain innuendoes, you just have to be circumspect in your choice of such things. Take into account that you will have told the parents it is now adult time so to some degree it's their choice to keep their children there, but never lose sight of the fact that it is their holiday.

This is something that demands a lot of thought and consideration being put into it and again is one of those things that gets easier with experience. The rule of thumb is, if you are not sure that a cabaret will be suitable – Don't book it. If it's not your job to book them, but you are unhappy about them performing at your venue- Don't let them go on. If you're not confident that a competition or part of it is appropriate – Don't use it or change that part. If a routine in one of your shows doesn't sit well for such an evening – Drop it!

You may be young and single but you know what's decent and what's not but if you are really not sure about something then it's probably because it's not right, so air on the side of caution. If you're completely stuck on any particular issue ask someone with more experience at another park or consider consulting friends and relatives with children as to what they would think if they were at your centre being presented with the object of your concerns. Getting this wrong will effect someone's holiday and more likely than not many people's holidays. The result is that by the time the dust has settled and the extent of the fallout from your bad decision is clear you may well find yourself without a job – yes it can be that serious!

Cheer up though because as always I have armed you with the knowledge that these things can happen so you are in an excellent position to avoid it. Take a look back at the sample programmes and get an idea as to how a programme in a single venue works then just add your own personality and imagination to it and away you go.

Even though you technically may have only one entertainment venue to use in the evening there is quite often at least a small bar that is separate from that venue. This is where you can be a little creative so why not consider a more adult late night act in here. In that way you are clearly showing that you are doing your level best to provide entertainment to suit all tastes and ages etc. It is imperative however that you consult and work closely with the bars and possibly the catering manager on this one. They will need to ensure that a number of things are in place before you can even consider this venture. For starters they will have to have an appropriate licence to cover entertainment, the venue will need to definitely be adult only at least from a certain time at night, they have enough staff to cope with the number of guests expected and make no mistake about it – the whole thing had better be financially viable otherwise head office, the owner or camp manager will be after your guts for garters. But so long as you have included the other managers and it was a joint decision to give it a go you will be fine and even praised for trying.

Most centres do have at least a room for children i.e. to use as a club room during the day or while bingo is on in the evening. But unless it's a well equipped entertainment venue in its own right I would suggest bringing the children into the family room as soon as bingo is over. However if you do have a fully equipped children's, junior or teenage venue don't underestimate their importance to your programme. Make sure they are well staffed by the appropriate people and always attend this venue to ensure all is well. I have spouted off long and hard about the good children's aunties and uncles being worth their weight in gold but some of the excellent ones will even want to put their own programmes together. This can be a great help to the Entertainments Manager, if you feel they are of that calibre, but whatever happens anything they have planned MUST go through you before it goes into a printed programme or is advertised. The reasons for this are quite simple, firstly you need to maintain a quality control over all entertainment, secondly make sure it doesn't clash with anything you have planned and lastly you will have to supply enough 'coats' to staff any events they propose to run. For example they may decide to put on a pantomime one evening, which is a great way to entertain families by the way, but this will mean quite a few of your 'coats' being in the children's venue for the early part of the evening, and you still have at least one other venue to run at that time. Logistics have to be carefully worked out here but so long as it all goes through you there should be no problems dealing with it all. In fact you should try to accommodate and actively encourage your children's entertainment staff when they have ideas for enhancing the programme. This is an extremely important venue for you, the children and of course the parents. Advertise it! Staff it! Support it!

Here is as good a time as any to remind you to let your children's entertainers, aunties and uncles off duty at a decent time, normally after the march out. The reasoning behind this is that they will generally have been on their feet and with children of varying ages for much of the day. Having done many hours work and more than their fair share of keeping your guests happy it's time for them to chill out and unwind.

SO WHAT ABOUT TWO OR MORE VENUES?

Well you won't be surprised to learn that the pros and cons are almost the exact opposite to those of a single venue.

SOME OF THE PROS:

Separate adult and family rooms:

Giving your guests the choice to remain at one of venues for the entire evening or take the opportunity to visit both at various times. Many people enjoy going to the 'adult only' venue when the children have gone to bed, families quite often taking it in turns to baby-sit.

Distinct and diverse cabaret, show and competition choices:

Your dilemma of trying to cater for all tastes in a single venue is obviously alleviated here.

More opportunities for 'coats' to perform their own cabarets:

Do remember that some if not all of your 'coats' will be budding stars. This really is their apprenticeship so as part of their training you should be teaching stage craft and giving each of them ample opportunity to perfect it. It can be quite a struggle to fit this in when you only have a single venue but is actually an asset when you have two or more rooms.

Some 'coats' can start and finish later than others:

Dependant on how you have orchestrated your programme, and the make up of your guest population, you may find that a significant number of them may not come out until the 'adult only' venue opens. This is generally later than the family room at most centres so it is quite feasible to start a number of your 'coats' at a later time also. Because you

---

have staggered the time your 'coats' arrive on duty you can allow the earlier starters to go off at an appropriate juncture leaving the late starters to finish the evening with your guests. This has the affect of allowing you to build decent rest periods into their duties, the late starters having a longer break between the day and evening programmes. Be careful that you spread these breaks out among the team so that all get a fair share. It's all too easy to keep using one of them, to their detriment, because they are particularly good at assisting you in the running of either the early or late part of the evening. There will be those however that will volunteer to do one or the other and this is fine as long as they are not depriving others of the chance to develop in that area. Just be aware of these things and it will all come together for you. Of course you will need a number of 'coats' at your disposal to carry this one off in the first place. A minimum number of 'coats' are required at all times if you are to run a professional programme as we have discussed. Do also bear in mind that if you have 'coats' starting at two different times you must be available when the later ones come on duty to cover all the points from the meeting.

SOME OF THE CONS:
'coats' and guests are split up:
There's really not much to say here except that logistics, rules, etiquette, stage management and time keeping will all demand your full attention. I know we haven't covered them all yet but rest assured we will. You must ensure you have enough 'coats' at such a centre to put on a professional day and evening programme. If you have not you *must* tackle this with head office, management or owners. It's your reputation at steak after all but more importantly it's the guest's holidays that will be ruined. As I have previously advised, I would always recommend going to your park in advance on a fact finding tour and make sure the number of 'coats' you are being offered is enough for the number of venues you have.

CABARETS, SHOWS, COMPETITIONS:
The more astute amongst you will have noticed that this heading already came under the section of pros and no I haven't lost the plot entirely. The reason that these could be seen as a negative when operating with more than one venue is that inevitably some guests will miss out on some things. A bit of an obvious statement I know but you must give a great deal of thought as to what you put where and try to please as many of

your guests for as much of the time that you can. This, I promise you, will be one of the most difficult juggling tricks that you have to pull off but you can only ever do your best with this one because a perfect solution is all but impossible to achieve. For example you have a visiting 'star cabaret off the tele' and of course everyone wants to watch them but they are not suitable for a family audience so you should put them in the 'adult only' bar. What are you going to do? Ask them to tone down their act so that you can put them in the family room? What about those then that want to see the adult act they were expecting? What about the act themselves, they will have rehearsed the adult act or maybe that's all they do? What about the gap in the programme you will have left in the adult bar? Well the simple answer is that you can please all of the people for some of the time, you can't please all of the people all of the time and never be tempted to just please some of the people all of the time.

Shows and competitions are less of a worry when it comes to your guests missing out because as we have already covered you can and indeed must adapt these to suite the room you are entertaining in and therefore they could even see a version of these in both venues. Where these could be described as a negative however is where, as I have unfortunately witnessed over the years, entertainment teams mistake 'adult only' venue for adult entertainment room. Please don't be tempted to go down this route. The 'adult only' venue is of course a place where you can get away with a certain amount of adult humour and fun and games but don't let this get out of control don't confuse adult room with adult entertainment with all its connotations. Don't let your shows or competitions descend to bordering on the pornographic or book acts of that nature. Remember a lot of people use the adult only venue simply because it is child free and that's what they want on an evening out. Yes this is an 'adult only' venue but as far as you are concerned all the entertainment you put on should be professional, within the limits of decency and never tacky or filthy for the sake of it.

LOGISTICS

I have mentioned this many times in this chapter and just before we leave 'venues' per se I just want to touch on this subject very briefly. Basically it's that old adage of mine and a posh way of saying you have to organise everything and everyone so that everything is and everyone are in the right place at the right time with the right stuff doing the right thing! logistically speaking.

BINGO

You must be wondering by now what is so special about bingo because it has cropped up regularly throughout the book so far and has received much press from me in this chapter. The truth is that it is not special at all but because it comes with its own unique set of variables I have dedicated a chunk of a chapter to it later. Suffice to say here though that you will have to cater for it as part of your evening programme every evening and you generally won't have a choice which venue you hold it in because of at least one of those variables.

SHOWS - BANDS – CABARETS

Once again we will be taking a closer look at all of these and the various technical aspects surrounding them in a later chapter but for now it's probably enough to say that all the usual suspect rules apply i.e. start on time, end on time and stage management is all important in this area of your evening entertainment.

BANDS

If you have a resident band getting on with them is incredibly important. They are your life blood when it comes to backing you, your shows, visiting cabarets and playing a major part of entertaining your guests for large chunks of the evening. You will need them to come to band calls for rehearsals for some of the above also, so a good working relationship is essential. Trust me they will be the first people to get upset, and will let you know it too, if you let your programme get out of control and start running late especially if they have to extend their set over a prescribed time. Remember they are guided generally by musician's union rules but its just plain bad management and manners to expect them to cover for your programme not running to plan. Of course if you have built up the required rapport with them they will help you out of a tight spot in a situation that is not of your making, remember they are helping you out and don't abuse their friendship, or you will quickly wear it out. Having said all of that there are times in life when you can't see eye to eye with someone, it happens to me a lot but then I'm only 3'2". Seriously though there may be a point in time when you come across a band or just the band leader who, for whatever reason, you just can't get on that friendly footing. My best advice would be to try very hard to overcome whatever your differences are, to make it work for your guests. But if you really can't find that common ground to build on, you have no option but get them moved. To another centre if that's an option i.e. if there is one available and the only problem with them is a personality clash between you, if there's not and or there's more to the problems you are having than just a clash of personalities you will have to let them go. Personalities change from site to site, park to park, village to village so a change for that reason is a justifiable and grown up way of rectifying the situation but you should never send a *problematical* member of staff to another centre for any other reason and that absolutely includes resident bands.

This is such an important working relationship for your success, your 'coats' happiness and your guest's enjoyment that if it's all going wrong divorce is the only viable action to take.

I want you to take notice and remember what I am about to tell you. Because for as long as you are at that centre *YOU* are the boss, *YOU* call the shots and what *YOU* say goes! Because at the end of the day if you don't take control of a situation ultimately the buck stops with *YOU!*

Early in the book we talked about the 'coat' that tries to take over and how to look out for it happening. Well I have seen for myself and heard about band leaders or members that can cause you just as much grief for pretty much the same reasons. Do keep a watchful eye on relationships between your 'coats' and band members. This is almost an inevitability and of course they are all adults and it's their own business what they do in their private lives. You must however be that father or mother figure for the whole team so you will have to make it perfectly clear to all concerned that while they are working they will be expected to do their job without favour i.e. trying to orchestrate break times to coincide with the bands, leaving other 'coats' to perform the more arduous duties or being called up onto the stage by the band to sing numbers with them as and when they feel like it. All of these things must go through you so that they are monitored and managed. This is not you being some great ogre it's just that, left unchecked these little things can get out of control and will cause great friction and animosity within the team, between you and the 'coat' concerned and the band. Of course you want them to be happy but at the end of the day we are *ALL* there for the guests first and foremost. So do be fair but strong were necessary in this aspect of your management.

PRIZE GIVING

Having already highlighted that prize giving is one of those events that can take place each evening or at the end of the week, weekend or mid week break. You will know I advocate the one slickly run event that accentuates the guests winning conquests. To me it is paramount that the guest feels that they have achieved something significant and that you are recognising it in grandiose style while they receive the adulation of the whole camp. In short don't skimp on this one, we have already talked of the prizes and certificates and we will come onto house points later because they can play a big part in the overall prize giving by creating excitement and tension building to the grand finale of the presentation of the challenge cup to the winning house captain. But for this chapter I want to concentrate on the slick running part. Whether you decide nightly or weekly is right for your park is of course a matter for you but the way in which you present this event should remain the same and contain the basic ingredients to make it special for your guests and in keeping with that smooth running programme.

The basic ingredients are:

Good timing for event,

Be ready to start

Good Prizes and certificates etc

Plenty of enthusiasm from you and the team

Safety and dignity of your guests

Appropriate music for the prize

Presentation of cup and always...

Keep it friendly

Be ready to finish

GOOD TIMING FOR EVENT

Obvious really I know but you should stage prize giving when most of the centre will be there. During the early evening, just after bingo or between the junior events is normally a favourite time. Some people like to split the junior and adult prize giving's, again this is up to you however, timing must be a crucial factor.

BE READY TO START

No I'm not going to labour the points we have already been through in this chapter. Suffice to say this is as important an event as any other so have your prize presentation table set out ready to enable you to glide seamlessly into it from the preceding one.

GOOD PRIZES AND CERTIFICATES

Yes I know I have covered this as well but it is so important that, not to mention it here would be daft.

PLENTY OF ENTHUSIASM FROM YOU AND THE TEAM

This for me is definitely the clincher when it comes to a successful prize giving. No matter what the prize is for, you and the team should show exuberant joy that a person has won it. They deserve it after all, they entered *your* competition helped *your* programme to run effectively keeping *your* sponsors happy making *your* job all the more easy, it's *your* turn to show *your* appreciation not forgetting, of course, that they deserve it because they won it! Being overtly enthusiastic, at your prize giving, sends out the signal that the week has been a great one and that the team have enjoyed it as much as the guests. Some will be going home tomorrow and you want to leave them with a lasting memory of your village reminding them of that great week and hopefully they will even have filled out the booking form for next year before they depart the next day. For those that are staying another week it gives a clear indication that entering the competitions or fun events is a worthwhile and fun thing to do and they will in turn help you to encourage the new guests next week.

SAFETY AND DIGNITY OF YOUR GUESTS

Always have a 'coat' of both sexes on hand to assist a guest to come and collect their prize. There are many reasons why someone may require a little helping hand, such as those that are a bit unsteady on their feet for example. Whatever the reason, because of the excitement, they might try to go faster than they should. One of the 'coats' going to meet them from their chair and dictating a slower pace ensures this does not happen and the guest feels no pressure because they are with the 'coat'. You can help your guests even further by arranging for seating with easy access to the stage or dance-floor for those that would benefit from it.

APPROPRIATE MUSIC FOR THE PRIZE

It always amazes me when I go to a camp and they wiz through the prize giving as if it is some sort of inconvenience. We have looked at the selfish reasons why you should not be treating this as an irritation to your programme but an event in its own right. Of course the most important reason, as always, is that it is for your guests. It is a very special moment for those that have won a competition, being recognised for it in front of everyone particularly their family and friends. I have regularly witnessed it being rushed through at such a pace that one guest is just arriving at the table to receive their prize when the next person is being called while the one before them is still leaving the stage to return to their seat. The effect is total confusion, no one knows who they are applauding so they stop, you eventually end up with a bottle neck of people all standing around at the table because some people get their faster than others meaning the 'coat' handing out the prizes has to ask who they are and what they have won, inevitably someone ends up with the wrong prize and has the embarrassment of having to bring it back. In short it looks a total unprofessional mess and that's because it is a mess and whoever is running it is completely unprofessional. Instead of it being a wonderful moment to cherish for a guest it becomes a thoroughly unpleasant experience for them and in front of a large audience that includes family and friends. Take a step back and think about it for a moment, your family have gone to stay at a sister park for a week and you nip over to visit them. One of them goes up to collect a prize and they are treated in this manner and totally humiliated, how are you feeling? Right so why would you want to put anyone else through that. It really is very simple to create an atmosphere of Olympic proportions, what? Exaggerating? Ok I know but with a little forethought and simple stage management you can make it special. Firstly give each winner 'their moment' it doesn't have to be a very long boring one but 'their moment'. Make sure they all get to and from the stage safely not rushing them because the next person is on their way up etc. Take a little time to personalise the prizes, for instance find a piece of music that suites each one and play it as that winner comes to collect it. If you have one of the pros staying with you that day they will often be only to glad to present the prize for their particular sport etc. A lot of centres don't bother with anything at all or just chuck on queens 'We are the champions' for the whole thing. Don't be one of those lazy teams, there are many ways to bring life to a particular presentation some are as obvious as those above but I'm sure that old imagination of yours will come up with some brilliantly original ideas to make your guests moment a special one.

PRESENTATION OF THE CHALLENGE CUP

If you have worked it properly this will be the highlight of the prize giving for most of your guests. They have worked hard for their house points taking part in the competitions, doing ridiculous things just to get one extra point, hoping it will all make a difference and they have done it all for this moment, the moment you announce the wining house for that week. Whatever you do make sure this lives up to their expectations, make sure it mirrors all the effort they have made, make sure all the forfeits they and the 'coats' have had to endure are reflected in this final presentation. The fantastic thing here is that there is no actual prize just the honour of being on the winning team. Make a big thing of the cup being paraded around accompanied by a right royal fanfare. To fully understand the impact this has on your guests and future bookings flip forward to the chapter on house points and treat yourself to a little sneak preview.

KEEP IT FRIENDLY

You have had a great week everyone has had the time of their lives and here we are at prize giving. Line your 'coats' up in their respective houses and let them play about booing and hissing each other as the house points are read out in a friendly pantomime fashion just as they will have done all week. ***But*** as each of the guests comes out to collect their prizes ***all*** the 'coats' must clap and cheer with equal vigour for every guest no matter the house. It is imperative that this remains a fiercely fought but light hearted competition.

BE READY TO FINISH

I know! You must be sick and tired of me keeping on at you about it by now. If you've got the message great, but here, just once more (actually that may not be true, but anyway) once more I will badger you with the facts of a seamless evening. You have just put on a brill performance, the cup has been won, the guests and 'coats' alike will be on a high from cheering all the winners and be in a really good frame of mind because of the general atmosphere you have created with things such as the horseplay surrounding the winning house etc. You have just reminded them of what a fabulous week they have had, they should be putty in your hands – DON'T BLOW IT NOW! Have something ready to go the second you announce the end of prize giving, make it a quality event that keeps that vibe going. Move into the farewell party night without them even knowing its happening. Now that's how a great Entertainments Manager would do it.

PROMOTIONS & SPONSORS

Sponsorship can be the lifeblood of an entertainment programme, particularly at smaller or independent centres but even at the larger ones the income this attracts can be quite significant. Of course it's not just the monitory value and the quality prizes, that sponsorship brings, that's of interest to an owner or company. Attracting a major sponsor carries significant prestige and enhances the camps image, meaning that both parties benefit from the deal. The sponsor gets great exposure to a large number of people while they are having fun thereby associating their product with good times while the Holiday Company or Owner makes the most of being linked to a big named brand. It is for these reasons that both the sponsors and your bosses will send people to observe both the competitions or sponsored events and definitely the prize giving from time to time. Do yourself a massive favour and take the time to read the bumph that comes with any sponsorship package. Make sure any relevant posters, banners or other props are out on display or are available as required, particularly at your prize giving. Give each of the sponsored events the respect they are due and know what the product is so that you can advertise it in the manner they requested as part of the deal. Never use the product as the butt of a joke or try for a cheap laugh at the expense of a sponsor, you can bet your life the day you do one of their reps or someone from head office will be in the audience. Do you really want to be the one that costs the company that big contract or even cause them to pay compensation due to deformation of their product? I thought not. As always it only takes a little thought on your part to ensure sponsored events get maximum exposure during your prize giving and instead of being in hot water you can actually generate positive feedback to your bosses from the reps or head office 'secret shoppers'.

LINE UPS (HELLO - FAREWELL)

I have touched on this subject earlier and will again when we cover the art of a compere. Really the only thing I have to highlight here is that once again you must take these as events in their own right and adhere to all the general rules to keep your seamless evening on track. As I pointed out before, the tricky part of these line ups is diplomatically making sure everyone that should be, or wants to be there....is. This is something I can't teach you, but I am sure if you shove this book under the centre manager's nose and point out the fact that they will be the one that looks bad in the guest's eyes if he and other managers don't play ball, they will soon sort themselves out and bring the others into line.

PARTY DANCES

You will realise that I view party dances as an integral part of your evening programme by virtue that I have deemed them worthy of a chapter all to themselves. All I will say for now is that you treat these as second rate time fillers or worse, as an advertising vehicle for products from the shop, at your peril. The guests love them – don't abuse it.

YOUNG GUESTS - (BED TIME MARCH OUT - DON'T ENCOURAGE BACK ON DANCE FLOOR)

To be perfectly honest with you I wasn't entirely sure whether to add this paragraph or not. We talk about the subject in so many other places in the book that I felt I was nagging you a bit. So I sought advice from mates that have worked the camps with me and those that hope to work at a centre in the near future as well as a couple of friends that have no idea about entertainment, but who are proof reading this as I go along as a sort of quality control on the 'interest scale'. The theory being that if they are kept entertained and interested enough to want to read the next chapter those of you in the business should be able to stay awake through most of it at least. Anyway they all agreed that they had no idea whether I should put it in or not...... Yeah thanks for the input guys. Unfortunately that means I will be nagging you on this one after all.

Oh stop groaning now it's not all that painful really, it's just a gentle reminder of the camp I stayed at a couple of months ago, where they had the children's march out, characters and all, then proceeded to run a session of party dances with the lights out and the 'coats' wearing luminous bands, necklaces, earrings etc from the shop. Well you will recall my views on this but it is worth a thought for when you are at your centre because it highlights a situation you don't want to emulate. After all what is the point in having your children's march out and announcing it's now 'adult time' if the first thing you do is stage an event that encourages the little ones back onto the dance-floor. By the way did you see what I did there? Party dances, shop advertising and march out. Clever huh? Well I know it's not exactly Prime Suspect but there's a bit of a plot line there somewhere? Oh please yourself, anyway bottom line is, once you've decided on a time to have your march out and go into 'adult time' stick to it. Don't send out conflicting signals to the guests or this will become unmanageable and trying to enlist their co-operation in the matter will be a lost cause. I don't know maybe I will leave this in after all what do you think?

MINGLE

It won't have escaped your attention that many things I say at first sound ludicrously blatantly transparently obvious. Yep I can tell your way ahead of me already aren't you? Well I can't help it some aspects of the job are based in common sense obviousness. Such as the fact that, a large part of a 'coats' duty is to mix, mingle and dance with their guests. This statement for example could not be more obvious if you painted it day-glow orange, stuck a pink ostrich feather in its cap and had it singing 'I'm a little teapot' from the top of a big red double-decker bus. So that must be all that there is to say on the matter then? Well you would think so wouldn't you but you haven't got this far into the book without realising that even the most blatant of statements has its foundation stuck firmly in past mistakes made by others, normally me, so that you can avoid them.

For example the reason guests love a good 'coat' show is because they are watching people they like performing for them. They will even forgive the odd faux pas (cock up to you and me) because they know you are doing your best and have been doing your best while working your socks off for them all day. It is imperative that you keep this rapport and momentum up throughout the evening. In order to mingle with as many guests as possible you will have to practice the art of 'table hoping', quite simply this means when you're not involved on the stage or on the dance floor go and sit at as many guests tables as you can. Chat, laugh and joke the night away with as many people as you can. Wow it even sounds like a great job and let's be honest it is for those of us that love to entertain. But if this is something you can't or won't do your definitely in the wrong profession. A 'coat' busy buzzing about, doing all they need to do, and hopping to various tables between tasks always with that all important smile on their face is just about the most wonderfully infectious way to ensure you maintain a happy vibrant room full of guests, who crucially wish you to do well. As with everything else in life there are always the usual cautionary notes but on this occasion they are very straight forward:

Don't keep going back to the same table, it is very tempting to do this when you find a nice family that are easy to get on with or keep buying you drinks or even an attractive person you are trying to impress. Of course you will remember we touched on all this earlier in the book but it is important to mention it again here because you *will* build up resentment amongst other guests and this will have the complete opposite effect to the one we are trying to achieve. The other "coats" won't be pleased to find out you have undone all their hard work by ignoring this rule. Again already covered I know but you just know they will win a competition or bingo etc and you don't need me to tell you again what uproar this will cause. The same principles apply when it comes to getting guests up to dance. Obviously it's easy to head for the same old favourites to get the night started and this is not too drastic so long as you do vary it a bit. It is, after all, getting more and more difficult to find people that can do certain types of dance now, although there has been an upsurge in ballroom classes etc since the advent of 'Strictly Dance Fever' and 'Dancing On Ice'. Nonetheless do try to encourage male and female guests from all ages to take to the dance floor with you for a variety of dances throughout their stay.

GUIDANCE

You will recall my earlier anecdote regarding the 'coat' that did not know the mingle but would happily do the slosh etc. Well as humorous as this true story is it would be an idea if you Entertainment Managers bore it in mind here. In this era of increasingly solitary leisure pursuits such as Game Boys, X-Box's, Wii and other computer based activities as well as millions of conversations taking place by text or email instead of verbally and face to face it may be a growing fact of life that some of our younger entrants to the trade will need gentle guidance and a friendly understanding helping hand to find their confidence in this area.

DRINK

I touched very briefly on guests buying 'coats' drinks just then and I will cover this in more detail in health and safety. However each company, manager or owner will have their own rules regarding 'coats' drinking on duty. Have a peek at what I recommend in that chapter but ultimately you will have to abide by the rules set where you are working. As for you Entertainments Managers, I strongly suggest that you make it very clear what you expect in this department and constantly monitor the situation.

THE EVENINGS NEARLY OVER

You will be glad to know that there are only a couple of things left to mention on the subject of running the evening programme. In fact mention, them is all I will do because they both hold such importance that their own dedicated chapters are coming up.

COMPERE

Whether you are the compere for the whole evening or for just one event that night, you are an integral part of the smooth running of that programme. Please take time to read what I have to say about this role in a little while and understand that a compere contributes a great deal to the success or the downfall of an evening.

THE DISCO

This is literally a mention just to reassure you I have not got fed up with writing, gone for a cup of tea and a fairy cake and forgotten it. It goes without saying the disco is part of the fabric of nightlife at centres, but you know me I'm bound to have something to say about it all the same and indeed do so in a complete chapter on the subject.

E VERYTHING MUST RUN ON TIME

V ENUES CORRECT & STAFFED BY THE APPROPRIATE PEOPLE

E NSURE BREAKS ARE TAKEN AT TIME ALLOCATED

N O GAPS OR DEAD STAGE

I NCLUDE CORRECT PEOPLE IN LINE UPS

N AME AND MENTION SPONSORS THE CORRECT AMOUNT OF TIMES

G ET IN AMUNGST YOUR GUESTS.........MINGLE!!!

SO MY FRIEND THERE YOU HAVE IT!

A complete guide as to what you should rightfully expect from your evening entertainments programme. An insight into what every Entertainments Manager's thought process ought to be when setting out to provide you with that 'value for money' 'quality' entertainment. If you are getting this level of service then all's well but if your being 'dished up' anything like the dregs I have beheld of late, in my opinion it's time to vote with your purses and wallets. Let them know that unless things improve you will be trying somewhere else next time and that could even mean switching alliances to another company altogether. Trust me your custom is worth millions upon millions of pounds to these holiday firms and centres and they won't want to lose it. In the UK you are more powerful than ever in this respect because millions more of us are staying at home due to the economic situation, airline strikes and even volcanoes erupting in Iceland.

Accordingly you have the right to flex that fiscal muscle and not just accept a poor standard of entertainment programme or staff. You don't have to put up with it as if 'that's just the way it is these days' and 'there's nothing I can do about it anyway'. You now know what I believe it should be like again and that you most definitely can and should do something about it.......*viva le quality entertainment revolution!*

CHAPTER NINE

GREAT COMPETITIONS & TOURNAMENTS - DAYTIME

Now then! Let's embark on this subject with enthusiasm, gusto and with all the excitement of a child on Christmas morning waiting to open the presents that Santa has brought. Ok I can almost picture your puzzled face looking at the page wondering what's he on about now, what could be so special about a daytime competition or tournament? Has Superblue finally lost it all together and gone Mediocre-indigo? Well that's nice isn't it? Here I am trying to get you all fired up and interested in a chapter that mirrors the one I wrote with the intention of becoming every 'coats' daily companion come aide-memoir and you accuse me of going all light blue on you. No I can assure you I am still all here fully compos mentis and rearing to impart pearls of wisdom that let you into the secret world of what makes a great daytime competition or tournament.

Perhaps I should explain why I think you should be excited about daytime activities such as these although to be honest by now and you probably already know the answer. However I realise you have had a lot to take in thus far so just to make absolutely sure we are all starting from the same place on this one, and it is important, a very quick reminder won't hurt at this point. The fact is that this is where 'coats' can really get you on their side, interact with you over extended periods, set their stall out for forthcoming days and of course the evening programme where they will need you to, not only attend but, participate. A 'coats' actions, attitude and professionalism during these events will have far reaching positive results if they carry it off in style and with great personality. On the other hand if they get it wrong there is always a downside as you will know by now, to get this one wrong will undo all the goodwill they and their fellow 'coats' have achieved and conversely influence all that is to come.

No need to worry though because here we go with a complete and positive run down on all that they need to know, and therefore all you need to know, so that they breeze through the day enjoying themselves thereby taking your hearts and minds with them. We will go through the process step by step so that you will be confident that what you see them doing and saying is correct and if not you can tell them so. In 'Tales of Superblue' I remind them at this juncture not to forget that, camp managers, owners and most importantly their guests, i.e. you, will also be reading this.

THE TEN MINUTE RULE

They ignore this rule at their peril!

Yes I know it's another of those scaremongering statements that managers use for effect. But they just have to remember.....I am on their side.......I'm not trying to make the joyous job of a 'coat' appear unpleasant.........I do want them to go to their camp and have the time of their life so they provide you with the time of yours. So I ask them to please heed this little 'nudge nudge wink wink' of a warning. It's so simple yet I promise you it will save them and therefore you so much grief.

They Must Always arrive at any event they are running ten minutes earlier than the *advertised* start time.

They will need this time to ensure they are organised before the start time so that the competition begins on time, the importance of this will become apparent in a minute. I will refer to all events as competitions from now on for simplicity but the same basic principals apply to tournaments or indeed any daytime event or activity that a 'coat' is required to run.

The reasons for being ten minutes early, you would think, are so obvious they hardly warrant a paragraph. So I ask myself, why have I seen so many 'coats' come a cropper by ignoring the rule? Why have I seen so many guests upset and angry because of the result of their ignoring this rule? I can only surmise that they have just become so obvious to me *because* I have seen so many people come a cropper over the years. For that reason I have decided that it would be wrong of me to assume that they are obvious to anyone else and give them their proper and rightful place in this book. Hurray! I hear you cheer. Oh well we all deserve our 15 minutes of fame, why not these precious little reasons. Now that we have a happy outcome just to give the fable a moral ending I will admit that I have learnt a valuable lesson here and will try not to take anything for granted in the future because, as we all know, to *assume* makes an ASS out of U and ME...............**The End**

OK enough larking about because there are serious implications for a 'coat' not bothering to get there on time. On time for them being?...............good it's sinking in then.

For a competition to start on time, as advertised, they will need to be in control, have everything they need, taken all the names of those wishing to enter and be in a position to do a countdown and start working out the byes.

EVERYTHING THAT'S REQUIRED

What will a 'coat' need? They just turn up let you get on with it and take the winners name don't they? Well this is exactly the attitude that has got so many folk into hot water. The last thing they should ever do is let guests 'just get on with it' but I will touch on that in a moment. For now let's rewind and concentrate on them turning up at the venue. Ten minutes early, OK good start. Now they have to stop and think about what it is they are running for you today. Dependant on what that is they will need to organise any number of things before they even start to deal with taking care of you my esteemed guest. For example they will have to set up any promotional materials that the sponsors have supplied, such as banners, posters or little giveaways etc. Then liaise with the games room or arcade staff for things such as pool and ten pin bowling competitions. They will need to clear the equipment of other guests in time for your competition to start unhindered. What about payment? Have they thought about that? They will require these things to be free of charge for you to take part in the competition. Most places give them a key to release the balls after each game others supply tokens and some dish out cash as the games progress. Whichever it transpires to be you can already see how much of their precious ten minutes has been eaten up, especially if they have to track down that person who may well be dealing with a problem of their own elsewhere on site. Not everything is that complicated of course take darts or table tennis. Darts, bats and balls are all you need for instance but they still need to think about the logistics of it all. Some equipment while easy for them to obtain may not be readily available at the actual location where the competition is to take place. Tennis, archery and mini golf are good cases in point, the racquets, bows and arrows or clubs are generally held in the games-room or similar so even more time will be spent collecting these before making their way to that location in time to clear it of other guests. Please do not let them do as I have seen and have you running around for them, firstly you are on holiday!!! Scondly it's unprofessional and last but not least of all if you should go onto win?....Well you can work that one out.

They will need to be armed with a number of bye sheets I will explain what they are soon, at least two pens, or better still pencils and a rubber, because we all make mistakes as the Darlek said climbing off of the dustbin, a few sheets of blank paper and a hat. They must NEVER expect any of these items to be at the venue already. They must ALWAYS turn up and have ALL of these things with them. It is the only way they can be absolutely sure of being fully kitted out for the task ahead. I guarantee the day a 'coat' says "oh stuff it they've always got that there I can't be bothered to carry my own all that way" will be the very day they haven't got whatever that may be.... ten......nine.....eight minutes ticking away.

So you should be able to turn up ten minutes before any advertised start time and witness your 'coats' getting on with all of this, in order to start your competition *on time.......every time.*

The apparatus is clear, all the equipment they need is there and they have brought all the required bits, brilliant but having accomplished all of that they should still have at least five minutes left. They will need this and maybe a little more at larger centres in order that they have enough time to write down the names of the guests that wish to enter the competition. Yes the 'coat' writes them down! for two main reasons, one they can check any unusual pronouncements so making sure they don't embarrass a guest when they call you for your turn and secondly no-one can later say they had put their name down and the 'coat' must have missed it when they worked out the byes. You will see how much agro this could cause when I go onto the subjects that follow.

It is imperative that they now set themselves up in a position so that no-one turning up for that competition could possibly miss them. It is an absolute holiday camp sin to sit inside the little hut or office so that the staff can say they were there while hoping the guests don't notice them and go away. I know! I know! I know! I can never understand it either but, and you know what's coming, I really have seen this happen too. I tell them in 'that other book' that if they are ever even tempted to do this to please take some time off and consider their future as a 'coat'.

Right they've got all the names down. Unless they have so many guests wanting to enter that they are writing right up to the wire, at least one and a half minutes before the advertised start time they should begin to call for anyone else that wants to take part to give them their names. This has two main effects, one is that no-one is left in any doubt that a 'coat' is present and guests need to give them their name in order to enter and secondly this subconsciously starts the countdown towards the advertised start time of the competition and the closure of taking names. This is also the time for the 'coat' running the competition to really begin to assert their authority over the proceedings. This may appear to go against the ethos that I usually espouse in regard to everything we do must be directed towards giving our guests the ultimate holiday experience. However in the next few paragraphs it will become clear to you that unless the 'coat' takes control of these events *your* holiday fun can so easily be ruined!

THE COAT MUST TAKE CONTROL

Put your seatbelts on this could be a bumpy ride for your brain. Because I am about to turn everything I have told you up to now completely on its head or at least that's what it will seem like at first but my reasoning will soon became very clear. You see my one overriding objective at all times, as indeed any Entertainments Manager and 'coats' should be, is that every one of our guests has the best holiday possible and on most occasions we would bend over backwards to accommodate all of your wants and needs. However as in life itself there are times when you have to put the happiness and wellbeing of the population before any one individual. Sounds like politics doesn't it? And in a way that's exactly what it is. You see rules in society are there to ensure law and order and fair play for all. Now obviously in our little society we don't deal with law and order in this way but we do need to see fair play for all. To this end there are a couple of times throughout 'Tales of Superblue' when I will instruct them to be, well quite frankly, ruthless when it comes to sticking to the rules and this is most definitely one of those times. I can almost put money on the fact that most experienced 'coats' will have ignored this instruction and have most likely suffered the consequences I am going to describe for you now. As a guest you are about to realise why 'coats' take this action and so I hope they can count on your full support in the future.

Let's make it perfectly clear from the outset that the only reason for a 'coat' being 'ruthless' is that a guest has either turned up late for a competition or tried to take over one they running. They have put that 'coat' in a position that necessitates taking the stance that they have and I am in no way endorsing that they become a 'jobs-worth', in fact the contrary. They should carry all this out with their usual exuberance, charm and all important, smile intact. Remember no matter what ever happens they still have yours and all of the other guest's happiness to tend to. They must however take control and be in charge of these competitions right from the start. State that they are and assert their authority over the proceedings and remain strict about certain aspects throughout while being that cheerful happy 'coat'. Of course there's an art to it but a good 'coat' should be that kind of person in the first place.

SO WHAT RULES ARE 'COATS' TO BE RUTHLESS ABOUT?
Latecomers.

If they have written down the names of those that want to take part in the competition, and a minute and a half before the advertised start time they started calling for any others to join in giving everyone ample opportunity to make themselves known to them, then they have done everything by the book. Now here we are at the advertised start time and it's time to work out the byes. What they don't do now is slink off somewhere quiet so that no one can bother them and do the byes by them self. I won't insult your intelligence by going any deeper into that one. What they should do however is loudly announce that *it is* the advertised start time to all and sundry. Get you all to agree that *it is* thereby confirming that you will support them when the latecomer arrives, and arrive they will! Then, and please note I tell them to definitely do this, they should get you guests to do a countdown and explain that when you reach zero it will signal the end of names being taken for people to enter the competition.

Indeed once you do reach zero 'that's it' no more entries. While all of the above is going on the 'coat' should have torn the names into strips from the blank paper they have been writing them on. I bet you were wondering why they had to bring those along. Well now you know that, can you guess what the hat is for? Oh I just know you're miles ahead of me on this one. Of course they put those names into the hat now and get one of you to draw them out. The best way I have found is to get a bystander to pull out the first one then as each name is pulled out that person pulls the next one until no names remain.

Now I have talked a great deal about byes and will explain how they work them out soon but it is important that for now you remember that the 'coat' needed to have worked them out prior to the countdown and the drawing of the names. If anyone comes to join during the countdown a small adjustment can be made – no problem. Once the countdown hits zero they must get the first name pulled and write that name on the bye sheet immediately. *That is well and truly it!!! The 'coat' must not let anyone talk them into letting them join in after this time!!!!!*

They are surrounded by happy bubbly guests, just like yourself, eager to see where you sit in the draw, do you have a bye? Who are you to play? Will you make it through the first round? The excitement, the tension, the apprehension of it all and if they've done their job properly the atmosphere is electric. They've got their head down writing the names in their respective slots on the bye sheet, they've done it they've pulled it off, mission accomplished 'on time'. They are the conquering hero when suddenly the mood changes, there's an aerie silence as the crowd that surrounds them.... parts..... and heading straight for them is a figure a figure walking with purpose a figure with a determined look on its face. Who could it be? What do they want? Suddenly, as you and the rest of the guests look on expectantly, and right on cue the figure speaks "sorry I'm late can I put my name down" Oh no!......they have arrived.......it's horrible......... it's a nightmare...it's the 'coats' worst nightmare!....... it's....... it's the.......... It's the Latecomer..........................be afraid be very afraid.

Now you're probably sitting there thinking he's taking that poetic licence thing a bit too far isn't he? Well I could have just said don't let anyone join in after you reach zero on the countdown I suppose. I guess your also thinking miserable so and so, what possible harm could there be in letting that poor guest just slip on the end anyway. Well for starters once I explain the bye system you will realise that someone can't just join on the end that's not how it works unfortunately. Then there is the next latecomer. What next latecomer? Oh didn't I mention them? You see if they should succumb to the pleas of the first latecomer and allow them to enter there's always another one a short while later and the 'coat' now does not have a reasoned argument as to why this person cannot join in, and believe me there will be enough people there that will remind them that they don't, because they let the first one join in. So they are already in deep trouble when the third one arrives........ok now they are well and truly sunk.

We will get to the byes soon but I am sure you can already see that the 'coat' turning up ten minute early was all for nothing they will have to write and rewrite the byes over and over as they let people join in and that means re drawing the names each time. What a farce what a complete fiasco what an unprofessional way to run a competition and the saddest thing of all is that they could have so easily avoided it just by being strong, sticking to the rules and politely saying no. Just in case a 'coat' at one of the centres you visit is still contemplating ignoring this advice let me end the mysterious tale of *'The Latecomer'* with the sting that is unavoidably in its tail. The twist to this plot is quite simple but they won't see it coming until it's too late and they won't be able to do a thing about it..........their fate is sealed. The foreseeable future for that 'coat' is one of complaints, accusations and being in trouble. People will pass them in the ballroom and point as they whisper "that's the one who let the latecomer join in" and why all this bitterness? Well as anyone with any experience of such things will tell you, the second you let the latecomer join in your destinies were entwined. For you see the latecomer's destiny is that they always win the competition.... and the 'coats'? Not nice!

Seriously though, you guests who turned up on time will be less than impressed that they allowed the eventual winner to enter after you had gone to all the trouble to do it all so correctly. I tell them to do themselves a massive favour and follow the simple rules on this one. I know you will support them now that you know........and be a latecomer? What you?.....Never!

Other little rules I tell them to follow are: Don't let anyone take someone's place once the competition has started for pretty much the same reasons. Should anyone need or want to drop out of the competition then their name is simply scrubbed from the bye sheet and play continues. The same applies if someone should not be present when they call for them to play their game etc. If they can play another match at the same level and give them a chance to return from wherever they may be that's fine, otherwise they must scrub their name and carry on. Which leads me nicely onto the other biggest single problem when running competitions...................

THE RULES OF THE COMPETITION

It is imperative that any 'coat' that is to run a daytime competition knows the rules and never leaves it to a guests to explain them. You will always get the one who is an expert on whatever sport or game it is and will try to take over. The simple fact is that the 'coat' must dictate the rules to be played by at the beginning of the competition and they are the rules that they MUST stick to throughout NO MATTER WHAT!!

You will be with other guests from all over the country taking part and rules will vary on most sports dependent on where they live etc. Pool is a good example with different rules being played by different leagues in any one area let alone across the country. Many *sponsored* competitions come with set rules and these must be adhered to for obvious reasons.

A 'coat' must make sure they know the rules, state them clearly at the beginning of the competition. Ask if all understand and clear up any ambiguities and be in a position to act as arbiter in any disputes that arise. Making it perfectly clear also that their decision will be final.

I have seen 'coats' ask if all agree but in my opinion this just leads to confusion. For my money they should just tell you the rules you are to play by…end of conversation.

Forgive them for giving sponsors a really good plugging. I would expect them to do this just because it's the right and proper thing to do for that sponsor but should they be having a bad day and contemplate giving it a miss just this once, they ought to remember that sponsors do send people along to test that their money is being spent wisely. You know as well as I do by now that the day they don't do it……….ah! you have been paying attention after all. It's a fact that advertising is big money today so they must earn it.

They can and indeed will need to get guests to referee and or keep score for certain competitions because they just can't physically be everywhere at once, pool, snooker and mini golf for instance. However they must always be in control of the bye sheets so all winners have to come and let them know they are through to the next round. Any disagreements can be sorted out there and then by the 'coat' and only the 'coat'.

I will set out some general rules of thumb in a short while but let's have a look at those all important byes. Once you realise the complexity of these you will hopefully be more forgiving when you get a 'coat', particularly a young one, in a bit of a tizzy and I sincerely hope you will never be the *latecomer!*

BYES

The first and most obvious question to answer is what is a bye? Well at the start of most competitions they will need to let some guests go straight into the second round so that you end up with only two in the final. Don't panic because there are a certain set of numbers that will always bring you to that successful two person final and it doesn't take Einstein to work them out. The clever bit however is, knowing what to do with those numbers to give you that final.

You need.................................*The magic numbers*

Magic numbers?

Well that's what we call them because they represent the perfect number of participants in any competition or tournament that will always leave you with two in the final. *Magic!*

Of course life being what it is, how many times do we actually get a perfect number of contestants in anything?

Rarely if truth be told.

So what's the point in having the magic numbers then?

Ah good question I'm glad you asked.

The reality is that you need the magic numbers to work out 'byes' so that you definitely do end up with that perfect number of 'two' in the final no matter how many participants you start with. *Magic!*

So what do you think those perfect numbers might be? **2, 4, 6, 8, 10, 12, 14 etc etc etc?**

Funnily enough that would be most people's answer before they actually run a competition for real. It makes sense after all doesn't it?

Start with even numbers they split…er…well…evenly don't they?

Ok let's have a look and see how some of those numbers work shall we?...........

Let's take 10 for instance………….

You draw the names from the hat in this order

1) Wilmot, 2) Jones 3) Johnson 4) Wolfgang 5) Harvey 6) Gossling 7) Hartland 8) Hallam 9) Botterill 10) Ritchie

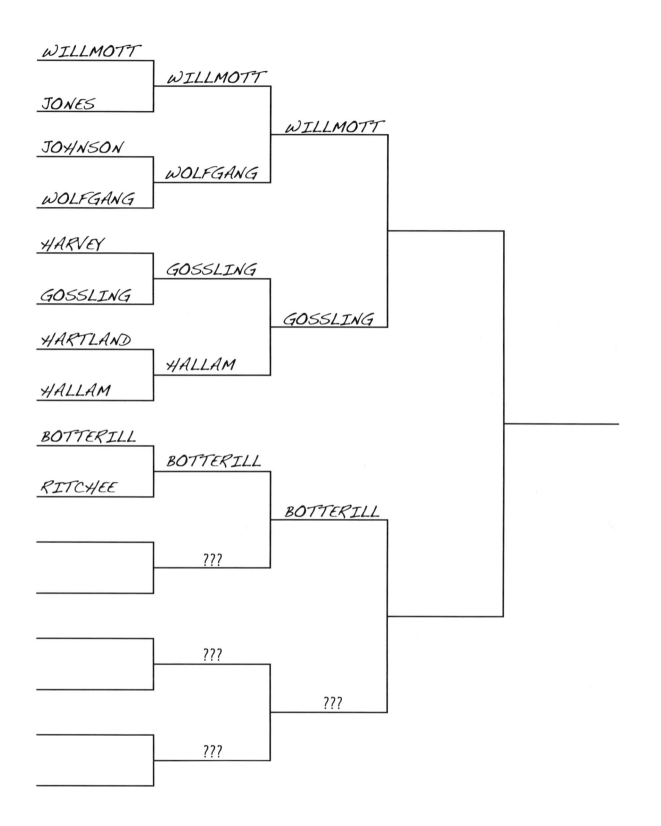

Oops…as you can see you are in trouble already and after only round one. You are left with 5 meaning that you will have to get four of them to play each other.

Consequently the odd one will have to play who? and where? In the final…WOW! Can you imagine the uproar when they win? No this number simply does not work it's not a *magic* number. The only way to make this scenario work would be a very complicated 'round robin' end to the contest. Not only is this an unnecessary waste of time but again a 'coat' running this is about to seriously upset the guests who were knocked out under the ordinary 'bye' system they were running.

OK TRY 12 FOR SIZE.....

1) Wilmot

2) Jones

3) Johnson

4) Wolfgang

5) Harvey

6) Gossling

7) Hartland

8) Hallam

9) Botterill

10) Ritchie

11) Walsh

12) Domingo

At least you got past the first round without grief this time but that's as far as you're going to go.

12 breaks down to 6 no probs. 6 breaks down to 3, oh dear, here we go again. As with the example above you are left with the dilemma of having more than 'two' in the final so who plays who? The 'round robin' is still the your only option if this does happen to a 'coat' and they now know they are going to have a lot of unhappy previously defeated guests to contend with and this is using very low numbers as examples imagine if you have 30 or 40 in your competition they play all those games over a long period of time just to find the 'coat' had not worked out the 'byes' properly. Oh dear!

This is where the *magic* numbers come into play.

So what are the *magic* numbers?

They are:

2, 4, 8, 16, 32, 64, 128, 256, 512 etc

How do they work?

To begin with, if the number of contestants for a competition corresponds with those above you can just run that tournament in the safe knowledge that you will end up with that *magic* 'two' in the final. Try it out for yourself and see.

Magically nonetheless using these numbers in the format I am about to show you will still ensure you end up with that all important 'two' in your final no matter how many participants you start with.

It will now become very apparent to you why it is absolutely vital that the 'coat' does the countdown on time and does not allow anyone to join in once they have closed the competition to entrants. Knowing how many competitors they are working with is the key to working out the 'byes'.

The basic principle is then actually quite simple they:

1. Close the competition
2. Know how many participants they have
3. Place all the names in a receptacle (the proverbial hat) ready for conducting a draw
4. Subtract the number of participants from the next highest *magic* number

5. The figure that that leaves them with is the number that, get a 'bye' to the second round. The rest of you play in the first round.
6. Conduct their draw (announce beforehand whether the first names out are to get 'byes' or will be those playing first)
7. Run a fun hassle free competition for you

Don't get flustered now it never looks straight forward when you see it in words like this so let me give you a couple of illustrations.

Let's take our number 10 again shall we?

OK then this time we take ten from the next highest *magic* number
Which is?

That's right 16

So 10 from 16 is 6

6 participants get a 'bye' and 4 play in the first round

The result is:.............

And what about that number 12?

Take 12 from next highest *magic* number which again is 16

12 from 16 is 4 - 4 participants get the 'bye' - 8 play in the first round and....

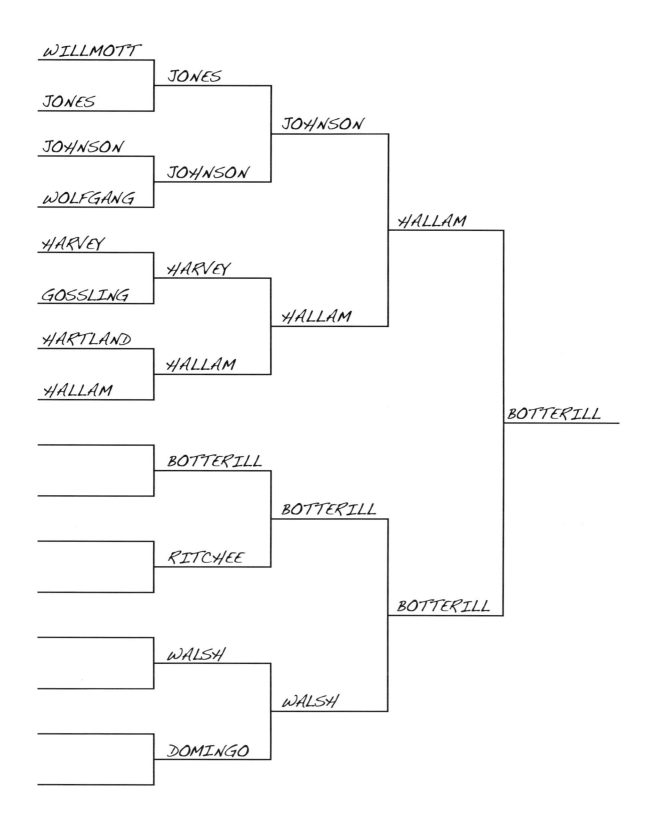

Hay Presto

THE MAGIC TWO IN THE FINAL

And this works for any number what so ever so if the 'coats' just stick to the simple formula I have shown them...........***abracadabra*** always two in the final.

We will take a quick look at what might seem a more difficult couple of numbers but I promise you with this straightforward process and all numbers just fall into line.

How about 15?

15 from 16 is 1

1 from 15 is 14

14 play leaving 7

7 plus the 1 'bye' is 8

8 play leaving 4

4 play leaving..........yipee!! yep its that lovely number 2

Let's go mad shall we?

You're at a large centre and everyone wants to take part in the very exciting tiddly winks competition.

They close with a fabulous 117 guests champing at the bit to tiddle

117 from, the next highest *magic* number, 128 is 11

11 from 117 is 106

106 play in the first round 11 get the 'bye to the second round

106 play leaving 53

53 plus the 11 is 64

64 play leaving 32

32 play leaving 16

16 play leaving 8

8 play leaving 4

4 play and yet again you happily find yourself with that wonderful

figure of.............. **two!!!**

From time to time there will inevitably be a guest that thinks that they have been hard done by and will complain about the bye system and in particular where they have been placed after the draw. The best advice I can give a 'coat' here is simply to follow the advice I have already given them, take charge and tell the guests the rules i.e. let you know up front that you are playing a bye system that may mean some of you will play one more game than others so you have the choice not to enter in the first instance. They must also make it clear that it will be totally random as to who plays who in what round. Of course they will deliver this information with all of their natural charm and whit which will disarm the situation but should they need a little back up I am always here to assist so they may well show that guest the book to prove a point (well you know every little plug helps). Anyway you are now on their side now aren't you? Well if they have done it all correctly and with a smile hopefully you will be.

I always threw in the line "but the best one will win anyway" which let's face it has to be true. Doesn't it?

GENERAL RULES OF THUMB

Do you know that's about it really for daytime competitions, not too complicated is it really? There are just a few rules of thumb that I think would be useful to know so will run through them for you before we move on. They are just in relation as to how they should structure a competition in order to get through it at a decent pace without detracting from your holiday experience and pleasure while at the same time making sure all have a fair crack at the whip. The inherent difficulty with these events is that they will always have a number of you who never play the sport or game from one year to the next but love to have a bash while you are on holiday and why not indeed, I would definitely be one of those number myself, you have paid to have the fun they are offering after all. They are not running the world championships they're running a fun competition and the fact is you are the very people that will transform a normal sporting competition into a happy and enjoyable couple of hours of fun. Although they need to take control re the organisation of the competition, for the good of the majority, I ask them to please never lose sight of the fact that it's your holiday so once they have it up and running I advocate that they do enjoy them self and have a laugh with you.

They will get those that, take it very seriously indeed and that's their prerogative of course. I warn 'coats' to be careful not to isolate this person or tease them for this, for a cheap laugh. We all get pleasure from different sources and it may be this person's once a year chance to shine, and they're loving it. So I say don't take their moment away from them!

Also some competitions are sponsored with very good prizes so winning can be a serious matter. The other main thing that tends to make people a little more competitive than they otherwise might have been is the chance to play the pro.

A good Entertainments Manager will always try to arrange the snooker competition, for example, to take place the day before the snooker professional is due with a game against the pro the added prize for the winner.

So what about those rules of thumb, well they are basic guidelines formed from tried and tested formats for certain competitions that you are most likely to enter.

SNOOKER

If you're lucky enough to be at a centre that still has snooker tables and hopefully a visiting pro, this is a great competition to run. As a 'coat' I had plenty of time to interact and have fun with my guests while they waited their turn on the table. Remember this is not a male dominated sport and ladies do like to play, you might even get separate ladies and gent's comps. The only problem with snooker is the length of time each frame can take, especially for those just enjoying their yearly bash at it. It would be impractical to play full frames from the start (I will tell you how I know in a minute). The tried and tested way of running this comp is to play 3 reds only until the semi finals, 6 reds for the semi finals and best of 3 full frames for the final.

Again if you do have snooker there are normally enough tables for the size of centre to cope with this, if not just play 3 reds for as long as you have to.

Another good way I kept it moving was to get a person who is waiting to play next to referee the match, with me always having the final decision in a discrepancy.

Of course I had told them all this up front so no problems there then.

IT'S NOT THE CRUCIBLE YOU KNOW!

I have expounded the virtues of asking about the rules, regulations and methods of running any of these events if you are not 100% sure haven't I?

And you will probably be only too well aware by now that when I give it large doses of 'it is important that you…' or 'it's imperative that this or that is done' or even 'the consequences of you not doing this will be….' it generally means I have learnt the lesson the hard way and made a complete pilchard of myself in the process. Well this is absolutely categorically emphatically unquestionably undeniably incontestably irrefutably indisputably incontrovertibly definitely no exception to that particular rule. This was a lesson well and truly learnt in no easy way, whilst I superbly splendidly magnificently superlatively outstandingly stupendously dazzlingly made a complete and utter pilchard out of myself, I was to inadvertently prove I possessed the stamina and willpower to conquer a feat of endurance to test the most aspiring of 'coats'. Not that I had any choice in the matter of course. No indubitably, oh don't moan I'm trying to look a bit intelligent before telling you how dim I could actually be back then! Anyway as I was saying, indubitably it was my first ever Entertainments Manager Richard Walsh, who I have already spoken of so admiringly, that made certain that this specific lesson was categorically and justifiably learnt by this brand new, keen as mustard, eager beaver, champing at the bit, rearing to go but thick as poo bluecoat.

It all started one wet and windy morning as a matter of fact it was blowing an absolute gale with dustbins, cats, dogs, a donkey and even the noddy train flying through the air as I crossed from the chalet line to the main entertainment complex. What? Oh come on, I am allowed to paint a picture of how windy it was you know. Exaggerate? What me? Never! Anyway it was only the third day of my very first summer season and I was enthusiastically ready and waiting to do anything asked of me to impress Richard and the rest of the experienced 'coats'. As I stood there soaked through to the skin completely bedraggled and windswept I realised this was probably not creating the image of someone enthusiastically ready and waiting to swing into action. However fortunately for me it turned out they had more pressing matters on their minds. Because if I was going to get into such a state after just a few yards dash we were going to be in for a real heavy wet weather programme. Happily Richard's programmes were so jam packed with brill stuff for our guests to do at the best of times that running a wet weather programme was never too much of a strain for him. He simply added a few bits here and there and joined the existing activities up seamlessly with these add-ons. One such brill activity was the very very popular adult snooker competition. Now this was always a well attended event at the best of times so you can imagine how many entrants we could expect from a camp that held three and a half thousand guests on a day that had gale force 36 winds, nonstop monsoon torrential rain interspersed with deafening thunder and blinding lightning strikes the sky's darkened by hoards of locusts and the ground trembled from the swathes of wildebeest.........ahum...yes well anyway Richard clearly asked, in his soft Irish brogue

"Do you know the rules of snooker?"

"Yes of course I do"

"Are you sure?"

"Absolutely"

Well I had seen it on the tele hadn't I?

"Do you know how many balls to play for each round?"

"Yes"

How daft did he think I was? You can only get 15 reds and all the colours on in any case. What a strange question to ask? Ah I get it! Richard was just testing to make sure I knew about snooker after all. Well I fooled him there didn't I?

"Do you want someone to come with you just to get you started?"

"No I am fine thanks"

"Are you sure, there will be a lot of guests there for it?"

"Yes really I will be fine, I know the rules and how many balls there are you know"

I said confidently. I could handle a few people turning up no problem. I had just come out of the Royal Air Force after all. I wasn't a baby was I? I had seen snooker on the box it didn't look that complicated. You can only get enough red balls on the table to fill that triangle thing and the coloured ones went on the spots, which spots I didn't have a clue but I was certain someone there would and actually as it happens that kinda went for the rest of the rules too to be frank.

I was armed with a clipboard and pen, wearing my pristine bluecoat, whites and big happy smile, overflowing with personality and enthusiasm, brimming with confidence and off to run my first major competition..........what on earth could possibly go wrong? Almost nothing really, almost that is!

Having watched a number of competitions being run by experienced 'coats' during the preceding Easter break and the first few days of this my inaugural season I knew what to do in order to get this thing off the ground professionally while keeping all the guests onside. So I pitched up at the sports hall nice and early, well before my ten minutes pre start time, to find over thirty men already waiting for me. There were very few ladies taking part in snooker competitions in those days. I took all their names, conducted my countdown and armed with my magic numbers worked out my 'byes', which everyone was well happy with because I had explained exactly what I was doing and how the draw would be conducted and who would get the 'byes' from that draw etc etc etc. I dealt with the usual couple of late comers politely but firmly backed by those guests that had been there on time so all in all I was on fire, I was the daddy, I was rocking and rolling, well deft man, cool, hip, far out there…..well I sort of had it under control to that point anyway.

Now nothing could go wrong could it?

You would think not wouldn't you?

But oh deary deary me! In my excited exuberance……….

I had missed one vital clue

I had failed to pick up on one tiny little hint

I had overlooked an obvious intimation

I had let a vital indication slip by unobserved

I had disregarded a fundamental pointer handed to me on a plate

In my eagerness to get out there and prove my worth, fly solo, show my metal, earn my stripes, and merit wearing that blue jacket I had ignored the importance of one fairly significant question.

When Richard asked; "Do you know how many balls to play for each round?"

I really should have heard alarm bells ringing

I should have seen the flashing lights

I should have been alerted by the Claxton

I should have been shaken into the real world by the simplistic enormity of his enquiry………………………..

Balls?

How many?

Rounds?

What? No erm what?

Only testing me? What a pilchard I was and so deserved every bit of what happened next.

There I was with my thirty-something men proudly announcing that we would play one full game all the way to semi finals when we would play best of 3 games and best of 5 for the final.

I remember the stunned silence as if it were yesterday.

After a few moments one of the men, who had been one of my most ardent ally's throughout the closing and 'bye' procedures, whispered in my shell like " are you sure you want to do that?" Again I avoided the obvious attempt of assistance and pretentiously proclaimed that I was in full control of my faculties and was abundantly conscious of my actions………………

Yep a real big pilchard!

One that wouldn't pass the Birds Eye test as their adverts say 'there's nothing added'

Well this flapping wet fish had something added alright …………..…….. Stupidity!

That kind man, trying to help me out, looked towards his fellow competitors for some further direction but they just shook their shoulders. Looking back at it I think that was probably half in disbelief and half at the thought of how much fun it would be to watch as it all fell apart around this young impetuous bluecoats ears.

So we set out on our epic journey together, me and thirty-something blokes. An expedition that would see us remaining together through thick and thin, through the trials and tribulations, through the ups and downs, through the good and the bad times of the next three days, yes you did read that correctly, the next THREE days!

After about 4 hours and me not turning up for the lunchtime sing-a-long and starting the event that I was designated that afternoon Richard came looking for me. You could expect him to be in a livid type state when he found out what I had done, and most people would have been but not Richard. He saw both the funny side of it and the lesson learning possibilities of my right royal bloomer. After consulting the thirty-something competitors, who were amazingly still with me, he decreed that I was to see this self made catastrophe through to its inevitable shambles of a conclusion. Which I needless to say did, surprisingly however the inescapability of the aforementioned shambles was not to prove to be the case. The prophecy of doom was, as it turned out, erroneous on this particular occasion. Not that Richard was very often wrong, indeed far from it, and certainly it had nothing to do with my cleverness, undeniably that was very far from the truth. No my saving grace had in fact been the culmination of a number of factors. Doggedness, these thirty-something men had embarked (see what I did there? dogged…embark….oh I hope you are taking note of all this corn…I do lead by example after all…lead by example….oh I just can't help myself) anyway we had embarked on a marathon of gladiatorial proportions and none of them was going to be the first to pull out of the coliseum before facing their destiny, their nemesis, the warrior, the foe that could take him down. Yes he was not going to be the one to back down from meeting his next opponent on that green field of war and do battle with…….. Mr Eric Swindlecost all the way from Pratts Bottom!

Curiosity played a massive part in my great escape as husbands, boyfriends and sons refused to leave the games hall in the fear of losing their place in this epic event their resolute mindset now being to finish what we had started, wives, girlfriends, mothers, sisters, aunties, dads, brothers, uncles, nephews were coming in search of their long lost loved ones. The word spreading through the camp as the days went by with all and sundry popping in at some time or other to witness these Olympians of the baize and the pilchard of a 'coat' that had committed this hideous faux pas in the first place.

Human nature being what it is meant that this would be another raison d'être that I was going to be saved from complete humiliation, disgrace, shame, mortification, dishonour, embarrassment and what was the other thing?

Oh yes….the sack!

Human nature meant that the whole escapade became an event, an event for everyone to have an opinion on, an event for everyone to chose their champion, an event where even the underdog might even win; in short it became a soap opera. Boy was I ahead of my time.

Kindness was something I was not expecting to be a bi-product of my outrageous gaffe but there it was all the same. The guests were wonderful throughout the three day event not only bringing red-cross parcels to their loved ones but even throwing a few scraps to the dim 'Bluecoat' whose fault it was that they had been incarcerated in that sporting tomb in the first place. They were lovely I never went without a meal, water or even, but don't tell anyone or copy me, but they even smuggled in a beer or two during my captivity.

I was also very lucky that there were four snooker tables at that camp or some would have had to book another week to finish the competition.

What did truly amaze me was the way even those that were knocked out in the early rounds would keep coming back to see how others were getting on. These people were total strangers at the inception of this blunder but the camaraderie that had built up between these guests was astounding to behold and something that I have never forgotten and have carried with me into every event that I ever ran from that day to this.

The final was truly phenomenal; this had become such a camp-wide event of interest with the players being given almost celebrity like status that everyone wanted to be at the final. The sports hall was just not able to cope with the numbers but something had to be done and consideration was even given to dismantling a table and reassembling it in the ballroom. In the end family and friends of the two finalists were joined by the others that had played in the half week long tournament earning the right to be there and then anyone that could squeeze in, did. The weather was still atrocious so we set up extra entertainment in the ballroom and had runners relaying the scores as the two last men standing potted their way into the holiday camp history book.

I have to say that it was a very long three days nevertheless I made fabulous friends during the experience and what an experience it was too. I hadn't created Superblue as yet, as a matter of fact he was born out of comments made by guests on the back of this, nonetheless I can honestly say that this was definitely one experience that this bluecoat was super grateful to his guests for. But not one that I recommend anyone else try as a character building exercise. Remember none of us knows everything. No matter how long we are in the trade we could and should attempt to learn something new every day.

The moral to this true story is simple however.....If in doubt........... a 'coat' must *ASK!*

Oh and you may be wandering what happened when the professional arrived. Well as a lot of you will know we normally hold the snooker competition the day before the professional is due to appear at our centre so that the winner of that competition can play them. This was what had happened on this occasion in fact, of course little did I know it at the time but we still had another two days to go before we would have a winner in this classic. Fortunately for me Dennis Taylor was the kind hearted fun loving pro that turned up that day. Guests always loved him as he has such a wonderful way with people and he was such a pleasure to be around. He would always have a laugh and joke with you and try to be flexible wherever he could and play more games than he was contracted to and stay talking to guests for as long as his busy schedule would allow. I made a break in the proceedings at his allotted time and we simply did a draw from names of those interested in playing him, which was everyone! God love him he just took it all in his stride, taking the Mickey out of me and generally giving the guests one hell of a good time as in truth he always did.

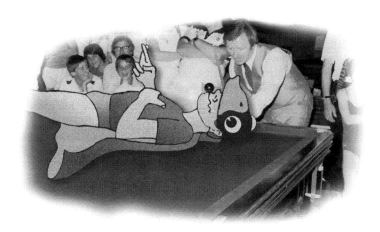

"Stay still Superblue" Dennis would then unbelievably pot the black ball from on top

of the chalk in my mouth.......incredible!!!

POOL

Unlike snooker pool is a much quicker game to finish but generally many more guests turn up to play because more play it at home so a 'coat' can't go mad. The best thing to do is see what the turnout is like and judge it for them self. Generally, though I have found one full game through to the semi finals, best of 3 full games in the semis the best of 5 in the final to be just about right for most scenarios. But if they have a low turnout they could consider best of 3 until the semis, best of 5 for the semis and best of seven for the final.   Pool does however have one main problem for them and that is the rules. The rules of pool change from pub to pub in the same village so what chance do they stand of compromising on a variety of rules with guests from all over the country? None at all! Trust me they don't stand an earthly. The only way to run this competition is to know the game them self. Then stipulate the rules that are to be played right up front, making sure they adequately cover foul shots, shots carried and the controversial number of shots and naming of pocket on the black ball and make sure all understand before the competition commences. Unless your holiday company or sponsor have stipulated a defined set of rules it doesn't really matter which ones they decide upon, after all the best player should win no matter what. But this comp is one where they must definitely set out those rules clearly and be in control. Once they have played a set of rules they must stick to them week after week because they will get guests coming back in the season and some owners every weekend, and if they have changed the rules for whatever reason they are just leaving them self open to silly allegations.

DARTS

Is one of the more straight forward of competitions to run but a 'coat' should not get complacent and drop they're guard re the stuff above, but it really is quite an easy one to handle. Generally one game of 301 straight start with a double to finish until the quarter finals. Quarter finals are best of three 301 with the final being best of five 501. As usual I got people waiting to play next to score each game until the final, then either me or a volunteer would score, but I made sure they were independent of the players. Most centres have built in machines with the dart boards these days however it is helpful if the 'coat' is fairly good at basic maths. It can be very embarrassing if they need to score and can't add or subtract at speed. They can use their discretion again here so that if they only have a few players turn up they can play best of three 301, best of five 301 then best of seven 501 in the final. Sponsor or company rules obviously apply. I won't mention this again either so just take it as read that whatever competition or event they are running, no matter what I recommend here sponsor or company rules will always apply including darts. Get the point, get it? Get the poin...oh I know but I bet it made you smile though .... moving on.

BOWLS

Is another sport where you will attract an 'expert' or two so they must know the rules and again do all the thingies we spoke about. I have found 3 ends until the final with 5 ends in the final tends to satisfy all parties involved.

MINI GOLF

Fun at its best this one. Definitely a great competition for messing around with my guests, yes of course you will get the odd serious person but in the main most people just want to have a go and enjoy a great time together.

Dependent on numbers, and there can be a lot of people, I sent them around the course in two's or threes marking each other's score cards. I mixed families and friends up with other people so the little minx's aren't tempted to cheat while I pottered from group to group for a giggle. If I only got a handful of contestants we all went around together and made a real laugh of it. I would expect any decent 'coat' to do the same.

TABLE TENNIS

So long as they follow the basics there really is not much to add to these competitions now. So with table tennis I think you will find one game through to the semi finals is quite enough then three games for the semis with five for the final keeping everyone more than happy.

TENNIS

One set until the final then best of three for the final.

This can take quite a time to play if you have a few people having their yearly or even first go at the game but if they deal with it correctly this can also be a good laugh.

FUN SPORTS DAY

Fete like atmosphere fancy dress etc.

It goes without saying that an Entertainments Manager should want to make the most of having the majority of their guests together, as indeed they should have if they have advertised this and things like the swimming gala properly. So they must make it a great atmosphere full of fun and silliness. But remember comedy is a serious business. The overriding factor here is safety and I talk more about it in the health and safety chapter but they must think every aspect of the day through before they even leave the office. Fancy dress costumes are great but do the ones the 'coats' are wearing create a hazard? If so they must change them for more suitable ones. They need to keep an eye out for the guest who has not thought about it and wants to enter something where their costume may be a problem and gently explain that to them. Keep a watchful eye for guests who may attempt to exert themselves more than their age or capabilities will allow or those who are getting over exuberant to the detriment of other guests in their desire to win and again diplomatically try to dissuade them for safety sake. This may be more prevalent when they are running a house system because you will go that extra mile for a few house points. They should always have a pre games check of the ground for any holes etc that might cause injury and on that subject not forget to ensure that appropriate first aid is on hand.

But all that taken care of what a great opportunity for them and the whole team to shine and bring a few hours of fun and frolics (I love that word) to a camp full of guests of all ages, families enjoying the day together, teenagers hanging out, all saying ah as the little ones do the egg and spoon or sack races (not that the big ones won't be doing that too). Hopefully everyone falling around with laughter at the comedic clown-like slapstick humour the team have carefully crafted and rehearsed so that it appears to be a load of off the cuff adlibs. If they are lucky enough to have a qualified sports organiser on the team they should liaise with them regarding what events to put in the sports day but must bear in mind they are not setting it for sports people but ordinary every day guests who are joining in for nothing more than fun. Events should be kept simple, silly, fun, easy, and not too stressful. As we have discussed before, they must take note of the weather and adjust events accordingly. Not forgetting to liaise with the catering and bars managers well in advance of any such event so that they can arrange for the appropriate refreshments to be on hand.

This is more a fun day than a sports day!

SWIMMING GALA

Well too many centres in my humble opinion have lost the good old swimming pool to water adventure areas. In my view there is a place for both at centres that are large enough to cope with them. Bulgaria have the right idea with two full size pools one for fun, loud music, noisy competitions and events and one just for chilling and relaxed swimming with a smaller one for the children. Anyway whether you are one of the lucky ones with a swimming pool that allows them to run a gala or are just, having to make do with water fun in the adventure pool the basic safety principles that applied in the sports day apply here. Obviously the added danger of accidents in the water and slipping etc are crucial in their planning of the event. The single most important factor, no matter which type of event they are running around or in a pool, is that there are enough *QUALIFIED* lifeguards on duty to cope with the number of guests present in the water at any one time. It is therefore imperative that the head lifeguard is involved with the planning of such events right from the outset. The number of lifeguards to the number of people is set out in law which varies from country to country. You can find all you need to know about British swimming pools at www.**hse**.gov.**uk**/entertainment/swim**pools**. htm However when you are holidaying abroad make sure you bottom this out. If you are going out to a reputable British company you can check with their solicitors and health and safety liaison at head office or in any case with the British consulate of the country you are going to. There are countries where no lifeguard is required or indeed supplied at hotels. In this instance I personally would not run any water based activities unless the company and or hotel have supplied enough *QUALIFIED* lifeguards as part of your team. As a guest I would always want to know the situation for my family's safety. Wherever you are be particularly careful when it comes to team water sports, water polo for example, they can very quickly get out of hand and become dangerous. Once again all that said there is a lot of fun to be had at a safely run swimming gala or water fun day. Entertainments Managers should still run these events in a carnival like atmosphere with fancy dress and slapstick fun (not enough of this at holiday resorts today) with silly games as well as races. There are any number of floating props that they can utilise from blow up canoes to giant dinosaurs, they just have to use that good old imagination I keep talking about.

FOOTBALL

Well hopefully you will have a sports organiser or at least a 'coat' on the team that loves football so they will run the competition knowing all the rules etc. Whether you are going to play this five a side or full eleven a side teams I suppose will depend on the size of the village i.e. the amount of guests or indeed the size of the pitch you have. Whichever it ends up being all the basic rules that we have covered in this chapter still remain in force here. The one main difference is that you may have groups of people turning up as teams trying to persuade the rest of you that their rules are the best. It's not an easy one but the 'coat' must stick to their guns and run the rules that they have decided or the company or sponsor have dictated are the right ones for this event. This is also one of those times when they may have to be harsh on the minority for the good of the majority. If someone is playing too rough they must deal with them before someone gets hurt, if that means sending them off, so be it. This and any similar sport can of course get very competitive. They need to remind those playing that you are on holiday and an injury is no good for anyone concerned. Again they should check any pitch or playing area for holes, ruts or damage that could cause injury before a competition starts and have the appropriate first aid on hand. Some centres still have end of the week Guests v Staff games, I fondly remember when cabarets such as Gary Wilmot would travel to my camp to get their weekly fix of the game and play in my staff side. Do be warned here though, whilst the majority of games are competitive they are also good natured and fair but from time to time we will get the one who takes it too seriously and wants to beat the staff at all costs or has a grudge against a staff member or just staff in general and tempers can flare.

If you have a football pro demonstrating at your centre, unless they or the sponsors say otherwise, the football match or competition should not be held on the day they are there. They won't thank the Entertainments Manager for being pressured to join in and play for a certain team.

SPECIALIST EVENTS

Now I'm no expert when it comes to these events but there are reputable companies that now have villages that incorporate a number of adventure type activities such as climbing walls, go karting, canoeing and archery etc. These should be well governed, organised, maintained and staffed by appropriately trained people so an Entertainments Manager can relax to a certain degree and run your competitions etc in relative confidence. As with swimming galas get their experts involved in anything they are contemplating doing around such activities right at the beginning of the planning stage. It would be unfortunate if there are any places left doing this sort of thing without those trained personnel. Whilst, I would hope, these would be abroad today I warn 'coats' to be aware of the ramifications of trying to run something without having the training to do so. Any kind of specialist activity in this field carries enough inherent risks without the added danger of untrained people running them. Archery is a good example; we take a lethal weapon then allow complete novices even children to get hold of it without any proper tuition. The possible results are obvious and I don't say this without some experience on the subject I have actually seen arrows land on the beach at one centre in Spain. There is only one piece of advice I could possibly offer on this subject and I know your way ahead of me but............................

I've started so I'll finish, as a nice man once said. It's quite simple if you're not trained and qualified to run any of these events …DON'T.

**'Coats' must always be there ten minutes early to ensure you get
the highest quality _FUN_ events**

YOUR 'COATS' MUST ABIDE BY THE RULES

Ten minutes early

Have all they need with them

Equipment and payment sorted out

Countdown done by guests

On time – Begin last calls one and a half minutes before and start on time

Magic numbers

Professionals

Everyone should be able to see the 'coat'

The latecomers

It's the 'coat' that stipulates the rules - rules do not change

The Sponsors - must be represented properly

If not sure ASK!

On holiday your guests are – as a famous Star Wars character once said

No complaints it's now an enjoyable fun competition

CHAPTER TEN

GREAT COMPETITIONS - EVENING

Ah! We have arrived at one of my most favouritest parts of the programme, the evening competition or comp. You've probably noticed I have been using the term 'comp' well it's not me being lazy although writing the word 'competition' every time does take up a few minutes in each chapter, but the actual reason is that it is a term you will hear 'coats' using at the camp so we might as well get used to it now. While these are evening comps they can of course run them at lunchtimes and in wet weather too but mostly they will be held in the evenings. I'm not going to go over old ground about the right comp for the right venue, start and finish on time and having all their props on hand when and where they need them etc etc etc. This is more about the mechanics of how they should be running a fun competition and it needs to do exactly what it says on the tin, it needs to be a *Fun* competition.

Fun for you to take part in

Fun for you to watch

Fun for them to run

The secret of a great comp is that it *is* fun, uncomplicated and nobody gets hurt or upset. See what I did there?

Fun

Uncomplicated

Nobody gets hurt or upset

Ok ok so it's not as clever as Einstein's theory of relativity but it gets the point across and anyway it is quit intelligent for me. The fun bit speaks for itself of course but they can easily lose the momentum of a good competition if it's overcomplicated and hard for contestants to understand what it is they want you to do, so I do urge them to think about it. They may have the bestist, funniest and most brilliantist competition ever in the history of, well, ever really, but it will all count for nothing if they haven't thought it through properly and someone gets hurt or anyone is insulted or upset by anything that is done or said during it. Apart from that they are quit straight forward. Your entertainer's imagination is the biggest tool when it comes to putting a competition together. They should make it interesting to watch, give it good pace and not make it last too long, half an hour to 45 minutes is about right for most comps. The ideal times for competitions are early evening when they can hold a junior comp and mid evening just before a cabaret or show so that the band can have a break and the majority of 'coats' can get changed if they are in a show or cabaret etc.

I am afraid to say I see less and less of these today as party and line dances are incessantly being used to 'fill the gap'. There should be no 'gap' to fill if they have put together a good evening programme which would include great competitions and party dances at the right times in the right measures.

Ok I have banged on about half the people want to watch the other half doing stuff, but if I am really honest with myself I will have to concede that the ratio is probably more 65% watching 35% doing these days. But that does not alter the basic premise of 100% enjoying it anyway. So while 'coats' picking the right guests is obviously important it really is nothing that can be taught in a book. Again this is where interacting and being that friendly professional 'coat' during the day pays off for them yet again. Most contestants will be picked on the night itself and if they have done their job properly during the day priming likely candidates all they should need to say is "only the first eight people to join me will be allowed to enter" or "the first four couples on stage" etc etc. So many times now I see 'coats' struggling to prize people out of their seats to take part in what is supposed to be a fun event. Half their allotted time has disappeared before they even get started. They should be 'geeing' you up during the day or even the previous evening while they are socialising with you, making it an exciting fun prospect to be part of this comp. If they're running a house system they should never have trouble getting equal amounts of each house to join in almost before they even announce it. There will always be the characters that will be only too pleased to be asked and 'coats' will get a sense of who will and who won't after a while. Other competitions of course will need a bit more organising and even a rehearsal. The adult and junior talent shows for example. While we will quite often find contestants for these will seek us out days before the competition is even due, there will be others that are reluctant to enter even though we are being told they are a good singer, or comedian etc. I would always speak to this person in private so as to gauge their true feelings without any peer pressure because a lot of people will happily give a quick rendition or a joke or two when at the bar with their friends or family, while the thought of getting up on stage fills them with absolute fear and dread. I would never want someone in a comp that didn't want to be there. On the other hand you quite often find that just being asked is enough to make someone's mind up to have a go, and they often do very well. Of course we will get the old favourites that absolutely revel in being asked and made a fuss of "well I wasn't going to this time, I was going to give someone else a chance, but seeing as people are asking me to……" Again this all comes with experience but it is a vital part of being a 'coat' and this is but one reason why there is no substitute for being out there and mingling with wonderful guests such as yourself.

There are many different types of competition and we will look at just a sample of them here but the principals for all of these competitions remain the same.

SO WHAT TYPES OF COMPETITIONS ARE WE TALKING ABOUT?

Well as I said we are just going to touch on a basic few to give you an idea of what standard of comp you should expect. Bearing in mind what I have said about their own imagination, fun and safety the possibilities are genuinely endless.

Three main headings cover evening competitions:

1) Talent based competitions.
2) Themed fun competitions.
3) Absolute outcome competitions.

I realise that if I changed numbers two and three around it would be a load of 'TAT' but even I wouldn't stoop that low just for gratuitous word play, well not this time anyway.

The order in which they have been placed is no accident so Einstein does not necessarily beat me on this one.

THE TALENT BASED COMPETITION:

Surely you're not going to give a whole section of this chapter to the talent competition are you Superblue?

I can almost see you rushing your finger down the page now to find out how on earth even I could manage to make a whole section plausible, never mind interesting, on this one subject alone. Well my friend I haven't gone completely bonkers just yet, take another look at the heading, it's all in the wording i.e. talent *based* competition.

While it stands to reason that the most obvious of these will indeed be the talent competition itself there are numerous other hobbies, sports, skills and disciplines that will fall under this banner and if you are at a themed week or weekend these could indeed be the mainstay of the entertainment programme with the 'coats' shows and cabarets coming in second place of importance to you. For example Baton Twirling, Model Making, Elvis Impersonations, Marching Bands, Fast Draw Shootouts and many many more.

The reality however is that in the normal fun packed programme there will still be a number of competitions that need to be treated with varying degrees of professionalism when it comes to setting them up, running them and crucially judging them.

These are competitions that entail the entrant having a talent or skill or having invested an amount of time in preparation of some sort as opposed to an 'ad hoc' fun comp.

Alright alright! I can hear you, so let's use the obvious example then shall we? **'The Talent Show'**

In my experience this is the competition that causes more agro, problems, near riot situations and subsequent complaints than just about all the rest put together (except the beautiful baby competition, but then if they're stupid enough to run a competition that pits mums against mums, dads against dads and worst of all grandparents against grandparents who all rightly believe theirs is the most beautiful baby in the world.......... quite frankly they deserve all they get).

OK then the Talent show.........I have to be honest here and tell you that I tried to write this for you so many times and in so many different ways. But kept returning to the fact that I really should just tell you what I think should happen. So after much deliberation and at the risk of upsetting your entertainers even further by giving you yet another insight into it all, I am about to let you immerse yourself into the mind of the Entertainments Manager, meaning you will be equipped with that same expertise........

Now I really am letting you know how I tick!

Well the first thing to remember when embarking on this competition is that by and large most of you adult contestants will believe, rightly or wrongly that you are very talented but in the Junior Talent competition **ALL** of you the parents **do** have the most talented kid I the world. A lot of you will of course be very good and will have worked very hard at putting your act together either over a number of years or during your holiday or even that day. However all will be taking part in my competition most of you will be very nervous and you all deserve the best chance that I can give you. This begins with ensuring you get a decent rehearsal time with at least some of the band or pianist and enough of my 'coats' to support the act with sound lights and technical equipment, many of you will have your own backing tracks that need setting up and playing at the correct time, for example I would always show each and every act the respect I would want to receive if I were a visiting cabaret. So long as your Entertainments Manager bears these points in mind they won't go far wrong with this part of the competition process. Should they let someone join in if they don't attend rehearsals? Well it's their call really, if they have stipulated that the rehearsals are all part of the competition and that's when names must be taken I would suggest not, remember the latecomer in the previous chapter..........same thing. But if the rehearsals were an optional extra.....up to them…it can throw a carefully planned competition into chaos however. The one time it's definitely not up to them is when they hold rehearsals involving so many contestants that even these are judged in order that a certain number go through to a final later. Only those put through to the final must ever appear on that stage, NEVER EVER should they let someone join in at this stage of the proceedings.

Having successfully steered myself, the contestants, band and my 'coats' through the rehearsal the next vital hurdle for me to overcome is the running order. Not many people like to be the first on stage and then there are others that just want to get it all over and done with, so I simply asked them which number they would like to be and all is lovely with the world.

What?

No of course life just isn't that nice to us poor Entertainments Managers is it. Seriously though I always always always have a draw to decide the running order. The ideal scenario of course would be to do it at the rehearsal and if I had everybody there at the end of it that was fab, job done. As is normally the case though people are rushing off to do other things once they have done their bit with the band etc so I would make sure to tell them a time and place where a public draw will be held and the order decided and made sure they understood it would not be changed after that time. 'Coats' should not try to orchestrate it so that they have a 'nice mix' of acts. Just keep it straight, transparent and above board.

They should always have a public draw, if it's just the adult acts themselves that are present so long as they are all there that is public enough. Should any be missing I would recommend the above and hold the draw at a stated time and place so that any interested parties can be present. The easiest way I found to manage this was during another event to ensure at least some guests will witness it, early evening bingo for example. The junior show is a different kettle of fish in as much as replace 'if all contestants are there' with 'if all parents are there' otherwise carry on as you would for the adults.

The next thing in the order of importance for me is to state a time that I want them all to be backstage so that I know I have the show that I have planned for and all is running smoothly. I would leave them in no doubt that anyone not backstage at that time will be disqualified from the competition. Once I have them there I keep them there not letting them go wandering off to the bar or to sit with their family to watch the other acts. I sound a bit harsh here I know but trust me it can all get out of hand very quickly if you don't keep a tight grip on it and people start going on stage out of sequence because I can't find an act when they should be going next etc. I looked after people back stage so they tended to be more than happy to stay and enjoy each other's company, I make them feel like important entertainers, because tonight they are! I find a few nibbles and some drink normally works wonders. You will get the odd guest that just refuses to do anything you ask and does the complete opposite, well your 'coats' will just have to deal with each case on its own merits but remember its one guests defiance against all the others enjoyment and fair play, and should this defiant and awkward guest end up going on out of sequence to the running order and then end up winning............oops!

So that's where my unusual harshness comes from.

The junior show of course is much more difficult to control and the best way I found to handle this one is to just try and get the parents on board and make it as happy a time for the children as I could.

Well here we are all backstage running order in place, the 'coats' have all the technical stuff on standby, the bands all ready to play and I am about to compare this marvellous variety show but wait a minute it's still a competition after all, I need judges don't I? Indeed I do and that is the very next thing on my list of importance. There are generally three ways of judging just about any competition we will ever run and one absolute way of finding a winner.

1) Get judges to score on score sheets – adding the scores at the end.
2) Get judges to hold up numbered cards after each act – so audience keep track.
3) Get audience to applaud at end of comp – loudest applause of course winning.

And the absolute way of coming up with a winner? Well this only comes into play when we run an audience participation competition, a little more about them later.

When it comes to talent shows my own personal favoured method is score sheets.

The score cards are ok for semi serious competitions if they prefer to use them with audience applause being reserved for the theme based fun comps.

Once I have decided which to use the next step is actually quite vital to the successful outcome of this competition and in turn to my whole evenings entertainments programme.

THE JUDGES:

I always tried to get at least one professional judge, a visiting cabaret or member of a band from another venue on site, a neighbouring Entertainments Manager or a local agent etc. If this was not possible I considered the camp manager, owner or local dignitary to add a sense of occasion to the proceedings. If it was sponsored, and the talent shows normally are, the area rep for that product was a good call and if I were at a private centre I would always invite someone from their head office as a matter of course. They normally only come to the finals but by doing this it shows I was taking their sponsorship seriously.

If I could make up my judging panel from such people all well and good but the reality is that most of the time your entertainers will have to select some, if not all, of the judges from the audience.

Now this is the one of those times I didn't want people rushing up and sitting on the three seats I had set out with a score sheet tantalisingly waiting to be filled in by the judges. I needed to manage this by calmly but firmly announcing that the judges are to be picked from the audience and that for obvious reasons no family or friends of contestants are allowed to be judges for this event. Sounds staggeringly obvious doesn't it? Well yes it is but it will amaze you how often this is exactly what happens. People will go as far as sitting in a different part of the venue for the evening just so they can be a judge in this one. Unfortunately I have seen some very ugly scenes caused by exactly this kind of behaviour. The best way to stop this happening is to know your guests and that is all well and good at a small or medium sized park but at the larger ones this can be more difficult of course. So what should your entertainers do to avoid it happening? Do exactly as I have said above and state clearly that judges are to be chosen soon, no family members or friends are eligible to be judges for this competition and that should it be discovered that a judge was either of those things…. the contestant in question **WILL** be disqualified. Being the professional that they are they should do all this in a way that sounds perfectly reasonable and keep it light hearted, you are on holiday after all. Then choose their judges. Now there are only a few ways to accomplish this task so they should use the one that they find appropriate. Once I had chosen my three judges I would sit them down and do my usual quick little chat with each BUT ended it with the words **"can I just confirm you're not a relative or friend of any contestant tonight?"** Now no one can be in any doubt that I had stipulated the 'no friends or family' rule several times and had done my level best to ensure it didn't happen.

I say three judges because this proved, over the years, to be the fairest and most manageable number. Fair because it's difficult for one person to impose their will on two strangers, to this end I tried to vary my judges in age and sex as well as ensuring they have come from different families or groups etc.

I needed to manage it so that I gave the result out as soon as possible after the competition ended. The best way to do this was to have this amount of judges so the scores can be added quickly at the end. Another way of doing it is to have a 'coat' adding the scores for each act from the judges as they go. But the problem with this method is that judges change their minds as they see other acts. So 'coats' must always make sure the judges are aware that they are going to mark in this fashion and don't change their score sheets without letting the 'coat' know. It can all end up looking very messy by the time they have finished of course and lead to allegations of 'fixing' so I strongly recommend waiting till the end to add the scores. Remember what I said about being transparent? Well now is the time to be really open, I always left the judges score sheets out so that anyone that wanted to could have a look at them. This is the quickest and most effective way of defusing arguments about who won etc. Please trust me on this one! It really is such a simple thing to do and *can save untold grief.* Your Entertainments Manager is a fool if they don't do this.

All that being said if they follow the simple steps I have shown you here 'The Talent Competition' is one of the best events of the week. It fulfils all the requirements, entertaining, guests watching guests performing, great variety, fun for the family and normally carries a substantial prize such as a free weekend at the final.

So why am I taking this competition so seriously? Well I take all competitions in this category this seriously! Why?

Because you contestants, your family, friends and the sponsors all take them that seriously and apart from giving you the respect you deserve for entering as I have already mentioned, getting it wrong can cost an Entertainments Manager or 'coat' dearly!!

The example above gives you the basis on which they should run any competition in this category, as you can see it's all in there. Get this one right use it as a template and they should have no problems with other such comps. Of course there will be subtle differences to each one but following the general concept they will come out on top every time.

It goes without saying some competitions will vary in relation to such things as judges whether or not they have rehearsals or indeed run heats leading to a final. Dance competitions are a prime example of the variety of situations encountered in this area. For instance if they are serious ballroom, line or sequence dance competitions they must have professional judges and will even have heats at special event weekends etc (I learnt never make the mistake of thinking these are remotely anything to do with each other and ensured I employed the correct judge for the correct comp). Often this means running different competitions for the various standards in each discipline. Some people just use the tea dance to brush up on their routine and you may be forgiven for thinking that tea dances are all but dead now. But the popularity of 'Strictly' and other shows has seen a massive resurgence of dance related events and the Entertainments Managers must keep up with such trends if they are to survive in the holiday entertainment world. Some camps now have professional dance tutors, again on the back of these shows. Even disco is back with a vengeance at the moment meaning they can have a brilliant 70's or 80's themed evening incorporating the disco competitions.

Weighing up the pros and cons the disco dancing competition can fall into this category in judging style or audience applause if it is not during a specialised dancing event and is just part of the weekly programme.

The dance theme is a wonderful tool to use as part of a themed fun comp too, i.e. getting you to dance highland flings, rock and roll, the cancan, Zorber the Greek and of course the classic old favourite of a bunch of blokes performing ballet in tutu's.

FANCY DRESS:

There is always an exception to the rule isn't there? And here it is; the fancy dress competition. Well the truth is it sits squarely between the talent and fun based comps. Talent because people go to a lot of trouble thinking up brilliant ideas and putting their marvellous costumes together and fun because....... Well it just is.

I have found that the people that generally enter this comp are good natured and just out for a laugh and don't take themselves too seriously at all. For that reason I have always used the audience applause method of judging it.

THE THEMED FUN COMPETITION:

The significant word here is definitely without doubt absolutely categorically positively downright unconditionally emphatically *FUN FUN FUN!!!*

So much of what would have given me a headache in the talent based comps has been removed here. That's not to say however that I would spend any less time or effort in the preparation of these types of comps. Indeed in some aspects they are a more difficult animal to control. For example health and safety will be a very big factor in many of the daft things that I would ask guests to get up. Guests that normally enter these comps are usually the more exuberant type who, enjoy taking part and hamming it up to the full. This is fantastic for 'coats' because they're not left struggling trying to drag unwilling volunteers out of their seats. If they find that they are in that predicament on a regular basis they really should be having a long hard look at their working practices. Because while we all go through difficult spells of a certain type of guest being absent from our audience from time to time they really should be able to rely on guests they have befriended during their everyday duties to help them out 99.9% of the time. If not why not??? Anyway back to the task at hand, that being, a safe and usually hilarious fun comp. The type of guest that they do pick for these comps is key to the outcome they should strive for. It's not always the noisy boisterous amongst you that is the funniest on stage, and can in fact ruin a nice comp by trying to take over or being too rude etc, so I always looked out for the nice quite one with a good sense of humour and would be game for a laugh, I found that 9 times out of 10 they gave a great comedic performance and the rest of the guests loved them. As I said earlier it's not an exact science and each week will be very different from the next but entertainers should learn, with time, who you want and don't want to see in a comp.

SO WHAT IS A THEMED FUN COMPETITION ANYWAY?

That is a fair question I think and the answer is quite simple really. It is any competition that is not inherently talent based and does not include full audience partition. In other words in plain English it's where we get a certain number of guests up on stage to perform for the other guests in a way that just about any member of the audience could take part if they wanted to. Themed? Well that's an umbrella term in truth for ease in identifying these comps as opposed to talent for example. The theme could be absolutely anything in fact for example in the ballroom / family room Man of the Week, Lady of the Week, Perfect Couple, Miss Lovely Legs, Battle of the Sexes, Elegant Grandmother, Werthers Original Grandfather (see what I did there? I'm even showing you how they should match and in turn attract a good sponsor for comps) Of course the list is endless and then you add on the ones they will be running in the adult bar and the possibilities are mind boggling.

But it's no good me banging on about these wonderful 'fun comps' and not giving you some sort of idea what they actually are, is it? No! So I've included a few templates of easy to follow and simple to run competitions at the end of this chapter. Yet again you now know as much as the entertainers.......
So make sure your getting your monies worth!!!

I mentioned health and safety and we do cover this in more depth later in the book but they must take their guests health and well being into account when planning one of these comps and give it serious thought otherwise what is funny one minute can be disastrous the next.

THE JUDGES:

If they have encapsulated all of the necessary ingredients to make this a truly fun competition they will have no trouble with this part of the exercise what so ever. You judges will be only too willing to vote for the funniest, cutest, most daring, cuddly, lovable or roguish contestant who has endeared themselves to you during the competition. But will the audience agree with your choice? Yes. So do they have to leave the score sheets out at the end to stave off complaints about a wrong decision? No. That implies it will be a popular decision then does it? Yes. Why? Because you the audience *are* the judges for these comps and you will choose the person who best fits the above categories in relation to the actual competition that you are watching. It's so simple they can't go wrong, so if they can't get this one right best they take up plumbing or secretarial work or even politics. At the end of the competition they just line the contestants up put their hand over each ones head in turn and monitor the applause. The loudest wins….told you it was simple didn't I. There is usually one outright winner but if they should find a tie break situation all the other contestants can return to their seats and then run the applause again for the two remaining they will find a winner here, if it is so close and both have given you a really good time they should consider giving both a joint prize, clearly you think that's what should happen so it keeps everyone happy. Even if it's sponsored they can always sort out the logistics later.

They should always ask for applause only as whistles, yelps and screams from certain contingencies in the audience only serve to drown out genuine impartial appreciative applause and is pretty much the only way they will get any aggro regarding the resulting winner.

There is always the exception to the rule of course but the exception here causes them no problems at all because basically the only time they won't use the audience as judges for one of these comps is when it's a *'first past the post'* scenario. In other words the first person to……… The person who collects the most……. The team who finish the task first……

I could run a whole comp using this scenario or just parts of one to get me down to a certain number of contestants or couples to 'play off' for the audience vote.

It's as obvious as the spots on your belly that when using 'first past the post' the winner will be the winner, so no need to dwell any longer here. But it does bring us nicely onto the last of the three types of competition in this chapter.

THE ABSOLUTE OUTCOME COMPETITION:

As plain as the spots on your belly, I liked that one, wish I had another like it now though. As plain as day - doesn't fit, as clear as a bell - to audible, as plain as the nose on your face – ooh no not another body part, it's as bright as a button – now that's just being daft. Oh well I can only hope I will come up with something suitably fitting and humorous by the time I get to the end of this bit. The fact is that so long as everything is run with all the usual provisos and is well and truly above board these really are absolute simplicity itself with a guaranteed outright winner every time.

Hence the title 'absolute outcome comps'. Of course I will show you a couple of examples as always but the amount of ways in which they can pull off this little fun time filler is again only limited by that good old imagination of theirs.

Time filler?

Well yes and that's the only time I would expect to see them running one literally just as a nice little time filler i.e. The programme running well early for some reason, while most of them get ready for a large show or wet weather etc.

Please do not let them get away with using these instead of proper talent or fun themed comps. And, on your behalf, I beg all holiday centre entertainers PLEASE PLEASE PLEASE and a thousand more pleases do not do what I had the misfortune to witness at that awfully ran place I spoke of earlier. Not only were they using this type of time filler instead of proper comps but were also running brainless versions at any and every opportunity they could and on top of that, can you believe it, they were actually charging the guests for the pleasure, an absolute disgrace!!! So please do use these comps sparingly only as nice little fun time fillers and not to compensate for your lack of entertaining abilities and most definitely not as a money maker for the centre and never ever for yourself, god forbid that that sort of thing should happen anywhere these days.

I know it's been a while since I had a little rant but it makes my blood boil when I see this sort of mindless excuse for an entertainments programme and as far as I am concerned when they then start taking money off you for this garbage it's nothing more than a rip off and you deserve much much better than that!!!!!

If you're an Entertainments Manager running this rubbish firstly you should be thoroughly ashamed of yourself and secondly I suggest you put it right ASAP as your guests will now be very aware that it's just not acceptable.

If you're a centre manager allowing this to take place, well ditto the above sentiments.

If you are an organisation, park manager or owner actually instructing your entertainment managers to behave in, what I believe to be an outrageous money grabbing fashion, then best you look to your laurels as well, your guests will be reading this and if that's making you uncomfortable then you know you're in the wrong, don't you!!!

As a guest reading this if this is the sort of excuse for entertainment you are being served up I would get myself to the camp manager's office straight away and make your voice heard on the subject if I were you.

I am not suggesting that they should never run a comp where money is collected from guests, there will always be times such as during wet weather programmes when games such as 'Hoy' are acceptable but still only as part of an overall fun packed programme designed to give a varied day of maximum entertainment pleasure to their guests. Being completely open and transparent about the amount of money taken and the amount being paid out or the equivalent prize you are playing for is, as always, absolutely imperative.

Right all that now being said let's talk about these comps as the happy jolly silly simple family friendly fun time fillers that they are meant to be.

Well for a start the title really says it all and these comps do exactly what the title suggests. They are designed to whittle down the audience, or as many of you that want to take part, to one single winner with no other possible outcome.....'the absolute winner'. The way to set about achieving this is for them to firstly pick the comp that they are going run, as I said they will be spoilt for choice. Because they are so simple they can quickly explain the rules and get on with it in minimum time. Run the comp in as brisk or slow a manner that befits the situation adding in all the hilarity that is suitable to their chosen comp. The winner will be the winner.

Is that it?

Well yes actually that's about all there is to it.

Ok I think the best way to explain is to run one of the simplest versions of it with you right now. It will show you exactly how easy they are to dream up, explain and run while giving maximum fun with little or no rules to worry about. The other beauty of these comps is that everyone can join in, no matter what and no one is excluded by age or disability etc. If this is not the case they've missed the point of the comp entirely so should go back to the drawing board and think this one through again. Of course it is only common sense that they can make them a tad more risqué for adult only venues.

You can run these sorts of comps at your own birthday or Christmas parties ect.

So here we go then - just about the simplest version of an Absolute Outcome Competition: Get guests dancing to whatever type of music suites the venue at that time ensuring that all that have entered can at least have a go at and enjoy the style. Not forgetting to take into account any disabilities. Introduce four aces on large cards, one at each corner of the dance floor. Held up by a 'coat' , another 'coat' will have four aces from a pack of playing cards and when the music stops all those on the dance floor have to chose an ace to go and stand by. The 'coat' then gets someone not taking part to pick one of the aces at random. All those stood by the ace picked are out and have to leave the dance floor. You repeat this as many times as it takes to get down to four players. Each then has to choose a different ace to stand by. As each of the four aces is picked by the audience member it is removed from the competition..... 3... 2.... 1 the winner.

You see it really is THAT simple. There is NO more to it. No catches. Just nice silly happy jolly family fun.

You will remember I was talking about injecting their own brand of humour and hilarity to suit the comp. Well this is a perfect example where it is just so simple to spice up any comp. For example, all they need to do as the contestant numbers become manageable and are easily viewed by the audience is start playing a variety of music getting you messing about and is bound to raise a smile from even the most hardened of you critics. Rock and Roll, Ballet, Russian, bob the builder, oh well you get the picture.

They don't even have to announce a prize beforehand just have access to a variety in order that they can give one out that best suits the winner. This is where they and the shop can work in tandem. But by way of promoting it and not by making everyone pay to enter the comp to get some cheap *tat* they are trying to get rid of. It's alright no need to panic I'm not going there again, I feel much better now. And anyway, believe me if they're doing it properly, you will be more interested in getting those good old house points…. Forgotten about those hadn't you, well not to worry we will be getting onto them soon.

It won't have escaped your attention that I have tended to mention the bingo machine quite a lot when it comes to this stuff. Well we will come onto bingo in its own right later in the book but I have seen the bingo machine used in a variety of ways including the same way as the playing cards i.e. as each number is called the person with that number sits down. Ok for wet weather fun I suppose but as a main competition in the evening? I think not, especially if again you're going to be charged for each number, sometimes twice over!!

Now then what about that saying that I was looking for?

I think it will be found that the grand style arises in poetry
When a noble nature
Poetically gifted
Treats with simplicity or with severity a serious subject
Mathew Arnold 1822 – 1888
I think that just about sums it up, don't you.

Here are a few examples of competitions as promised:

Remember these are simply examples there are many fun competition out there or your entertainers can make up their own of course.

***

Man of week
In my experience you love this one
Really fun competition that is one of those that is almost a mini show in itself
Simple to run but concentration required by compere and 'coats' throughout

Consider the jump through window if elderly, unfit or anyone with disability enters
(Always have an alternative)

6 males is a good number

Take them back stage give them a choice of sayings as alternative to "My name is Bond James Bond"

E.g. My name is Bond

Basildon Bond

Brook Bond

Premium Bond ....Etc

Tell them to stay in character throughout the competition either serious or funny, it's up to them

Bring them out one at a time let them walk to the mic in the stand and announce themselves i.e. "My name is Bond...."

Then quick interview by compere

James bond is a very good dancer so get them to dance to a disco number for 30 seconds

James Bond is great with the ladies so get them to pick someone from the audience and have a smooch for another 20 seconds

Then announce 5 agents have come into the room Bond must take the lady back to her seat (don't tell them to kiss her this will get them extra applause at the end if they do)

Bond must now dispose of the 5 agents – the funnier the better

You announce another ten agents have arrived, too many for Bond so he has to jump out of a window to escape (again the funnier the better)

Give them something funny like a space hopper or toy scooter to escape on at the end.

The 'coat' will firstly demonstrate how the sequence goes using karate on the invisible make-believe 5 agents (you can come up with your own comedic ideas here) The compere gets the audience to count as the each of the 5 are dispatched

The compere keeps it going nonstop so each piece of music needs to be set and ready to go on cue and the props need to be reset very quickly after each Bond has had his turn

---

The winner is the one with the loudest applause at the end.

Props

James Bond theme tune

Mattress or similar

Space hopper or similar

Disco numbers on tape – disc etc

Slow smooch numbers on tape – disc etc

Look at the guest's faces as Superblue demonstrates Bond jumping out of the window
They are so enjoying themselves - **That's what it's all about!**

What?
The bed?
Ah! Well that's another story, don't worry all good clean fun!

***

Lady of week

Not a beauty contest just bags of fun
Keep it simple, fast moving, get the audience supporting the ladies etc
Make sure its kept safe
Minimum of 6 ladies:

Part one:

With balloons between their knees they complete as many laps of a laid out circuit as they can in 1 minute or 30 seconds dependent on numbers. (Trust me it's much funnier than it sounds)

Minimum 2 people are out here.

Part two:

Photo session

Each lady has to pose with four objects

Have silly objects as well as things like a feather bower and the appropriate music playing in the background

Minimum 1 person is out here.

Part 3:

Showtime

The remainder of the ladies are to dance/mime to a suitable showstopper

Two top scoring ladies go through to the final.

Part 4:

Final dash

The two remaining ladies have to burst as many balloons as possible on the laps of two men sat on chairs at the end of the dance floor. Trust me this one is as funny as it sounds and then some.

The time for the final dash is 1 minute.

Winning lady of the week is the one who bursts the most balloons of course but boy has she deserved the accolade by then!

This is a real fun competition!!!

Props

A large amount of inflated balloons (20 will be your minimum requirement)

Hats, skirts, tops other props for mimes

4 props for photo shoot (comedy)

Camp photographer (I mean a photographer working at the camp)

Suitable records/tape/CD

***

Perfect Couple

Very funny but simple to run

Start with 4 couples end up with the winning pair

Go through the stages below keep it tight and fast moving

Ensure safety of all

But a great family competition that is almost a mini show

Once again I know you love it!

Part 1:

Four couples (not necessarily married or even together)

Men sit on chairs – Ladies stand behind

Men are covered with a cloth to protect their clothes

Ladies are blindfolded and then handed a tin of shaving cream and given 20 seconds to prepare men's faces with cream

Ladies then given a plastic spoon **BUT** told it is a razor

They then have 1 minute to shave their partner (hilarious)

One couple to be eliminated.

Part 2:

The remaining couples are presented with an assortment of ladies cloths and make-up.

The ladies are given two minutes to make their man up into the best 'lady' they can.

Simple but oh so funny!

One couple to be eliminated.

Part 3:

The two remaining couples have to prove they are the perfect couple and are asked to dress and feed a baby (one of the staff and usually me!).

A large sheet for a nappy, talcum powder and a large safety pin all add to the comedy factor.

Give them 1 minute to dress the baby.

Then they need to feed and wind the baby (I always used a bottle of beer here)

The couple that make all of this the funniest are just about always voted winners by the audience and I have seen some ingenious impromptu comedy routines pulled out of the hat over the years.

Props

4 x blindfolds

4 x covers

4 x shaving cream

4 x spoons

Assortment of ladies clothes and make-up

Make-up remover and towels

Sheets

Talcum powder

Large safety pin (comedy)

Bottles of beer

Superblue comperes the beginning of perfect couple at Club Tropicana

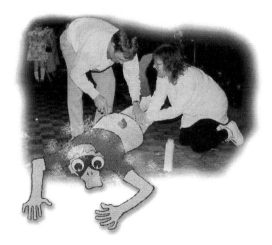

I always ended up being the big baby though Hey watch what you're doing with that pin!

It had its compensations though

That's my sixth beer...hic!

***

Team Chase or Battle of the Sexes
They don't come any simpler than this one
The secret is in great compering
Keep it fast moving fun and noisy
Noisy?

Yes this one really works on the whole place being involved and supporting their team
This can be a knock out competition or just see who finishes all the elements first
Choose your teams to reflect how you are going to get the audience to react

Men v Women - House v House - Left Side v Right Side
Split the room even further and have more teams if you want – after all it's only for fun
Then get them to go through either a number of single challenges so as to eliminate the
losing team each time

Or run the challenges continuously so that you end up with an outright winning team

These challenges are extremely simplistic for a couple of reasons

They are easy to explain and easy to understand

They are quick and safe

A good example of such an uncomplicated competition would be:

1. Passing a balloon through the team using their knees only (Definitely no hands)
2. Passing an orange through the team under their chins (Definitely no hands)
3. A space hopper (or similar) relay race around the dance floor
4. Passing a ball over one persons head and between the next person's legs. Once it reaches the last person they run to the front and start it all over again. This continues to take place until all have been and the original person is back at the front
5. A non alcoholic drinking round starting at the front person when they finish their drink put the **plastic** glass upside down on their head and next person starts their drink and so on
6. Passing a spoon tied to a piece of string starting with the first person. The spoon travels up through the first persons clothing and down through the next person's until it has travelled through the last persons clothing and they have hold of the spoon and the first person still has hold of the other end of the string (which must be still attached to the spoon).

    We can really get the audience going because if at any time a team fails in any way i.e. drops a ball or an orange, the string comes off the spoon or we just catch one of you cheating the whole team have to start that particular challenge again…oh the agony!

Props

Balloons

Oranges

Space Hoppers (or similar)

Balls, Spoons & String

Quick thinking compere and great music

SPONSORS

I have touched on these lovely people a few times in the book now. But it is so important that we managers and owners realise their worth and our responsibility to them.

Their input into the industry is literally worth millions of pounds. All over the country sponsors are paying hard earned cash to have their product presented in the best possible light to thousands upon thousands of holidaymakers at hundreds of centres, villages, parks, hotels and camps. The 'coats' at your holiday camp will be amongst hundreds tasked to do this, so why should they bother too much about it? No one will know will they? They can't make that much difference can they?

Well for starters it shouldn't matter whether or not anyone would know. They may be only one of the many but they know why they should bother, and if they don't by now they should go and get a copy of 101 things I wish I had done before I died and add 'became a fabulously happy and professional 'coat' at a holiday centre' to it. No one will know? Not that it should matter to them but the reality is that firms that spend their money want to know what they are getting for it in return, which is why they send people to check out how their product is being advertised at a number if not all the sites where they have sponsored a competition. They can't make that much of a difference though, can they? Well actually a company can and will pull the plug on a sponsorship deal if they believe they are being misrepresented or just not getting the type or amount of exposure they are paying for. Now on a small or private centre that would be bad enough but imagine being the one who is responsible for a major company withdrawing all that lovely dosh because you messed up. Imagine you didn't take it seriously, imagine you didn't mention the product the specified amount of times or when you did, you thought it would be funny to say something derogatory about it just to get a cheap laugh or imagine you didn't think it necessary to put up all the posters or placards or imagine you belittled the prize for yet another cheap shot at a gag, *imagine being on the dole!* That's what I instilled into my teams and is as true as ever today.

Just to reiterate then. I tell them to take all sponsorship very seriously indeed. Find out what the sponsorship deal entails i.e. what is expected of them in relation to it. Know the product so they can advertise it properly and to the full. Always be enthusiastic about the sponsorship and the prize. That is why when a 'coat' is exuberantly emphasising the virtue of the sponsor I ask that you have a little patience with them.

However they are not a puppet or a robot so should they believe there is a moral reason for not having a particular sponsorship they should raise this with the appropriate person and if they are over ruled but still feel strongly about it they should ask not to be involved in that comp. After all not only are we, the company, camp owners etc representing and advertising that sponsor but conversely if they should turn out to be unfavourable bedfellows with our guests, all the moral issues aside, we are scoring a home goal in the bad publicity department ourselves. A 'coat' or you highlighting something like this could just save a lot of people a lot of unnecessary grief.

WHERE ARE THEY GOING TO GET COMPETITIONS FROM?

This is one of my main gripes about, what appears to be a lack of training and apprenticeship at a number of holiday centres these days. Absolutely one of the best ways to learn about the types of competitions they can run and get a basic idea of what makes a good comp into a great one is to see as many as possible being run for real. Hence being a 'coat' under a good Entertainments Manager is worth its weight in gold. So if they are lucky enough to be or get into this position they must make the very most of it. Look listen and learn then use their own imagination to come up with new variations.

While nothing can compare to learning from experience it's always useful to shop around for inspiration. The internet is of course the place to find an abundance of ideas for all sorts of foundations on which to build competitions on and there are a wide variety of books available to stimulate the little grey cells as Hercule Poirot would say. Sometimes, as you will learn for yourself, it's the oddball or the wacky idea that creates the most fun and hilarity so they should not be afraid to try something new or be put off just because it seems silly or no one else has done it.

I'd rather have a fool to make me merry, than experience to make me sad
William Shakespeare 1564 – 1616

Children's competitions, normally, held in the early evening follow pretty much all the same rules, but Entertainments Managers should always double check the health and safety risk assessments re dangerous objects or the likelihood of children running into things etc. An adult can think for themselves to some degree but kids don't always see danger and are nearly always eager to please so 'coats' must **think for them**.

A good rule here is.....er....to try to have as few rules as possible.

Now that we have reached the end of the section of the book dedicated to competitions here is a little something for you to use should you find it necessary to defuse a situation.

For when the One Great Scorer comes
To write against your name
He marks
Not that you won or lost
But how you played the game
Grantland Rice 1880 – 1954

CHAPTER ELEVEN

THE CHILDREN'S PROGRAMME

A child is a precious thing
Never to be let down
Always allowed to sing
A child is priceless
Not to be ignored
The prince or princess
A child is valuable
That's for you to remember and ensure they are
Never allowed to be vulnerable
A child is full of potential
You the role model
Your behaviour exemplary and exceptional
A child is the future
Treat with respect and dignity
In return fond childhood memories will nurture
Superblue 1957 – 2011 (so far)

Well I really don't intent to spend too much time on this subject.

That's not to say that it is any less important than any other that we are covering, in fact it is just about the most important there could be. No the reasons for not dwelling here for too long are quite simple: I have covered almost anything to do with the day to day running of any programme elsewhere and there is precious little else to add to any of that. What I do have to say to you however I feel is so very important that I want to make it short sharp and to the point. So I'll save all the funnies for other chapters and get stuck straight into it.

The first and most crucial thing to say is that only the right people should ever work anywhere near children in any capacity whatsoever. Whilst it is up to the entertainment executives in large companies to ensure the recruitment and vetting process for these posts is correctly adhered to, it could easily be down to the Entertainments Manager in a small company or private centre. Should this be the case, because I don't know what the status may be by the time they are reading this, my best advice to them has to be to contact the local council and police to enquire about the relevant qualifications needed by persons that are to be working with children of varying ages in a variety of capacities. There is also a requirement that persons applying for certain jobs in a number of professions, where children are involved, to now have their names checked. Again due to the ever changing regulations within this arena the only proper advice to give anyone with this responsibility is to contact their local police as well as the council for the latest procedures etc. It may seem a bureaucratic nightmare when you first think about it but let's get things into the right prospective *ANYTHING* that helps to protect children in anyway can only be something that we should all applaud and wholeheartedly embrace.

You can find out what employers may require at **www.direct.gov.uk/employment**

Just by way of example of the variety of qualifications needed by different companies or local governments at home and abroad here is an extract from an expired Thomson Holidays advert for Holiday reps/childcare staff.

To work with 0-3 year olds you will need Nursery experience and a level 3NNEB or equivalent.

To work with 3 – 12 year olds you will need an NVQ level 2 or equivalent.

(If they are applying to work with children in the UK they should definitely be required to undertake a CRB check, this varies from country to country)

So as you can see even the biggest of companies do take this aspect very seriously as indeed your holiday company must.

Once the company, Entertainments Manager or other designated person has covered the above requirements, as we have already discussed it is absolutely imperative that they employ the very best in children's aunts, uncles and entertainers.

I will use 'them, their and they' from here on in but I am referring to the Entertainments Manager, all 'coats' and children's aunties, uncles or entertainers. No matter the title if they have anything to do with the welfare of your children they must.......

Always do everything they can to keep the children happy.
I always remind them that children are the guests of the future

Happy children = Happy parents = Happy holiday centre
I always remind them children are the guests of the future

NEVER LET CHILDREN DOWN

If for some reason beyond their control an event is unable to go ahead they must make sure they have something ready to take its place.

I tell them to never promise anything they may not be able to deliver.

If they have 'characters' i.e. a Crocodile or Tiger etc etc at your centre they must make sure they turn up to events as advertised or promised appearance.

I keep reminding them children are the guests of the future

NEVER IGNORE A CHILD

No matter how busy or rushed they might be they must always make time for that young person.

For example my nephews recently went to one of the big '3' it was their first venture into the holiday camp world and I could not wait to hear their excited blow by blow account of the fabulous time had by all. Unfortunately their overriding memory of the entire holiday was that the Entertainments Manager ignored them one day when they went out of their way to say hello to him.

I keep reminding them that children are the guests of the future – ***or not!***

Make sure parents always know where their children will be, especially if the venue changes for any reason.

Always have enough staff to cover the amount of children particularly for excursions and trips etc. Health and safety is never more important than when dealing with children.

Sports events, swimming galas and the Noddy train are perfect examples of the amount of conscious consideration and thought that needs to be expended on this subject.

When putting their programme together always divide it into manageable and realistic age groups for their guest's enjoyment. Have a quick look at the example I provided a while back for guidance.

Never forget to make sure it knits in neatly with the adult and teenage programmes so that families can be together when appropriate.

It is very important that the Entertainments Manager keeps a tight rein on the junior, children's and teenage entertainments departments to ensure that, the staff running them are, disciplined in the art of keeping those programmes running on time. Lose track of this and their adult programme can very quickly and easily be thrown into disarray.

I'm not going to harp on about it but, as you know, I do dislike children being used as pawns to abstract as much money as possible from you adult guests while on holiday. If however, they are running events where money is required to change hands I strongly suggest that they ensure a parent is on hand to give them that money. I won't insult your intelligence by pointing out the many pitfalls of doing it any other way.

THEMED DAYS:

This is one of those occasions where the children's enthusiasm is one of their best friends. If they get them excited and on board for these days they will bring you parents along with them and enhance our chances of carrying off a successful fun filled day. Children will dress up, join in and drive the day forward with their exuberance. So 'coats' must spend time explaining to them what is in the programme, what they can do to join in, what they can do to get you lovely parents to do to take part in all the fun. They can also enthuse them to want to watch the in-house 'coat' shows and fun comps and even help to get you fun loving mums and dads to take part.

CERTIFICATES AND PRIZES:

I have of course covered this in greater detail previously but when it comes to recognising children's achievements at their park triple everything I said before. This is an aspect of their programme that is of such consequence that it cannot be overstated. It holds such magic for the children while at the village and means it remains a fond place in their memories ensuring they become guests of the future. They also advertise for that centre when they get home from holiday, i.e. telling friends and relatives and showing off their trophy etc. I'm sure that it is suitably indelibly imprinted in their minds by now, but, I warn them not to dare to forget those all important sponsors.

I hope they are going to take notice of what I have to say about 'House Points' and if they pay particular attention to this when dealing with the children's programme the youngsters will take this very seriously and every point a 'coat' gives out will be heeded so they have to make sure they note down who has been given what points and add them to the scoreboard when most of the children will be there, early evening probably being the best time to carry out this ceremony.

PARTY DANCES:

Children love party dances and it's a great way to get many people up onto the dance floor early in the evening programme. We will be talking about this particular subject soon but there are a couple of things to mention here;

They should not run party dance lessons at the same time as another junior event, as I say many do enjoy these and will want to be at the lessons.

And

Never use party dances instead of junior competitions or as a method of abstracting even more money from the poor old parents.

CABARETS AND SHOWS:

A subject that is increasingly becoming a problem at all holiday centres, not just with children but also among some adult guests, is people walking across the dance floor while cabarets are on or shows are being performed. I am going to speak more about this in the chapter on 'Stage Management' but here is a very good place to start the education process instilling into their future guests the fact that to do this is nothing short of rude ignorance. To this end they should have enough 'coats' to sit with the children while cabarets are on and other staff members doing the role while they are all performing in the 'coat' shows. It will also have the knock on effect of telling those adults that need telling (that's not you of course) that it is something they're not prepared to tolerate in their entertainment venues.

Larger centres with theatres will not usually have this problem of course.

BIG TIME DO'S and DONT'S for all Entertainment Staff:

Do not have children anywhere near staff accommodation – **EVER!**

Do not be left with a child for extended periods of time – you are not a child minding service – make sure parents know what time to collect their children after each event – never agree to look after a child for the day.

Do think about everything you say and do when you are around junior guests – The younger ones will actually look up to you as a 'Role Model' – consider such things as smoking, language and alcohol – also things such as appropriate language of others i.e. cabarets or even lyrics of music played at the junior disco.

Don't treat children as fools they are very astute little human beings:

In the early days of Superblue I thought I was doing well fooling the children into believing that I was an entirely new person who joined the team when they called for him. That was until the day a very wise young 6 year old boy came up to Superblue in the middle of a stunt and proclaimed to the world that Superblue was in fact none other than 'that daft Bluecoat'. Assuming my costume and disguise were good enough to carry it off I protested my innocence to this deception and proudly announced "I am Superblue and I only appear when you boys and girls call for me, I don't know who this Bluecoat is" The little boy looked me up and down with a thoughtful look on his face then announced "Well I know your that Bluecoat" not thinking it through I stupidly, and in a voice that made the 6 year old look completely grown up, said "How do you know that then?" The young man gave a great big huff and rolled his eyes as if to say how daft do you think I am anyway. Then came the killer "I know Superblue is actually that Bluecoat because you're wearing his shoes" He didn't finish it with so there! But he might as well have. The whole place was in stitches it was just one of those magical moments. I'd love to know what he grew up to be, maybe people that remember Superblue as children will drop me a line and let me know what happened to them. But I digress, the point being I forgot and treated that lad as if he was somehow less intelligent than me for that moment in time and he made me Pay for it – large style!

Do always let children's aunties and uncles etc go off duty at a reasonable time in the evening. After the children's march out would seem to be sensible wouldn't it. Why? Well if they are working properly they will, quite simply, have worked extremely hard throughout the day with young people of one age or another baying for their attention just about every minute of that day. They absolutely deserve to finish before anyone else and have some downtime to themselves.

So a quick recap on how they should run a successful children's or junior programme. All they have to do is stick to all the rules and advice as we discussed re the adults.

Then stick to my extra rule of keeping young people H.A.P.P.Y.
H - Having fun

A - Always safe

P - Plenty of staff

P - Parents always know where children are

Y - You're a role model, act like it

But hay the kids don't have to wait for holiday time to have fun......visit

Where they will find their very own section

Packed with stuff just for them

Including how to become one of my junior..........

Super Agents

With a spy back-pack full of everything they need to report back on the junior aspect of your holiday

CHAPTER TWELVE

THE TEENAGE PROGRAMME

You will be surprised to find out that this promises to be the shortest chapter of all which is ironic because it covers a subject that I promise is in many ways the most difficult of all. Why such a short chapter then? Well pretty much for the same reasons as with the children's programme i.e. I have said all there is to say about most things regarding programmes being in sink and running on time da-de-da health and safety yakaty-yak appropriate staff blah-blah-blah house points hi-di-hi and so on and so forth. There are however some points to highlight that are no less important than those we have spoken about in the adult and children's programmes.

The first thing to recognise is that teenagers will come to most centres with their parents and are generally a good natured group of people despite the bad press they tend to get these days. So for the most part we can organise a teenage programme safe in the knowledge that if we make it interesting and varied enough they will respond positively and enjoy attending the events we have set for them. Provided we have done our research properly and are running events that are relevant to this age group today we should provide a happy and enjoyable working environment for the people within a dedicated teenage department at larger companies and for the 'coats' in general at the smaller or independent ones.

I say 'should' because there is always the chance that we may get a rogue teenager or two at times and indeed it has been known for large groups or families, to cause a centre many problems. If this is compounded by allowing them to take control in any of the areas that we have spoken about, it can be nothing short of disastrous, but letting anyone do this with the teenage programme would be an absolute recipe for that disaster. As with anything else we will encounter, it is something that 'coats' as individuals will learn to deal with. They will learn to be tuff with those young people that need tuff handling but should this ever get out of their control which of course it can, after all they are a holiday camp entertainer not a police officer, they must make sure they know the company, camp, managers or owners strategy for dealing with these people and ensure they fit in with that ethos. It is imperative that they have support from those said entities and it should be made clear, from the outset in any literature, website and verbally if necessary that anyone behaving in a way that disrupts the happiness, safety and comfort of other guests or staff will be dealt with in a very strong and positive manner indeed. The penalties for such behaviour are of course not a 'coats' responsibility; they just need to ensure they exist for their protection and your holiday enjoyment. I add this little section in this chapter only because it needs to be in the book at some point and here is as good a place as any to put it as the teenage contingency of any unruly party are as likely as not to give some of the first indications that such behaviour could manifest itself.

That's not to say of course that a disruptive teenager automatically signifies any such thing about the rest of his or her family. Remember the vast majority of teenagers are there with thoroughly decent parents and family and are caught in that twilight zone between the children's and adults programmes. All they want to do is have fun the same as everyone else but in their own way, being treated as young adults and having events that are catered specifically for them. Large centres can and many do cater specifically for this age group with climbing walls, quad bikes etc and will have done the research allowing the Entertainments Manager to run age specific events for our teenage guests.

The fact is however that after all said and done there are many events in the other programmes that teenagers will happily enjoy if it's for their own age group only. Things such as Talent shows, pool, snooker, tenpin bowling, table tennis, disco, their own club room and trips etc. Well that doesn't take a genius to work that out does it Superblue? Well no but that's what I mean about this being a short chapter. It literally is mostly working on the same principals as we have done for all the other programmes and then just adding a touch of common sense, taking firm control and being clear about the rules, treating them with respect and remembering they are young adults, embracing the fact that they want to be very grown up while ensuring safe and legal parameters in which they can develop. Never lose sight of the fact that they are still at an impressionable stage in their lives therefore our responsibilities as role models are as great as ever.

And that's about it………

CHAPTER THIRTEEN

THE WET WEATHER PROGRAMME

Sunshine is delicious, rain is refreshing, wind braces us up, snow is exhilarating; there is really no such thing as bad weather, only different kinds of good weather.
John Ruskin

Rainbows apologize for angry skies.
Sylvia Voirol

If you have ever been a boy scout you will know the motto and it's a motto that will save your bacon now if you attach its importance to the wet weather programme you will.....

'BE PREPARED'

If you were a girl guide.....I have just looked them up and your laws and motto could have been written especially for a 'coat' in any weather..........

Because the Guide Laws are:
A Guide is honest, reliable and can be trusted.
A Guide is helpful and uses her time and abilities wisely.
A Guide faces challenges and learns from her experiences.
A Guide is a good friend and a sister to all Guides.
A Guide is polite and considerate.
A Guide respects all living things and takes care of the world around her.
And the Guide Motto is again:
Be prepared.

WOW bad weather should be a doddle for you girls!

I jest boys of course the Scout oath and laws are cool too!

IT RAINED FOR FORTY DAYS AND FORTY NIGHTS:

This was of course the exception rather than the rule but Noah was still prepared and had his ark ready on time to save the day.

So how many days can you expect to have a wet weather programme in a week?

Well that's the thing isn't it no one knows how many do they.

With the climate going through so many changes in recent years it's totally unpredictable.

I know the weather forecasts are much better than they have been in the past but you still have to be on your toes for that sudden ridge of low pressure being pushed by a cold front from the polar cap with a whole load of nasty isobars to boot.

You didn't see that lot coming did you?

No nor me, I just got carried away there for a moment.

Anyway the fact still remains we never can tell how many days wet weather programme we will need in the future so Entertainments Managers must.....BE PREPARED.

Have at least a couple of day's worth of indoor events that are at the ready and can swing into action at the shortest of notice. Have many more, in the back of their mind, that they can start to get ready should the inclement weather look like settling in for a long spell. If they're on a park that incorporates owners that are on site every weekend and most holidays they will need a fair array of different activities to be able to deliver a number of diverse wet weather programmes to keep everyone entertained and happy.

HAPPY FAMILIES:

Is one game that they can lay on to amuse down hearted, housebound and very subdued guests but I'm not so sure how impressed you would be with that one unless they turned it into a great game show of course.

No, what I am getting at here is the fact that wet weather generally tends to throw families together all in one room all wanting to be entertained all wanting to be made happy all waiting for the 'coats' to come up with a brilliant wet weather programme to take their rainy day blues away. I know some villages will have more than one venue, including adult only bars etc, and we can utilize these to achieve the best results for our guests in this situation but Entertainment Managers must be mindful of the amount of staff available and that this could turn out to be a very long day so the more guests they can entertain in one place the more likely it is that they are going to be able to cope with prolonged periods without needing breaks in the programme.

It stands to reason then, that for the most part a wet weather programme should cater for fun for all the family.

I am sure the Entertainments Manager at any holiday centre you will attend will have many ideas of their own, that they will bring into play when the time comes. But the reality is that with very little or no warning they can find themselves with a couple of thousand guests of varying ages all looking to them to chase the rain away. So I am going to run a few little things past you that I set out in 'Tales of Superblue' and should at least point them in the right direction to get off to a good start allowing them time to think of their own unique little rays of indoor sunshine. This is the very basic of wet weather programmes I would expect any centre to provide for you on holiday. So don't you think it's the least you should expect too?

GET READY.... GET WET.....GO:

Very good indoor family fun sports days typify what constitutes a 'real winner' for wet weather programmes. They involve the entire family while at the same time being a great spectator event. Therefore they accomplish 'the some like to do while others like to watch them doing' philosophy. There are so many other events in this vein that will keep families happily ignoring the weather outside for hours and are so easy to set up and run; indoor bowls, skittles, quoits and indoor donkey derby (one of my favourites) to name but a few.

THERE'S NO BUSINESS LIKE SNOWBUSINESS:

See what I did there? Good ah? Oh well please yourself but putting on a show or pantomime, seemingly, out of the blue is a sign of a very good Entertainments Manager and you will really appreciate the fact that they are taking this programme as seriously as any other and are pulling out all the stops to ensure the continued enjoyment of your holiday, despite the weather. Now I know it's sometimes hard enough to put on a variety of shows, as it is, at some centres but if they do the best they can it is so worth it when they pull it off. Do remember that they are unlikely to have the use of a band at this time so will have to make sure extra shows are on backing tape etc with at least one back up copy that are checked regularly to ensure they play properly and are compatible with the machines and consoles that they have to work with and that they are made up of family friendly material and are flexible enough so as not to be unworkable, should a certain 'coat' be on a day off for example. So now you know how much goes into putting one of these 'extra' shows on for your wet weather enjoyment, you will appreciate it all the more. However if your team aren't bothering to even try to perform one for you, how uncommitted to your holiday happiness are they? Where _is_ your money being spent?

That being said if they have already put at least one on for you a really novel and fun way of putting on another wet weather show is to get you guests to do it for them. Yes I am serious and it's actually very simple and easy to do. It just needs backing tracks, DVD's, CD's or records of famous stars that everyone knows, Tom Jones, Elvis, Shirley Basey, Madonna, The Spice Girls, Elton John, Michael Jackson etc etc. Put you into costumes to suite the star and you're away. Run it like a comp in that they pick the guests that will go for it, get you together early to run through what is going to happen, keep you backstage once they start the show, announce each star onto the stage. Run it like a show in that the sound and lighting is fab, they can have set routines with some of the entertainment teams dancers for effect, give you a great build up for a final bow at the end. They can run this as a comp if they like, getting the audience to applaud (remember the themed fun competition?). However I personally wouldn't because this form of show brings so much fun and laughter and let's face it, it has given them a brilliant entertainment spot for anything up to an hour in their wet weather programme that I think people who take part in these shows for them should **all** get a prize as a way of thanks and of course will go down very well with you in the audience too, another little ray of indoor sunshine!

Hopefully you are beginning to see what it is I am trying to get them to achieve. Each little event should build on the last until suddenly the day is over and you are in your rooms, caravans, chalets excitedly getting ready for your evening programme while talking about what a great day you have all had. Rain what rain?

ANYONE FOR LUNCH:

If they have taken heed of my advice on lunchtime entertainment they will now be putting a cheque in the post to me, yes of course I'm only joking, really, some people are so tight.

Seriously though they will be thanking me big time and patting themselves on the back for taking that advice and putting it into practice because they will just have realised that they already have a good hour or two of the wet weather programme taken care of and they may even be able to expand this at times. They will have a band, duo or pianist in place with whom, they are on good working terms, which we have already established is a crucial element, will quite often help out during the day (And yes I know about musician's union rules but they are not always compromised by this).

The only real difference between this and any other day should be the number of guests that will attend this lunch time session so be prepared to be switched to a larger venue if necessary.

TAKE TWO HUNDRED AND TWENTY FIVE:

Something you guests don't actually want; repeated films.

Bad weather can eat up a collection of films very quickly so they must make sure they either, have more than enough to carry them through the worst case scenarios or easy access to fresh titles when they need them. Making sure any film they show is appropriate for the time of day and venue.

Ensure the advertising stipulates the censors grading of all films to be shown.

Show as varied a selection as possible so as to, at least, try to please some of the people some of the time.

Always make sure they have all the necessary licences etc to give a public performance of films in the first place.

USE WHAT THEY HAVE TO BEST EFFECT:

For example if they have children's competitions on the programme for that day anyway consider moving them into a bigger venue if they are not already being held there because many of these comps are very entertaining for all guests and so can be a very good source of light hearted fun for many people on a wet day.

OH! THAT'S NOT FAIR DAREN'S MUM DOESN'T MAKE HIM DO THAT:

The same is not necessarily true with the teenage programme. Generally this age group like to keep their activities separate from the adults and children's programmes after all that's the whole point of it, it's their programme. Many of them will also not want to 'perform' in another arena. So they should bear them in mind when running a wet weather programme and think it through before deciding what to do for them.

NEVER EVER MOVE ANY COMPETITIONS:

If they have other competitions indoors on that day all well and good but they must NEVER EVER move a competition from another day to try to please their wet weather guests. The fact is that a lot of you holidaymakers do plan your week around the competitions you or your families want to take part in and rightly take them very seriously indeed. If for example their programme shows the snooker competition will be held on Thursday those that want to take part will arrange to take your families to a local attraction on another day, Wednesday let's say. They have a wet weather day on the Wednesday and decide to make life easy for themselves by moving indoor competitions like the snooker to the Wednesday in the hope that Thursday will be sunny and they will get away with little effort on a wet weather programme. The next morning the sun is out and it's a lovely hot summer's day, they're feeling really clever and pleased with themselves aren't they? Well that is until about 10.30 am when they suddenly find yourself surrounded by angry guests, including you, who turned up at the 10am snooker competition only to discover that its already been held the day before while you were out! They changed it, it's all on their shoulders so what are they going to do now? And if they've been really lazy and daft they've got the pool, darts and table tennis comps that they changed to deal with later as well. They may well find that they will have to run the whole lot again to keep you happy, especially if it's a sponsored competition, remember what I told them about those? But the fact is, sponsored or not they've managed to upset a good number of guests including you and your family just by trying to make life easy for themselves!!!

Remember they're not there to make life easy for themselves…. It's all about you, the guests and wet weather days are where they really earn their money and what's more any decent Entertainments Manager would love having all those guests in one place for so long….just think of the fun to be had…marvellous.

PARTY DANCES AND TEA DANCES:

Are always popular of course, dependent on the type of holiday they're catering for, but they must not do them to death just because they can't think of anything else.

FUN QUIZZES:

Are another obvious asset here but again there is nothing more annoying than yet another fun quiz just to fill the time. When they do run one however they should make it fun and ensure the questions are varied to cover their audience so all can enjoy taking part.

FUN GAMBLING:

Prize bingo, horse or dog racing on film, non licensed bingo, hoy etc are all great ways of contributing to a varied wet weather programme, but that's what they must be, a contributory factor in a successful wet days entertainment. They must not fall into the trap of running these events one after another throughout the day. There are many reasons for this, many of which we have eluded to already but two of the main ones are plain and simple lack of variety for you holidaymakers, either because of their laziness or insufficient knowledge or imagination to run anything else and secondly *MONEY*. I have touched on the subject of using the children in, what I believe is, an unethical way to drain parents dry of every last penny. Well wet weather is another of these occasions where they not only have this leverage with the children wanting stuff that costs money while stuck in because of the weather but the parents themselves will want to pass the time and some of those pastimes will cost them enough as it is without Entertainments Managers adding to their anxiety by running a complete days programme that you will have to pay to take part in. It is imperative that they never lose sight of the fact that you have already paid to come on holiday at their village because they advertise that they supply free entertainment in the package as this is a massive incentive to would be guests with families. I know as well as them that they may come under pressure from the camp manager (often called operations managers or similar now) to squeeze every last penny from the guests and the only advice I can give them, as I did before, is to be strong, polite but firm and explain that guests only have so much to spend and putting them under pressure to spend it quicker or on things they don't want to or making them have to say no to their children only serves to make them unhappy....

the complete opposite from what a holiday company is supposed to be all about. They should explain that if they are just allowed to run a decent, varied and fun wet weather programme that does no more than entertain you guests then guess what….you will come out of your chalets, caravans, rooms and apartments and join in the fun. While you are doing that what do you think is happening to the bars, restaurants, shops and take-aways? That's right they are taking money with no pressure on you. You are just there enjoying yourself by being entertained for free as promised and this spending is just natural holiday expenditure. Money, by the way, the camp manager wouldn't have in those tills if you are sat in your chalets etc because the wet weather programme is rubbish or you just don't like the pressure they put on you to spend spend spend. Trust me a good Entertainments Manager runs a team that bring in more than their fair share of the revenue at that centre, just take them away and watch the takings drop like a stone. So they should stand up for themselves and their guests on this one.

ALL HANDS ON DECK?

In general terms the centre needs as many 'coats' on duty as it can muster on a wet day and for the Entertainments Managers wet weather will of course be the busiest days of all and can be quite stressful. But if they plan well ahead as I have laid out in this chapter and stick to the basics they will be fine, tired but fine; but hey that's the job we signed up for isn't it? Yes indeed it is so they should just enjoy the challenge when it comes. So they're tired are they? What about the rest of their team? One of these days every now and again is no great shakes really and most people just get on and take it in their stride. But they have certain responsibilities in relation to their staff welfare and that includes the hours they work and the stress of any situation they may be working under, remember mid season blues for a start. Wet weather programmes can obviously sap the energy of the most energetic and enthusiastic of 'coats' during this time or just on an off day of course but should you get more than one wet day in a row it can start to affect everyone on the team to varying degrees. This is one of the challenges the Entertainments Manager will have to manage and it will depend on the size of the team how they achieve this. The most obvious and by far the best way to accomplish it is to split the team into shifts so that everyone gets decent and equal breaks during the day. For example they may have to decide whether to have a morning and afternoon shift etc or completely split them into a day and evening shift. The reality, however, is that at many holiday parks across this fine land they will only have a very small team to begin with and wet weather mercilessly drains their resources even on one wet day. So Entertainments Managers have to do the best they can with what they have got. Run a programme that has all the elements we have talked of but needs minimum staffing levels, consider leaving at least one 'coat' off duty in the afternoon so that the Entertainments Manager, yes Entertainments Manager, and they can cover the late night session in the adult bar and or disco in the family room. This allows them to let those fabulous hard working 'coats' off at a sensible time that evening. They must not forget the children's department! They are very likely going to need extra people to help them through this day, another reason to combine programmes when they can.

Whichever way they ultimately end up dealing with this tricky issue and get through the long day they now have a camp full of happy and appreciative guests and they are getting a pat on the back from grateful resort, bars, shops, restaurant and take-away managers. While the Entertainments Manager is getting all this praise they ought to remember who carried it all off for them and always let the team know how grateful they are. No need to limit this to just verbal thanks either, trying to respond to all their hard work by arranging extra time off over the next few days, especially if they have covered more than one wet day is always a good thing to do for the 'coat' and means that they will be fresh and ready to deliver you the best possible holiday fun again and so it's good value for your money too. There are many ways of making this happen, the Entertainments Manager doing some comps for them for example. Tired? now they're tired but now they are also changing, changing from a good Entertainments Manager into a great Entertainments Manager.

SIGN OF THE TIMES: OR LOCATION LOCATION LOCATION: OR COLD CROSS BUNNIES:

Oh the humour of it all, anyway back to the case in hand, it's pouring with rain, cold, windy, getting more overcast by the minute so I tell Entertainments Managers to.... Imagine you're the head of a family of guests snuggled up in a nice warm comfortable caravan or chalet. You've got some nice beer, lager and wine in the fridge, plenty of snacks and sweets for the kids and a stack of good DVD's to watch. There really is no need to venture out into that nasty cold weather at all. You've got everything you need right there but you think what the hell "we're on holiday" so you drag your husband or wife and kids kicking and screaming out of their nice warm comfortable home from home into gale force nine winds and just as you are leaving you hear it!!! As they wrap themselves in their thermal gloves, scarf's and thick Eskimo hooded 'coats' you hear your spouse angrily utter those fateful words…… "This had better be worth it or else" but as you bravely lead the way across the holiday village a whole half mile trek through the golf ball sized hail stones you're not worried; Oh no the entertainment has been great so far why should a little iddy biddy hurricane make any difference? Why indeed! As you march up to the main venue, supremely confident, obviously cleverly looking to see that there are no signs or posters saving you valuable time and much needed dignity in front of your already disillusioned family by telling you the wet weather events are being held elsewhere. Happy in the knowledge that you are about to be the hero that has delivered them into the entertainment Shangri-La that is...

'THE WET WEATHER PROGRAMME'

You fling open the doors to be met by the deafening sound of……silence. "Ah?" You nervously utter as you turn to look at the family from hell, if looks could kill! What could have gone wrong? Well no matter they must be in one of the other three or four venues or perhaps the swimming pool or games room and so you set off in search of the illusive lost tribe known as the entertainments team as you traipse from venue to venue the family is getting wetter and wetter and colder and colder until they are a soaked through dishevelled unhappy mess. Imagine 200 heads of family going through this nightmare. Imagine all those thoroughly fed up, wet and cold people traipsing around the camp getting colder and wetter by the minute trying to do no more than find the entertainments team to be.....well..er..entertained. Won't the team be glad to see them when they eventually turn up? Oh yes of course they will, more lovely people to entertain. Only they're not so lovely anymore, they're angry, they did venture out in that nasty weather and went to the most logical or nearest venue to their chalet to see what wonders the team had in store for them on this dank day, only to find the Entertainments Manager had let them down. Not only did they let them and the other 199 mums and dads down but they let themselves and the 'coats' down badly too. What should have been a triumph of ingenuity and superb entertainment management dexterity has disintegrated into a soggy damp squid of a palaver. Why? What did the Entertainments Manager do that was so wrong? Why are all these guests so angry at them now? Why is it that they won't bother to venture out to any venues again tonight once they get their family back into the warm and comfort of their own little abodes? Why? I will tell you why. Because the Entertainments Manager and 'Coats' ignored one of the most basic of rules from all that time ago when we spoke about 'How to advertise their programme', remember now? Of course you do and you will recall the fuss I made over the importance of having posters, signs etc at prominent locations especially on wet weather days and the many other ways of advertising they should consider using to catch as many guests as possible in their information trap for this exact reason. Ok I think I made my point and you can see how absolutely imperative it is that they heed that advice or risk losing great chunks of their audience for that entire day or worse, for the rest of the week, they could even lose the goodwill that they should be enjoying from regular and loyal guests.

So if you ever encounter this situation at a holiday centre you will know exactly what stance to take and show your disapproval. There really is no excuse for this happening.

DON'T GO OVER OLD GROUND:

Ok then I won't but I must just touch on as couple of things we have spoken about before or you will think I have just forgotten about them. It goes without saying all usual rules apply. They must have all the right things at the right times in the right places etc. Having everything ready to go in the right place at the right time is even more important when running an ad-hoc programme like this. They ought to run all advertised comps and events on time and finish them on time.

BARS, TAKE-AWAYS, RESTAURANTS, GAMES ROOM AND SWIMMING POOL ETC.

They have to liaise with catering, bars, casino, games room and maintenance managers before they embark on a wet weather programme and always check that the swimming pool has enough qualified staff to cope with the influx of guests and any extra events they might want to run on these days.

HEALTH AND SAFETY.

Same as any other time of the week as we will discuss in a later chapter, except that they have the added factors of wet floors, electricity and water etc.

TOO HOT TO HANDLE:

I know I have concentrated on wet and bad weather for this state of affairs and let's face it it's the most likely case scenario. But in this ever changing world of global warming we have had some **stonkingly hot days** over the past couple of years so I tell Entertainments Managers to remember that everything in this chapter can also be used as guidelines for **extra hot weather too.**

CHAPTER FOURTEEN

HOUSE POINTS

"I kinda see everyone as competition. I'm a very competitive person. But I think that's good. Competition is great. And as long as it's friendly and not a malicious thing then I think it's cool."

Janet Jackson

I can imagine many of my younger readers thinking thank goodness for that, I'm finally going to find out what these 'house points' are all about and why that Superblue keeps going on about them.

And my more mature readers saying thank goodness for that, he's finally going to tell them youngsters what 'house points' are all about!!

Boy-o-boy everyone's a critic!

Ok ok the time has finally come for me to indeed explain what 'house points' are all about and moreover how important they can be to the overall success of an entertainments programme while creating so much fun for you.

The basic premise is so simple it's scary.

It is no more complicated than.....................Just splitting the camp, centre, village, hotel or park into two teams the most obvious and easiest way being to use the chalet, room, or caravan numbers to determine what team you are in; Odds v Evens......See told you it was simple.

WHAT THEY THEN CALL THESE TEAMS DEPENDS LARGELY ON A COUPLE OF FACTORS.

1) If they have managed to secure sponsorship quite clearly that's what your house names will be. For example when I started at Pontins all those years ago the house names were Embassy and Castella so you can see straight away they were sponsored by a tobacco company which in itself shows it was some time

ago but it also demonstrates the advertising power of a brand being the name of one of the 'houses' and that it can attract some of the top adverting spenders in the corporate world.

2) That does bring us onto the other aspect in the choice of the house names and a very important point it is too.

Suitability; There's nothing wrong with the Entertainments Manager rubbing their hands together because they've been a clever little sausage and managed to entice a corporate giant to sponsor the houses etc. Oh no indeedy, however nothing more than plain old common sense should prevail here and to remain a smart little chipolata they simply have to remember that they are generally operating in a family environment and therefore whatever names they end up using, sponsored or not, they must be wholly acceptable to all ages.

Nothing too dramatic there was there? No the 'House System' really is that simple.
So why do I get so excited about it then?
Well that's quite simple too!
You guests get excited about it that's why!!

HOW DOES IT WORK?

Simple….Now I know you're expecting me to say "but nothing is that simple is it" but no not this time because this really is that simple.

The Entertainments Manager runs the House System during the week or over however many days they have this set of guests for.

You get 10 points for winning and 5 points for coming runner up of every competition, game, tournament, bingo win, race at sports day and swimming gala etc etc.

Points are taken off for not joining in events like the best dressed table or chalet for example and anything other opportunity that presents itself for such a painful forfeit, and believe me it brings on the pains when the teams are close and someone loses points for them.

Score boards are placed in all entertainment venues and restaurants if full or half board or even all inclusive and a portable set for outdoor events. An announcement will be made about the times of day that these will be updated with the latest results thus far i.e. at breakfast or first thing in the morning if not full or half board, at lunchtime and for maximum effect at the start of the evenings proceedings when the vast majority of guests are in one place (or at least they should be if the Entertainments Manager has worked this system to its full effect).

The boards can be added to directly during the evening after each event building the tension as they go.

What is all the fuss about? Why do you guests love it so much? Why will you go all out for a few extra points? What is the big prize at the end of it all?

'The Trophy' of course, The Pride, The Honour of your house winning back or keeping 'The Trophy' for that week, weekend or short break. The length of the stay is immaterial what counts is the fact that you, your team, 'Your House' did it, you took part, you got the points…. YOU WON!!!

Q) Yes but who gets 'The Trophy'? A) Well no one actually.
Q) No one? A) No, no one.
Q) So what happens to it? A) It moves across the room.
Q) Moves across the room? A) Yes.

OK I can see I am on my own here so let's take a step back to the first night… imagine the page rippling like they do it when they go back in time on the television back….back….back we go to the first night you arrived. The Entertainments Manager has done the welcomes and now it's time to explain the 'House System'

Because they are doing such a great job after reading 'Tales of Superblue' they should be getting a lot of repeat customers who already know how it works and you have indeed actually booked your accommodation to ensure you are in the same house as last time. Whether that house won or not, people stay loyal to a house or odds or evens should the name change (I tell them not to change the name if they can help it though. They can always have **'Superblue house'** sponsored by British Airways this year and **'Superblue house'** sponsored by South Eastern Railways next for example).

Where was I? Oh yes introducing the house system. Well for a start they build up the excitement in the room in their own inimitable fun packed way until you guests are champing at the bit to find out which house you are in and get on with winning those points for that house. I'm not going to spoon feed you all the way now, they can do this in so many ways and they should know how best to do this at their centre using their imagination and own personality.

Then they **Present** the Trophy for the first time that week and announce last week's winning team with a fanfare. This has the effect of guests in that team wanting to keep the trophy on its rightful place on their side of the room and the guests in the losing team determined to take that very same trophy away from them and place it in its new rightful place on their side of the room.

The Entertainments Manager then parades the trophy around the room again with great pomp, ceremony and pageantry finally making a big deal of placing it into last week's winning teams place. The best way of adding to the sense of achievement is to have a small trophy cabinet up on the wall either side of the stage for each team along with their scoreboard. Now the Entertainments Manager has you hooked. You will turn up to events just to make sure someone from your team does and there is no 'Cheating' going on.

I ask Entertainments Managers "Does that all seem a bit much to you?" If the answer is yes I wish them luck in their new career because holiday camp entertainment is not for them. If on the other hand they were excited about the idea I look forward to visiting their camp.

It really is no good going at this one half heartedly, it has to be all or nothing, you guests will only take it to your hearts and join in the spirit of the thing if the Entertainments Manager and their team of 'coats' do. Entertainments Managers and 'coats' must join in, play along, cajole, excite, try to cheat, wind up the other team and generally have complete fun with this concept ALL OF THE TIME!!

I mentioned 'Cheating' a couple of times there and you will know by now that I would never cheat a guest out of anything, let alone hard earned house points and of course you'd be absolutely right I never would. So what do I mean by cheating in relation to house points? Well as part of their 'coat' introductions on the first night they will have told you which team each of the 'coats' are in and they will wear badges etc showing that team throughout the week. They should organise it so that you have a major cheat on each team who will always try to steal points or goad members of the opposition etc but of course always fails. This creates an endless source of fun between you, them and other guests. There are four golden rules here that Entertainments Managers must follow however;

1) Always choose this person very carefully, they must understand and abide by the following 3 rules implicitly.

2) They must always be found out when they try to cheat and never actually obtain any points for their team.

3) All 'cheating' must be overt, in other words must be so obvious to all guests that it is a fun bit of attempting to 'Cheat' and is silly enough that it is doomed to failure.

4) All points that are actually awarded to a guest even in jest must stand. This is especially important if given to children. If points have been given in error during a cheat add more points IN A FUN WAY to the other team. DON'T TAKE POINTS AWAY THAT HAVE BEEN AWARDED.

Don't forget they can deduct general points from a team score as a penalty as described above but taking individually earned points away defeats the entire object of the house system being nothing but another way of supplying you guests with that magical ingredient of your holiday............... **FUN FUN FUN!!**

I was recently at a park in Devon run by a major holiday company where they 'sort of' ran a house system in the evenings and for the children only. While this is a very good way of introducing the young ones to the concept and certainly ensures repeat and indeed their future custom as adult visitors, I do feel they are almost playing at it and missing out on the adults being able to join in and build that all important fun factor and not just in the evenings but throughout the day also. They did use characters as house captains, which is brill for the kids and again instils the brand into them at an early age, obviously weighing up the pros and cons they have decided on this as the best commercial direction for them to take. They can always take this route of course but have to remember it's a long term plan and if they're astute they can still build in sponsorship deals.

HOUSE CAPTAINS

These are very important people in the Entertainments Managers master plan right now. They are absolutely integral to the ongoing and enthusiastic support of the house system. Each captain will need to be a personality that engenders loyalty and tirelessly enthuses about their team. There are three ways of trying to ensure they get the essential house captains of that calibre.

1) One of the 'coats': As I have already said the team will be split into houses so it would be easy for one of them to be a 'House Captain' as well. The upside of this is that the Entertainments Manager knows that personality and therefore can control their exuberance or lack of it.

2) Run a fun adult competition with equal competitors from each house the winning member from each house being 'crowned' the house captain for that week or length of stay. The downside of this is the exact opposite of above. They don't know that personality and so will have to monitor the situation as it goes. The upside is that guests generally like to have one of 'them' as the captain. It feels more like a team effort that way. And less anything to do with the Entertainments Manager or 'coats'.

3) Choose a guest. Seems simple doesn't it and it can be. But the Entertainments Manager must beware of a number of pitfalls including the obvious one if they don't know them. They have no idea about their personality so have no idea what they may or may not do at any given time or in response to any given scenario. At least with a fun comp you and the other guests get a feel for a person. What if they do know them? Well that could be ok because they are not likely to choose someone they don't trust to do a good job for them are they? But the downside of this approach is that they could be accused of cheating for a friend later on. It would also be easy for them to keep picking the same person or people each time they are at that camp but you and other guests will soon get fed up with this.

So whichever way the Entertainments Manager decides to go they will have to keep a watchful eye as the week, or length of stay, unfolds and monitor the captains in particular.

I previously mentioned characters being used as house captains and in my opinion they are fine as figureheads for the children but I honestly believe that nothing can beat those good old human emotions and loyalty, so if they do go down this route this would be my advice. Use the characters as figureheads and choose a human team captain, as above, to engender all the other aspects that can make the 'house point' system so successful.

Ripple *ripple ripple ripple ripple and your drifting, drifting back, drifting back*......and a click of the fingers and you're here.

So that's how the Entertainments Manager starts the week and carries on with that fun system right up until the last night when they put up the final house points of the week and discover that .... Oh my! It's a draw....well how did that happen?

The fact is that it won't always be possible but most weeks the houses will be fairly evenly matched by this point and there are ways of giving a couple of silly points here and there to get you to a draw situation or near enough that either team can still win on the last fun comps of the week that evening. You have to have experienced the electrifyingly tense atmosphere when this occurs to appreciate it. It is an Entertainments Managers finest hour if they can pull it off. It makes your final night one of excitement and unforgettable fun and emotion. Yes it really can be that great!!!

(But I tell them never to do this at the detriment of fair play, and to use their judgement as to whether it's a reasonable thing to do or not).

Then they parade the winning House Captain around the room and place the trophy into the winning cabinet for the last time that week. Present the Captain with his own little trophy...*and the crowd go wild*...cue for a *great party* night to finish with...............
Job done!

A couple of little points I tell Entertainments Managers to bear in mind are:

Keep the scores straight: Guests will *always* be keeping notes of the scores. So make sure that all your competition scores are handed into a central point or person each day by a certain time so they can be added to the score boards that evening.

The only person who can give extra points or take points away as described above should be the Entertainments Manager or their deputy on their day off otherwise the whole thing gets out of hand and descends into a debacle.

Most importantly:

Remember to make sure it is ALWAYS made clear that it is only for fun and that the only real reward at the end of the day is fun fun fun. Never let anyone get so serious that they are spoiling the enjoyment of others and **UNDER NO CIRCUMSTANCES** ever let it descend into a feud and or any kind of violent behaviour. It's a wonderful tool at your disposal so don't lose the right to use it, control it for the sake of everyone.

Now my mature readers will be saying "fantastic memories bring it on" you younger members should be saying "fantastic I want those memories, bring it on". Camp Managers and Owners should be asking why this is not happening at our centres, parks, villages or hotels etc?

If this is all new to you, you will be utterly amazed at yours and your fellow guest's response to it, your support and involvement for comps, tournaments etc. The way you will give a natural cheer or round of applause without constantly being asked for one which really annoys the hell out of me, as an ex Entertainments Manager, never mind you poor holidaymakers. So much so that I cover it later so look out for 'NAFF'.

CHAPTER FIFTEEN

PUTTING ON THEIR OWN SHOWS OR CABARETS

THE OTHER CHAPTER ONE !!!

Well let's be completely honest about it now shall we. In 'Tales of Superblue' experienced and budding Entertainments Managers and 'coats' will have turned straight to this chapter as soon as they got hold of the book.

Well there is nothing wrong with that because, let's face it, for most of them this is what it's all about, the hard work, the exhausting long hours, the constant never-ending smiling, competitions, tournaments, weird and wonderful sports and events they had never even heard of before arriving at a holiday centre, bingo and the myriad of bits and bobs that make up an entertainment programme........for them all this is a means to an end, to get where they really want to be......because for them it's all about *show-time!* Let me assure you that there's absolutely nothing wrong with that nothing whatsoever. **ALL** of the things I have mentioned are so vitally important though, because they **are** what ultimately allows them to get up on that stage and perform, do their thing, strut their funky stuff, sing their heart out, dance their legs off, amaze and bamboozle with their magic, razzle dazzle them and they'll beg you for more, twinkle twinkle little star, the cheers, the applause, the adulation, the audience are on their feet it's a standing ovation, they're going wild....what?..oh...ahum..er..sorry...yes well anyway you get the picture.

Of course this is their motivation and that's perfectly natural so they should embrace it and, as we have discussed, always give the rest of the programme 110% and use it as a platform to proudly announce that they will be on that stage, in that show or performing their own cabaret. I genuinely do mean this, they need to remember you will be getting to know them during the daily events etc and will come to support them all the way. So, if they sell themselves then they can celebrate and repay your support in the best way possible…….. By putting on a show they can be proud of……every time and I do mean *EVERY TIME!!!*

DO IT RIGHT

As I lay here on a sun lounger in my Caribbean paradise in the pouring rain, oh yes it's a monsoon, a constant down pour. Bouncing off of the clear blue shimmering surface of the pool and what a magnificent sight it is, a water ballet with each wonderful droplet, out of the millions that must be falling every second, hitting like a tiny diver just reaching under the surface of this large expanse of its own kind, exerting just enough presence to force a reaction, one that you will have seen many many times before. Yet I bet that you have never stopped and taken any notice of it or even given any thought to the actual beauty of this little event. So next time you see a dripping tap, stop and observe the pretty pearl shaped particle of H_2O fall majestically from the spout and land on the water in the sink or bath. Experience the tiny little bomb burst as an equal amount is forced back up into the air like a minute nuclear explosion followed by the ripple effect. It's incredible to think that something resembling anything with such a terrifyingly devastating force of death and destruction is actually being formed by the liquid of life itself.

But here I am in the Caribbean in the pouring rain, I must be so fed up mustn't I?

Well actually no quite the opposite, remember right at the very beginning of the book where I told you how I had started to write again because of being here….

What?

No?

Oh yes, of course I forgot a lot of you budding Entertainments Managers and 'coats' came straight to this chapter didn't you?

Dear guest please forgive me for a moment while I digress and address this group. You will quickly see that it is ultimately for your benefit.

So 'coats' I do understand why you came here but I would recommend that you nip back and have a look at the chapters that come before this. Everything really will make a whole lot more sense and you will appreciate that, while this chapter is important to you, and rightly so, your whole being as a holiday camp entertainer could very well dictate your success or failure in this aspect and therefore your entire future in showbiz.

You would also have been completely aware by now that I am prone to wandering off the point at times……… as indeed I have just done yet again haven't I? Oh dear… Sorry, where were we then?

Oh yes…. Fed up?

No not at all. It may be pouring with rain but it's warm and sunny at the same time and I am sat here completely mesmerised by this synchronised liquid dance from the heavens being choreographed right before my very own lucky eyes. I feel so privileged to be receiving this fantastic personal show, being performed just for me, well everyone else has scattered for cover, huddled up in bars or watching TV in their rooms. Me? Well for the last half hour I have been happily sat under my coconut palm thatched canopy thinking. Thinking, how this magical display, a natural real life spectacular is my own little moment of peaceful joyful inspiration. It brings back inspiring memories of last night's 'Broadway Show'. Inspiring indeed, in fact one of the main inspirations to start writing again. But of course you know all that now, don't you? Well those of you who have started at the beginning will do anyway.

Far from being fed up, here I am writing with enjoyment in my heart and a new zest for what can be achieved on stage at holiday centres anywhere in the world. So on we go, as the page gets soggier by the minute and the ink begins to smudge, here we go with a subject that really matters to Entertainments Managers and 'coats'. Get it right though, as they do out in this part of the world and they will be amazed at how much it matters to you dear guest too. Done right it is such an emotive medium, done right it is powerful enough to conjure up every emotion imaginable skilfully woven into the very fabric of a single show that masterfully navigates you through a passionate affair with your senses. Laughter, tears, joy, sorrow, romance, pride, nostalgia and at times during your magical journey evoking all sorts of memories, hopes and wishes.

Yes in the right hands a show is so powerful that it can even move a despondent Superblue to start writing about this wonderful subject again.

So here we are at the very point in the book the Entertainments Managers and 'coats' have been waiting for. Putting on their own shows and cabarets and the first thing to say is so obvious it's hardly worth saying. You might as well spell it out in fairy lights on a giant thirty foot chicken suspended from a hot air balloon in the shape of Pavarotti being pulled along by 500 pterodactyls with a purple giraffe at the helm and the whole ensemble accompanied by the sounds of that famous one hit wonder 'It's an obvious thing' by the Obvious Orchestra from Obvious Island just off the coast of Obvioustainia. But for the sake of clarity here goes anyway…..It's THEIR first step to stardom, THEIR chance to shine, THEIR moment of glory so I tell them DON'T WASTE IT!!

There I feel so much better now that's out of the way.

It is nevertheless not as daftly obvious as it may at first seem and you will have a better understanding of how it could affect their future in the chapter 'How to be a Star'

But in this chapter we will be hitting the subject of staging their show or cabaret from some basic standpoints:

1) The guests

2) Entertainment Managers

3) The teams

4) The individual entertainer

5) The support staff

6) The park management or owners

You would probably expect that I would now go on to categorise the chapter to fit these differing viewpoints and needs. Well you wouldn't be alone because that's exactly how I did begin to set it out. It very quickly became evident however that, the needs, requirements and expectations of all six were so inherently entwined and dependent upon one another that each would want, indeed need, to know about the others in order for any show or cabaret performance to be of an acceptable standard…and there is only one acceptable standard…the highest possible…and nothing less will ever do.

That is why you can sit back and just carry on reading whoever you are. Follow the path of bits and bobs as we meander our way through various aspects, necessities, rules and best practices. Be carried away on a journey around the enchanted forest of **show-time** home of the elusive 'stage tree', well you've heard the term 'treading the boards' where do you think the boards come from? Anyway these trees branches all merge in the centre to give a dazzling display of majestic beauty, constantly changing with the seasons to remain alive but always one of nature's perfect shows. Whoever you are you will belong to one of those branches and only by all of you coming together at the right time in the right place with the right attitude and respect for each other will you be able to emulate nature's perfect example. A little like my rain storm, one tiny droplet on its own would have gone completely unnoticed by the world but millions of them together…. *wow what a show.*   So read on now and soak up the advice I give everyone else along the way. You will then understand that, when the branch's meet your tree will be so much stronger, giving you a healthy respect for each other's wants needs and talents. To that end I will give you another look at a direst lift from 'Tales of Superblue' in the hope that by the time you get to the end of the chapter you will not only know the amount of work and effort that has gone into a good show and appreciate it, when they do that for you, but also when and why to complain when they don't. Enjoy the dominance of knowing exactly what I tell them…………

ESTABLISHING CAPABILITIES

Whos?

Well firstly you must know your own, terrifyingly obvious again isn't it? Well of course it is but the temptation is to over egg your talents to impress your new Entertainments Manager or others on the team. But let me warn you straight away that this is the easiest way to make them very unimpressed with you very quickly.

Why?

Well the Entertainments Manager will be relying on this first collective self assessment from each 'coat', sometimes before they even arrive at a centre, when trying to decide what type of shows he or she can attempt to stage with the talent available to them. If you have told them that you can sing or dance to a certain level of competency and they plan or compile a show and build in sophisticated routines based on that information only to discover you can't actually carry a tune or put a few decent steps together at all.....well you fill in the ending of that scenario for yourself. Not a pretty one is it?

So be honest about your strengths and weaknesses, after all you should have passed the audition or at least the interview stage to be chosen to be there. So you have something that that company or individual saw in you. Bring whatever that is to the party and enjoy doing what you are capable of doing at that time. Don't forget your Entertainments Manager should be working with you to develop your skills as your time there progresses. So don't run before you can walk. On the other hand don't hide your light under a bushel either. If you feel you have a strong talent or one that could easily be developed in a short period of time be proud of it and let them know. There is nothing better for an Entertainments Manager than to know exactly what you have to play with when putting your programme together.

One of the highlights of the week, as far as the guests are concerned, are the 'Coats Own' homemade shows. Homemade? Well yes and I'll talk about that more shortly.

It does not so much matter to an Entertainments Manager how many singers and dancers they end up with on the team. What does matter is that they know what strengths they do have and then they should be experienced enough to compile shows based on those strengths at their disposal. Once again this is where a great Entertainments Manager is worth that proverbial weight in gold.

The Entertainments Managers among you should be daring with your staff shows, and I will come to other staff shortly too. Look for the unusual in your team, don't be blinkered and just stage shows full of singing and dancing, particularly if you only have a couple of 'coats' that can actually carry this off. All this serves to do is over expose those 'coats' and put the others in their shadow. It does not make for a happy team and the guests get fed up with the same people constantly performing too. Guests love variety, particularly in the staff shows. If you do have someone who is adapt at choreography then you absolutely should be using them to the fullest so that you are being adventurous when you do put on those all singing all dancing numbers. But also look for magicians (often found in the children's entertainment team) comedians, baton twirlers, jugglers or even speciality acts such as ventriloquists, escapologists or plate spinners for example, in fact just about any talent that you can put on a stage and make it entertaining. That good old furtive imagination of yours should be working overtime in relation to using these 'coats'. I have to say I have seen some pretty ingenious ways of slotting the most unusual of talents into a show and making it interesting and entertaining. I am pleased to say I myself have had my share of little brainstorms in this department. The amount and variety of shows you should be putting on should give you plenty of scope for inspiration. For example lassoing in a country and western show, escapology in sketch or Thriller show, magicians in a Harry Potter number….oh I could go on all day but you get the idea. Once again the only real limits on who you can utilise or where to utilise them are the limits of your own creativity.

Never rule out utilising staff from other departments, they can in fact be a godsend at smaller parks. Just because someone has arrived at your holiday centre via a route other than joining the entertainments team, it does not mean that they aren't talented. Remember talent comes in many forms too so don't just be looking for those singers again. A volunteer is generally worth using in one capacity or another. I have had a laundry lady that loved costume making, handymen that adored nothing better than creating stage sets in their spare time and an arcade manager that came up with the most amazing special effects. Sometimes they just want to be involved but have no natural or learnt talent, well that's no problem either. Be grateful for their enthusiasm and make them feel appreciated by asking them to assist in some role or other. What that transpires to be will depend largely on what they are capable of and what you need doing, to be honest, but with a little thought I am sure you will place the right person in the right role. As I have indicated above many people are more than happy to be taking part in an offstage activity, which could be anything from spotlight operator to costume changer or from stage hand to sound and lights. Of course there will be those that will want nothing more than to be performing on that stage with the team. The best bit of advice I can give you here is simply never rule anyone out before you have given them a chance because sometimes the most unlikely of people end up being your biggest stars…literally. Always allow them to audition for you when guests and other team members or staff are not around, just in case they are not quite as good as they may think they are. It's never in anybody's interest to find yourself in an embarrassing situation particularly for that individual so keep it as private as possible. If they do turn out to be…..shall we say a little over optimistic in their hope for fame…..do let them down gently and in a way that doesn't shatter their self confidence and then encourage them to stay enthusiastic about entertainment and take part in one of the other tasks we have talked about. Remember to always approach their manager before you agree to even look at what they have to offer. As I have already described in an earlier chapter you can cause a lot of unnecessary bad-feeling between departments and your fellow managers if you take their staff on without this courtesy being observed.

Staff stars!!!...... oh yes there really are some undiscovered major talents amongst those other departments so don't be snooty about the fact they are not a 'coat', in fact you should never put yourself or team on a pedestal, your just setting yourself and them up for a fall and people will actively seek to knock you off of it....and hard. You should lead by example and be open and sociable with the rest of the people that work there with you. They do a brill job too you know and if it wasn't for their hard, sometimes not so glamorous, work you would not be able to enjoy your privileged position on the entertainments team. So show them respect and be grateful to them. I learnt very early on not to get bogged down by the 'Hi-De-Hi Peggy Syndrome' and good job I did too because I have had the pleasure of working with lovely people from all sorts of departments in all sorts of roles who so enjoyed just being part of it all. And then there were the stars.....I have had bar-staff, shop assistants, people from all aspects of the catering department etc who have gone on to have careers as performers in the entertainment industry. A case in point is a lifeguard and a really nice geezer who went on to appear on New Faces where Nina Mishcow loved him........

THE SHOW
Now that you have established what talent base you have, and remember that includes your technical support too. You can begin to create your masterpiece. Do utilise all at your disposal e.g. sound & lights, graphics, cartoons, PowerPoint etc. As I have already said many centres do actually employ someone with these skills to be part of the entertainments team these days. But if this is not the case where you are......trust me it's not too difficult in this age of hi-tech computer wizardry to enhance your stage presentation to maximum effect with little effort. We will cover this a bit more in stage management in fact quite a bit of many chapters do cross over into stage management so it should all fit together quite nicely in the end. I would like to claim responsibility for this and say that I have cleverly interwoven this integral part of holiday centre entertainment in and out of those chapters that required it's presence.....I would like to but the truth is it

just naturally occurs, oh well I feel a bit clever today anyway…I have just finished a jigsaw puzzle and it's only taken me six months, that's not bad seeing as it says for 2 to 3 yrs on the box…... Anyway you now have your talent base so time to get creative and I am not going to apologise for regurgitating one of my favourite sayings and you can probably see it coming a mile off but it's just so so true. You are only limited to what shows you do produce by the limits of your own imagination. Think big (you can always scale it down but start with a great idea), think professionally (there is no compromise here), think variety, think razzamatazz, think spectacular, think comedy, think old favourites, think innovative, think original, think novel, think tangential but above all think about entertaining your guests. Never lose sight of the fact that that's what we are there for, to entertain our guests. So think about all the afore mentioned and then make it entertaining for the audience you are playing too. It's no good getting all excited because you have put together a really great heavy rock type show and then wonder why you have been hauled into the bosses office the next morning because the sequence dancers that have taken over the centre for that weekend really didn't think it was their cup of tea, now is it? I am sure that there are sequence dancers that love a bit of Ozzy Osborne but you get the message. It's not about what you like so make sure you are aware of the type of guests you are expecting and play to that strength. Of course most of the time you will be catering for a mixed family audience so no excuse not to make the best of it.

THEMES?

I have gone on about variety, I know, but that does not mean you can't base a show on a central theme. Indeed as we have discussed you can centre a complete day or evening around a theme with the show as the great crescendo of a finish to it all. I was just sat here thinking about how many themed shows I have put on or been a part of over the years, it is quite staggering when you stop and take stock of them all. There have been so many, country and western, variety hall, rock and roll, round the world, 70's, pantos, nursery rhymes, musicals, comedy, sketches, thriller, horror, battle of the sexes, films, television, events in history……boy-oh-boy the list is endless. I have seen some great ones of late too so by all means carry on using the many tried and tested themes that are out there and do visit other centres to get inspiration from time to time but please make it just that….inspiration. Be original, creative, and ground-breaking, take the theme and work it. You should never resort to exactly copying someone else's show or routine it should be yours or a collaboration of you and your teams ideas even if the inspiration came from elsewhere.

CONTENT

Do think about all subject matter and satisfy yourself that it fit's the criteria. Never let a routine or staff cabaret go live on stage until you have seen it for yourself and are happy with it. Then if it is the wrong choice for that audience, well it's down to you. Don't just think that's a catchy little pop song or rap, listen to the words even look the group or artiste up on the internet etc if you don't know anything about them.....

Rule of thumb.......if you're not sure........don't let it go on.

Always better safe than sorry.

M = Appropriate material

V = In that venue

T = For that time

SKETCHY ADVICE

I will quickly mention here that if you are going to work abroad, you could do yourself a big favour and learn as many sketches as you can or even create new ones before you leave. If you are in Spain for example many guests from European countries, Germany in particular, love the sketch show format. It also allows you to supply comedy entertainment, to a point, even if there is a language barrier.

COSTUMES

It always amazes me when people skimp on this aspect of the biz. Please don't be one of them because it is so important to the success of your shows. Many of the larger centres do supply costumes, so if you are at such a centre for goodness sake do take care of them; they are a vital tool of your trade. I was at a centre recently that had fabulous costumes and was pleasantly surprised to find out that it was the head house keeper who made them as a hobby, ooh the nostalgia.

If you're at a small or independent park you may be lucky enough to find one of these wonderful people but to be honest they are a dying breed and unfortunately everything costs these days. That's why it is always worth considering becoming one of those enterprising entrepreneurial types like myself and decide to have 'back up' costumes of your own just in case. You will have to buy your own wardrobe which can be a very costly affair, it has to be said, but there are ways of getting bargains from costumiers, theatrical outlets and specialist sales or auctions and build up a nice little collection to work from. I am always on the lookout at car boot sales or even in second hand or charity shops where you can often find a period piece for a few bob. I have a loft full of assorted costumes including sailors, clowns, cowboys and Indians, cats, ghost buster jump suits, cops and robbers, shimmering shiny skirts, trousers and tops, a multitude of hats and headgear there is even a complete set of ostrich feather showgirl outfits up there. The payback is that you never know when you might just get that offer of a lucrative job somewhere and having your own costumes and props to go straight in and get on with it can be a godsend as indeed it proved to be for me a couple of times over the years.

QUALITY

I still have fond memories of my first season at Pontins and that fabulous Entertainments Manager, Richard Walsh, getting us to sit in the sunshine sewing sequins onto all sorts of silk shirts, trousers, skirts etc etc. It took hours upon hours of fiddly painstaking work but the end result was quite staggering. He would not let any item through his stringent personal quality control unless it reached the standard that you would expect from the best professional suppliers. It did mean however that we had hands on input into the production and quality of our own shows from the very outset while producing costumes that looked brilliant on stage at a fraction of the cost.

Why share this little nugget with you? It's not as if today's entertainment teams will be doing this now is it? No I doubt it very much but whatever input they do have into the costumes for any show or performance the main principles will always remain the same. The first thing to say, I suppose, is that they need to be able to costume anything they intend to put on the stage. A palpable statement of course but it means being realistic in the first instance.

For example can they afford what they have in mind? Is it feasible to make or buy what it would need to stage that number in a professional manner? Can someone actually perform wearing it? These are all blatantly obvious when you stop to think about it but you would be surprised at the number of times I have seen one or more of these issues scupper what promised to be a great show just through lack of forethought.

As I mentioned above some large companies have corporate costuming of corporate shows but many of the entertainment teams at independent sites for example, will be expected to provide this on a budget. Hence the story above, they can costume very well by choosing the right numbers, routines, sketches for their shows and then buying what they need for them wisely. A good way of achieving this is to source the material, sequins, ribbon etc etc and seek out a seamstress in the local area. Shop around is my best advice to them in this matter on both the material front and the person. The Internet and The Stage are always at hand but they could do as I did and go and ask their local fancy dress shop where they source their outfits from, they may be pleasantly surprised at what they can get for a reasonable price. On one lucky occasion it actually turned out that the lady who owned the shop was a seamstress and she costumed my entire summer season shows magnificently and very affordably. Now I have mentioned cost quite a lot in this section and it would be stupid of me not to acknowledge that this is a big constraint on many of the teams and Entertainment Managers as indeed it was for me when I started out. What I would urge them to do in this respect is to speak to their park, resort, village, centre or hotel managers, show them this book, and try to elicit as much dosh as they can from them to buy what they need. Explain that they want to put quality shows on so as to keep their guests in the camp to spend money at their bars, restaurants, casinos and shops etc. Once they have done their best there and they know how much they are getting my advice is to then to rethink their planned shows. Why? Because they may just have to re-adjust those plans one way or the other.

It may be that they have been given more money than they expected and can consider even more dramatic numbers than they had planned.........er well yes that could happen.

It is more likely however that they have not been allocated as much as they were relying on and have to think a little cleverly on how to make it stretch to cover all the numbers etc. I know I have pointed out ways of accomplishing this feat but let me put a word of caution in here. It is always far better for an Entertainment Manager to cut a number or two from their show and spread the cost on the other routines, than to keep the same amount and compromise on the quality of their costumes. There is nothing worse than a half dressed half hearted attempt at staging a number it just comes across as tacky and tacky is the last thing they should ever want to portray. So whether they are lucky enough to have great financial support, a less than bulging purse or even making some of thier own costumes they must remember to dress their shows to a professional standard. Pizzazz, colour, glitter, sequins razzmatazz feathers, headdress's etc etc all a little cliché I know but all so necessary when it comes to giving you guests the best West End type production possible. It goes without saying that not all of their routines will be glitzy, a number from Les Miserables for example, but they will still demand that big stage presentation.

ALWAYS THINK HEALTH AND SAFETY

I do urge Entertainment Managers and 'coats' to please consider all aspects of safety when they make or buy any costume or associated accessories. For instance are they fire safe? Are there any loose items that may cause tripping or strangulation? Eliminate sharp or jagged edges? Always know the makers recommendations for specialised items and ensure they are adhered to, for example the amount of time a character head may be worn without detrimental effect. This is not meant to be an exhaustive list but rather a base on which to get them thinking health and safety around this subject.

PROPS

How do you think obtaining, making or buying props differs from costumes?

It doesn't? Well to be fair that's about the size of it. In fact if they treat props with the same deference as they do the costumes they won't go far wrong. Now I am not going to insult you by spoon feeding you on what props they should consider having with certain numbers or shows etc that comes back to that good old furtive imagination of theirs. But the same limitations do apply as with your costumes and health and safety most definitely carries at least the same significance too.

They ought to try to maximise their spending power again in the same ways but this time add brick-a-brack shops etc for places to find that unusual item at a bargain price and the maintenance, arcade and catering departments to the list of places to try for bits and bobs and most importantly people to assist or make things for them.

BACKING

You will know by now that I am whole heartedly of the opinion that every centre should have at least some sort of resident live music in its venues. Unfortunately this is increasingly becoming the exception rather than the rule. So this will be one of the first things to establish if the Entertainment Manager is to produce their own shows. If they are to require backing soundtracks they are going to be limited by a number of things. For example: what tracks are available, do they match the capabilities of the entertainments team, what keys are they in, are they allowed to reproduce them. These are just the basics that they must be considering at a centre without live backing. By far and away the best way to overcome this is to pay for professional backing tracks or have some made for them but we are of course back to that old conundrum of cost again aren't we? I do add a little ray of sunshine here though when I remind Entertainment Managers that once bought they are theirs to use at other centres in the future. There are without a doubt many karaoke type tracks available at varying levels and some of very dubious quality indeed. By now you will know my feelings on Entertainment Managers or 'coats' putting on anything less than the most professional it can possibly be for you. So I will leave this one with you, you can decide what action to take (i.e. How much noise you're are going to make and how high up the chain you are going to make it) if you're getting anything but that!!!

I remind Entertainment Managers to bear in mind that whether they use live music or recorded backing performing rights will need to be paid for but don't panic I did cover this in 'Tales of Superblue' and will mention it in a later chapter just so you know what all the fuss is about.

KEEP MUSIC LIVE

Even though I am not a musician myself, I have to be honest, this is a bit of a soapbox subject of mine I am afraid. Quite simply there is nothing that can ever compare to live entertainment of any kind at a holiday park and absolutely nothing, nought, nil, zilch, zero comes even close to live music and when it comes to backing for your shows….well what do you think?

This is where Entertainment Managers having a good working relationship with their colleagues comes into its own. Much of the time they can set really great shows between themselves and the resident musicians. Who will, most likely, have a lot of the music they will want in their repertoire. They will be able to translate this into the necessary keys for their team and allow them to keep the shows fresh by changing numbers at regular intervals or as new members join the team.

SHEET MUSIC

If their resident musicians do transcribe music I would seriously advise Entertainment Managers to pay for this service. There really is no better or more cost effective way to obtain a complete set for a number of different instruments. It's also worth having a copy of all the numbers in the show, no matter the keys because they can have them transposed easily enough and have them in their possession when they move on. For guests and 'coats' I sincerely recommend that you buy a copy of any numbers that have been put into your key, often for the talent show etc, and even more so if they have been orchestrated especially for you.

Please please please don't take this service for granted if you're lucky enough to have musicians that will do this for you, be grateful be very grateful. They don't have to do it unless it's in their contract, which you will find it almost never is. This means they are generally doing it in their own time and for 'goodwill' so I tell Entertainment Managers to be grateful and show their gratitude, not just in the financial sense but more crucially in the way they treat them. It all adds up to premier all round happy, professional and value for money holiday entertainment for you to enjoy.

It is always advisable however to have music for a show or cabaret spot when you turn up at a centre whether you are a guest wanting to enter the talent show an Entertainments Manager or 'coat'. It can then be transposed into the right keys. To this end there are many outlets that supply sheet music around the country and naturally there's the internet but I always find Foyles of London an exceptional source of sheet music for just about any genre you could think of. Use whatever source is right for you but here are their contact details in case it helps:

They have other stores across the country but good starting points are

Foyles

113-119 Charing Cross Road

London

WC2H 0EB

Tel: 020 7437 5660

Foyles Book Department
Selfridges
The Dome
Trafford Centre
Manchester
M17 8DA

Foyles at Selfridges

London:Tel: 0800 123400 ext. 13678 or 13670.

Manchester: Tel: 0800 123400 ext. 41157

www.**foyles**.co.uk

And I must not forget the great Chappell's of Bond Street either even if their address is

152-160 Wardour Street, London

W1F 8YA

They supply all sorts of instruments etc

But there direct line for sheet music is 0207 432 4400 (select option 1)

REHEARSALS

Stating the obvious is obviously an obvious occupational hazard when writing some books obviously I don't do this intentionally but it's obvious that sometimes you can't help but talk about a subject without....well...being obvious. Obviously they will need to rehearse their show but to what standard? There is only one standard they should ever be striving to attain, nothing less will ever be good enough, they **MUST NEVER** put a show on stage until they have rehearsed and rehearsed and rehearsed and reached....**perfection**. I have to be honest here and say that if this is something that is not automatically obvious to an Entertainment Manager or 'coat' or they are happy to get it to an ok standard and say "oh that will do" they are most definitely in the wrong job. When and where to rehearse varies greatly but is something that needs to be a 'well thought out' detail when setting their programme. It's absolutely useless to rehearse a show to perfection and then just let it run for weeks on end without taking a look at it and at least rehearsing a number or two from time to time. It may be their 100th time of performing it and they are probably getting very blasé about the whole thing but its tonight's audience's first time of seeing it and you deserve the same excitement, exuberance and energy that their first night audience received. So they should have built in rehearsal times in their programme. Not only to freshen up existing numbers to keep it all tight but add new ones or even change a complete show from time to time. This injects enthusiasm back into the team and stimulates the creative and performing juices. Us entertainers love nothing more than learning something new to show off our talents it's what makes us….us.

When I first started out we used to rehearse when the guests had gone to bed, yes honestly, we would work all day and at 1 am be there ready and waiting to put another 2 or 3 hours in on a number or two. Especially if the Entertainments Manager was unhappy with the performance of anyone in a show, it really was a very serious matter and rightly so. But as I say they just need to think smart and incorporate rehearsal time into their working rota. Rehearsals should never be a chore it's another fun part of their chosen trade. Anyone that moans about this should just remember there are people in factories getting paid less than they are, or even unemployed in these tough times!!! They would do well to remember how lucky they are and give it their all in rehearsals and enjoy……….
show-time.

STAGE MANAGEMENT

Of course a large part of their productions will obviously be down to stage management and, as I say, some centres employ specific people to do the job but many Entertainments Managers and 'coats' will yet again need to be a Jack of all trades in this respect but we will cover this in a chapter still to come.

Staging Your Own Cabaret

If you are an aspiring cabaret performer or intend to use a cabaret performance as a platform to showcase your talents and move onto greater things such as the West End stage, TV or films all of the above advice will be equally constructive for you. Eg; Know your capabilities, M.V.T. dress appropriately, utilise props wisely and rehearse rehearse rehearse etc etc etc.

If you are considering beginning this journey as a 'Coat' (which by the way is a great place to start so long as you choose wisely, and yes we cover how to do that later too) you will also be uniquely placed in that you don't have to travel from club to club, theatre to theatre or holiday centre to holiday centre to watch, listen and learn from already established cabaret artistes…….they actually come to you! So don't waste one second of this on tap resource. Observe, digest, critique, dissect, scrutinise, analyse, and absorb as much as you can from them. Pick out what you think would work for you and your act, discard what you don't like and work the principal ideas into your performance. Don't just copy someone's act…….you will come a cropper!!! Use your own personality.

Entertainments Managers should always vet an act before allowing a 'coat' to perform live to an audience. They should be looking for the suitability of that act for that venue (M.V.T.) and constantly be looking for ways to enhance the 'coats' performance so that both the 'coat' and their guests benefit from their knowledge and experience.

CORPORATE SHOWS

I can just imagine you sitting there thinking......what's that?......corporate shows?..... not allowed to make your own up?.......well yes and there are as always pros and cons to such matters. The pros are quite simple, your entertainers should have been taught great dance routines by a first rate chorographer, been supplied spectacular costumes and props and if done correctly this can be very affective. The cons, for me, are that a great deal of the time these days it's all on disc so no band is required, a show always lacks something without live music, I also find that because some of these are churned out like a factory production line those delivering the end product find it a little soulless and that of course shows through to the audience. But as I say, done well and kept fresh, **being performed by the resident 'coats',** they have their place and don't forget this does not stop them putting on their own cabarets of course.

VISITING ROAD SHOWS

However these are totally different kettles of fish! And on the whole I *HATE* them!!

There that was a bold statement wasn't it? Well yes it was but I genuinely don't like them. This of course will not be popular in some quarters...particularly with those making money from them........

But I am entitled to my opinion and having spoken to a large number of guests just like yourself over the years and again particularly those at that holiday park I was so disappointed with at the beginning of the book, where there was no resident band, no real talent in the entertainments team and the only real form of entertainment apart from a visiting cabaret a couple of times in two weeks was the ramshackle, second rate, poor excuse for organised entertainment of so called 'Visiting Road Shows'. Which I was to learn, consisted of a group of last year's 'coats' who believed they were now mega stars. However the awful production, content, costuming and lack of talent was, only matched if not actually outdone by the unprofessional, ignorant and downright rudeness of those alleged performers. I watched in absolute disbelief and anger on many occasions as they fumbled their way through routine after routine in clothes (and I do mean ordinary clothes not what I consider constitutes costumes) that had quite clearly had had no care taken over them still bearing battle trophies from previous outings such as things written, in chalk, on the back of jackets etc.

Presumably they found this all very amusing??? I found it wholly distasteful and insulting to the profession.

Rudeness? Yes they treated their audience with utter contempt, remember I was part of that audience so I know what I was feeling, and as I say, discussed it with many others at the time. They were quite simply there for their own egos, I would not mind so much if they deserved to have one.....but they didn't, they messed about amongst themselves on stage, it was all a big joke when one of them got it wrong AGAIN! They strutted about as if the world should look up to them. If only they knew what I, other guests and the staff in that showroom actually thought of them.

As a member of a paying audience you have the right to expect an advertised touring troupe taking the place of live bands, cabarets and a 'talented' entertainments team (if there is one) to be outstanding 'top notch' entertainment. They should be professional, polite and worthy of your money. Unfortunately all that I saw at this and some other centres in the past few years was no more than cost cutting garbage.

Ok there's a bit of letting off steam there but it serves the purpose of highlighting to management and holiday companies that you and your fellow guests actually resent being treated in this manner. You will support the resident entertainments team when things go a little awry and will even appreciate somewhat less than sophisticated props or scenery because you know and like them. You know how hard they have worked the rest of the time before getting up on that stage and you know the team respect you too. I have been involved and performed in travelling shows that incorporate the resident entertainments team that have worked well on some levels. But to be honest I will always have my reservations until I know how much they are designed to support the resident team and who is putting them together etc.

It is important to acknowledge that there are many great professional 'Road Shows' on the circuit and I will not insult your intelligence by describing them. It's enough to know and recognise that a GOOD road-show, that does NOT purport to be anything other than a standalone cabaret event, whether for a couple of hours or a complete evening is exactly that and in no way short changes you or other guests.

There are numerous formats that your Entertainments Manager and 'coats' can utilise and again the only limitations are that of their own imagination!

Below you will find a few examples I laid out for them in 'Tales of Supedrblue' and as you will see the topics are endless. But with a basic a start as I have given them to work from you surely must be getting magnificent shows by now.........aren't you?

For instance:

VARIETY SHOW
Utilising the talent pool available to them......simple ah?

COUNTRY AND WESTERN
There are hundreds of up to date numbers to choose from of course but a fun little family show where they can add a lot of comedic sketches to tell a story throughout would be something like this-
1) She'll be coming around the mountain
2) The Deadwood stage
3) Raindrops are falling on my head
4) Black hills of Dakota
5) I'm just a girl who can't say no
6) Anything you can do I can do better
7) There a hole in my bucket
8) Achey brakey heart
9) Billy don't be a hero
10) 3 wheels on my wagon
11) Wandering star
11) Deep in the heart of Texas
12) I wish I was in Dixie

AROUND THE WORLD

Well they can literally go anywhere they like with this one

Costumes, scenery, special effects and a splattering of comedy can have you searching for your passport and sun cream

Oh my, another endless list to choose from but just off the top of my head…Now let's see….

1) We're all going on a summer holiday (good old Sir Cliff) 2) I'll go where the music takes me 3) From Russia with love 4) Born in the USSR 5) America (West side story) 6) New York New York 7) I'm a lumberjack and I'm OK (Monty python) 8) Do you know the way to San Jose? 9) Haitian Divorce (Steeley Dan) 10) Loco in Acapulco 11) Rio 12) Barcelona 13) England Swings 14) Slow boat to China 15) Japanese girl 16) Turning Japanese (The Vapors) 17) Africa (Toto) 18) Down under (Men at work) 19) Tie me kangaroo down 20) My boomerang won't come back 21) Cuba (Gibson Brothers) 22) Don't cry for me Argentina 23) Zorba the Greek 24) Sitting on the dock of the bay 25) Sailing 26) Leaving on a jet plain 27) London calling (The clash) 28) Caribbean queen (Billy ocean) 29) The Can Can 30) We are the world……………Oh so much world so little time!

That just gives you an idea of what they can achieve if they put their mind to it, I have literally just sat here and typed what came into my head re that one.

WEST END OR BROADWAY

Again the worlds their lobster isn't it

I will try to do it again, straight from my head but also try to instantly chuck a running order together that will be vibrant, fun, colourful, lively, flowing and very very entertaining

So here goes……how about

1) Let me dance for you

2) Fever

3) Memories

4) Star maker

5) Razzle Dazzle

6) Nothing like a dame

7) Beauty and the beast

8) Circle of life

9) Send in the clowns

10) Your never fully dressed without a smile

11) Don't laugh at me

12) There no business like show business

13) Its not where you start it's where you finish

14) Side by side

Not bad huh?

No I don't think so, not for just rummaging the little grey cells for a moment or two

So imagine what they should be coming up with after giving it some real thought

There is so much fabulous materiel out there too

Again off the top of my head let's quickly name a few shows with classics in them:

West side story, Cats, Oz, South Pacific, My fair lady, Chitty Chitty Bang Bang, Beauty and the beast, Annie, Oliver, Grease, The sound of music, High school musical, Saturday night fever, We will rock you , Mamma Mia, Tommy, Lion king, Mary poppins, Phantom of the opera, Little shop of horrors, Moulin Rouge, Cabaret, Wicked, Les Miserables, Spamalot, Chicago....................

Oh somebody stop me!

I could go on forever but that's just a taster of what they should be considering.

FILMS

Endless fun, endless possibilities just like the West End shows above....they just have to go for it!

ROCK AND ROLL

Well the possibilities for a fast paced up beat colourful show are infinite here

So I will leave you to ponder over that one!

DISCO

The colour, the fab music, the clothes, the campness and the memories and oh what great memories of the 70's in particular.

They can produce this in so many different ways

A history of

70's

80's

I can't wait to visit and see what they are doing with it

THRILLER

One to have enormous fun with

Start with Michael Jackson's timeless classic

Then I would take you guests on a wonderfully comedic scary musical journey

Monster mash

Time Warp

Phantom of the opera

Any number from little shop of horrors

This house is haunted (Alice Cooper)

I put a spell on you (Screaming J Hawkins)

Witch Queen of New Orleans (Redbone)

Men in black

Ghost town (The specials)

Ghost busters

Well you get the idea, your Entertainments Managers and 'coats' just need to have fun with it and you will too

I do of course tell Entertainments Managers to keep any show that they produce professional, slick, rehearsed, choreographed to perfection with great scenery and stage management and then they can have as much fun as they like

HISTORY OF THE WORLD

Oh I wish I was putting a show together right this very minute

All you have to do is consider this topic for a millisecond to get excited about it

Just take all that I have said up until now, the counties, the themes, the comedy, the costumes, the scenery etc

But with the added dimension of time................Wow oh wow oh wow

I won't even get started on this or we will be here all day

They could begin with Dr Who for instance

He travels back to......

Oh I have to control myself

They on the other hand don't have to.....so I sincerely hope they have worked a great one out for you to enjoy on this fabulous holiday that you and your family are surely having, now that you have put them straight on what you expect for your money!

COPS AND ROBBERS

They will be like a kid in a sweet shop here

There is just so much great stuff to pick from

Jail house rock

The heat is on (Beverly 's cop)

Gee officer Krupke (West side story)

Pink panther

Murder by numbers (The police)

Green green grass of home (Tom Jones)

Folsom prison blues (Jonny Sach)

Tie a yellow ribbon round the old oak tree

I Fought the Law and the law won (Bobby Fuller Four, and the Clash)

Chain gang (Sam Cooke)

The laughing policeman

Policeman's song (Pirates of Penzance)

Mumma take this badge from me (Eric Clapton)

Oh I went and did it again didn't I? Sorry just can't help myself, OK then I will just move right along now then.

MOTOWN

As much as I adore Motown music on this occasion I am simply using it as a header They can choose any genre of music they want and happily build a great show around it

---

Motown though is one I would personally have in my armoury because it contains an abundance of all the essentials that we have spoken about up until now plus the music, musicians and artistes are just wonderful.

BOY & GIRL BANDS

Speaks for itself really

Not one of my favourites I have to admit

But if they have enough talented 'coats' to carry it off, why not

They can engineer a double wammy here though

With either bands or famous artistes they can produce an interactive show where you, the audience vote on the best performance

They can then call it 'Battle of the Bands' or 'Fame Face-Off' or similar and there you have another little winner......oh I'm on a roll now

SKETCH SHOW

If you are holidaying abroad your Entertainments Managers will need to have a couple of these under their belt due to the language barrier and because European counties simply love them!

There are numerous sketches that are old favourites

Such as:

The lamp post

The Airplane propeller

The doctor's office

Rubber balloons

Caught in bed with wife (not rude at all)

Give back borrowed clothes (compere)

The rope

These probably mean nothing to you at the moment but look out for them your Entertainments Managers should know and be using them and loads more besides

CHILDREN'S SHOWS

Now I am not going to insult you by stating the obvious

But I tell Entertainments Managers to just construct good wholesome funny, colourful shows for the little ones.

In this day and age of children's TV being such big business and a new children's or family film hitting the screens every few months they have no excuse for failing on this front. They just have to make sure, like any production, they have the correct permission to use any characters such as Bob the builder etc

PANTO

Almost the same as children's Shows really except they can get all sorts of humour in there,

They can use one of the old favourites Mother Goose, Cinderella, Captain Hook etc or write their own, or have one written for them

They must keep it very family friendly however

COMEDY NUMBERS

It is all very well them having a team of talented vocalist, but just throwing one song after another at an audience is not producing a show, and you will very soon get bored with it...No matter how good the singers are!

They need to construct a show that travels along, intertwines, tells a story, brings a tear to your eye, makes you laugh, scream or whatever......but construct a show they must!

Comedy is a marvellous tool and in my opinion, almost, no show should be without its lighter moments. They may not seem so obvious at first but I used to get a laugh by subtly introducing people in numbers the audience would not expect to see them in such as the life guards and gym assistants performing a fun version of ballet (swan lake always hits the funny bone)

Any number of staff members, in skits like

The ugly duckling

Little white bull

Puff the magic dragon

(All of the above can be performed properly for the kids show too of course)

Reading the news (in Two Ronnies type tribute)

Always look on the bright side of life

I'm a lumberjack and I'm ok

I even had a ham fisted, accident prone, DJ bounce a ball to the Harlem Globe Trotters tune for 1 minute one season in Spain. He was all over the place and couldn't even get that right. But because the guests all knew and loved him it brought the house down!

Comedy comes in all shapes and forms not just stand up, in fact the sketch shows are nothing but well honed comedic tales one after the other. So Entertainments Managers should look to use some of these sketches and treat their comedy numbers, sketches or segments with as much respect as they do their best vocal performance, which do you think you will remember the most?

I did have a little debate with myself regarding whether or not to talk about the next two types of show. I came to the conclusion that if I don't I am denying you the chance to make up your own mind about them. Therefore just so that you are aware of their existence and what they are all about I will touch on the 'Old Tyme' Music Hall and ENSA shows. If they are not your Entertainments Managers cup of tea and they don't think it's your cup of tea either then fine, they can leave them be.

But here they are so you can make up your own mind:

OLD TYME & MUSIC HALL

I've not seen one of these staged for some time now, It's another one I had a lot of fun with. A master of ceremonies always cleverly strings the thing together for comedic effect using very long or unusual words he has looked up in the dictionary to describe a variety of acts. A lot of the numbers have humour at their core too!
I would probably do something like:

1) Old Bull and Bush
2) On mother Kelly's doorstep
3) Heart of my heart
4) Bye bye blackbird
5) My old man said "follow the band"
6) They tried to tell us we're too young
7) Dream dream dream
8) You made me love you
9) Lambeth walk
10) Maybe it's because I'm a Londoner

11) If you were the only girl in the world

12) You are my sunshine

13) When you're smiling

14) Get me to the church on time

15) Waiting at the church

16) Lily of Laguna

17) By the light of the silvery moon

18) Underneath the arches

19) What a lovely bunch of coconuts

20) Mumma he's making eyes at me

Or a combination of those and many others like

Burlington Birtie – Sisters - Any old iron - Don't bring Lulu - Five foot two eyes of blue - Baby face - Couple of swells - Daddy won't buy me a bow-wow - I'm Henry the 8th I am - Sweet little dicky bird - Daisy

Oh I could go on and on but I hope this list has intrigued some of your Entertainments Managers enough to give it thought and have a go especially if they're at an all adult centre.

E.N.S.A OR DADS ARMY

The Entertainments National Service Association or ENSA was an organisation set up in 1939 by Basil Dean and Leslie Henson to provide entertainment for British armed forces personnel during World War II. ENSA operated as part of the Navy, Army and Air Force Institutes. It was superseded by Combined Services Entertainment (CSE) which now operates as part of the Services Sound and Vision Corporation (SSVC)

I am proud to say I have worked for these entertaining our troops abroad and hope to do so again in the near future.

For those of you that had no idea about the numbers in the Old Time Music Hall show these will be just as mysterious to you. They are basically feel good songs or morale boosters during the wars. Again with the right working, costumes and poignant use I would pull an unusual and moving show out of the bag. Not forgetting that humour was also widely used in those good bad old days. So I may centre my production round, something like: 1) Goodbye Dolly Grey 2) Pack up your troubles 3) It's a long way to

Tipperary 4) Run rabbit run 5) This is the army MR Jones 6) Bless them all 7) Roll out the barrel 8) Siegfield line 9) Who do you think you are kidding Mr Hitler? 10) When Irish eyes are smiling 11) I belong to Glasgow 12) We'll keep a welcome in the hillside 13) Keep the home fires burning 13) Land of hope and glory 14) Rule Britannia

If your Entertainments Managers are going to give either this or the 'Old Tyme' music hall a go it is a good idea for them to hand out song sheets or have the words on a screen so that you the audience can join in.

By the time this book comes out, what I am about to tell you will be history. But oh boy what a historical moment it is for entertainment. I have just had the honour of being one of a couple of billion people to watch the Beijing Olympics closing ceremony live. I have sat for about half an hour with tears in my eyes taking in all that astounding colour, precision, drama, love, warmth, fire, passion, hard work, choreography, dedication, stage management on a mammoth scale, acrobatic wonder, bravery, beauty, creativity and history in the making. I can honestly say that that breathtaking awe inspiring extravaganza is the second most magnificent piece of theatre I have ever witnessed in my life, only being surpassed by the Beijing Olympics opening ceremony. If any Entertainments Managers truly want to know how to put on a great show they should get the DVD of these two events and watch them over and over again until they feel it, until they get it, until nothing less than that will do. Then start to think about putting their shows and cabarets on. They will of course only be able to work to the limits supplied to them but if they remember all that we have spoken about and do the very best they can….but with the fire and passion in their sole that those men and women had and be true to themselves, their 'coats' and most importantly of all *YOU,* they will justly deserve the accolades when they bring the house down!!!

CHAPTER SIXTEEN

STAGE MANAGEMENT

"Perhaps, therefore, ideal stage managers not only need to be calm and meticulous professionals who know their craft, but masochists who feel pride in rising above impossible odds."

Peter Hall

This is a chapter that, as a guest, you really should not have to be concerned about if your Entertainments Manager and 'coats are doing their job properly. In fact you should not even realise stage management is taking place. I feel so strongly that this should be the case that I was actually thinking of leaving it out altogether. But then it dawned on me that this would only be the fact 'IF' they were indeed doing their job properly. So if they weren't how would you know? How could you tell why it was that you could hardly hear what was being said in one part of the ballroom while being deafened by the overpowering volume from the speakers in another part of that very same room? How would you know if it was their fault that the visiting cabaret was seemingly awful due to props, lighting or any other number of incidentals going wrong? How would you know the show was an absolute farce because nothing was where it was supposed to be when it was supposed to be there? Well you wouldn't would you! But I honestly don't believe that to try and explain all the intricacies of what to look for purely from a guest's point of view would really give you a good enough insight into it all. So at the risk of being called a lazy little Superblue and because I feel very passionate about what I wrote and told them in 'Tales of....well that little blue fellow' I sincerely feel that you ought to be allowed to read, what they should have, for yourself.

I therefore decree that from this day henceforth let it be known that in the kingdom of **Holiday Land** you shall Have the all knowing, all seeing power of stage management insight and may use this force to elicit respect and deference from all tribes collectively known as 'holiday companies'. Since once you digest and comprehend the recently discovered (in my bedroom draw) manuscript, originally destined only ever to be viewed by their Entertainment Chiefs, you will be a crucial member of little known but growing clan of your own. A surreptitious group fast becoming the scourge of any Machiavellian that may attempt to deceive you or worse 'rip you off. For you are now one of those known to them as the dreaded band of the............

'KNOWLEDGEABLE GUEST'

Now close your eyes, hold your nose, spin around three times chanting the revered mantra of "whaaaaat diiiiiid yoooou teeeell theeeeem Superbluuuuue?" and cross the threshold into this mystic world of....er....well what I did tell them actually..........ok then pretend you're an Entertainments Manager and......Read on Macduff.

WHAT IS STAGE MANAGEMENT?

In its purest sense it would be exactly what it purports to be and in a theatre that's precisely what it would be, the management of the stage and all that it entails. But at a holiday centre the definition is slightly misleading because your stage is pretty much the entire place really, when you come to think of it. So whereas the stage manager in a theatre has that one domain to rule over and maintain your responsibilities are far greater.

But don't break out into a cold sweat now at the thought of it because in essence stage management is quite simply having all the right things for the right performance or event in the right place at the right time. There easy isn't it?

Indubitably it is, nonetheless it befalls to me as the keeper of the sacred fire curtain to impart upon you the darkest most fiendishly cunningly and shrewdest secrets of the

Clandestine order of the board treaders and backstage masters

Since it is written that it is my destiny to entrustment upon you of that sacrosanct knowledge and wisdom passed down by many generations of masters and treaders.

WHO DOES THE STAGE MANAGEMENT?

Well in the absence of a master you will actually. The reality is, that at most centres you, the 'coats' will do the stage management and most of the time you will do it without even thinking about it. Of course the Entertainments Manager will direct it to be done a great deal of the time to begin with but you will soon find yourself running on autopilot and just getting on with it. At some of the larger centres they will have stage managers and the relevant staff but… ***beware less they break the code of the ancient order***

What?

Oh leave me alone I am having fun

You must be used to me by now?

Anyway moving on…..

So generally you will be carrying out stage management duties throughout the day to varying degrees just to get your job done.

So let's carefully open the book of………...

'Numinous showgeschäft durante la sua gestione'

What?

You're really not playing along with me today are you?

All I was trying to do was make the subject a little more interesting that's all!

Ok you want it laid out in plain English, that's fair enough.

The book?

Oh that translates as the book of 'Numinous' is 17th century Latin and kind of means mystical, 'showgeschäft' is German for show business and 'durante la sua gestione' means under his management in Italian.

So now we will carefully open the book of 'Mystical show business under his management'

Doesn't have the same ring to it does it?

Oh well let's knuckle down and look at the variety of aspects that constitute stage management in an Entertainments Managers or 'coats' world in plain English.

SOUND SYSTEMS

Firstly it is important to say that you should be fully trained on the equipment at your centre before you start to 'play around' with it. Secondly **don't** play around with it!

You are so dependent on this equipment for such a large amount of what you do that you need it in good working order all of the time. Never have drink or a liquid of any kind in or near a sound or disco booth or anywhere else your centre houses this stuff, it's a sure fire recipe for disaster. You should always know what volumes to set, whether it be for individuals during shows or the late night disco session for example, and the only way to be sure of this, is to have tested it by working through all scenarios.

Remember that although you may set sound levels at rehearsals this will be in an empty room so you are most likely going to have to adjust them slightly when you have an audience. The same goes for the disco what may be very loud in that vacant venue could well be a somewhat subdued noise when full.

When putting your shows and cabarets together you should designate a particular channel to each radio mic or mic and lead, simple colour coding using tape will do the trick to keep the various sets together. Once they are set, make up a template diagram for each show etc.

- If you have regular visiting cabarets do the same for them too.
- Keep all equipment in safe storage so that only the appropriate people can get hold of it. Treat it with the utmost respect these are the tools of your trade
- Always stow them away properly
- Don't tie leads up in knots
- Put radio mics on charge or remove batteries as per manufacturer's instructions
- Turn all equipment off when not in use
- Test everything everyday
- As soon as anything appears to be faulty or becoming so call out an engineer
- Never start any session, day or evening without these checks
- Don't forget that the speakers around the venue are part and parcel of your sound system and should also be checked for signs of blowing and general wear and tare
- You should also ensure that they are placed in the optimum position or simply facing the right way for best effect without deafening your audience
- Always have spare mics & leads to hand
- Once you have used a back up item replace it ASAP
- As part of your training on the system make sure you are told about and understand what the terms reverb, echo, fold back and feedback mean
- You should know when and where to use reverb and echo, the importance of a fold back and how to eliminate feedback

Never take this equipment for granted I cannot overemphasise the importance of daily testing but do remember also to try out any new equipment delivered to you when it arrives. I recently witnessed an incident where a centre took delivery of such equipment and installed it. Parts of the setup were fold back speakers and they just would not play ball at all. So they were left unplugged. No problem! However when they were later needed the 'coats' tried plugging leads in, pulling leads out from this socket into that one taking the speakers away, bring them back again, I have no idea what this was meant to do? And as if it could not get any more like a scene out of a keystone cops movie....suddenly we were treated to the entertaining voice of Bridget, the local taxi firms controller desperately trying to get cab number twenty six to pick up Mrs Hargreaves from number twenty six, Institute Drive and take her to Horgrove Hall, where she was joining her friends of the Women's Institute for a whist drive. I am not sure who was having the worst time of it Bridget or the 'coats' but I do know that while it was funny to begin with the guests soon became tired of the joke and wanted to get on with their evening's entertainment. I can't imagine the bars manager saw the funny side of it much either as he watched his profits walk out of the door.

Always test everything

Make sure it is ALL working as it should be before you need to use it

Make sure there is an engineer on site when you know you are receiving any major installations or very different new equipment

Please take all radio equipment out of its packaging and test it out – even the backup stuff

Remember health and safety –NEVER open or tamper with any equipment you are not qualified to. ALWAYS call an engineer.

LIGHTING

To be fair there is not much difference between what I have just gone through with you in sound systems but the two are inescapably linked anyhow. So just as before be fully trained before attempting to use equipment, check everything is working every day, understand the various terms for different lights and effects such as super trooper – strobe – black light etc etc, position the spots and others for maximum effect for your shows and cabarets and have a template diagram or similar, Set them so as not to blind your guests, keep spare bulbs, halogens and gels (colour slides) etc to hand. Do seek advice if you have not been taught how to handle bulbs particularly halogens before attempting to fit a new one.

Remember health and Safety – NEVER open or tamper with any equipment you are not qualified to. ALWAYS call an engineer.

Never try to fit a new bulb, change a gel or even reposition a spot with the electric power on ALWAYS check it is off and have a colleague remain with the power source until you have finished to ensure no one else turns it on accidentally.

If you are going to use special effects such as strobe lighting or black light **DO** tell the audience beforehand. Different lighting can affect people in a variety of ways, those that suffer from epilepsy or migraine for instance, may be affected by strobe lighting.

If you're not the dedicated stage manager but are to cover that role for a particular show, cabaret or competition your attendance at rehearsals is just as important and in some ways more so than if you were performing on the stage. Whether you are doing this by yourself on a smaller centre or a couple of you are working together at a larger one the importance of your role is the same. Your colleagues are depending on you to provide them with the best lighting and sound possible, to have props in the right place at the right time and be there to help with quick costume changes etc.

Entertainments Managers; obviously one person can't accomplish these feats single handed so you will need to ensure you have resourced enough assistance back stage to allow this to happen. On smaller parks you may have to enlist the willing help that I have found comes from colleagues in other departments. Please always follow protocol however and speak with that department head before approaching any of their staff or promising someone who has approached you, a part to play, on or off stage.

I would heartily recommend that you obtain the numbers of local sound and lighting companies. Make contact with them, in person, at the earliest opportunity in order that they get to know you personally and will come to your rescue at short notice and know they will be paid a fair sum of money for that service.

I personally always did this, even if I worked for a company that had a contract with the equipments suppliers or major contractor covering the country. I have lost count of the amount of times these people are not able to 'despatch an engineer' to your location until 'at least' the next day. This is absolutely no use to you when you have a ballroom full of 2000 guests sitting in silence waiting to see and hear the 'big star named cabaret' they have paid for.

I can tell you that the amount of times I have offered the solution that I get my friendly local company to come and fix it on 'their' behalf and our company claim the cost back from them has been 'music to their ears'. Excuse me but a complete pun intended.

You would probably expect the opposite to be true wouldn't you? Well yes that's most people's reaction but the truth of the matter is that by me taking this action I get them out of an embarrassing situation, one which could also prove to be very costly for them. You see these contracts can be worth hundreds of thousands of pounds a time and every time they fail to deliver the nearer they are to losing that contract.

So is that why they don't mind you paying your local company on the night and claiming the cost back from them? Well yes partly, but unofficially I believe it's because quit often the local company will charge less to do the job than they would have to pay to send someone out to you. Never take this decision unilaterally however, always have the full support and agreement of the centre manager at least but if you can get it, head office too.

PROPS

Wow where to start?

The definition of the term 'Prop' in the entertainment sense is:

'Object used in performance'

It comes from the mid 19th century and was simply a shortening of the word property.

Props to you will have the same meaning except that your performance covers a vast array of entertaining activities. That could be anything from bingo to a full floor show or from sports day to a visiting star cabaret and from the darts competition to a ramble in a national park.

In terms of a holiday centre entertainer a 'prop' is literally every object that you or a colleague will need in order that an activity takes place, takes place on time, takes place and runs smoothly, takes place and ends on time, takes place with anyone having any part in it being safe and sound.

In the chapters on running a day and evening programme I drummed into you the significance of having such things in place, at the right place, at the right time and in full working order. As well as the consequences of not achieving any one of these because getting two out of three just isn't good enough. Miss out on one of them and the whole thing falls apart and it can have a more dramatic effect than any play you are putting on…trust me! I won't go into it all again now, I am sure you will have had enough of that in those chapters. But it is all part of it and you must see 'props' and their effective use and deployment as a major part of the overall 'stage management' of your entertainments programme.

I do allude to props, in particular in relation to stage productions and fun competitions, in other chapters, where I recommend talking to your colleagues from other departments. It's amazing just how many have talents in this field and are usually only too happy to have their work seen on stage. In my experience the maintenance department and arcade are not bad places to start this search. But if you generally let it be known that you are open to offers of assistance in all aspects of 'stage management' I think, more often than not, you will be pleasantly surprised.

CONTROL THE ENVIRONMENT

No I don't want you to go running off being an echo warrior although doing your bit by recycling etc is always a good thing. Getting your guests to join in, particularly the younger ones is even better. But that's not what I mean in this instance. What I am talking about here is your working environment and keeping it safe, in order and happy. In short, whatever event is taking place with however many guests, spectators or colleagues involved, as the stage manager elect or at least one of the stage management team for that particular staged part of the entertainment programme, it is incumbent upon you to have a control on that environment in such a way as to instil an atmosphere that engenders natural good behaviour within those taking part without them even being aware of it most of the time.

We have talked about running a day time programme competition, for instance, and the merits of controlling the start time, rules and byes etc thus setting your stall out for all to see. You are plainly in control of the situation, hence subconsciously allowing your guests to enjoy the tournament in an atmosphere of relaxed confidence in your ability. Another example would be where you purposely show your guests that confidence in your management abilities and that you are taking your role very seriously. This is sometimes the case when we need to enforce a subtle or sometimes not so subtle control over the very few to ensure the enjoyment of the vast majority.

The dance floor would be a magnificent case in point! The dance floor is for all of your guests to use most of the time. But that does not mean that it does not need to be managed. It is part of our domain so for the preponderance of those guests we need to keep it an enjoyable and safe place to be when in use. Just as we must keep it a guest free zone when, required as a constituent of our stage. In other words we need to be in control and enforce the rules of dance floor etiquette. Of course you can and must try to do this in your usual friendly and entertaining manner but if this should not work.....well that is what security is for.

We don't want to be ogres or little tyrants but we must lay the foundations of decency for others to follow so, as I say, the enjoyment of majority is not spoilt by the few. It's not too difficult really, take this paradigm for instance. There are many people on a dance floor when being used for that purpose so to ensure rhythmic harmony exists without any aggression breaking out make certain you promote a code of conduct such as no drinks to be taken onto it, no outrageous behaviour that would detract from others dancing pleasure, no children on the floor after a certain advertised time etc. Unfortunately these days we have to educate some of the general public in the etiquette that is in reality, just plain good old fashioned manners, when it comes to cabarets, competitions or show-time. So often now I see people just rudely stroll straight across the middle of the dance floor to get from their seat to the bar or elsewhere....but normally the bar.

I can tell you this does make my blood boil especially when they wander past a troupe of 'coats' or in front of a visiting cabaret as they are performing. Ladies and gentlemen we should not have lost control of this sector of our core business. Educate your guests particularly the younger ones as they are your future adults, but do educate all of your guests, that during these periods the dance floor is out of bounds to them and that for the enjoyment of all they are expected to walk around the carpeted areas to get anywhere......even the bar!

Now I know you will do this in a nice way and rightly so....but do it you must. Reinforce this message by sitting with the children at the front of the dance floor to watch said shows, comps or cabarets and verbally deter any of them or the odd stray adult from crossing it. If you have enough staff an Entertainments Manager should always post a 'coat' to sit at either side of the stage for the same reasons but with the added dimension of a visual deterrent and reminder of this significantly noteworthy rule.

As you will be all too well aware by now I always expound that you show a well mannered respect towards your guests with their fun and entertainment at the heart of everything you do and I expect that you will carry this through into these types of stage management scenarios with your usual gusto.

HEALTH AND SAFETY

We cover this subject in depth in its own chapter later on but please do bear it in mind. In the course of your stage management you may well find yourself working at height, making all manner of props, swiftly followed by using all sorts of props, hanging scenery, negotiating slippery or wet floors after a competition for instance, dodging wires laying around backstage or across the ground on the sports field, and you don't want to be holding that mic when the heavens open up. Seriously though please do consider yours, the guests and colleagues safety. Never tamper with or open anything and I do mean *anything* that you are not trained to use, refit and or repair.

CHAPTER SEVENTEEN
DISCOS

"I think music in itself is healing. It's an explosive expression of humanity. It's something we are all touched by. No matter what culture we're from, everyone loves music." -
- Billy Joel

Oh Superblue now you're being very obvious

Discos?

You put the record or CD on, people dance, that's it.

Surely even you can't make more of it than that?

This one has to be that straight forward, doesn't it?

Well, yes actually.

Well almost actually.

The fact is this chapter could have been so much more in depth, but, all I would be doing is going over old ground, and that's just wasting both our times. So as we take a quick look at a couple of points in relation to discos consider the chapters on Compare and Stage Management in particular as much of what we talk of in them overlaps into Disco and being a DJ.

It has to be said that some centres employ people specifically for the role of DJ and even some light jockeys, but these tend to be the big ones (Butlins for example). Generally speaking the job will fall to the good old hard working multi skilled 'coats'.

Your Entertainment Managers are warned that whoever is running the disco or associated events, they are still responsible for all that takes place regarding guest enjoyment so they need to ensure all the rules we have discussed in other chapters as well as the few mentioned here are adhered to.

I have found that DJs have historically thought they are a law unto themselves and have required a very tight reign at times, so took control from the outset, laying down the law and enforced it.

Disco time, although if run properly can be a lot of fun, is in fact just an extension to a very good evening had by all. Generally however they are at the end of the evening when a fair amount of alcohol has been consumed and so there is always the potential for trouble. As well as making sure that their staff are not the catalyst for the said agro, they have a duty of care to them also. So because most staff will be off duty at that time they must make sure the centre, park, resort or camp have made provisions for adequate security personnel to deal with transgressors and ensure the safety of their team as well as you 'John Travolta' and 'Olivia Newton' look-a-like guests. The Entertainments Manager is not in charge or control of security personnel (unless they are the duty manager) but must step up to the plate re their duty of care responsibilities. This sometimes means they will need to be robust with the camp manager or owner, but hay that's the job.

DJs/Coats- may never have done this before but I tell them not to get flustered by it. After all it's just another form of compering and we cover that and all the same rules apply here. Being prepared is one of the easiest ways of allowing themselves to DJ with confidence and be just as entertaining as they would be with any other performance. It is imperative that they use appropriate records, CDs, tapes, jingles, party dances etc. This will include your tea dances and ballroom sessions being played at the correct speed etc. They should utilise a wide variety of music types when they can, but they need to be thinking about all aspects of their stints 'On the decks'. Props, spot prizes, little things like pen and paper for requests or dedications. If a 'coat' takes a dedication, particularly during the day they must make sure they give it to the DJ to play on the correct evening and make sure that DJ does announce it.

Again a lot of what we talked about in stage management will come into play here also so I won't bore you with that again. I tell them to use their compere skills though; there is nothing worse than someone just putting on one track after the other and nothing being said in between, you may as well have your "I pod" on. They need to build up the atmosphere that they want to achieve for that particular session, so as I say they can just keep a great ambience going from an already good night's entertainment. I do say however never talk so much that people get fed up with their voice. On the flip side to that, get it "flip side"? Oh I know I sound like broken old reco....oops I've slipped into DJ cliché mode now...oh dear!

If all that's required is some background music during a meal for example, then they should do the complete opposite and stay quiet. I know it's difficult for some people once they get a mic in their hands they just want to talk for England, but they just have to learn to play to their audience and indeed what they are being asked to do by the entertainments manager or whoever is running that particular event or part of the day.

VOLUME is quite simply one of the biggest sources of complaint!!! If people are moaning that they are too loud then they *ARE TOO LOUD*. It's that simple, you are the audience, you know what you want, and you can hear what they are pumping out from their side of the box. They are stuck behind the speakers in their own little world with their headphones on half of the time, again this is where knowing their workplace pays dividends, in 'How to Compare', I tell them to stand in a variety of places in the venue so as to learn what it sounds like from there..... The audiences' point of view? Well they should be putting that into practice even more so if they are to be the DJ. They will of course get the lovely little elderly couple who will insist on sitting right on top of the biggest speakers they have at the front of the room and then complain that they are too loud. Tact and diplomacy, tact and diplomacy, enough said I think.

I did touch on the fact that larger centres may have lighting jockeys these days, well they know their job so generally the Entertainments or stage manager will just keep an eye on how they are performing. At most centres the lighting will still be another little string to the 'coats' bow. There really are no hard and fast rules here and stage management comes into play, but I tell them to try and vary their lighting to co-inside with what they are playing, don't just put one sequence on and let it run throughout their set. If they're going to use strobe lighting they must make sure you guests know that it may be used during a certain part of the evening. Some people can be seriously affected by this and may wish to move to another part of the venue, in fact I say it may be just as well to make you aware of dry ice, bubbles or any substance that they may be going to use.

M.V.T.

No I'm not going to harp on about this again, just a quick reminder, that DISCOS and DJs are no exception to the rule so as always they must play the correct material at the right time, in the right venue.

Going back to being prepared, they will need to have enough material to cover a number of sets and avoid playing the same music over and over again night after night. Vary it to suit the theme of that particular set and play what people want to hear or dance to. Not just what they like for example Guns and Roses may not be the first choice for people on an Elvis Presley weekend.

MAILING LISTS

For the more enterprising among them or those who wish to take their career along the DJ or music TV paths etc. They can be among the first people in the country to get hold of new releases before they are ever released, if that makes sense. Pre-releases or trial records, CDs etc are often known as white labels i.e. sent out by record companies for pre-release market research. They can quite easily get onto their mailing lists and receive white labels which come with a score sheet or questionnaire, all they require in return is that they play the track and return the score sheet or questionnaire containing info on audience reaction. They will be kept up to date with new trends and artists as well as established acts. White labels can also become collectors' items; I actually have a couple from my early days that a collector would pay handsomely for.

CHAPTER EIGHTEEN

TEA DANCES

Whilst this form of entertainment is rapidly returning to Britain it may well be a completely unknown term to some of you so let me explain where it comes from. In years gone by people used to literally flock to dance halls or large hotels in the afternoons to while away the hours with Ballroom Dancing. Unlike today however, the licensing laws were very strict and you could not serve alcohol for most of the day and polite society dictated this was a fashionable thing to do. So tea was served as the preferred refreshment hence they became known as Tea Dances. Of course holiday camps followed suit and for many years Tea Dances were a staple and popular afternoon programme activity, normally just before the afternoon bingo session. The larger dance halls and hotels would have bands or even orchestras playing at the most swanky of venues but entrepreneurs such as Billy Butlin, Fred Pontin and the Warner Brothers soon realised that people on holiday would happily do a Viennese Waltz with a Viennese whirl to go with their cup of "char" (that's an old fashioned term for tea you know) to records. And so another great British institution was born 'The afternoon holiday camp tea dance', immortalised in that wonderful training program 'Hi-De-Hi'. Yes camps actually had 'ballroom instructors' on the entertainment team who would run these sessions; experienced dancers that would give lessons to the novices before judging the evening ballroom competitions.

I did say they used to be a staple part of the programme didn't I? But with the advent of Strictly Ballroom, and other dance based shows currently on the TV there is a serious resurgence of interest in the genre, so whilst there may not yet, and may never be enough of an interest to warrant these experts full time on the team some serious thought should be given to at least holding tea dance sessions for those of you that are interested. I implore Entertainment Managers to give a little consideration to possibly even employing local dance instructors who will come in a couple of times a week and give you lesions. Of course on most cruise ships they are still very much a part of the entertainments structure.

I mentioned competitions there and if they are running ballroom competitions apart from all the other aspects that we have discussed with such events, right place, right time, right staff Blah Blah!! Entertainments Managers will need to ensure that they are taken VERY seriously by any staff concerned, because they will be taken VERY VERY seriously by the aficionados of ballroom dance. Of course I mean all types when I say ballroom I just use this respectfully as a generic term for all styles such as Latin or modern for instance.

A professional judge is a must!

If they are not using a band (why not!!!) but if they are not Entertainments Managers must make sure they have a system that plays exactly the right speeds to get the correct tempo of dance, that also goes for the tea dance sessions or they will be teaching new comers at a slightly wrong pace and the experienced dancers will have their guts for garters.

This is also something I tell Entertainments Managers to bear in mind when they are recruiting team members. Many of them will have learnt all or some aspects of ballroom in their early years or at stage school etc and of course Entertainments Managers should always encourage all 'coats' to take part and learn these dances. During the evenings many of you guests will be only too pleased to show them the ropes and of course this is another great way of interacting and socialising with you as well as at the tea dances, when they can pick up tips from the professionals and other 'coats' too.

WET WEATHER

Yes indeed, Tea Dances are a great way to pass an hour or two on wet weather days especially if Entertainments Managers have more than one venue at their disposal. There is nothing better than being able to offer a varied program of events for our guests and these can be relatively light on our labour distribution, possibly just the right 'coat' with the right equipment playing the right music at the right speed.

SEQUENCE DANCING

Not to be confused with line dancing as this is a whole other ball game, my best advice here is unless the Entertainments Manager is a sequence dancer them self or they have a 'coat' who is......DON'T even attempt to run anything to do with this genre of dance. It is so specialised and those that play an active part in it are, in my experience, extremely indignant to anything less than pure sequence dancing professional involvement and practices.

This however is where having the right band....live band....live music at their centre can greatly help an Entertainments Manager and will play the correct music for this past time.

All of the above being said I have seen quite a few people taking to the floor and enjoying their sequence steps at Warners centres of late. It just has to be the right music at the right speed again and so easy to get wrong if the 'coat' does not know what they are doing.

CHAPTER NINETEEN

PARTY DANCES

I suppose the first thing to do is identify what a party dance is.

The party dance is steeped in holiday camp history actually. With camps springing up after the second world war in particular with the whole British nation looking to shrug off those dark years of death and destruction and replace them with fun, laughter and frivolity. The traditional division of our class system begun to break down here too and meant that people from all walks of life and family backgrounds were, for the first time really, all in the same place at the same time in the pursuit of happiness. One of the telling signs of this would turn out to be on the dance floor. Whereas different lifestyles meant a varied way of doing just about most things holiday camps stood for togetherness, equality and the same fun time to be had by all. So how do you blend all these diverse cultures on a dance floor and guarantee that everyone from the ballroom experts, to the most reserved city gent or from the Saturday night palais rock and roller to the lovely hard working housewife will fill it and all enjoy themselves while being assured of the fact that they would never be embarrassed because they couldn't do a particular sort of dance? Well there was a way, a very good way indeed and so……..
The holiday camp party dance was born

It was an instant winner, with classics like 'the slosh' 'the gay gordons' 'Lambeth walk' 'oke koke' and they continued to thrive through the years with numbers such as the 'birdie song' 'time warp' 'superman' 'agadoo' and 'night fever' etc leading onto the present day with fun little ditties such as the 'one eyed purple people eater'. Of course it had a massive overhaul a few years ago when the country and western fraternity got hold of it and the so called brand new craze of 'line dancing' swept the nation and many of these line dance routines are now solidly based in the regular holiday centres party line dance section of the programme. And it wouldn't be the same without our yearly summertime novelty hit with its fun dance steps like Spitting Image's The Chicken Song ("hold a chicken in the air, stick a deckchair up your nose"), Aqua (Barbie Girl), Lou Bega (Mambo No.5), Kaoma (Lambada), the Macarena, The *Ketchup Song* and the Cheeky Girls' *Touch My Bum*.

So party dances or line dances were invented in Britain at holiday camps just after the war then? Well of course not, you've only got to stop and think back through history to realise that dancing together in lines to the same beat, doing the same moves was being practised by the earliest tribes and continue to this day, some carrying a serious message of culture and history.

But purely to galvanise a war torn nation, divided by class, wealth and background, into getting onto the dance floor together and jiggling about to music just for the sheer fun of it!!!!! Well I would say that was a pretty important and impressive mile stone in the history of dance wouldn't you?

In practise what does it mean to you today though? Pretty much exactly the same as it would have done to those very first Butlins, Pontins and Warners guests as well as the Red, Blue or Green 'coats' believe it or not, yes, you are carrying on the great holiday camp tradition of filling the dance floor with lines of happy campers (guests as we call you today) all doing the same simple dance steps that you have come to know and love over the years or brand new ones you have been taught that week.

As we move into the 21st century with luxury accommodation and fine food, not to mention the horrible recession. We are once again attracting new first time holidaymakers from a variety of backgrounds that have not considered a British Holiday Camp to be 'their thing'. I recently watched a very 'posh' family having the time of their lives in fits of laughter as they learnt the steps to 'achy breaky heart' at lessons in the morning and was delighted to see them giving it all they had, with no inhibitions all that evening. These dances are quite simply gold dust to an Entertainments Manager and their 'coats'!

If they play the right party dance or line dance song they instantly turn an empty desolate dance floor into a thriving mass of happy people putting the whole venue in the right frame of mind for an evening of fun. Filling a room with such a fabulous atmosphere should always be their ultimate goal at all times. So they must never waste this wonderfully simple universally 'John Travolta' enabling music. They should embrace it, enjoy it, have fun with it. There are times when a 'coat' may think oh no not that tune again, but if that does happen.......

I tell them to just stop and consider two things:

(1)   The alternative is an empty dance floor and that means THEY!! Will have to go around trying to drum up enthusiasm in the room and even end up dragging unwilling participants onto that floor. Now I ask them, which would they really prefer?

(2)   it's not about them anyway!!!

So as long as you guests keep getting up and enjoying yourselves to whatever tune it may be, from the good old Birdie Song to the latest summer craze, the Entertainments Manager and 'coats' ought to keep playing and dancing to it and by gum they'll do it with a great big smile on their faces too.

Won't they?

You bet your DARN TOOTIN Country and Western Boots they will.

I tell Entertainments Managers and 'coats' to have fun with this. And I do mean have fun, because this is a part of the programme that lends itself to silliness and high jinx, they should play on it, you guests are relaxed, the whole family is in the venue having fun and Entertainments Managers and 'coats' have the opportunity to be a little bit daft and exuberant. So they should treat this like any other show time, plan, organise and scheme, get dressed up for certain numbers, be wacky. Add to the overall feeling of Party Time, it really does pay dividends for them in the long run.

But they must always remember! You are following THEIR lead, so if it's their turn on stage or on the floor they have got to stick to the dance moves or they will quickly empty the floor.

The party or line dance has no interest in age, sex, height, shape or size, it loves everybody and everybody loves it (except for the odd grumpy person anyway). Your entertainments programme should always contain some form of lessons in these dances, most centres tend to hold these in the morning after keep fit, and they again tend to be family affairs, and just as much, if not more fun than the actual evening sessions. It is of course up to the Entertainments Manager to decide when the best times for lessons are at their park but ought to make sure they don't clash with other family entertainments.

Which dance they choose to teach and use in the evenings again is a matter for them but I would personally be guided by the age mix of guests that week, sometimes for instance there may be only a handful of children and more senior citizens at the centre and the next week during half term, well they have their hands full don't they. So they need to be realistic about what they choose and temper it to fit their audience.

I advise them to listen to requests from guests of all ages and try to accommodate whereever possible and look out for the latest dance craze too!!!

Routines should always be kept at a reasonable level of difficultness the simpler the better is a good rule of thumb, although this has to be tempered with keeping it interesting. I remind Entertainments Managers that a lot of 'coats' are trained dancer's, the guests are not, in fact for most of you this will be your once or twice a year foray onto a dance floor of any kind. So all the steps in the routines have to be very achievable for every man or lady, boy or girl.

'Coats' should never add bits on to a dance that they have taught guests, just so that they look clever in the evening session, all this will serve to do is clear the dance floor and they will alienate you guests because you can't follow them.

Trust me this will make them very unpopular with the band, DJ, Entertainment Manager and their colleagues on the team and most importantly all of you guests. Keeping it simple being the lead in a session of fun dancing for guests is all they need to do to fulfil their entertainment ego.

I do also warn them that during the lessons they should be aware of anyone from a dance club etc, they can sometimes try to take over and teach other guests more complicated routines. I instruct them to diplomatically try to dissuade them from doing so; as yet again this can put a lot of people off from joining in during the evenings because they feel they could not master those routines. If you are one of these fine folk however I edify the Entertainments Managers and 'coats' to talk to you and see if you have any new or different steps that you can teach them and consider utilising in a dance they will teach other guests. I tell them to watch you on the dance floor in the evening too and pick up what you can. This shows your important to them as indeed you should be, while they remain in control.

Larger holiday centres or villages or those that belong to a company such as Haven or Parkdene Holidays etc will very often have a few set corporate routines, generally to go with their characters, but if they are on a small or independent site or hotel for example, there is nothing stopping them creating their own "Club Dance" This is something that is very popular out in the Caribbean, and guaranteed to fill the dance floor, not only do they teach this at the lessons but also make a big thing of it at children and teenage activities so that many of the guests learn this dance routine to accompany a certain lively tune or song and then they play it at the start of the evening dance session, after a competition in the evening to get ready for Showtime and always play it at the end of their 'normal' evening session leading into disco time which is a great way to use it to maximum effect.

The club dance is a real winner in so many ways

(1)   It fills the dance floor

(2)   As soon as people hear it they need no explanation 'they are up'

(3)   Transcends all age groups

(4)   Leaves lasting memories of a great holiday - repeat bookings,

(5)   It's that centre's dance, if you go elsewhere that does not do anything similar, you will be back.

As always this necessitates making it easy to learn, but full of fun moves to go with a great song and tune for all the family to enjoy.

So who chooses what line/party dances to do each evening or indeed what ones to teach at the lessons? To be honest it's a bit of collaboration really. As always the Entertainments Manager should be in overall control of everything that is being presented to you for your enjoyment, and if he or she is going to regularly lead the evening session then it maybe that they have more of an input than another manager who is happy to let their team take the limelight on this one. Whichever category they come under here Entertainments Managers must supervise what is being taught to the guests and that a good mixture of party dances or line dances are being played in the evening. So they must at least dip sample the lessons from time to time to ensure the correct level of difficultly or should I say ease is being maintained for their guests enjoyment and keep a watchful eye on the evening sessions for the same correctness and good mixture as well as that 'coat' that always gets carried away and starts to show off adding bits in for effect.

But really the answer is that anyone can decide after that, so long as all the above is in place any 'coat', the band or the DJ can decide what party dances should be played when, not forgetting the main part of that collaboration.......You the guest!!!!!! I have to be honest and say that I do forewarn the Entertainments Managers and 'coats' to be mindful that a handful of vocal guests might like one particular tune while the majority of you may be getting sick of it being played repeatedly every night or even more than once a night.

Who teaches the guests and the 'coats' the dances? Any of the 'coats' that have not got two left feet can take the lessons, and actually that's not a bad way of judging if a dance is right for all guests. If the worst dancing 'coat' can cope, you should be OK. As with anything else we have discussed Entertainments Managers will find their best dancer/teacher in the team and the temptation will be to post them to that duty day after day. I would just reiterate that while this would appear the easy option at the outset, the long term affects are that they are not affording the rest of the team its chance to develop in this area, and may run the risk of that one 'coat' becoming fed up with that daily posting and them losing their enjoyment of the dances and so their excitement to teach and that will come through massively to you, the guest. Generally though they will have at least two or three that love it and will happily share the assignment and also bring the others along until they are up to speed and ready to take lessons on their own two left feet.

As for who teaches the 'coats'.........

I have already mentioned the corporate stuff and this of course will come from head office and passed on from 'coat' to 'coat' as they join the team or at corporate days etc. But the party/line dances are generally something that many people bring to the party. The majority are passed on as new 'coats' join the team, new 'coats' quite often bring a new one or two with them from stage school, dance clubs etc or others from previous camps, hotels, villages, and centres they have worked at. If an Entertainments Manager is starting up a completely new team they should bear this important aspect of their guests daily enjoyment in mind when recruiting or auditioning people to join them as 'coats', but I do ask them to please do remember 'personality first'.

Of course one of their biggest teachers will be you, the guests, so long as they take into consideration what I have said about too difficult dance steps and not letting a guest or group of guests take over. Quite often the first they will hear about that latest dance 'craze' is when a five year old asks them to play it and starts to dance, quickly followed by another 100 people....AH! A new party dance. Enjoy!!!

I am sure your Entertainments Manager has the best team in the world and your party dances are second to none. But just in case someone at another centre, park, hotel, club or village has managed to find a step or two that are worth looking at, I do advocate they go and visit any that may be near to them or in fact not even that near.

A fresh approach from another team's perspective is always worth a little effort on their behalf.

Entertainments Managers should under no circumstances rest on their laurels when it comes to party and line dances, they are obliged to keep an eye out for new ones or to improve the ones they have (but not change standard dances that you guests will know and love from over the years. That will only mean another empty dance floor). Keep the 'coats' fresh and alive to learning new ones whenever they can. They should buy as many compilation CD's or records as they can and use the ones that best suite where they are working at the time. Watch as many music channels as they can to pick up latest hits or golden oldies. Picking any great moves they can use, and get hold of music DVDs for the exact same reasons.

Whilst this is a huge amount of fun for you it must be run as professionally as any other part of the programme. So the Entertainments Manager should make sure whoever is running either the lessons or the evening session is prepared, whether using the disco unit or band they know what dances are to be used, all music, costumes and props are ready well in advance and in the right place ready to use.

Remember for the most part you guests will be looking to them to lead the dance so they can follow, no matter your experience. So again during both the lessons and evening sessions Entertainments Managers need enough 'coats' on duty to cover all aspects of the dance floor, so that no matter which direction the dance steps take you in, left, right, back or front there is always a 'coat' in front of you leading the way. Too often I see a couple of 'coats' on the stage for the glory of the audience sitting down. Well I counsel them to forget that now as their priority is the guests on the dance floor. The better they do this job, the less guests they will have sitting to show off to in the first place, because you will all be up joining in with them.

I recommend that they vary the music as much as possible, obviously certain songs or tunes are tailor made for a particular dance or visa-versa but other than those, for your enjoyment they ought to be trying to work out what dances will go with as many songs as possible and not fall into the trap of playing their favourites. You will soon get fed up of them doing this and it will have an adverse effect. They should pick up on what the guests favourites are at the time and what will get you out of your seats and onto their Dance Floor without doing it to death.

They must Never Never Never do what I am so sad to say I have seen recently at more than one centre, belonging to more than one company, and seems to be a growing trend in the business. And that is they must NEVER use party dances to replace live music or live entertainment, or visiting cabarets etc. Of course if you are a 'coat' or Entertainments Manager reading this, you can only do as you are told if working for one of these companies. But please keep the pressure up whenever you get the chance to have your voice heard and show your disapproval at the situation. If you are a guest or future guest, well, you can have a massive impact on this aspect of your holiday. Firstly: when booking ask if they have a live band and cabaret **EVERY NIGHT!!!** If they don't, vote with your feet and go somewhere that does. There is nothing like dwindling profits to concentrate the minds of those moguls from holiday companies. Demand the entertainment you deserve, after all YOU ARE PAYING FOR IT!!! If you are an owner on a site then you know how strong your voice can be, don't put up with it let the management know of your displeasure. If you're a manager, owner or company director in charge of one or one hundred camps, centres, sites, parks, villages or hotels. Well sit up and take note...... people want value for money, taped or recorded music is not it!!! You know what's right in this respect so do the right thing by your guests and staff alike and 'KEEP IT LIVE'. Don't use party/line or character dances to replace Bands, Cabarets or Shows.

You now know the guests know. It's up to you!!!

Of course party dances are brilliant in wet weather situations for an hour or so, but again not to be done to death and they must have plenty of other activities for you to take part in or watch that day.

EDUCATE THE CHILDREN!!!

We touched on this in the chapter about stage management but it's important to reiterate it here. There is no point in an Entertainments Manager announcing it and it stating in your programme that children are to be off the dance floor by a certain time in the evening if they are going to play party dances for them after that time. They only have themselves to blame when other guests complain that there is no enforcement of this rule. Especially if, yet again, the whole operation is designed to sell glowing, flashing or spinning merchandise from the shop. Oh don't get me started on that subject again. Not too many centres now have this rule, but some have to because of the makeup of their venues and the different types or ages of guests they need to cater for. So if you're at a centre that does have this rule, the Entertainments Manager should enforce it nicely and with humour and gentleness...... But enforce it!!!

You can greatly assist here though buy keeping your children off the floor or supporting the Entertainments Manager or 'coats' when they ask others to do so. Not that I advocate personal input at the time but complaining to the camp or duty manager at the time or even the next day helps.

Party dances are called that for a reason. So they should be professionally run, with a fun, party carnival atmosphere that you will ... ENJOY!!!

CHAPTER TWENTY

A GREAT COMPERE IS CRUCIAL

I suppose the best way to start on this subject is to ask the obvious question:

After all Confucius say
"He who asks the question is a fool for a minute; he who does not is a fool forever"

So what is a compere?

Well no matter what that Chinese bloke says that *IS* obvious isn't it Superblue?

Oh is it now?

Cop this for obvious then;

Compere: The host of an entertainment show. A transitive and intransitive verb (3rd person present singular comperes, present participle compering, past and past participle compered) coming from the Mid-18th century. Via French compère 'godfather' & medieval Latin compater & Latin pater 'father'

So there ner!ner!ner!ner!ner!ner! (In a very childish told you so voice)

Oh well…er… yes…sorry Superblue I had no idea I hear you confess, I thought it was just the person who did all the talking between things going on, I imagine you admitting. And do you know that's probably what you guests do think too and if that's all you do think that's a very good thing.

What???

I know I know I was just trying to look like a clever little academic type for once but I didn't really pull it off did I? No I rarely do.

So let's forget the dictionary and history's definition and get down to what a holiday centre, park or camp compere really is all about.

Without a doubt one of the outward signs that a great compere will display to their guests is that they are just 'doing the talking' between things going on, why, because it means that their audience is not aware of any kind of stressfulness in that person, no flapping or panicking, no indication of harassment, alarm or distress just an ease of transition from one event to the next.

I fully expect seasoned entertainers to know that there is much more to compering than merely chatting between other things going on but if you don't or just haven't given it much thought before now………Go make yourself a nice cup of tea or coffee grab a couple of chocolate biscuits or a big slice of yummy cake or both…well why not? Bring them back here sit down, relax and be prepared to see the role in a whole new light, one that will enable *YOU* to recognise a compere of note and therefore one of the most valued members of the team and a very important person in the entertainment manager's arsenal of professional weapons of mass enjoyment.

Right I'm off for a cupper see you in a few mins……

Oh your back already mmm that cake looks nice and I am on a diet too.

So here goes…….ahum

Right here goes….er

Ok the first thing is…..

Oh it's no good I just have to have some, right you stay there I'll be back in a minute…..

Ah that's better three chocolate digestives a lovely big chunk of triple choc gateau and a raisin and biscuit Yorkie bar.

What are you looking at me like that for? Oh I'll start the diet again tomorrow, hungry work all this trying to be clever you know.

Right as soon as I get that piece choc chip out from between the G and the H and that dollop of fresh cream clear of Back Space and Enter on the keyboard we will be off and running.

There all spick and span.

So where was I? Oh yes compering…well firstly you need to be aware that being a compere is as much a discipline as anything else I have talked about and indeed in many ways one of *the most disciplined*. After all its *The Compere's* job to gauge their own performance and be flexible enough to instantly extend or shorten their time on the mic in order to control the all important timing of those gaps between major events in order that the programme runs efficiently and on time. This can mean cutting short a nice piece of well planned and rehearsed comedy in order to bring the next event back in line with its scheduled time slot or adding that quick throw away audience participation silliness so as to 'pad out' an unexpectedly long break in the proceedings.

This is where adlibbing is an art of its own and those of us that have been naturally blessed with it are truly lucky individuals. So I ask them to please use this gift wisely, don't get carried away with them-selves and start to love the sound of their own voice turning it from a thing that others are in awe of into something the other 'coats' and guests are sick to the teeth of.

I tell *Compere's* to never get so wrapped up in 'their own press' that they believe they are invincible, that everyone loves them and they can get away with anything they like, doing and saying anything they like to anyone they like and definitely avoid, like the plague, the one that catches many a Prima Donna out.....Actually starting to believe they are indispensable........*NO ONE IS!!!*

Yes I know they should know that and I know that you and they know what's coming next but.....I have seen it all before and I would be wrong not to pass that experience on to them. I won't bore you with all the variable scenarios I have witnessed but I will tell you about one to illustrate how bad it can get.

THE DAY HE WENT TOO FAR!

The atmosphere in the massive ballroom was lovely it had been a great sunny day, all the morning competitions and fun and games have been well run and a very enjoyable atmosphere was abound in the village, the lunchtime sing-a-long was packed and everyone had sung along to just about everything and to cap it all in the afternoon, apart from everything else we had on, the donkey derby had been a roaring success of family fun and mayhem. The capacity audience of around 2000 were buzzing we were buzzing the band was buzzing it was all set to be one of those brilliant nights. We had a really good show to put on for the guests and we were really looking forward to performing it for them too.

So it would take something truly major to transform that fabulous ambience of friendship and harmony into one of hate and hostility wouldn't it? Well yes is the plain and simple truth of it.

How quickly and easily one 'coat' managed to do that though was amazing not to mention very very frightening for the rest of the team. One minute all was well the evening was flowing beautifully and one of the youngest 'coats' had been given his chance to run a competition. This would surely never be the catalyst for such ferocious venom directed towards an entertainments team? It couldn't have been the Entertainments Manager had played it safe after all. He had given this young 'coat' the 'Glamorous Gran' competition to compere. There just could not be any simpler a competition to cut your teeth on for goodness sake. All those marvellous ladies dressed to the nines looking smashingly glamorous. Quite often their proud grandchildren would be in the audience cheering them on. While the rest of the guests sat in awe of the stories that the compere would elicit from those delightful ladies, and they had some great tales to tell, many hysterically funny while others would bring a tear to the eye but all told by genuinely charming women. Surely that cannot have kicked off? All the compere has to do is ask their name, where they are from, how many grandchildren do they have and tell us something about yourself. They were already primed off stage to think of a little story to tell. That's it! There is no more! What the Sam Hill could possibly have gone wrong?

A 'coat' getting it all so wrong that's what!

This young 'coat' clearly hadn't watched and listened enough, hadn't taken advice on how to run this competition, had got it into his head that he could say or do anything that would get him a laugh at the expense of anyone and it would all be ok.

I wasn't in the ballroom when he uttered the dreadful words to one of the enchanting contestants but I was soon to find out how the guests had taken it, as where all the 'coats' on duty that night and over the days to come.

"It's all kicking off in the ballroom that young 'coat's' really messed up" said another hysterical 'coat'. Well similar wording anyway, using his name and an expletive or two as you can imagine. I rushed over from the adult bar to find the place in, what I can only describe as a state of uproar.

A large group of people were trying to get back stage, security and other male staff, were trying to hold them back and all around the venue 'coats' were visibly shaken as they tried to calm other gusts who were remonstrating with them.

Oh my word! What the hell could have caused this disorder this chaos this turmoil, what on earth could anyone have done to create such havoc such pandemonium such bedlam? Be rude to one of those lovely lady contestants that's what!

Rude, bang out of order and downright insulting is what that young 'coat' had been.

The group trying to get back stage where the relatives of the lady concerned, as it turned out, and they had come to our camp on mass to enjoy their family holiday which had just been completely wrecked by this one young 'coat'.

Little did they know that he had been whisked away out a back entrance and put in a location, unknown to the rest of us at the time, accompanied by security for his own protection because that family were baying for blood, I know that sounds ever so dramatic but I genuinely don't know what they would have done if they had got hold of him that night.

While this was going on the rest of the 'coats', including me by now, were in all sorts of conversations with groups of other guests regarding the situation and endeavouring to restore their confidence and regain their trust whilst reassuring them that we found what had taken place unacceptable too. The rest of that night was a write off, we put our show on to a half empty room and those guests that had remained were so subdued it was horrible.

Although there were some heated discussions, particularly and understandably with the members from the family, I have to say that at no time did any of those guests make any threats to the rest of us 'coats'. Even so it was an experience I would rather never be subjected to again for all concerned especially the lady, her family and all of our guests. It did indeed take a couple of stressful days before 'normality' was re-establish between us and all of those guests but we were a strong team and we pulled together and got through it. By the end of the week, when there had been no sightings of the young 'coat', people began to trust that he had been sent packing as was their wish.

What had he done that was so terrible? He alluded to this 'glamorous grandmother's' size in such a demeaning fashion, making remarks such as Michelin woman, that it just incensed all in that venue at that time. Little wonder the family reacted the way they did!

Entertainments Managers should be watching for this type of behaviour forming and put a stop to it at a very early stage. Even if that means removing a person from that duty until lessons are learnt or completely if said lessons aren't learnt after they have been given the chance.

The rest of the team have some responsibility too however. Imagine being a 'coat' at that holiday village that week. It was far from pleasant I can tell you, but many comments had been made about this young 'coats' behaviour, "out of control" "no respect" "thinks he's god's gift" "going to go too far one of these days" "going to come a cropper" are just some that spring to mind now. So what did I, a fellow Bluecoat, do about it?.....Nothing.... that's right nothing!!! Remember this is as much about learning from my mistakes as it is from other people's brilliant ideas and ways of working. So ashamedly I have to accept my failure in respect to my responsibility as a team member so and tell them about it in 'Tales of Supeblue' so you hopefully won't have to ever witness such unpleasantness on your holidays. No I did nothing and so that young 'coat' did go too far, was out of order and paid the price as indeed did the rest of us 'coats'. But most importantly insulted and upset that particular family as well as any number of the 2000 other guests on holiday at the time.

It would be stupid Entertainments or camp manager that did not take very seriously anything you or another staff member tells them about any fears you have regarding how any 'coat' is behaving in this respect, even if that person is the Entertainments Manager themselves.

The absolute rule:

Rudeness, inappropriate behaviour or language and swearing are NEVER justified and wholly unacceptable at ALL times.

So did I answer the question; what is a compere?

Well after a shaky start I think I did redeem myself and spoke proper common sense like what I does and we got down to the bones of what a compere is. So let me sum it all up, how about this for Superblue's definition of what a compere is?......

"A compere is a personality that cleverly manipulates time between events in an entertaining fashion, making it appear seamless, they are master wordsmiths who articulate the positive when introducing acts and wizards of controlled hilarity during competitions, artfully bringing the gift of the gab to sparkling life on the dullest of days while all the time they are performing this linguistic feat with panache they engagingly and compellingly interweave useful and instructive content into their oration without so much as a guest being aware that they have momentarily stepped out of being purely entertained"

Superblue ....circa 2010

And so onto the second question ~ the second question? Oh dear I do make life hard for myself don't I? But then if someone had written this book 30 years ago when I was in short pants, incoherent and dribbling everywhere, wow that brought back memories of me being at my mates stag do last week, anyway if someone had written such a book when I was starting out I would have been so much wiser. So don't worry far from feeling sorry for myself it is a privilege to think that someone like you thinks this one is worth reading. I thank you for the compliment and with a smile in my heart get back to question number two…**Who compares what?**

The fact is, as I have already indicated, quit often a natural contender will emerge from the team, but not necessarily the person who was originally employed for the role. In the UK however we, too often seem to, stubbornly stick to the tradition that the Entertainments Manager and assistant (on their day off) compere all of the big events (those with most exposure). While abroad they will do many of the short links because significantly they recognise that a good compere can make or break a situation, competition or large event and so it tends to be the best person for the job – does the job. Something I believe we need to wake up to in Britain. That being said you know I am passionate about everyone getting the chance to learn all aspects of the trade and I was pleased to see this taking shape to some degree at a centre I was at recently, however I'm not sure how much that was down to using this philosophy and how much was due to lack of staff.

The fact is a couple of people hogging the mic night after night, day after day not only frustrates other members of the team but firstly begins to bore the pants off guests before it becomes downright annoying to you.

So yes they can utilise the most natural talent for the most part but should give everyone a chance until they find their comfort zone and capability then mix and match. Some will love it but will just not be that good at it, others will not like to be on the mic at all but may be really good when they are, it really should be just another part of the overall entertainment stratagem to bring you variety and quality holiday entertainment.

Question three:
Question three?
Blimey how many are there?

I don't really know to be honest I think I have run out of answers after this one so I hope there are no more but only time will tell I suppose.

Question three:

Can they learn to be a good compere?

And what a question it is too.

The simple answer is yes they can.

While some of them instinctively know just what to say and when to say it others will have to work on that aspect beginning with learning to use tried and tested stock in trade set pieces for a variety of situations. So comparing sounds quite simple and straight forward doesn't it? Well do you know, you will be pleasantly surprised to know, it actually is.

"Superblue"

"Yes"

"Can I ask one last question please?"

"Of course you can"

"Oh goody, in that case can you tell me how one becomes a *great* compere so I know what to look for when I am on holiday?"

"Well I can and will certainly give you all the basic tips and tools that they need to become a *great* compere. But firstly we need a little break so, go and fill your cup and grab another choccy bic and we will get started. Now where did I put that giant toblerone?"

Ah there you are!

Wipe that bit off of there, no to the left a bit, that's it you got it.

So you want to know what it takes to be a *great* compere? Good because it is nice to see the best in 'coats' as well find fault in whatever we talk about. So the following is what I chronicle on this essential subject in the 'other' book. Do you know what, I recon you will be applying for a job as 'coat' or even Entertainments Manager once you have read this book. And why not it does not matter how old you are it's never too late to start a new career, a new chapter in life, a new adventure. I am living proof of that. Why not read this next bit as if you were going for that 'coats' job? Imagine how good you would be? "Never say never my friend"

We have touched on competency levels and you will find yours so don't worry about that for now and certainly don't panic if you find you're not a natural compere your talents will lie elsewhere and the 'gift of the gab' comperes, other 'coats' and guests alike will be in awe of you then. You should never put that kind of pressure on yourself and an Entertainments Manager should never expect it of you either. Of course you want to do the best you can and following what I am about to tell you will make you much more proficient than those that choose not to. You will have a very good head start on them and trust me you will be very happy with yourself and your compering.

So let's start by forgetting the word *great,* oh controversial Superblue!!! Well no not really; instead let's concentrate on what will allow you to compere with confidence and professionalism at whatever level you settle at.

"What do you say?"

"Go for it I think I hear you shouting, it's difficult to tell through a gob full of doughnut, you really are letting yourself go now you know" But a good answer so as requested here I am going for it.

The fact is that most of your compering will be conducted on a microphone otherwise known in the trade as the 'mic'. There learnt something already, what? Not impressed? Stick around kid you'll be walking the walk and talking the talk when I have finished with you.

Always on a mic? No at times a strong interesting voice is a distinct advantage so long as it's clear and backed up with personality. Everything else we talk about will be relevant to compering on a mic or not. But learning to use a microphone professionally is learning to master the basic skills in the use of the basic tool in your chosen vocation.

If you have never been on a mic before it might actually startle you to hear your own voice coming out of a large sound system. Don't worry this is a natural reaction. We very rarely sound like we think we do. It's a good idea to tape yourself talking at home and play it back to hear yourself as others do. This will also come in useful later when we talk about habits and mannerisms etc.

Imagine you are compering a show, introducing acts or running a fun competition. Go for it as if you are up there on stage in front of a 1000 people. Go on give it a go right now if you can………

So what did you think of the sound of your own voice? Wow is that me? Yuk is that me? That sounds awful? That sounds brill? I was too loud? I was too quiet? I fumbled my way through that? I was so slick? Is my accent really that strong? I thought my accent was stronger than that?

Your reaction could be any number of the above in any combination. The fact is you now know what you do sound like and how others hear you. Everything after that can be worked and improved upon. Please remember what you have heard and temper how you use that tool and that there is a fine line between being enthusiastic and being loud. While you should always be enthusiastic you should never be too loud and having to shout means you have lost control.

Ok now moving onto the real thing won't be so much of a shock to the system. Even so when you get to your camp get yourself on the mic and try it out as many times as you can while no one is around. Just get used to the feel of it and how your voice fills the room and how certain things you say come across in that environment etc.

A point to remember is that a fair amount of sound, reverberation or echo will in essence be deadened by the pure fact that people are in the room. Their bodies, sort of soak up noise so that when you do have an audience you may think you are coming across quieter than you actually are. You will have to bear in mind that they are sat out there amongst all of those speakers set up to cover that venue and some will be right on top of them. Don't be tempted to shout to overcome this. On the flip side of that coin don't rely on the volume you are getting from your fold-back speakers or other stage monitors because while it may sound as if you are coming across as clear as a bell on these you may well be unintelligible in a part or all of the rest of the venue. You will, in time, learn to trust in the mic settings that you have set for yourself or that have been set for you and I would advocate, where feasible to do so, check these at the beginning of any event or show you are about to take part in or compere. We will talk about what the sound is like when your venue has people in it in a mo and we covered mic settings also in 'Stage Management'. Bringing me nicely onto the next step in this exceedingly valuable learning process.......

WATCH, LISTEN AND LEARN

We have already established that that there will be some very good and some not so proficient comperes already at your centre so, not only is, there no shame in it but you would quite frankly be absolutely foolish not to watch, listen and in fact study all of these people. Try and identify a style that suites you, oh yes there are many styles out there, learn what works for the audience bearing in mind you will have to adjust for various audience demographics.

Note that those that are too loud tend to hold the mic right up to their mouth, while those that you find hard to hear may well be holding it under their chin or even further down for example. This is normally only a confidence thing but you are already one step ahead of the game in that department because you are learning from their mistakes. Take note of how many good comperes will constantly work the mic, just like a great vocalist, moving it closer or just far enough away for effect and always without resorting to shouting. Go and stand in various parts of the venue and judge for yourself how well the speakers cover that area. This will give you that confidence allowing you to perform on stage in the knowledge that everyone can hear you just fine. If you find an area that is not well covered or has a dud or blown speaker bring it to the attention of the Entertainments Manager and stage manager, if your centre has one, at the earliest opportunity.

MASSIVE RULE

Watch, Listen and Learn......But **Never** Steal.

By all means soak up ideas on how to run competitions, introduce acts or link events. Make a note of what humour works with what occasion. Even put things in the old memory bank for use at another place at another time. But…..................................
....

Don't go on stage and use someone else's repertoire

Don't go on before anyone and use one of their lines, jokes or catchphrases

Don't use gags or any material that you have picked up from visiting cabarets

Don't pinch someone's fun competition or audience participation idea and use it before they can

---

Do use all of the above to inspire you

Do use that inspiration to make you an all round better performer

Do pay attention to professional artiste's acts and learn how best to structure your own

Do be yourself and let your personality dictate what type of material will work for you

Of course there are some standard trade competitions, events and ways of making mundane things such as bingo a whole lot livelier etc that an Entertainments Manager should be passing onto his or her team and it goes without saying that a certain amount of patter will be handed on with this. There is no problem with this at all in fact it is one of the things that keeps our industry alive and kicking with highly professional, vibrant, fun entertainment that guests have come to expect and depend upon.

Now is also a good time to be getting constructive criticism too, it's nice and early in your development but do encourage your peers to continue to give you feedback no matter what stage of your career you are at. You can augment this with self critical appraisals from time to time. Basically you want others to give you honest opinions on your performances in general but as compere the things they are looking for are clarity, style, correct use of humour etc etc not forgetting to ask them to point out any annoyances or repetitive habits that you may not be aware of. Remember these little habits left unchecked can transform into whacking great big habits that can at best make you look daft and at worst completely ruin your performance. The most common are verbal, with the obvious um's and er's, but there is an infinite number of words, phrases, coughs, throat clearing or noise repetitiveness that one can fall into without realising. As for the physical aspect, well the mind conjures up all sorts of ways of getting us to embarrass ourselves in the form of a 'stressful habit'. Some of us shuffle about like demented penguins others constantly scratch our bottoms like a flea bitten gibbon or worst still keep touching ourselves like Michael Jackson on heat. I for example used to habitually touch my nose, thankfully stopping short of actually picking it. But the mere action of my hand constantly reaching for my face and my forefinger searching out my proboscis was enough to ensure audiences were beginning to concentrate on that act, counting in the next recurrence and being very pleased with themselves when they got it spot on. It was almost as though I was performing a second little game-show just

---

for them. Of course the problem was that while they were taking part in that hilarious new version of 'take your pick' or were justifiably being bugged to distraction by my automated involuntary movement, they weren't paying attention to anything that I had to say. A bit of a hindrance for a compere wouldn't you say? Yes indeed it was and even more so for a comedian. Good friends did point it out to me at an early stage but, luckily, when I continued to do it without realising they went to the trouble of filming me to prove how annoying and distracting it actually was for someone sitting in my audience.

You have no excuse as these days being filmed is almost a daily event with everything from mobile phones to the spy satellite passing thousands of miles overhead, from CCTV to the X-Factor….well you know what I mean. The fact is it's so easy to get yourself filmed while on stage now I highly recommend that all of you do exactly that in fact you'd be mad not to. There really is nothing better than this firsthand experience to see what you look like on stage and work out those traits.

So do actively encourage constructive criticism, have audio and visual recordings so you can look at and listen to yourself, and remember if you should catch yourself flicking your nose I am living proof that it is curable. Although I will let you into a little secret……I do catch my digit having a little wander in that direction from time to time. Thank goodness for good mates!!!

Ok you're on the mic, used to the sound of your own voice, all habits eradicated, volume is perfect, found the style that, suites you and you have a nice piece of patter to use……You're a compere!!! Bravo – good for you.

Wow is that it then? Is that all there is to this compering malarkey?
Well that is the basics covered really but you know me I wouldn't leave you to fend for yourself from there. So let me give you a few simple tips to guide you which, if you adhere to, could be the difference between you being just an ok announcer or that **great** compere.

KNOW YOUR SUBJECT
I cannot over emphasise the importance of the statement 'Know Your Subject'

No matter what you are about to compere be it a short link or running an entire competition, calling bingo, introducing a major celebrity, fronting the horse racing on DVD or a family sports day…. 'Know Your Subject'.

Getting the message yet?

I sincerely hope so because many a debacle has ensued when some smart Alec thought they would just wing it! Thinking how difficult can it be? After all it's not as if the guests know if it's all going horribly wrong is it?

You think not???

Well that would be your first big mistake right there. Guests go to holiday centres for years on end. A lot of them know the rules of just about everything inside out and are only too well aware when a competition has gone wrong or if the way people have been allowed to be judges has meant a family member or friend wins, as we talked of in another chapter, and you don't want to chance the ramifications I warned you of there, happily though this is all very easily avoided if you just 'Know Your Subject'.

So what do I mean by 'Know your subject?' Do I mean study it? Well to some degree, yes, that's exactly what I mean. Bingo has its own unique pitfalls compared to darts, snooker or table tennis for example. But not KNOWING any of these subjects before you attempt to compere any one of them will result in that debacle. Fun competitions are fun because we take them very seriously and KNOW the rules and procedures of that competition before we go anywhere near a mic to compere it.

You will already have found many of the do's and don'ts for a myriad of events in this book and there are many more to come in chapters that follow. But once you are made aware that you will be required to compere a particular event that you have not compered before, seek out the 'expert' in that field. A sports organiser, life guard or children's entertainer for instance but it could just as well be your Entertainments Manager or fellow 'coat' that usually runs that event and don't forget what I have said about watch, listen and learn either. Make sure you KNOW the rules of that event, be in no doubt that you KNOW exactly how a competition should run in order that you end up with a winner and more importantly the fair and rightful winner. Quite simply do not ever try to compere any event, show or competition without 'Knowing Your Subject'. If you were ever to be stupid enough to be tempted to try and do this when it involved anything where your guests have to pay money, for example bingo, hoy, horseracing on DVD or any gaming activity for that matter.... I have one very good piece of advice for you...

DON'T

When it comes to visiting cabarets go and talk to them well before they are due to go on. Find out if there is any particular phrase they would like you to use when you introduce them. Don't forget some acts have their own unique catchphrase that they probably won't thank you for using. They will want it to have its full effect the first time they use it in their act. Others will want you to use it as part of a warm up for their entrance...the point is you won't know unless you ask. When you talk to them get a little background history e.g. any TV, radio, cruise ship or major venue appearances and what they have been doing recently. There is nothing better for a visiting cabaret than to have a big build up delivered by a professional compere.

A good example would be something like:

"Ladies and gentlemen Camp Superblue is proud to present one of Britain's funniest men, his talents have seen him make TV appearances on such shows as Live at the Apollo, QI and Have I got news for you. He has thrilled audiences at packed venues including The Royal Albert Hall and The London Palladium. But tonight we are fortunate enough to have him right here with us in the sunlight lounge. So it gives me enormous pleasure to introduce to you, direct from his highly successful tour of ships on the Royal Caribbean Cruise-line, please welcome the one and only MR Charlie Giggles"

Also if it's a vocalist, comedian or magician for example always check that any material you may be thinking of using, by way of an opening song, a quick throw away trick or a few silly gags to get the audience warmed up for instance, isn't going to clash with their act. To be honest my attitude to this has always been don't do whatever the visiting act is doing when 'putting them on' If it's a vocalist leave the singing to them, comedian does the gags that night and your magic will still be clever a few days later. I have recently seen the exact opposite at a centre and I have to say it made me feel uncomfortable to be truthful.

Always KNOW when they are ready to be 'taken off'. Most acts have a 'be ready' point that they will tell you about. It will be very recognisable and that is when they want you backstage and...well...er...ready.

It is very important to be aware of any false endings in order that you can elicit the correct response from the audience and enable the act to return to the stage and perform that 'oh so unexpected' encore. Although it needs to be no surprise to you and you don't get caught unawares when they suddenly go into another five minute routine either. Talk to them, KNOW what they plan to do and what they expect and want from you. In this way you can confidently 'take off' all acts with the same enthusiastic exuberance that you used to 'put them on' extracting the appropriate audience reaction of rousing, thunderous applause, cheers, whoops and even the odd standing ovation. Yes I can tell you from bittersweet experience that the compere really can induce the response that an act deserves with a little enthusiasm from him or herself or kill a room stone dead just as they are about to stand on its feet by their alternative lacklustre indifference.

For example in September 2010 I stayed at an adult only centre, which I do regularly and generally have good comments to make about the entertainers as well as the rest of the staff. However on this occasion I had gone specifically to see the inimitable Elki Brookes performing to celebrate her 50th year in showbiz. It was an amazing show and she was absolutely fabulous spending a lot of time with the guests who had travelled from far and wide to witness this. Unfortunately the previous evening one of the 'coats' had announced that Elkie would be performing two 'one hour' sets. Regrettably the compere did not seem to have checked this fact before she went on stage and Elkie went on to complete a fantastic very long set. Sadly as she left the stage the compere did not allude to this and showed no real enthusiasm about what had just taken place. Therefore we in the audience subconsciously referred back to the last piece of information we had been given on the subject even though that had been announced on the mic the night before. This alas meant we believed this was merely the end of the first set and so gave her a decent round of applause but were holding back on the....big cheers and whoops....not to mention the standing ovation and calls for more and encore encore for the second set.

This then became an eerie silence as the compere, who was still not on the stage but talking from behind the scenes somewhere, realised that Elkie and her band were now waiting in the wings for that very response. While I and the rest of audience were now being hit by the realisation that she had gone on for so long that a second set was impractical. Oh the agony of those seamlessly long moments. It was heartbreaking to think she had done all that time, given a magnificent performance, put her all into it and we had not responded as she had every right to expect us to, and the awful angst as we now got to our feet in order try to rectify this atrocious situation. We the audience bought Elkie and her band back onto that stage, we told her that she was brill, we told her that we wanted more, we told her that we appreciated what she had done for us that night and indeed for the past 50 years.

It was nothing short of disgraceful that the compere (who was in fact the Entertainments Manager) in my opinion never did actually recover this, but he did remember to tell us all about his fabulous 'coats' show the next day. Well it was ok but I have seen it that many times now that it's all wearing exceptionally thin. He also found time to let us know how much he wasn't looking forward to the up and coming 'Tinsel and Turkey' breaks which was a shame, because he was supposed to be promoting them.

I will never know if this was a genuine mistake (can't think why it would be) but the resulting embarrassment felt by all concerned should have been picked up by the compere and put right with flare, gusto and enthusiasm...not as it appeared, to me at least, with indifference.

Visiting and resident bands should be dealt with in exactly the same manner as a cabaret and although you will get used to a resident bands sets don't get caught out by being complacent.

Cabarets, bands and any other specialist performers or demonstrations etc must be made aware of the start and end times that **YOU** want them to perform. **YOU** are in control of the programme **NOT** them. Some will try to dictate to you for their own benefit but you **MUST** be strong in this aspect and always remember **YOU** are the client, **YOU** are representing the camp, firm, company and most importantly the guests who pay for their services. So they comply with **YOUR** wishes or they don't get to perform and don't get paid…..*it's as simple as that!!!*

Talking of specialist performers such sports stars or demonstrations for instance. Now is as good a time as any to cover this aspect of the role of a compere. There are so many varied types of course that it would be impossible to go over them all individually. Wrestling however would be a very good example of how you should approach this crucial side of your entertainment programme. That reminds me of a very essential point that I want to make at this juncture and you would do well to head my advice here, not very often I talk to you like that is it? No but I feel very strongly about it and it's at your own peril that you act any differently. The fact is that these lovely people, such as the wrestlers, are as much stars of your entertainment programme as the top named vocalists or comedians are in the evening. Indeed on many occasions they will provide more than their fair share of family fun and hilarity as well as dazzling or instructing your guests with their chosen skills be it snooker, darts, football, judo, swimming, dancing or......

Oh I did it again didn't I? Rambling off the point a wee little bit.....ok ref I'll take a warning.

Wrestlers as I was saying before I so rudely interrupted myself, wrestlers, yes indeed the wrestlers, well I have been incredibly fortunate over the years to have had the pleasure of working with some of the great names from this sport. When I started out there was a great group of men that would light up the lives of so many people when they rolled up to the camp. Mine most definitely, the other 'coats' and staff without a doubt, but the guests?....absolutely! Fabulous showmen such as the incomparable Billy Stock (sadly no longer with us but his memory lives on), the ever so controversial (but in a brilliant showmanship way and with great effect) Dave Heinz, the hairy scary one and only Tarantula, the fun loving Sanchez brothers, the man with many strings to his bow the personality that is Mel Stuart and then of course there is my old pal Brian Manelli who was the 'Guvnor' of one of the best British wrestling firms I ever had the pleasure of working with. In fact he very nearly got me onto the TV as a wrestling compere and or referee, me and some of his top wrestlers that is. You see TVS were going to bring back 'Saturday Afternoon All Star Wrestling' for grapple fans. He staged a free show at my centre, Romney Sands, and I compered some bouts and refereed others. They liked what they saw and it was all looking so good but unfortunately they went and lost their franchise. Oh well back to the drawing board. I have lost count of how many times I had come close to making it! Oh well that's entertainment. But getting back to the real stars, above are the names of but a few of them from that golden age, thankfully all of whom I am proud to say were or are friends of mine.

Visit SUPERBLUE HAPPY HOLIDAYS.com the home of honest holiday reviews

These magnificent athletes, yes athletes. There are not many 50 year old men that can get thrown around or even out of a ring three times a day every day. Take the smashes, cuts and bruises, sprains and even broken bones and keep going to make sure the show goes on. Trust me having been in that ring with them and come a cropper on more than one occasion for being in the wrong place at the wrong time.....it hurts!

These athletes astounded me with their agility, showmanship, kindness and warmth. Their stage presence was as massive, impressive and influential as Elton John playing the Albert hall. They would pack a whole ballroom on the hottest of summer's days in the middle of the afternoon (I have seen some so called big names fail to do that). If you were lucky enough to have them for an evening booking they would arrive, set up the ring (no mean feat in itself) causing little disruption and in no time at all, give a magical performance for all the family and then break the ring down, again with little fuss. Amazingly and professionally they would do all of this and be within minutes of the start and finish times you gave them keeping your advertised programme on track.

In short.....These people deserve your respect!!!

When dealing with specialist acts etc not all will be so professional and will try it on from time to time. The same rule applies here as before...you pay them...you're in control. Don't neglect all the other aspects we have discussed, talk to them, and find out what is going on, what they need from you, when they need to be taken off, How individuals (wrestlers for example) want to be announced, what they want and don't want you to say. 'Know Your Subject' if you don't know anything about the sport or discipline find out about it!!! If in the case of wrestling, darts, snooker, judo or any other event where you may have a professional referee or adjudicator NEVER announce a result until they have indicated to you that that is in fact the result they are giving. There are many intricacies that go with these specialised events, so bide your time and wait for that direction.

There are times of course when you are the compere and or referee for such events, as indeed I used to be while in the ring with the wrestlers, and this is when you really do need to 'Know Your Subject' or you can so easily end up in all sorts of serious trouble.....Talk....Ask!!!

Just before we move on I can feel your eyes keep flicking back up the page to the wrestlers, what is there that intrigues you I wonder?

Kindness and warmth!!! Oh I see well make no mistake about it these are hard men. They have to be to go through those daily rigours and then there are the hours upon hours of training that they put themselves through to perfect their skills, but those that I have come across over the years do an awful lot for charity, will come to the assistance of a friend at the drop of a hat (as I have had the fortune to discover on more than one occasion) and the humanity that I have witnessed firsthand has brought me to my knees on occasion. You see because they are what they are they don't need to 'big it up' they don't need to pretend to be hard and tuff, they don't have to try and scare you into respecting them. They are who they are and you find yourself respecting them for that and not what they seem to be.

There is probably another complete book about the times I spent with them and other artistes like the time we went sea fishing with Gary Wilmot, Shane Ritchie, George King and others: that was such a funny Story with Gary having one over on Shane 'big time'. Or with John Virgo, Cliff Wilson and Ray Reardon on the way back from a Pontins seminar in Devon and a very silly policeman. Then there was the brilliant 'let's get Superblue good and proper' end of season fable where I ended up naked in the ring or the ghost at Pontins Holiday Centre 'Dolphin' tale and so so many more.

But one story will always have a special place in my heart and will stay with me forever. Mel Stuart was being his usual nasty self on stage when he was thrown out of the ring into a screaming audience. He was met with the usual boos and hiss's and of course hit with an umbrella or two by fearless old ladies who would then scamper away before he got up off the ground. On this occasion he had landed on a table and was breathless for a few moments, an occupational hazard. When he looked up there was a terrified young boy, who had down's syndrome sat under the table. He was one of a group of similar youngsters that were staying with us that week. Mel quickly realising that his presence at such close proximity was causing the young man distress immediately got to his feet, made his way back to the ring and continued the bout with all the lively entertaining heart stopping acrobatic gusto and fighting spirit that we, audiences and his opponents had come to expect and admire from this baddy. But after the bout when all was packed away and the rest of the audience had gone out to enjoy the sunshine Mel noticed this group of people still sitting in the ballroom. He beckoned one of the carers (another fabulous group of unsung heroes you should do all you can to assist at all times) anyway he beckoned her over and asked if all was ok. She told him that the young man had been very frightened and didn't want to move for the time being so they all had to stay with him until he felt alright again. Mel went straight over to the group and sat with them for absolutely ages and all we could hear from them for the next hour or so was excited laughter as he did magic trick after magic trick or some silly stunt or other but mostly just putting himself out to make that young man happy again.

Did it work?

Well now let's see…..would you call this it working?

A few months later Mel was booked to perform at a town hall, where many wrestling shows are put on, he got himself backstage nice and early as he always did, honed his concentration after pulling a few magic tricks on the staff then got down to the business at hand he changed into his all black Mr nasty wrestling outfit and began to psyche himself up for his bout against a blonde haired pretty boy who was Mr nice guy personified. No matter Mel was well used to the wrath of the audience, hardened to the boo's and hiss's, even philosophical regarding the fact he would undoubtedly get a bashing from a brolly or two before the night was over. He steeled himself as the time for the bout drew neigh taking a few last deep breaths and a last couple of hard swings at the punch-bag. He made his way through the long corridors that lead to the auditorium, the coliseum in which these two gladiators would do battle and as he approached the end of the tunnel he could see the bright lights shining onto the ring of war, feel the anxious anticipation of a couple of thousand hardened wrestling fans baying for him to be defeated and not just beaten but completely crushed by this pretty boy that they would love as much as they would hate him. He felt the tension welling up inside of him as he heard the master of ceremonies begin to announce the vicious, mammoth fight that was about to ensue. He straightened himself up and marched fearlessly into the thunder dome to the sound of his heavy metal signature tune and the deafening noise of all star wrestling fans screaming abuse at him at the tops of their voices. He sprang into the ring over the rope like a leopard relishing the fear of its prey as it attacks, he eyed his opponent with a stone face that said "you are a dead man" the scene was set, this was it, the tension was excruciating as the two men took to their corners awaiting the sound of the bell the crowd hushed in excited anticipation and in that moment of calm…it happened…"we want Mel" " we want Mel" "we want Mel"…what the!!!

The whole auditorium was brought to a shuddering halt…a two thousand strong, hyped up, angrily worked up, anti Mel Stuart mob turned and fixed their furious stare at the source of such dissent. What would happen next? How would this nightmarish scenario end?

As the crowd rounded on the centre row of seating in the east wing of the hall to espy the Stuart cohorts they were confronted with the wonderful scene of a large number of young people, led by the boy from under the table, with dozens of homemade banners and t-shirts emblazoned with slogans such as "We love Mel Stuart" and chanting similar sentiments at the top of their very happy voices. What was this embittered lynch mob going to do? What could they do? The next few moments seemed to go in slow motion, just like the matrix, as everyone stopped looked at each other then back at this little band of cheering banner waving baddy fans then back at each other then at Mel Stuart who by now was stuck to the spot his mouth wide open and his brain in disarray working overtime trying to decide what the best course of action would be. Surely one way or the other he was going to upset one group of fans or the other. Was it to be his young band of, by now clearly to be, devoted followers or two thousand aficionados of the sport? What to do? What to do?

Well just like in the matrix that momentary slow motion moment passed and as the scene began to speed up to normal speed an excited buzz went around the room like a giant bee telling everyone what to do next.....and then it happened....it really happened......just like in any good Walt Disney movie....it happened. The whole place erupted into 'Mel Stuart Mania'....yes these stalwarts of bad guy detestation had had their stone hearts melted by the sincere enthusiastic love that these young people obviously had for Mel. All the hard work that had gone into the banners t-shirts and other sundry items they had made for him had not gone unnoticed either. What was there to do?..........Nothing except, maybe just maybe for one night only, maybe give these young people their hero.

And so it happened just like that. The whole auditorium filled with cheers and whoops every time Mel made a descent wrestling move and big heartfelt ah's resounded if the pretty boy got the better of him from time to time. But it happened on this cold winters night in a packed two thousand seat venue Mel Stuart, the baddest baddy of them all became the crowds favourite all star professional wrestler of the night. And for a small group of young people who would remain fans he could never be anything but the good guy.

What?

Did he win?

Oh I think so don't you?

I CAN'T REMEMBER THE RESULT OF THE BOUT THOUGH!

As if that were not touching enough a little point that I forgot to mention before and makes this an even more extraordinary story is the fact that; when Mel was thrown out of the ring, over the top rope, and landed on that fateful table it was no wonder that he was winded for a time and shows his selfless act of retreating to allow a frightened boy to recover and then going to spent so much time with them in their true perspective. Because you see it later transpired that Mel had actually broken a rib or two in that incident...................Incredible!

It is with great sadness that I add this entry into the book. Unfortunately that great man and fabulous friend, Brian Manelli, passed away just a few days ago. Fortunately he read all that I have written about the wrestlers and him and we actually met up just a short time ago at a Holiday Village to catch up. Thankfully he was very happy with the result. I am honoured to have known and worked with such a lovely person and will remember him with affection. I respectfully dedicate this chapter of the book to him. You will be missed my friend.

THE THREAD THROUGHOUT:

As I have said, probably more times than I actually needed to, there are going to be parts of chapters that are going to overlap others and this is one of those times, but.......... My granny used to have lots of balls of wool in the house, much to the cats delight, and as a little boy I would see those balls of brightly coloured softness on many occasions. Sometimes just one on its own and at other times there would be a whole basket full of them with a myriad of dazzling colours and shades presenting this little fellow with a spectacle of technicolor. But it didn't matter how many times or how often I witnessed these stringy bits of sheep's clothing, it wasn't until Gran got to work with those magic needles that I realised they were actually integral parts of a jumper, pair of gloves, babies outfit a scarf or even an early pair of swimming trunks. And so it is with my little stringy bits, on their own their ok, they're not bad even mildly interesting at times....but together they form the thread that glues so much of this book together. So as I carry on knitting let me tell you about a number of things we have discussed elsewhere but are definitely part of the romper suit that is the chapter on comperes and compering.

The swimming trunks? Ah yes well they were ok when they were dry.....but as soon as they got wet...oh dear! Still never mind I was only a baby after all.

M.V.T.

As the master of ceremonies you will have a big influence setting the standard and tone of material that will be used during your part of the programme. So never forget M.V.T. and consciously think about it every time you take to the stage or pick up a mic.

The right   **M**aterial

In the right **V**enue

At the right **T**ime

As a compere you will be thinking on your feet much of the time and it is easy to let your mouth overtake your brain. Don't let this happen, remind yourself of where you are and use language, behaviour and material appropriate for that venue at that time.

Enough said.

NAAFA

Not always asking for applause.

Now I don't mean to keep on but this one drives me mad at the best of times as you well know. But as a compere I expect you to be a professional and not drive your guests to distraction with this. You will have control of the mic for large amounts of time while compering and so be in control of the degree of annoyance you force upon your audience with this really awful practice for large amounts of time.

I honestly don't know why we have ended up with the situation as it is now here in the UK. So many other countries I have visited have evolved a far better ethos altogether. They have learned to let the audience applaud what they feel is a natural time to show that appreciation.

For example Americans and Canadians will go mad, cheering, whooping and clapping as soon as their country is mentioned. This is generally just good healthy, friendly rivalry and a smattering of patriotism and believe it or not you can, in point of fact, learn from this. For instance when using the 'house point system' you can elicit a similar reaction for any participant without ever using that unnecessary and annoying "let's hear it for" or "give them yet another round of applause for just being here". Unfortunately however the reality is that here in the UK we have spawned a culture amongst holiday centre entertainers that they should AAFA instead of NAAFA i.e. Always Ask For Applause...........and I do mean **ALWAYS!!!**

To the extent that.....

She's just won money at bingo.......round of applause!!!
He's just picked a raffle ticket.......round of applause!!!
A youngster said please.........……….round of applause!!!
The baby just smiled...……………. round of applause!!!
They just had a round of applause... round of applause!!!

You see the fact is that;

"And applause for...."
"Give them a round of applause for….."
"Let's hear it for….."
"Put your hands together for……"

Might well be what you can hear yourself saying.

But your guests hear;

" And yet another round of applause for someone who has done nothing to deserve it"

"Let's hear it for someone who has just won *MY* money"

"Put my hands together because they picked a raffle ticket out of a hat...WHY?"

"You want me to applaud yet again today? Is that what you call Entertaining Me?"

"You want me to applaud everything all of the time….for what?"

Good question, why are you asking the audience to clap every time someone so much as turns up? Well that may be a little exaggerated but only a little. Because all this, now enshrined ritual, does is really! Really!! REALLY!!! annoy the hell out of your guests and actually devalues the highly significant act of clapping someone.

So it should come as no surprise when you are trying to get a decent thundering round of applause for an act or one of your own shows or a contestant that has earned their moment of glory to find that the audience give you no more than they would had they just won bingo…….they are tired of clapping everything all the time. They now see it not as a show of enthusiastic approval but merely something the compere says to fill the time.

It really is high time this practice was called to a halt to reclaim the round of applause for only those occasions when someone has actually earned it. It's time you comperes became more imaginative and filled your time on stage with intelligent entertainment. You can always set an audience going with verbal team support e.g. men v women, left side v right side, adults v kids and of course there's always the good old house points.

So please refrain from boring your guests to death with incessant requests for a round of completely unnecessary, unearned and downright annoying applause.

A good compere is a NAAFA compere;

Not
Always
Asking
For
Applause

ADVERTISE

I won't dwell here for too long, we have talked of it elsewhere and it is really common sense but, as the compere it is your job to make sure guests are made aware of forthcoming events and themes etc. Use your time on the mic to inform them of particular items of interest such as special guest appearances, trips of note, fancy dress, talent shows or indeed any occasion that you or the management of other departments would like them to take an active part in.

This is where you will be required to utilise that flamboyant personality of yours. The Entertainments Manager will have liaised with other dept heads, bars, catering etc and will be asking you to promote tonight's cocktail, 2 for the price of 1 pizzas or a sale in the shop etc etc etc. Please don't see this as a chore or interference in your patter but rather remember that at the end of the day we are all part of a team and the reason you are up there in the first place is because the guests ARE spending their money at the bar, cafeteria or shop. So put passion and conviction into your efforts to promote what you are asked and keep it entertaining, trust me it's very easy. But please remember what I have said about not 'ripping your guests off'. If you feel this is happening make your voice heard with the management. **Your guests will definitely be, after reading this!!!**

CONTROL THE DANCE FLOOR

This is a hugely important yet underrated part of the compere's repertoire.

It is such a massive tool in the entertainment manager's arsenal. Amazingly however we never actually teach anyone about its magnitude or how you can in fact dictate the behaviour of your guests on the dance floor before they ever even leave their seats.

So please take note of what I am about to tell you.

If you have everything else right, you're entertaining, you're NAAFA, you're clear and you're interesting you will be in control and have the audience's attention every time YOU are on the mic.

Now's the time to lay down the law…well nothing heavy in reality just a few basic rules that the guests are expected to adhere to while in this or any other venue on the centre. Once you have relayed these points in a clear, concise and firm manner you will find that the majority of guests will, in fact, give you support and backing if you subsequently have to deal with transgressors afterwards. It obviously goes without saying that the compere will deliver this vital and serious information with a pleasant personality and, where possible, humour. But DO get the message across that these ARE RULES…….NOT REQUESTS!!!

If a rule is broken while you are on the mic use it to good effect to show you won't tolerate the transgression. The most effective way to do this is to take a leaf out of any good comedian's book and make the person the subject of appropriate jokes or comments etc to enforce the point. Do what is right for you and the moment but always try to do it in an entertaining manner. You need to get that point across but you don't want to offend the guest who may have simply forgotten the rule. We don't want to impose many rules, after all they are on holiday, but those we do ask them to abide by are necessary for the enjoyment, safety and general good of all.

Rules such as;

No walking across the dance floor during cabarets, competitions or shows.

The time children are to be off the dance floor – Adult time.

No drinking on dance floor etc etc etc

SAFETY

What's this got to do with the compere?

A lot as it happens.

Who do you think everyone will be looking to for quiet, calm guidance and leadership in the event of an incident?

That's right…..**YOU!**

Don't panic now because it just comes right back to that god old fashioned… 'Know Your Subject'.

For instance

Know where exits are

Know where emergency equipment is

Knowing these two things means that, if you have to, you can direct your guests out of the building or the appropriate personnel to the necessary equipment without panic. You will *only* be able to achieve this life saving feat if you **Know** where these things are without having to think about it.

KNOW THE EMERGENCY CODES

Every centre should have set phrases or words that relay a certain message to the staff without panicking the guests. For obvious reasons I am not going to give examples here but it is absolutely imperative that all staff know what they are.

But as the compere you are very likely to be the one delivering that coded message to the majority of staff on duty over the mic. So it doesn't take a brain surgeon to work out the importance of, not only, knowing what they are but also what action is needed to go with each of them. This is in fact imperative as you will be the one directing the guests and at times staff to comply with those actions.

Health and safety dictates that you will have systems in place for such eventualities. You, your managers and camp owners are obliged by law to ensure it is adhered to. One thing that is universal however in these situations is the calmer and more controlled you remain the calmer and more controlled your guests will be. You could actually be SAVING LIVES by your actions.

While most security staff and management have radios there is no substitute for an immediate response to a situation that is getting out of control. Again you can't beat a good old fashioned code phrase to alert them to the fact that you need their assistance. This carries the same proviso though: keep it calm and controlled. You can often feel trouble brewing in the venue well before it sparks off into physical contact between your guests, so calling security to show a visible presence at an early stage often defuses a potentially violent confrontation in the first place.

For working abroad please see that chapter but it's basically all the same as here except you will need to speak other languages or have translators.

What is a comperer?

A compere is the happy vibrant face of the Resort, Centre, Hotel, Park, Village or Camp

They are always in control
They are always professional
They always 'KNOW' their subject
They are always entertaining
They are NAAFA

WHEN THEY TALK OTHERS **WANT** TO LISTEN
Superblue 2011

CHAPTER TWENTY ONE

HOW TO BECOME A STAR

We have sort of touched on this subject elsewhere in the book haven't we? Well yes touch on it we did but it's time to take a look at it in its own right now.

But I have to be honest and say that I was sorely tempted to cut this chapter out all together. After all it is really aimed at those in the trade but then I thought, nah, I hope that many of you reading the book may indeed go onto become 'coats' in the future. So should I remove this one? Would that, in fact, just be me being lazy or would I actually be depriving, some of you at least, of useful information?

We established that the ultimate goal for many of you thinking of taking this journey of entertainment enlightenment is becoming a Star, a Celebrity a Household name but can it really happen to you?

Yes of course it can.

It has become a reality for many others like you over the years. We have already mentioned a few names in a variety of places in the book such as Shane Richie and Gary Wilmot. In fact there are two good cases in point.

Let me think about Shane for a moment, Mmm well let me see now we were both working at Pontins at the same time he was a blue 'coat' just like me, we had the same fun, drank as much as each other, danced and socialised and I was even appearing on the same stages as him. The Oldham Coliseum was one such occasion, seems like only yesterday, he gave a blinding performance of a plane lost in the fog, and I remember agents coming up to him at the bar afterwards and ....well next time I saw him he was well and truly on his way to stardom, but the hard work, heartache, pain, sorrow and joy was only just beginning for him. I'm not talking out of school here, just read his book to find out (actually I really recommend it).

Is Shane a star?

In my eyes he most defiantly is. Even though we met as bluecoats all those years ago and he has gone on to great things whenever I have met him since it's just been good old Shane, no Prima Donna, no look at me I'm too good to talk to you, just the great personality that is Shane. In fact a few years ago he went even further than that when he was appearing at the Road House, Covent Garden. He was doing a charity gig for Help a London Child. They had set up a highly guarded, raised area next to the stage for all the 'stars' that were there and believe me there were some seriously big names in town for that one. Anyway I was there, in the audience with a large group of special people (that's another story) when suddenly there's a tap on my shoulder and to my surprise Shane had not only seen me in the midst of the hundreds of people in the audience, but had taken the time to come down from the ivory tower of celebrities and seek me out. The look of amazement on the faces of those in my group summed up the moment really. He invited me up onto the 'All Star' Stage area and proceeded to introduce me to all and sundry as if I were one of them. The 'names' I met that day were all very nice to me and I enjoyed a few drinks with them before rejoining my group on the dance floor.

So there was Shane up amongst all those really famous names and he was well in demand at that time as he is today. He could have looked down his nose at me, just ignored me altogether, or even tried to big himself up at my expense, but no! He was a true gent and went out of his way to 'big me up' and in front of the other 'names', my friends and all in the Road House.

But of course I did mention another magnificent person who I have the absolute honour to remain friends with to this day and that is the outstandingly talented Gary Wilmot. Now there is a 'STAR' in every sense of the word. He can sing, dance, act and impersonate just about anyone. But unlike most 'jacks of all trades' he performs each and every one of these varied and demanding artistic disciplines with consummate professionalism, the highest degree of talent and panache that the likes of us mere mortals can only watch in wonder and enjoy.

I remember Gary from his early days on a TV talent show, but it was as an incredible visiting cabaret act in the 1980's that I was to get to know him as a person. And what a smashing person he is too, from right back in those happy days at Pontins he was a supreme performer and would fill whatever room he was appearing in. But he was always the friendliest of people whether it be spending time with the guests, hanging with us 'coats' or joining in the weekly 'staff v guests' football match. He always had that lovely cheery smile that we have come to recognise and love.

I remember the day I discovered he had been given his big break. He was to have his own television show....oh boy everyone that knew him was over the moon. If ever anyone deserved to make it big it was Gary. The show was of course a great success and he was as brilliant as ever, we couldn't be happier for him.

But what would Gary be like now? Would he still spend time with us and the guests? Would he talk to us or even turn up at holiday camps at all now that he could command, what must have been, larger fees from now on? Well happily Gary is Gary and on his return or I should say triumphant return to the holiday centres, where as he used to fill the room before, the guests were now hanging from the rafters to see him. Yes his TV show had been a great hit, yes he must have had offers flooding in and yes I'm sure he could command a much higher fee elsewhere but......... This was Gary Wilmot and Gary Wilmot is an honourable man and so it was that he honoured his contract and never missed an appearance at my centre for the rest of the season. I mentioned it to him once and he said "it was just the right thing to do".

I have always remembered this and trust me when I am an International Star of Film and Television.......what? Oh that's nice isn't it.....ok I'm going to ignore that and carry on regardless.......there's a good film title......anyway.....uhum......

Anyway as I said I am extremely privileged that Gary and I are still in touch and do you know over all those years of Staring in the West End on Television and Radio not to mention touring with his own shows as well as alongside the biggest names in the business, he remains one of the nicest down to earth individuals I have ever had the pleasure of meeting. It was in fact Gary that introduced me to a saying that I have tried to live my life by and still do to this day.

"Be nice to people on the way up....you never know who you will meet on the way down".

Gary certainly does not have to worry about the 'on the way down' bit and I can't go any lower so I try to emulate this fabulous man and concentrate on the 'be nice to people bit'.

Is Gary a Star? Oh goodness me yes and here is a perfect example of a person being a true star in so many ways. So much so that I know he would not expect it and hope he won't tell me off for it. But.............

I would like to dedicate this chapter to him

Cheers Gary

Why tell you these stories here? Well you see, you can be a massive 'name' and you might be having your 15 minutes of fame, but that does not make you a 'Star'! What you do with that 15 minutes, how you treat people, if you make the most of it, enjoy every second of it and respect yourself and others throughout this time is what will ultimately prove whether you are a true Star or not. Generally the bigger the 'name' I have met the nicer the person. So before we crack onto the ways you can help yourself become a 'star, let me please ask you to do yourself the biggest favour of all. Be a nice person and stay a nice person, it's not a weakness it's a strength and it will get you so much further than being a 'legend in your own lunch time'. It's a job, a way of life like no other. So if you are one of the lucky ones that manages to make a living out of it, be humble, be grateful, be proud but most of all be nice!!!!!

FAMOUS?

I did mention famous there didn't I. Well the fact is that people are famous for all sorts of reasons. Trust me you don't want to be famous; you want to be a 'star'. If you just want to be famous, don't bother with all the hard work, blood sweat and tears, the heartache, the ups and downs, the long hours, the long weary drives through the night in the wind rain and snow, the hard audiences that just want bingo to start in some working men's clubs. The long lonely days and nights travelling from one town to another trying to get a handful of people to clap at the end of a song or raise a smile at just one of your jokes. Oh yes this is what all so called 'over night' stars have gone through, it's what makes you resilient, it's your training ground, your apprenticeship. It's where you learn to be tough, and where you learn to appreciate it when you get your break, and the reason you really should be nice, you have earned the right to be there, you have earned the right to be a 'star'. So be proud. Others do like you, they want to like you when they meet you, be nice and you will inspire those others to want to be like you.

Famous?

If you want to be famous.............. Go on big brother!!!

THE JOURNEY

I painted a bit of a gloomy picture of being a cabaret artist there, but you really do need to know the truth if you are just starting out in the business. Life can be very hard at times on the road, but this is a vocation you have chosen and like anything worthwhile its worth working for, it's an apprenticeship like no other on the planet, but while it has its hard times, I found they are far outweighed by the good times when they come. The fun, the laughter, the lifelong friendships, the stories that you will tell your grandchildren and bore your mates with time and time again, stories of true life adventures that will have people captivated for hours. So yes it can be rough, but the people you meet, the places you see, the things you will do that you would never ever have done otherwise, are all worth every minute in the end analysis. So next time you find yourself dropping off at the wheel as you drive back from some terrible night that you would rather forget and are thinking of packing it all in. Pull over, sit for a while put some really cool music on and think. Think about how many people you know that are lucky enough to be sat out in their car at 3am in some quiet spot, the stars putting on a show for free, and you can set off again any time you like and have that clear road ahead of you getting home and chilling, just as your mates and neighbours are getting up with hangovers, cutting themselves shaving, before rushing down a cup of lukewarm coffee and clambering into their cars and zooming off just in time to sit in a traffic jam for the next two hours, or crammed into that packed train, squashed between the smelliest and boniest man in the world standing for the next three hours because of a signal light malfunction just outside Clapham Junction, just like there was yesterday, and the one outside Vauxhall the day before. Only so that they can spend the next 8 to 12 hours in an office or a factory doing a job they hate and will do every day for the next 30 years.

As you put the lid back on your flask, and sip the coffee you had made for you by those nice people at the club, you know the one you were at tonight, the one where you did not go down so well, the one you would rather forget. The one where the club sectary, said "don't worry son their a hard bunch here, you did ok, they didn't throw anything did they" just as his wife hands you back your flask, full of piping hot coffee she has made for you. Yes that club!!!

Now that wasn't such a bad night after all was it?

No not in the big scheme of things my friend!

There will be stinkers, make no mistake, but hay that's life.

But as those same friends and neighbours trudge home again from their dreary sad unhappy days work, downtrodden, tired fed up, annoyed that they didn't stand up to the boss again, who picks on them relentlessly, and wouldn't let them have a pay rise or that week off they wanted, back on the same train carriage stuck between the same people they were stuck with this morning, or on that road not moving again for the next 3 hours, in the same traffic jam as this morning and every morning, only going in the opposite direction as it does every evening. There you are!!!! Setting out on another adventure in life, off to some wonderfully named place, on a clear road, to meet some lovely new people, see some brill new things and perform in a new venue and be a star.

Be a star?

Oh yes, remember, famous = big brother, being a Star = being worthy of your art, being a nice person, being liked, being a star. And if at the end of the day you are one of the lucky few who do become very famous because they are a 'star' then you really have had the ultimate blessing, and good luck to you, and as Gary, Shane and many others have proved to me over the years, being a 'Famous Star' comes from being a nice person first.

YOU'RE IN THE BEST PLACE OF ALL

Holiday centres are so fantastic for giving you the chance to find your feet, learn an act and how to be with people, while in a safe, happy environment with experienced entertainers all around you, cabarets, bands and even the other 'coats' that have been out there.

So as obvious as it sounds my first real piece of advice is to soak up as much as you can during this time. Watch, listen, ask and learn. Go to the camps, summer shows, theatres, in fact any performance you can get to, to see how others that have made it 'do it'. Use your time at any holiday centre to try out new material or even put an entirely new act together, you will never have such an easy going audience who will forgive you tomorrow if you don't go so well today, but remember M.V.T.

That's where I really learnt my trade; remember right at the beginning of the book? Empire Ballroom Leister Square? Auditions for Pontins? No? Oh of course some of you will have turned straight to this chapter too. If you are one of those people, that last sentence will mean nothing to you. So here begineth lesson one, 'Always start at the beginning' it's the only way, there are no short cuts to being a great act, here endeth the first lesson. For the rest of you, yes that day in Leister Square at the Empire Ballroom, still sends a tingle through me, yes it was a long lonely walk across that massive dance floor to the sound of my own feet, but boy what a wonderful long journey I have been on since then. You may recall the reason for that long walk was actually all my own fault. Having ticked every box in the book, saying I could do absolutely everything from the tango to trampolining, from rugby to ballet, from Country & Western to opera and of course there were those terrible jokes that I tried to get away with in front of a couple of thousand people, all willing me to die on my feet, because they wanted that exact same Blue Jacket that I was fighting for. Oh yes they were willing me to fall flat on my face and I didn't disappoint them, did I? But as you will also recall I was so incredibly lucky and a few weeks later there I was in my lovely shining new Pontins uniform at a camp that had a couple of thousand gests that wanted to be entertained. I can tell you that I did not waist a moment and grasped this lucky break with both hands. I did exactly what I am telling you to do, I watched, listened asked and learnt, not only did I very quickly become an Entertainments Manager, but I put together quite a nice little stand up routine early on too. You see it turned out that I was quite good at it after all. Well!! I still count my blessings to this day. I tried, joke after joke, routine after routine, gimmick after gimmick until it all came together and then took it on the road, which is where you really start to learn so much more about different types of acts, for example comedy can vary from place to place venue to venue. This is where you really learn to deal with aspects of life on the road and specialised little intricacies like hecklers etc.

Once you have something resembling an act get out there and see what happens when you try it out on a non-friendly non holiday camp audience. There are many ways of doing this, enter talent shows, there are quite a few around the country, so try a varied amount of these, see how you do in a working man's club up north, a pub in London, or a theatre in a seaside resort, The 'stage' paper is possibly the best starting point for these. Please take my advice here, and never pay to enter a contest.

Volunteer for charity shows, again in your local area. But spread your wings, let it be known that you are willing to do this when you talk to visiting acts or bands, and any time you talk to an agent. Now this is a bit tricky because while you want to get out there and show off your talent, you don't want to become known as the cheep or even free 'fill in' act that gets agents 'off the hook' when they are asked to send someone for a charity event, just to keep a good customer sweet. So just be aware of who you are doing what for and if you are finding that you are getting calls from an agent or agents to do a lot of this kind of work but not paid gigs, and I do mean decently paid bookings, it's time to call a halt to it. We all want to do our bit for charity and once you reach a certain level I hope you will do, just as Gary and Shane have. But if you're doing nothing but free shows, you are being used and used badly and it won't be long before you might need the help of one of these charities' yourself. In short do your bit. It's useful to get your name and face known by agents, bookers and other acts, but keep control of it and if it's getting out of control put a stop to it until you can control it again. Use the contacts you make from these to network as much as possible, if someone says "call me" get their number and do just that. Keep in touch by phone or email but don't become a pest or it will have the opposite effect from the one you are after.

Whether at a centre, a talent show or a charity event once you feel ready to move up a gear and take this act on the road, get as many agents to come and watch you perform as you can. If you are getting them to come to the centre, village, park, hotel or camp where you are working please remember the following rules. Not is it only common decency and respectful to your peers, but if you don't and it all goes horribly wrong because someone objects to them being there and decides to make that objection known, either overtly or covertly (by messing up your act or verbally destroying you to the agent) Your career as a cabaret act and therefore your chance to become a 'star' will be over before its even begun.

So always clear it with your management, both the Entertainments Manager and the Centre Manager. Let the bands, other acts on that night and all of your colleagues in the team know that there will be an agent in the venue. Again only common courtesy and hopefully you will get full support from them if you have done it openly in this manner. Make sure they are aware that you will be fully supportive of them in the same situation and then please do be supportive!!! What goes around comes around!!!!

If you are fortunate enough to attract an agent to your centre, make their stay as comfortable as possible. Do everything you can to make it a very pleasant experience, not just hope they will wait around and be amazed by your talent.

START AT THE BEGINNING

When they arrive make absolutely sure that they are expected by whoever it is they have to report to in order to enter the premises and for that person to be able to contact you immediately on their arrival. Ensure there will be no problems whatsoever re this part of the operation.......

Operation?

Oh yes this needs to be a slick, well thought out and executed operation.

Make sure their first impression is a good one. No problem getting in. They are completely expected and treated with respect and dignity. You are alerted and turn up to welcome them ASAP, by that I actually mean immediately if not sooner.

Ask them before hand if they would like overnight accommodation, and if they do, have this in place for them too and have their bags taken there. It's the little things that count. You want them to be in the best frame of mind they can be when they eventually get to watch you perform. But for now you are showing them the person, the 'star' potential behind the act. It's up to you who pays for this, sometimes the centre will have a very good concession rate that you can afford and if you really want to impress this agent or booker a free room is not a bad start now is it?

Ok back to their stay being a pleasant one. Once you have them settled. It is always a brilliant thing if you have managed to sort out something at the bar for them. This could be as simple as they don't have to queue at a busy camp to putting some money behind the bar yourself, so they don't have to pay for drinks. This really is up to you. Please please please do always go through the bars manager for anything like this otherwise it can lead to all sorts of un-pleasantness, just what you didn't want, and do the same with the restaurant or food outlet. In short do whatever you can to make them feel welcome and important. They are important to your future. Don't however lose sight of the fact that you have paying guests to take care of and they must always come first no matter what!!!! A good agent or booker will completely understand this anyway.

You can't and don't want to be hanging around them all night, they will want to observe you not only on stage, but with people in general, how you interact with other staff and guests. So it's worth taking note to see if they are travelling alone? Are they planning to meet anyone else for the evening? Do they already know people at your centre who will be socialising with them through the evening? If not it is a good idea to have someone lined up to be with them during that time. This could be the same person, a friendly 'coat' who is off duty for example or a number of different people from the team taking it in turns but **not** at the expense of your guests. This has a number of positives, it ensures that pleasant experience we talked about, someone is there to facilitate the little niceties I have mentioned e.g. the bar and restaurant etc. They don't feel uncomfortable sitting alone in this family environment and they are not pestered by others vying for their attention at the expense of your performance.

BE SEEN BY AS MANY PEOPLE AS POSSIBLE
Have a DVD, CD or tape made of your act or part of it at least if you don't want to give too much of a unique one away. Complement this with professional photographs and promotional material including your CV to date. Please do not skimp on these things because you are selling yourself and if these look cheap, you look cheap. If these are classy, professional well presented and quality then guess what.........exactly!!!!! Get these sent out to as many agents, bookers, cruise lines, TV companies, holiday centres and companies as you can.

A good email address is vital these days so keep this as simple as you can, and change it as few times as possible. Never to change it would be the best option because your details could lay in an agents files for ages before the right gig comes up, and if they can't get in touch now, you could have just blown your lucky break. The same goes for your contact telephone number. If you have to, get a second phone, a pay as you go for example; just a cheap one that you would never need to upgrade will do, but it will always keep the same number!!! Whatever contact details you do put on this material it is your life line to those people, if it changes and they don't know, you are lost to them so it's all been for nothing.

Consider very carefully having your own website where, not only can any of the above find you at any time and see what you are up to, but you won't need to send out DVDs or CDs etc just your literature and photos with the web address and they can go on line and see the act. It will save you a small fortune and look professional at the same time. If you are going down this road, the same rules apply re being professional, slick etc etc. Don't make it look cheap. Don't forget to visit www.Acts-R-Us.com and advertise on your own web pages for a ridiculously low price.

You can make your own website quite inexpensively if you look on the net there are a number of domain companies that will allow you to do this if you have the inclination. However if you decide to have one built for you….shop wisely. Don't take the first offer you are made. You generally don't need all the expensive extras they offer. You just want to get yourself out there to start with. After a while if you build up a following, as you can do working at a holiday centre, you can set up chat forums etc.

Something that I can't impress upon you enough is that if you are going to send out any material or place it on your web site or any other web site and you are the only one on it that's fine., but if there is any other person on it e.g. other 'coats', bands or acts you must get their permission to do so. It's that good old common decency again at the very least. Be very very very careful that you're not breaking any company rules or worse copyright laws.

EQUITY CARD

Every self respecting act will want to own an equity card. There will be many a door shut to you and your future journey towards stardom without it so visit www.**equity**.org. **uk** for advice on this.

Equity has seven offices which between them cover the whole of the UK. Usual office hours are 9.30am - 5.30pm Monday to Friday. Staff in these offices deal with issues on behalf of members based locally or who are working in the area. Staff at the Head Office cover, national matters and industrial agreements plus issues arising for members based in London and the South East and where the central helpdesks are also sited. In addition there is a network of Equity branches currently comprising 31, which have regular meetings and events for members and student members within their area. A full list of Equity direct contact numbers and emails is available in the Members and Student Members areas of their website above.

So you want to be a 'star'?

In this chapter I hope I have explained what a 'star' is and how you can start on the road to becoming one. I hope that you reach it safely and soundly and that when you get there you will remember all that I have said about being a nice person. But while you're still on that journey take this as your motto;

WORK HARD FOR THE FUTURE- BUT HAVE FUN AND ENJOY THE PRESENT.

Remember these are the best days of your life!!!!!!!!!!!

CHAPTER TWENTY TWO

ETIQUETTE

'Étiquette means behaving yourself a little better than is absolutely essential'
Will Cuppy (1884 - 1949)

Throughout the book I have talked about the 'right thing to do' 'common decency' and 'showing respect' etc etc etc and it's all very well going on about it without quantifying what I mean isn't it? Indeed it is!

It is high time I put my money where my mouth is and confer upon you the rules set for the Entertainment Managers and 'coats' in that other book. I really didn't intend to insult their intelligence or belittle their natural well mannered kind selves and so much of what I tell them I would sincerely hope they would do or not do as the case may be without my pontificating. The reality is, however, that if I translated the obvious into factual documentation via the printed word those that may not be as sociably responsible won't be able to use the excuse "I didn't know".

Hence as you peruse this chapter you will probably have to forgive me for much of its content. Nevertheless you may find yourself being grateful to me for it in the future when having to deal with one of those socially inept individuals that we do come upon, even in this trade, from time to time.

Again we have touched on many aspects of this throughout the chapters in this book but we need to consolidate all that we have talked about in an easy to read, easy to find and easy to quote format.

So let's take a look at what I deliver to them in 'Tales of Superblue' on the subject known as:

THE 'COAT'S' ETIQUETTE

1) **Never use inappropriate language or behaviour**
   Remember **M.V.T**.
   Swearing is an absolute No No at anytime
   Always remember YOU are a role model to the kids and even teenagers

2) **Always be clean and tidy**
   And **S.M.I.L.E**

3) **Always show respect for your guests**
   I would feel insulted if after all we have talked about I had to elaborate here
   Also see #8

4) **Always show respect for other staff**
   As I have pointed out many times, you are not a star, a Prima Dona or better than or above anyone else. The only reason you are allowed to enjoy your job, having the fun you are having, being able to get up on that stage performing in the first place is because of all of those hard working staff members, who have less glamorous jobs than you, working very hard to ensure the guests, their guests, YOUR guests have every amenity that they could wish for. You must show them the respect they deserve. You must support and stand up for them when anyone is wrongly having a go at or being rude to them and they will do the same for you.
   You earn respect……not expect it!!!

5) **Always show respect for visiting cabarets or bands**
   As long as they show you respect
   Remember it's always YOUR programme
   They are getting paid to fit into it

6) **Never Upstage**
   Never do anything to distract while another artiste is performing
   No matter if visiting cabaret or another 'coat'

This could be as simple as unintentionally talking too loudly at the bar or intentionally trying to be funnier than them while sitting in the audience

My view is staggeringly straight forward on this point............
The unintentional should be warned ONLY ONCE then sacked
The intentional *SACKED*

7) **Mingle**

It's part of your job to socialise with as many guests as possible
You know this all too well and indeed a good 'coat' loves nothing better than doing just that. While it may not come as easy at first to some of you trust me and work on it.
Don't spend all or even most of your time with one family or group.
It is very easy to fall into this trap because......
They are nice to you
They are easy to be with
They will always get up and dance when the Entertainments Manager is paying attention
They always buy you drinks
You fancy one of them
Or any combination of the above
The simple fact is that not only are you committing a holiday camp sin by neglecting your other guests but you are on your way to agro.
The other guests **will** resent this ignorance and the out and out snub on your behalf.
They have paid the same amount of money to be there. Little Jonny or Suzzy are sad because their favourite 'coat' always sits at the other children's table.
Remember it's not about you!! It's all about the guests!!! All of the guests!!!!
God help you when one of them wins a competition or bingo let's say.......
And if it's the one you have made it clear to the world you fancy..........
Oh dear oh deary deary me!!!

And PLEASE PLEASE PLEASE don't ever imagine for one second that you are so talented that this rule does not apply to you.

They will soon let you know how much that does not matter to them.

If you were on my camp with that attitude on the first night you would be on the Dole by the second day…no decent Entertainments Manager would tolerate this.

8) **Don't get drunk**

I think it goes without saying that this is a coverall statement and most of you realise that getting drunk on duty would be unacceptable.

However there are a couple of points to raise here.

For instance being drunk off duty can be just as detrimental to your career if you lose control and break any of the other rules. Best practice is to stay away on nights off.

You need to bear in mind that you are a role model so be particularly careful if around children or teenagers.

Many holiday companies these days don't allow the drinking of alcohol while on duty. But even when it's a soft drink that you are accepting from a guest, and let's face it you should be getting offered them if you are doing your job properly, don't abuse their generosity.

Only ever have a small 'whatever' and don't keep going back to that table for more. That's not doing your job, it could be financially embarrassing for them and as we have covered, you are leaving yourself wide open to so many allegations and at the very least you're not socialising like you know perfectly well you are supposed to.

9) **Be discreet**

No matter what you may hear when socialising with guests or colleagues unless otherwise asked to do so…KEEP IT TO YOURSELF.

People being people will tell you things because they have let their guard down and feel they can trust you due to your friendliness and natural communication skills.

This is sacred…you never tell another living soul.

Be proud that they feel they can confide in you and honour their trust.

You tell one single person, no matter how much you beg them not to tell anyone else and it will be around the entire village before you get back to that table.

Well a slight exaggeration maybe but the sentiment fits.

If as above you have feelings for anyone and anything takes place.......
Keep it to yourself!!!
Show them the respect they deserve..never boast about what you may crudely see
as a…. conquest……
When dealing with internal matters of your own department and or another's keep
schtume….let the relevant information be relayed by the relevant person.
Don't leak anything whether or not you're sure of the facts.

10) **Never gossip to guests**
Never discuss internal matters
Policies, Gossip Or what you see as problems
This will cause untold grief as you will see in the chapter on guests & owners

11) **Visiting other villages, parks, centres, resorts, hotels or camps**
Always call first and get permission from the Entertainments Manager
Ask your operations manager or camp owner if they would like to put in a courtesy
call to their equivalent at that village
Once there act in a respectful manner
Just as if you where on your own park
All of the above rules apply
You are representing your own camp, company and above all yourself
You never know who may be there…they will remember you
You never know when you may need a job
You never know when you may have to work with one or more of them
You never know when one might actually be your Entertainments Manager
Be remembered for the right reasons

12) **NEVER NEVER NEVER NEVER!!!**
Have you got the gist that this might just be as important as it gets???
Well it is…..and then some.
There is one rule that there is never ever an excuse for breaking…
And this is it…..

NEVER NEVER NEVER NEVER HAVE A CHILD ANYWHERE NEAR YOUR ACCOMMODATION

That is all there is to it!!!

They will from time to time find out where you live and visit unannounced
Should this happen you MUST get another 'coat' to assist you and return them to their parent's with the explanation that this is what occurred and make it clear it must NOT happen again.

<u>**UNDER NO CIRCUMSTANCES EVER**</u> allow a child into your room, chalet, bungalow or caravan etc

13) **All of the above**

All of the rules apply whether you are on or off duty
Enough said.

CHAPTER TWENTY THREE

GUESTS AND OWNERS

Superblue says "They must always put their Guests First"

You are probably sick of hearing this statement by now and I make no apologies for that because if Entertainments Managers and 'coats' have learnt nothing else from the other book but to put their guests first.... At least whatever they do from that stand point, their motivation will be right.

I just know you are waiting for the 'but' or 'however' and I am never one to disappoint So..........

However, there are couple of scenarios where they will be more than justified in not putting certain guests or owners before them-self, colleagues or indeed other guests on holiday at that time. But... (See what I did there?) I tell them not to worry about them for the moment and concentrate on the 99.9% of the guests who are lovely people and for you they will.... **Always Put The Guests First.**

There is absolutely no problem with the fact that a 'coat' is having the time of his or her life and loving every minute of it. In fact I would be seriously worried if they were not and if they are having that kind of fun you guests should be having that kind of fun by definition. It only becomes a problem, and actually a massive problem in my book and this is my book so it would be a massive problem, if they start to have fun at the expense of their guests.

This is their job, their way of life; it doesn't get any better than this. They are actually paid to have fun, they are paid to have fun with their guests, they are paid to give you a taste of that wonderful lifestyle for a week or two in what is otherwise a 'normal' life. I am not saying for one moment that all or even nearly all of you aren't happy with that life, but this is your escape into a world of fun, laughter and just plain relief from all those cares and worries for a short time. You have chosen to come to their place; you have put yourself and your family into their hands for your holiday. You have paid good money to be there, so *grateful* 'coats' must enjoy sharing that fun lifestyle.

As I write this chapter the economy has had a massive down turn, Northern Rock went bust, then banks all over the world followed suit, banks going bust? House prises are slashed and tumbling faster than any time in 30 years, food prises are rocketing, We are in a recession but the fact is that while now is a particularly difficult time for the nation and the holiday industry may well suffer for a while. This should make them even more humble when you still chose you to spend what money you do have after tightening your belts at their centre. Economic downturn or not many of you will have worked hard all year to be able to afford to bring your families away for a holiday. It's a massive expenditure and one that you will have thought about and planned for very carefully, not to mention looked forward to immensely. You have done them the great honour of entrusting them with that most precious of things 'Your Happiness'. Of course 'coats' are just a part of the team at any camp that should be working together to bring this about but I hope by now they will have realised just how much difference they can actually make to any guests' day, just by being themselves and following all the steps we have spoken of in this and 'Tales of Superblue' thus far.

You will know by now that every guest is as important to me as another. I don't care if you have spent your last penny getting there or if you can afford to buy the entire holiday centre and neither should any Entertainments Manager or 'coat'. You are all their guests, you have all paid to be there, you have all chosen their village, park, resort, hotel, camp or centre........ In short you have all chosen them!!!!!!!!
They must not let themselves down by letting you down!!!!!!!!

Actually I do care if you have spent your last penny to get there, because when I was a little boy growing up that was my family, that was my one week a year holiday, my mum worked so hard to give me that one week of wonderment and I loved her and the Redcoats for making every magical moment of it.

Many of you guests treat it almost like a ritual returning year after year, quite often the same time every year. Some of you will even contact head office and find out where your favourite 'coat' or manager is working that season, and book up there. This happened to me on occasions with a particular group following me for quite a few seasons to camps owned by a variety of companies and finally to an independent, they used to enjoy playing practical jokes on me. They were a great crowd and I enjoyed their hi jinx which was just as well because they got up to some mad stuff, one year putting my car in the middle of the sports field fully decorated for all to see, now I had grown to know this particular group and they were sensible and took care of my things properly when they played any such prank but Entertainments Managers and 'coats' must be aware not everyone is as thoughtful. Remember this meant these guests getting the keys of that car from my chalet somehow on this occasion, so 'coats' must choose wisely and not become a guest's or set of guests 'pet'. But as I say these were great families and once again what a massive compliment! They don't come much bigger than people actually following Entertainments Managers around because they think they are worth it and are guaranteed to give them and their family a good holiday and value for money.

If you are a guest that does this or find yourself wanting to ensure the quality of your holiday entertainment by going to a centre where a particular Entertainments Manager has gone, please respect his or her privacy and time off. As we have already discussed, while the best of the best will be the most sociable and interactive people you will ever come across, they will also be working very long hard hours. Give them the break they deserve and never feel that they owe you any of their spare time because, even though many give it up, they don't have to. Most importantly please remember you never 'own' an Entertainments Manager or 'coat'. They are people doing their job, hopefully very well and they see it as a vocation. But it is their job and they must not be treated as anything other than professionals giving you as much time as they can whilst on duty. I would also not advocate going near their property or accommodation, I had a very special relationship with my group of guests built up over a number of years.

But for those of you that return to the same holiday centre year after year. You know what to expect and if an Entertainments Manager was there the previous year you will want the same standard of entertainment (providing they were good of course) but even better with different shows etc. If you have a new Entertainments Manager this year they should stamp their own personality onto the entertainment and of course having read this book they can't help but make a great success of it. I will mention it further when we talk about 'owners' but I tell them not to allow themselves to be persuaded to change tack just to please a few regular guests who feel they 'have a right' because they go every year and they like it done a certain way.

Nothing personal and I do tell them to listen though as they never know when they might just pick up something worthwhile and it is always nice to make a guest feel special and let you know that we value and respect your custom. So I advise that they never disregard anything out of hand. Take it all in make their own decisions and act accordingly.

I warn them to bear in mind that some of you have been going to that camp or with that holiday company since you were children, through your teens, into adulthood and are now there with children of your own. Not customers they would want to lose!

OWNERS
Now you are a different kettle of fish altogether!!!

What do we mean by an 'owner'?

It stands to reason that the holiday centres such as Butlins, Warners or Pontins are owned by those companies, although those companies in turn maybe owned by even bigger ones and so on and so forth.

But the 'owners' that we are going to be talking about here are the caravan, chalet or room owners.

If this concept is all new to you then let me explain.

There are people who actually own caravans at a holiday park for example, a chalet at a village or a room in a hotel. The latter being a fairly new phenomenon. They have chosen to base their holidays around one camp' paying ground rent to the company for certain utilities and amenities. It's fair to say that they do have some perks at centres but this is one area where an entertainment's team and in particular an Entertainments Manager needs to be diplomatic but robust when dealing with certain 'owners' in certain situations.

Yes you own a caravan or chalet, yes you bring regular revenue into the centre, yes you visit whenever you can, and yes this can be every single weekend and entire school holidays in some cases. Yes you _may_ have certain owners' perks such as swim times or discount at the sports centre or Bowling Green etc. But you don't own the village and you most certainly do not own **The Entertainments Manager or 'coats'!!!!**

Of course you do have a vested interest in the success of the holiday centre, park, resort village, camp or hotel after all you have chosen that particular place to spend a lot of time and money. Many of you will also use this as a source of revenue by 'letting out' your caravan, chalet or room. So it stands to reason you want everything to be as good as it can be in order that not only do you, your family and friends get what you have all paid for but that the people you have 'let to' have a holiday to remember and become regular paying guests.

For this reason we (Entertainers) can find that some owners try to be a little bit more intrusive into our affairs than we would like them to be and even attempt to dictate how things will be done. At some centres I have known there to be owners committees for example.

Now I appreciate that this can be a fine balancing act. On the one hand we have you 'owners' who have invested in property of one sort or another and expect a certain quality of service in return but on the other hand we have our visiting holidaymakers who have paid just as good a monetary sum to be there. Both sets of people are looking to us to entertain them and provide quality entertainment for that money. Owners at the end of the day are paying guests as far as we are concerned. Our job is to entertain ALL of our guests to the best of our ability and of course that will always be to the highest standards.

By the pure virtue of the fact that you own a caravan or chalet etc and will normally visit the holiday park fairly regularly 'coats' will come to know many of their 'owners' personally and will build up a rapport with those they like and at times can become wary of those that they are not so enamoured with............But Entertainments Managers must remember you are All paying guests. I have to be extremely honest and forthright here and state that you 'owners' can be an Entertainments Manager's best friend or worst nightmare (dependant on your level of support or interference). I hope that has not upset you now but it needed to be said and you know me I am nothing if not straight with you.

NEVER FEAR SUPERBLUE IS HERE

You will know by now that I never give Entertainments Managers problems but rather the reality of a situation and then provide them with solutions that allow them to deal with any dilemma. I have given them some simple guidelines that I will map out below so you can see how they should be working to become a success in your eyes no matter which faction you fall into, that is to say either a paying guest or owner.

I honestly believe that the single most important rule in this respect is to 'Always be in control'. It's another of those statements that's so staggering in its obviousness that you would think there would be no more to say about it. It might be useful however if I tell you a couple of true stories to illustrate what the consequences can be if the Entertainments Manager does 'stay in control' or if they 'loose it' much of this section will mostly effect Entertainments Managers, in fact, but will have an impact on all 'coats' therefore you fab guests in some form or another.

STAY IN CONTROL

Of what, who and when?

The when is simple:

Entertainments Managers must always be in control.

The what?

Well that's probably best described as any situation that involves their department, particularly the Entertainments Managers. I do urge them to support other colleagues when they are in the right but not to get embroiled in arguments or disputes involving other departments. This may not always be so easy for Entertainments Managers as part of the management team people will complain to them and expect them to take some sort of action. It's always best if they can relay the complaint to that department head and ask them to deal. But of course that person may be the subject of the complaint in which case the Entertainments Manager will need to refer it to a senior manager to deal with. There is no easy way out of this, it comes with the territory and particularly if the Entertainments Manager is actually the duty manager at the time.

'Coats' should not get involved in arguments or disputes in relation to their own department either. They must refer any situation, that has even the tiniest amount of potential to turn into one, to their Entertainments Manager ASAP. The sooner they can get a handle on it the easier it will be for them to defuse it, if that's possible. If their Entertainments Manager is not available then refer it to the next appropriate person on the camp.

THE WHO?

It would be so easy just to say 'everyone' and that's kind of the answer really, if they are in control of the situation by definition they are controlling the people involved.

Let's examine some of the 'flash points' though and discuss a few individuals that Entertainments Managers might like to give particular consideration when thinking about controlling that situation. A 'flash point' is where a normal situation, conversation or enquiry from a guest has the potential to turn nasty. Of course we can't legislate for the individual, couple or indeed an entire family or group that just complain for the sake of it (sorry my friends but they do exist). Entertainments Managers can however be aware of the phenomenon and handle it professionally in an attempt to halt it in its tracks so that it stays just that 'some people complaining for the sake of it!!! These incidents are a lot rarer than you might think and most of you that wish to make a complaint or highlight something to the Entertainments Manager that you feel is wrong do so because you genuinely believe something needs to be said and put right, whether that is something personal to you or something in general. I hope this is also rare but, even if an Entertainments Manager thinks what a guest is saying is petty or indeed just plain wrong, I strongly implore them to remember that the guests believes it to be important and or true. If you have paid to come away on holiday and you're not getting what you have paid for 'That Is A Big Thing To You!'.

So who do you think an Entertainments Manager should control first? The couple who have gone to them yet again because the tap in their chalet still isn't fixed? The mum whose little angle didn't win the junior talent show? The family who liked last year's manager and just complain about every single thing that he or she is doing this year? It goes without saying that all of the above have the potential to hit a 'Flash Point' at just about any time and the controlling of those situations will be vital......... But who do they need to be in complete control of first?

Would you believe none of the above actually

None of them? Who then?

THEMSELF!!!!!

Yes that's right 'Them selves'

You see Entertainments Managers and 'coats' can, and to be honest most of the time will, be the difference between a general complaint or remark regarding just about anything being dealt with in a way that makes you feel valued and listened to or.............. a 'Flash Point'. Honestly it could be the most mundane of issues raised by a friendly 'on side' guest, like you my friend, that can turn into a full blown out of control angry delegation of guests banging on the camp managers door wanting the Entertainments Managers head amongst other things. So it's themselves that must be the first person they need to be in complete control of, at all times, but with heightened thoughtfulness when dealing with a problem of any kind.

We will have a look in a moment at the sort of the salient points that an Entertainments Manager should be working to in order to remain in control in a firm yet approachable manner whilst remaining calm and professional at all times.

There are a few key individuals or groups where the skills we have spoken of will be of particular benefit if the Entertainments Manager needs to bring them into play and these people will be their secondary concern when it comes to controlling the situation. You see, just as they can affect the outcome by their positive actions, attitude and professionalism these people can have the same or opposite effect on that same situation. Obviously the Entertainments Manager will have passed this onto their colleagues in the team so I would expect them to be acting in the same manner as the Entertainments Manager, but if they are not the Entertainments Manager must 'TAKE CONTROL'.

If it is staff, from another department that are not being professional a 'coat' should highlight this to their manager, who should pass that onto theirs. Try not to get involved them-selves there and then, although this is not always easy because if they're doing their job properly the guests will know them and see them as a reasonable person to have as an ally. Remember they must not take sides but if this means they can calm the situation for the moment and inform guests of the best way to resolve the issue, by reporting it to reception or department head etc they should do so. If there is any chance of it getting seriously out of hand they are duty bound to call security or senior manager. I do counsel them to bear in mind that some guests or owners are not always what they appear to be to the Entertainments Manager or 'coat' and it could be they have been completely out of order to that member of staff. Also not all staff will be taught how to deal with confrontation or have a 'coats' friendly disposition in the first place..... hence the volatile situation. They don't want to be 'piggy in the middle'.

Rude guests (oh yes there are some in this day and age I am afraid) can be a tricky one because the Entertainments Manager or 'coat' doesn't want to sink to their level even though sometimes they really feel like it. There are many ways of dealing with these people, dependent on whether they are being rude to the Entertainments Manager them self a 'coat' a colleague or other guests. We are going to talk about how they should deal with situations in general in a moment, but the one thing to mention here is that neither, they, their colleagues or guests have to put up with abuse so they always have two ultimate remedies at their disposal. The first being to have them removed from the holiday centre (a 'coat' must never do this them self) and secondly via the law. (I urge that they always go through management for this one unless for some reason things have got so out of hand they need immediate assistance of the police).

RING LEADERS

If trouble is brewing it normally means someone is orchestrating it. I advocate Entertainments Managers try to identify who this might be and then follow the points that we will go into soon, don't single them out for 'special treatment' of any kind. Flag them up to senior management who should also deal with them in the most appropriate manner, but if necessary alert security and the duty manager. This rarely transpires to be a violent situation more often or not just a delegation to the camp manager's office to complain.

I think it's safe to say that by following much of what I have already told them in the book they will be safe from many of the errors that I or others have made before them. Fortunately however we are all learning all of the time and if there is one thing that I have learnt for definite – It is that people will be people and as much as they will do everything in their power to give you guests the very best of everything, at the end of the day.......... you are people. You will probably know the saying 'you can please some of the people all of the time and all of the people some of the time but you can't please all of the people all of the time'. Basically there will be times when for no logical reason whatsoever someone will complain about something or other and they're going to have to deal with it. Now some of what I am about to say will look familiar to you because we have spoken about that or a similar point in other chapters. It is however important that they sit here in this particular part of this particular chapter as this part of their job and how they handle it crosses over into so many other aspects of being a 'coat' and most definitely an Entertainments Manager. So here goes-:

Entertainments Managers and 'coats' should *Always keep their composure, sense of humour and dignity.*

Never lose their temper- while all around them are getting agitated and upset, possibly even saying things they are going to regret. They must remain calm self controlled and impassive to such behaviour. Once they have lost control of themselves, the situation is out of hand.

Always treat people with respect and respect their point of view whether they agree or not it's clearly important to the guest. In return they should find you show them respect. This won't always be the case as there are people in this world that don't respect anything or anyone but as long as they have remained respectful in their dealings with those people the end result will be that they are fine and any action that needs to be taken, should that arise, will be against those people and not the Entertainments Manager or 'coat'. It is also a way of eliciting the support of other guests. If they can show they are prepared to listen to the other side of the story or complaint and remain calm and respectful no matter what state others get themselves into, you and other guests will, importantly, support the Entertainments Manager or 'coat' you if necessary.

They must always know what they are talking about. When it comes to any complaint they must be absolutely sure they know exactly what the correct answer is before they say a word in relation to it. If it's a competition or event they are running they know they should KNOW that competition or event before they run it. If it's someone else's event tell the person making the complaint they will hear them out and listen to the complaint. Once they have established what it is they can decide if they KNOW the answer there and then or need to go and clarify the point. If this is the case they simply tell the complainant that and that they will return to them with the answer or someone that can supply an answer for them.

An Entertainments Manager or 'coat' must never say anything that they are not sure of. There are so many aspects in a 'coats' trade that they can't be expected to KNOW the answer to everything off the top of their head. There are rules and laws etc that may be at the heart of a guest's grievance so they must ensure they KNOW the answer to that particular guest's angst before they blurt anything out. Never guessing or making anything up because they are under pressure. This will only come back to haunt them and very often makes matters worse because the guest will, rightfully, see being lied to and getting fobbed off as disrespectful. The reality is that they can cause themselves even more grief with the other 99.9% of their guests who aren't complaining yet, because you have supported them up until now. They will have deserved to lose your support if they have taken such an action!!

They must always know the programme. I know it sounds really basic doesn't it? Well it is! The reality is that a lot of complaints begin as very small annoyances such, as guests being sent to the wrong place at the wrong time and missing their favourite event. This is silly basic stuff we have talked about before but by getting the basics right Entertainments Managers can save them self and their 'coats' so much grief in the long run. It's only good old common sense after all. Don't forget this should include changes to the programme, special events and cabaret details etc.
Always find out the facts before making a decision.

Whilst this will mostly affect the Entertainments Managers I advise every 'coat' to have read its counterpart in 'Tales of Superblue'. My reasons for that are twofold. The first is that they may well find themselves as the entertainments assistant or even the Entertainments Manager unexpectedly as I did very early on in my career and suddenly there they are in charge of dealing with the situation. But secondly as a 'coat' they will understand why the entertainments or other management might take the steps they do in order to deal with that situation.

So as I was saying they must always find out all of the facts, both sides of the story and any aggravating factors such as rudeness, violence, drunkenness etc. As well as factors that could offer an explanation such as faulty equipment, illness or age of the persons involved for instance. Then take their time to speak to any independent persons that may have witnessed an event if they need to before deliberating on their final decision. Snap decisions are fraught with danger!!! They must make their decision for the right reasons and stick to it and never give in for an easy life. Again all they will achieve is to turn the rest of the guests against them and they will lose the respect of their team and other management.

Giving in for an easy life rarely ends up being that, an easy life I mean; in fact it normally means the exact opposite. For example a park I was at recently ran a game using the bingo machine whereby each guest would pay a £1 for a number between 1-90 and as each number was called that person would have to leave the dance floor until only one remained and they were given a choice of prizes from the shop. On this particular evening two little girls were left standing on the dance floor. One had the correct raffle ticket number the other ones number had been called during the game and so should have left the dance floor. The 'coat' running the event initially took the correct course of action and explained to the little girl that her number had indeed been called and showed her on the machine where it had been lit up. The 'coat' did this in a lovely manner and did not make the girl feel silly or upset because she had missed the number telling her there would be many other games for her to play during her stay etc. The next event started and I noticed the parents of the little girl at the disco consul where this 'coat' now was. They were from a large family and so many other adults from the family were also making their presence felt. To be honest it was one of those occasions that could have turned nasty at any time and was particularly scary for the 'coat' involved. The conversation was clearly one way with the 'coat' not being allowed to explain their side of things. When the Entertainments Manager turned up I fully expected the family to be told calmly but firmly, that those are the rules of the game (not that I agree with the game itself) and that unfortunately their little girl did not have the winning number and that is actually all there is to it, in a nice and respectful way of course. And for a while this is what it looked like they were doing, but the family became more animated bordering on aggressive and so the Entertainment Manager actually gave into them and gave the little girl a large cuddly toy from the shop. Well you could feel the mood change in that venue the instant that happened. Whereas before the other 99.9% of the guests there were completely on the side of the 'coat' and entertainment team even ready to support them if the situation did indeed get nasty, they are now outraged that the Entertainments Manager has taken that support and rammed it down their throats, sticking two fingers up to fair play and respect for the rules of that and any other event of their holiday and if they are owners, well for ever really!!!

Entertainments Managers and 'coats should never under estimate the strength of feelings these situations can conger up and dependant on how *THEY* deal with it that can have a positive or negative out come for them, the team and the majority of you terrific guests. We have spoken of this before of course but you can see how easy it can all change if they make the wrong decision and giving in for an easy life, in my experience, is always a wrong decision.

What?

What happened at that park?

Oh well it wasn't pretty I can tell you!

Because the family were so animated, loud and getting close to aggression the entire venue had noticed what was taking place and was monitoring the situation, as I said in order to support the Entertainments Manager and team if necessary however when they witnessed the Entertainments Manager handing over the large cuddly toy, they were all but incensed. How many other cuddly toys do you think had to be given out by the senior management after they had an almost riot situation on their hands. What about all those other children whose parents had stuck to the rules and accepted their child just hadn't won? What about all the tears they had to deal with? What about the explanation they had delivered, to that child, telling them that they were out because their number had been called? What about the little "it's just all part of life's rich tapestry" pep-talk? Only to have it all thrown back in their faces by the Entertainments Manager giving in to this boisterous family. Then having to explain to that same child why that little girl got this big cuddly toy when she had lost, just as they had. I am sure it cost that park a lot of money that night not just in stock from the shop but at the bars and restaurants etc, as many people left in disgust not to mention future bookings and word of mouth negative advertising.

The 'coats'? Well that was a horrid night for them and a very difficult week but the Entertainments Manager funnily enough did not see the rest of that week out and one of the 'coats' had to step in until a replacement arrived (See how easy it can happen). The owners are very unhappy because they have revenue paying guests there who they will most likely lose because of such an event. Other staff are also effected, the security team being at the brunt of aggressiveness were put in a very bad situation, bars, restaurants, shop, arcade, chalet cleaning staff, reception, sports hall, managers and just about everyone working there cops some sort of fallout from this decision and its aftermath.

So much for an easy life!!!

If there is a right decision the Entertainments Manager, in particular, should make it and stick to it. It may annoy or aggravate one person or a small group of people at the time but the end result should be that they will then be supported by everyone else including the company, owners, other guests, staff and their team.

They must never promise anything unless they are one hundred and ten percent sure they can deliver what they are offering. If they are trying to sort out a situation that has a solution but they are not sure that they can actually bring about the result that you would like Entertainments Managers or 'coats' should never say "leave it to me I will sort this out" "I promise that will happen for you" or anything similar. If they know they can't give you what you want, they should say so, it's far easier than leading any of their guests on with the promise that they might be able to. They will only have to tell you they can't sooner or later anyway.

If they are not sure they should tell you so. Then go and find out if what they had in mind in order to sort out the problem is a realistic proposition. Consult those who they will need to help them in order to make it happen. Then and only then give you an answer. Of course they will tell you that this is what they are going to do for you so you at least know they are trying on your behalf.

One such regular problem that illustrates this very well is - Football!

Yes football, rarely does anything cause so many problems as football. It is impossible to please everyone when certain games are being played on TV. Not only do we get fans of a number of teams that may be playing on opposite channels but at times we also have more guests than you might think that don't even like the game at all and have in fact taken their holiday on those exact dates to escape the onslaught of TV coverage of a particular sporting event (The World Cup or FA Cup Final say). So if it's not written into their programme, showing a particular game, at the expense of another or an advertised event could cause them more problems than they solve and remember I tell them not to 'give in for an easy life'. They ought to make sure they can show what you want bearing this all in mind before they tell you they will. Football is only an example of course the sentiment goes for anything that a guest or group of guests want outside of the advertised programme.

DON'T GIVE PERSONAL DETAILS OUT

You will inevitably get close to some Entertainments Managers and 'coats' if they are doing their jobs properly and because you owners are at the centre a great deal of the time you will get to know them fairly, if not very well. I am going to be totally impartial here and at the risk of upsetting everyone give you all the same advice, by all I mean you're the Entertainments Managers and 'coats' and they're their guests (I don't mean you of course you're a perfectly nice person, I mean the others) So in regard to those others I highly recommend that you don't give out your personal details to anyone until you are absolutely sure they are someone you can trust to keep those details safe and are a person you will want to see or hear from again. It is so easy to give a mobile number out these days without giving it a second thought. But the fact is that it leaves you vulnerable if you then don't wish any further contact from that person and a great deal can be found out about you from that number including your home address. The same can be said of email addresses as well. So think before you give any details out whatsoever. I would not advocate ever giving your home address to anyone unless you genuinely want them to visit that address and again you can trust them with its security.

Never be under any illusion, If you give out these details certain persons will call, write and visit. So be absolutely sure before you give anything personal away. Holiday's are very easy places to let your guard down.....Keep your private life private.

The Two 'BIG' No No's

I feel that it is very important to touch on, what I believe to be extremely serious matters, not just at holiday centres but, in society in general at this time.

(1) NEVER. Violence or Abuse

It goes without saying that I would never expect Entertainments Managers or 'coats' to ever use violence or abuse of any kind towards anyone.

However they are NEVER to except such behaviour directed towards them.

I would never expect them to retaliate either.

However the law does allow us to use reasonable force to defend ourselves.

SELF-DEFENCE

At common law the defence of self-defence operates in three spheres. It allows a person to use reasonable force to:

(a) Defend himself from an attack

(b) Prevent an attack on another person

(c) Defend his property

REASONABLE FORCE

A person may use such force as is reasonable in the circumstances for the purposes of:

- self-defence; or
- defence of another; or
- defence of property; or
- prevention of crime; or
- lawful arrest

The Crown Prosecution Service says that in assessing the reasonableness of the force used, prosecutors should ask two questions:

- Was the use of force justified in the circumstances, i.e. was there a need for any force at all? and
- Was the force used excessive in the circumstances?

Go to the CPS website for further legal details **www.cps.gov.uk**

Should any such incident take place and Entertainments Managers or 'coats' have acted correctly, it is my submission that management should give them full support and take decisive action against all violent or abusive individuals in every instance.

(2) Entertainments Managers & 'Coats should <u>NEVER</u> Discuss Internal Matters or Team Politics

One of my biggest bugbears ever is anyone spoiling your holiday with needless tittle-tattle so of all the things I urge them not to do in 'Tales of Superblue' this ranks right up there with the most serious offences.......I quite simply say to them:

Don't gossip with guests or owners re internal matters or team politics. No matter how friendly you may become with them. You will honestly be amazed at just how much trouble this can generate for the guests, owners, management, colleagues and You!!!!!

The last thing you want is an audience or a camp full of guests taking sides.

THEY ARE ON HOLIDAY LEAVE YOUR TROUBLES BACK STAGE.

Go Out And-

Spread your time evenly and send out vibes of happiness

Make as many people's dreams come true as possible

Ignore people's backgrounds or status: treat everyone with the same decency and respect

Leave your troubles backstage

Employ diplomacy: enjoy yourself and they will follow

Make Them-

Have the holiday of a lifetime

Applaud because they want to

Put the pressures of life out of their mind during their stay with you

Pleasantly surprised with every event or show: give them quality and value for money

Yearn to return as soon as possible

CHAPTER TWENTY FOUR

GAMING AND PERFORMING RIGHTS

It is a fine thing to get a peck or a bushel of gold by betting for it,
the tremulous rapture of mingled hope and fear is almost compensation
enough even if one loses. Next to the pleasure of winning is the pleasure of
losing; only stagnation is unendurable.
Hubert Howe Bancroft 1888

Eyes down look in, klickety duck, two fat….don't even go there, Kelly's legs eleven, unlucky twelve - well it will be for someone won't it, key to the top of the shop. Oh what fun we had with that silly old game of bingo and we did have fun. We used to mess about play daft pranks and use it as just another fun part of the day to entertain our guests. Things have seriously changed over the years and while your entertainers can still have a laugh or two in between the bingo games themselves it is strictly forbidden to do anything and I do mean anything during the game itself.

So what happened to change all of this fun into so much seriousness? Well to be honest – continuity, transparency and fair play are probably the basic reasons for the instigation of the Gambling Commission.

Who?

The Gambling Commission was set up under the Gambling Act 2005 and was formally established in October 2005. It has taken over the role previously played by the Gaming Board for Great Britain in regulating casinos, **bingo, gaming machines** and lotteries. The Commission also has responsibility for the regulation of betting and remote gambling, as well as helping to protect children and vulnerable people from being harmed or exploited by gambling. The Commission is also responsible for advising local and central government on issues related to gambling.

The Gambling Commission is a Non-Departmental Public Body, sponsored by the Department for Culture, Media and Sport. They operate at arm's length from government and their advice is independent. They are funded mainly by licence fees from the gambling industry.

You can contact the Gambling Commission at:
Victoria Square House
Victoria Square
Birmingham B2 4BP
Tel: 0121 230 6666 - Fax: 0121 230 6720 info@gamblingcommission.gov.uk

Wow that is serious stuff isn't it?
Well kind of but it really shouldn't bother your entertainments team so long as they know what they are allowed to play, where and when. Of course once they know these things they must KNOW the rules of whatever gambling activity it is that they are running.

I would be very amazed these days if you ever went to a centre that did not have all the necessary licences, permissions and people in place to legally cover you to play at the very least bingo. No matter how big or small the company or indeed an independent. I cannot imagine they would slip up on this fundamental business practice.

This is really for the Entertainments Manager to establish on arrival at any holiday centre but any 'coat' can request to see the necessary licences etc and question the their validity and the legality of any gaming activity they are being asked to perform if they feel it is right to do so and if they're still not happy or sure should contact the Gaming Commission above and ask. The centre will also have a licensing officer at the local District Council and within the Police Service for that area.

WHAT IS GAMBLING?

The Gambling Act 2005 defines betting as: 'making or accepting a bet on the outcome of a race, competition or other event or process; the likelihood of anything occurring or not occurring; or whether anything is or is not true'.

While not losing sight of the actual definition it might be that you could consider the term gambling at a holiday centre to mean;

The doing of any activity that a member of staff at any holiday centre etc will take money from any guest in order that they (or any person) may participate in an that activity in the hope that they will win a prize due to the fact that that activity involves an element of chance.

Simply put; if they're taking your money for a chance bet, they're gambling.

If they treat everything they do under this umbrella with the same respect and caution they won't go far wrong.

I tell all Entertainments Managers and 'coats' not to 'GAMBLE ON THEIR JOB' but to always ask and make sure it's legal and above board.

Obvious examples would be bingo, horse or dog racing on DVD, hoy, derbys, raffles, casino nights, lotteries, all manner of using the bingo balls or playing cards for one off knock out games etc.

Entertainments Managers and 'coats' should check that it is allowed, legal and ethical before they set anything in motion.

No matter what the reason, If they are handling money that belongs to you, you must always know what is happening with that money, you must be aware how much goes where and why, how much has been taken and how much is being paid out again, how much is going to a charity for example, how much goes to the centre as a participation fee for instance.

THE GOLDEN RULE

Whenever an Entertainments Manager, 'coats' or anyone else working on behalf of the centres is handling your money they must be: OPEN AND TRANSPARENT Perks? There are none!!! I really don't mean to insult Entertainments Managers or 'coats' regarding this but it's something that needs to be said. All of your money belongs to you….All of your money is either paid back to you or otherwise distributed as described above. Not one single penny is a tip, a perk, a donation to the 'coats holiday fund' or any other euphemism.

BINGO

Where did bingo actually come from? Well a potted history would be that the game appears to derive from Lo Giuoco del Lotto d'Italia back in 1530. The actual game of bingo is more closely akin to a French game called Le Lotto - said to be being played in 1778 which was developed into an educational style game. The term bingo has one of those nice stories behind it, as fun things in history often do. Edwin S. Lowe had played a Lotto game called Beano at a carnival and introduced it to his friends. One of them getting the name wrong uttered the immortal word 'Bingo' (instead of Beano) and the game was born. It developed thanks to Lowe and a fun loving professor who assisted in the development of 'bingo cards' allowing multi player games.

Bingo has certainly come a long way since Lowe's 'Beano' days and in this new technological era of online bingo and linked games between bingo halls. It is a testament to its growth in popularity from those humble beginnings that more people play bingo than to the cinema each week in the UK, hardly surprising with the huge cash prize jackpots now on offer.

Now I don't intend to go into everything on the obvious list but this is one activity that will be ran at just about every single centre, club, hotel, village, park, resort or camp and quite likely twice a day too. So it is vitally important that you know what Entertainments Managers' 'coats' and other experienced guests know about this subject because you will soon discover that some guests do know a lot about it and if Entertainments Managers or 'coats' should get it wrong all hell will break loose. Why? Because it's your money of course!

Why are so many of you so wise as to the rules of bingo? For the very reason I have highlighted above, it is played everywhere and not just at holiday centres either, it's a massive part of the leisure industry in this country with halls all over the country and is now fast becoming the number one gambling activity online. So you know the rules, the rules that they will have to play by or else, the rules that if they were to deviate from could well be their last ever action as a 'coat' or Entertainments Manager, the rules that govern this major aspect of their programme and have dictated that there will be no fooling around during the game anymore, the rules that have put paid to the little sayings such as I played with at the beginning of this chapter, the rules that will save them when they have an irate looser in their face wanting their blood because they missed that all important cry of bingo. Because the rest of you players will happily point out to that person that their claim is void because the Entertainments Manager or 'coat' calling the game................**STUCK TO THE RULES!**

So considering all that I have just said would it surprise you to know that in fact there are.......
NO RULES TO BINGO!

Yes I thought it might and you think I have well and truly lost the plot now don't you? I don't blame you and you're probably not far wrong in general terms but on this occasion I can claim sanity as a friend.

'There are no legal definitions of the game of bingo or a standard set of rules under which the game is played. But the game and its rules have evolved over the years to the point where, despite the absence of any formal industry standard, the way in which bingo is played is the same throughout Great Britain'.

Well I'll be?

I can just see hundreds of well seasoned guests, 'coats' and Entertainments Managers now staring at the page in amazement and scratching their heads.

For years, as the 'GC' statement above suggests, we have indeed been working to a very stringent set of rules as have the whole bingo industry. In fact one of my first winter season jobs, when there was such a thing, was as a bingo caller in a large north London Mecca Bingo venue and these same rules were drummed into me almost as a matter of life and death. Come to think of it if you messed up there as the caller that's exactly what it could be. They were hardened professionals those ladies and they played there every day. God help anyone that wandered in from the street and haplessly sat in one of their seats by mistake.....oh the fury of a bingo player whose lost her lucky seat is frightening so imagine the dread as a caller if you missed one of their calls.....I am breaking out in a sweat just at the thought of it. For instance one caller at a London hall not a million miles from my own was actually assaulted and another had his car wrecked, serious stuff indeed.

It's no wonder that the bingo establishment did not wait for the government or any gambling body to put rules in place it was probably more a matter of self preservation. We all needed to be working to the same standards, playing the same game and abiding by the same rules or it would have all descended into a shambles, a confusing mess and of course from the industries point of view a massive loss in revenue. No link games would have been possible for a start but even more basic than that was the fact that customers would just simply chose the game they liked with the rules that suited them and voted with their feet and purses. I am not being sexist when I say purses apart from the fact that a man can rightly carry a purse if he wants to its also a well documented fact that bingo is the one single gambling activity that is played more by women than by men.

Of course it may also have been that if the industry hadn't come up with something of its own the government or a gambling organisation such as the 'GC' would have, and perhaps they would have been very stringent or even draconian. Who knows? Anyway all you need to worry about on your holiday is that these rules exist and they WILL play by them or ignore them at their own jeopardy.

There are different forms of bingo, cash or prize etc so I remind them if they're not sure what they are allowed to do at their village…ask and if necessary go online to the 'GC' and check. I would suggest that they don't differentiate between them when it comes to the basic rules of the game but again they can find out more about prize bingo for example online.

I intend to stick to their core business in this arena and go through the rules that have come to govern 'cash bingo' at holiday centres, which are basically the same as the large bingo companies use in the high street and have done for many years now and, as I eluded to earlier, you will be completely comfortable with this because most of you definitely do know these rules.

Some sites will also play a flyer which is a single game separate from the 6 page book. Pretty much all the same rules apply to this so I won't confuse matters by going into it. It's just something they should check that they know and understand and are allowed to play.

Eyes down look in and let's begin.
And where better to begin than at the beginning…………

BINGO BOOK SALES

Firstly a person must be 18 years or over to have anything to do with the playing of this type of bingo and that includes the buying of books. They must never sell any books to a person under 18 years. It is one of the strictest rules of all. I have seen 'coats' fall foul of this because they knew the family and knew the books were for mum to actually play. I have even witnessed the 'coat' ask others in the cue if they minded. Of course they don't mind then and there.....but when that mother wins oh boy oh boy oh boy. But it's not up to them anyway, it's very simple....they are not allowed to by law and that's that.

Nearly everywhere you will holiday particularly in the UK you will need to produce a chalet key, wrist band or similar to prove that you're a resident in order to be allowed to purchase books to play bingo at your venue. Again if this is the case where you are this is a must they don't have any discretion in the matter no matter how well they know you they MUST see that item before they sell you a single book.

We play a six page book each page has a different colour to identify the game being played. They contain a mixture of numbers between 1 and 90. They do come in strips of six and some players will play all six or even more. All the numbers from 1 to 90 are contained on every game in a strip of six books so someone playing all six will be crossing a number off of their set each and every time the Entertainments Manager or 'coat' calls one. This is why very often we see people playing at the same table and they will ask for 2 sets of 3 books but will insist that they are from different strips of six. Because if they are from the same strip while one person is playing the other cannot, as they only have one set of numbers between 1 and 90 between them for every game. Clear as mud? Don't worry it will be.

Entertainments Managers should ensure adequate advertising of the place of sale, the times of sale and the price of books very clearly in the programme, on posters and verbally. Making sure that that is exactly where those sales then take place. Being ready to start the sale of bingo books at the time advertised and close the sales at the time advertised. Again on the mic they can let you know there is ten minutes left, five minutes left, one to go and then a ten second countdown to close the sales. No one will be left in any doubt that that is it......no more books to be sold.

I think it is best then to take the cash and remaining books out of sight. Not that they are doing anything underhand and I will explain in just a moment how they are going to be open and transparent throughout the entire process. By taking themselves and the books away they negate the possibility of being pestered by the latecomer who will badger the life out of a 'coat' to sell them "just one book, oh go on just one, that odd one there will do, how could it hurt? Please just the one no one will mind, ask them" and when the 'coat' does succumb to their pleas and asks the room if anyone minds. Of course you don't not now you don't but when that one and only book wins the big full house........oh boy oh boy oh boy.....see how much you mind then. When sales are closed they are closed and that's that. So I say let them take them self out of the public area and then they can work out the prize money etc.

HOW DO THEY WORK OUT THE PRIZE MONEY?

Once again there are no rules set down regarding this unless their company have stipulated any. So basically they just have to be sensible and divide the total cash that is to be paid out in prizes into acceptable sums.

For instance they might allot £10 for a line on a page and then £30 for the full house. Or they may only play the line on that page and the full house on the next. It is best practice to keep these figures the same for the first 5 games and then allot a larger amount for the last game whether for a line and a full house or just a full house.

They ought to be realistic and not make the figures wildly low throughout the game so that you get a wildly high payout in the sixth game, keeping the difference between a line and the full house reasonable. They should never lose sight of the fact that it's YOUR money not theirs to muck about with. At some centres a member of the accountancy staff or similar will deal with the money side of things for them.

Books should always be sold from a batch so that the numbers run consecutively otherwise their working out will be all over the place and leave them open to criticism at the very least. If for some reason, they have to start a fresh batch due to volume of sales say, they must show start and end numbers for both batches on the display I am about to talk to you about below

---

Visit SUPERBLUE HAPPY HOLIDAYS.com the home of honest holiday reviews

Once the figures have been worked out they MUST be displayed to the players so that all can see them clearly and MUST remain on view throughout the session. The media for displaying them is not important it can be on a board especially made for that purpose or on a computer generated screen as I say it's not important. What IS IMPORTANT however is that it's clear, visible to all and remains visible to all throughout the session!

IT MUST DISPLAY THE FOLLOWING INFORMATION;

The start number - the number of the first book sold

The end number - the number of the last book sold

The number of books - self explanatory? Just take one figure from the other don't they? Yes indeed this is the actual number of books that doing that would give you BUT THEN THEY MUST SHOW……..

The number of spoilt or void books - any damaged or books not sold for any reason between the start number and end number must be shown here. And vitally must be available for scrutiny. Then they can show the true total of books sold.

Total number of books sold - exactly that.

Money taken - This is the total amount of cash taken

Less tax - if tax is to be taken as it is in some countries they must show the amount and percentage here, if none then obviously they don't

Less participation fee - again this can be taken and amount must be shown here

Total prize money - This is the figure left after deductions

Prize money for each game - as we discussed they will divvy it up and show that here

Total prize money - some places like to show this again after the prizes for each game just to show that all of the prizes for those games added together equal the total prize money……**if it doesn't they're in real big trouble**….so they must check and double check before displaying the figures. Because I know you will be!

A very simple example would be:

Start number -	1
End number -	110
Number of books -	110
Spoilt or void -	10
Total books sold -	100
Money taken -	£100
Less tax of 10% -	£10
Less par fee of 10%	£10
Total prize money -	£80

Game 1 line £4   full house £6
Game 2 line £4   full house £6
Game 3 line £4   full house £6
Game 4 line £4   full house £6
Game 5 line £4   full house £6
Game 6 line £10 full house £20
Total prize money   £80

Remember they won't always need to deduct tax or participation fee so it is even simpler. Once they have worked out and displayed the figures and before you play any part of a game they **MUST** also read them out so that all participants or any other interested party can clearly hear them. This is normally read out by the first caller.......

WHO IS GOING TO BE THE FIRST CALLER?

They all are!

That's right any of them can be the caller in fact it's a foregone conclusion that they will all be taking their turn. I don't want to upset any of my readers who are avid bingo fans but I am sorry to say that this particular part of the programme tends to become very tedious after a while and is best shared amongst the 'coats' equally. Unless there is someone who really enjoys it of course, however in all my years thus far I have still to come across that individual. Seriously though this can be a very dangerous situation because it carries such a high boredom factor, after some time, that a couple of things can very easily occur:

1) The 'coat's' mind starts to wander and they miss the winning call, trust me very easily done.

2) They begin to mess about, whether calling or checking and they miss the winning call, trust me even easier to do.

So I would always advocate a rotation of 'coats' calling each day and break that down even further to two 'coats' calling three games that afternoon or evening. Yes it's monotonous for the 'coats', yes they will get bored with it very quickly but it's a big part of your programme, it's very serious, they should be professional! And most importantly it's your money they are playing with and….

YOU GUESTS LIKE BINGO……end of story.

Whenever they are going to be the first caller there are two things that they MUST do EVERY TIME.

Before they ever start to even contemplate calling a session of bingo as the first caller they must check that the machine is working correctly. They should DO THIS IN FRONT OF 'YOU' THE AUDIENCE as part of their setting up procedure. Most of the electrical ones will have a self testing programme that they can run while setting up for that session or they may need to go through the motions manually. Whichever the method they must go through this ritualistically before every session and once they have completed the test all 90 lights or indicators must be lit or functional and in full view of the audience. 'coats' and Entertainments Managers should then leave these exactly as they are until they are literally about to call the first game then and only then clear them away to leave a blank machine that is ready for a completely fresh start.

If they are using a machine that delivers balls or any other ingenious form of randomly selecting numbers 1 to 90 (normally only abroad these days) they must have all 90 balls or whatever article carries those numbers on view in sequence and again leave them on view until they are ready for the first game. Then invite at least one member of the audience to come and physically check that that is exactly what they do have. Then and only then drop them into the machine, box, bag or whatever. If they are using a wind blowing bingo machine, you know the type that pushes ping pong balls up the chute, they MUST NEVER pull the ball restrainer at the top of that chute to one side so that the

balls fly out of the chute just as their colleague is about to call the first game.................
Hysterical prank isn't it?

No actually it's not they are interfering with a gaming machine a machine that their colleague spent time testing to make sure was working and that all 90 balls were there. Now guess what they have to do? Yep round up all 90 balls place them back into the machine and go through the whole procedure again in front of a now very impatient audience and not only are you impatient but most likely very very angry. You will recall I spent some time at the beginning of this chapter informing you of the seriousness of gambling and bingo. Well that was not for my own health....it was however for theirs, Entertainments Manager's and or 'Coats' must get it into their heads that they are playing with other people's money it's not theirs to do what they like with. They must get into their head that bingo is a massive pass-time for many of their guests, they must get into their head that many of you love this part of the day and they really really really must get into their head that you will crucify them and create merry hell if they mess up in this department. What they have in fact done, by their little jape, is to change the course of how that bingo session would have gone they have cheated probably at least six people out of money that is rightfully theirs.

How?

If that 'coat' had not messed with the machine and sent those balls flying that would have been the order that they would have been called for the first game. But because they did do that the first true game was lost. That means that the next game will be lost too because the test procedure has to be run again.........you getting the picture yet? The game that the guest's actually get to play as game 1 is in fact the true game number 3. Yes they have actually altered the results of the games you have paid for.

It's for exactly these reasons that they don't mess with electric machines either. Once they have run the testing procedure and its working fine with all lights lit etc....... they should not go near it, just leave it on view and only clear it when ready to call the first game and NEVER before then.

You guests will be up in arms over this and I hope they took notice earlier in the book when told them how bad it can be when a holiday camp full of guests turns against them. It's SO SO SIMPLE.....I tell them in 'Tales of Superblue' DON'T DO IT!!!

Sorry a little bit heavy that wasn't it? But I promise you it's entirely for their own good and things don't get too much lighter with this subject I'm afraid. That's one of the reasons 'coats' tend not to enjoy bingo but please never fear we know you do so they must always make an effort to be their usual happy jovial self, just not while the games are actually being played.

So they have decided who is to be the first caller the machine has been checked and all is well. The second thing they need to do is inform you of the rules, facts and figures. The facts and figures could not be more simple they just read what's on the board or screen etc the rules are something else however. There aren't many rules but they MUST be read out before every single bingo session without exception. It is important that they do this with absolute clarity ensuring that you and all of their guests have understood them at each juncture and while it can be done with some gentle humour, such as getting you to all jangle your chalet keys at them to prove you have them with you, it is in fact a very serious business. The reason for clarity and checking will become very apparent very quickly when they are at a centre because they will soon realise that no matter how many times they tell you the rules and ask if everyone understands there will still be that odd one or two who won't have a key or didn't call on the right number or did but not loud enough. Now this is not a problem if they have done as I say and read out the rules in a clear concise fashion before EVERY session because those one or two people soon become isolated with their angry assertion that it's 'all the 'coat's' fault' because the rest of the players will support them if they have acted correctly from the start.

THE RULES

1) A person must be over 18 years old to play bingo

If a person under 18 years is seen to be marking a card that card WILL be confiscated (Note not given to an adult in the party but confiscated)

2) The colour of the ticket must correspond with the game being played

3) The serial number on that ticket must be between the start and end numbers

4) A player making a claim must produce a key, wrist band, hotel card etc to as proof of residency - membership or their bingo book will not be checked and their claim is void

5) & 6) Right!!! pin back your lug holes and pay attention because these two together cause 99.99999999% of all the grief at bingo

5) The Last number called must be on the claiming book and that once they have started a number they must finish it

6) It is the player's responsibility to call loud enough to stop the caller on that number

Let's take a look at those for a moment shall we?

The last number called must be on the claiming book or flyer etc. Quite simply it is what it appears to be. If the last number was ten, for example, then ten must be on the winning book being claimed not on a book either side on the same strip....the winning book being claimed!!!

If it is not it generally means that the player missed claiming on the number that made up their line or full house. This in turn generally happens for one of two reasons

  a)   A simple lack of concentration
  b)   Or they did not stop the game in time by not claiming loud enough to be heard by the caller

As sad as that is the only and I do mean the ONLY course of action is for the caller or 'coat' checking to gently tell them that their claim is void and move on. Of course it can be hard when they have the nice little old lady at the back and it can be very tempting to ask the rest of you players if they mind them paying her out on that claim…oh boy oh boy oh boy would that not turn out to be one of the biggest mistakes of their life? Yes it would believe me because again you might all seem to agree at the time but are they in for a rough ride in the camp manager's office when loads of your fellow guests go to complain afterwards. And what if you can see the next number on the machine and it's the one you are waiting for? What sort of situation do you think the 'coats' have just created now? Not a good one that's for sure.

No there is ONLY one way to play this and that is straight....the last number called must be on the actual book and page being claimed.

The last number called?

This one can cause eruptions and it sounds so simple doesn't it? And indeed it is if they stick to what I have told them about 'how to call bingo' and will share with you in a moment. The basic bottom line here though is that if they are calling and no one has stopped them with a claim, once they begin to say the next number (not when its shown on the machine but when they actually begin to say it) they must finish that number and that WILL be the LAST NUMBER CALLED.

It is then the responsibility of the person claiming on that number to make sure the caller, NO ONE ELSE BUT THE CALLER, hears their cry of bingo, housey housey, here, yes, oh my goodness I've won or whatever they care to shout. It doesn't matter as long as they make the CALLER stop on that number. All too often they will tell the person next to them and then shout or just put their hand in the air and by the time anyone notices or the friend shouts it's all to late the caller has started the next number and they must finish that number.

They should place 'coats' around the room during bingo but remember their job is to check the claims not to stop the game for that person and again this should be made clear from the start. In reality of course they should be paying attention and ready to shout if they do hear a claim to assist the caller but that's not their role and the onus is squarely on the player to stop the CALLER not let a 'coat' know.

Now can you see why we don't mess about during bingo?

Why do we bother if it causes so much grief? That's a very good question and the reason is that without this rule believe it or not the grief would be so much worse. I know, hard to believe huh? Imagine if we didn't have this rule and two people claim just as the caller starts to say the number ten. When the books are checked one of them has number ten on it but the other has number twenty the previous number called on it and not ten.

Who are they going to pay what to? Half and half? Doesn't the person who is claiming on the first of the 2 numbers called deserve more if not all the money? And anyway the caller didn't even finish saying the number ten did they so it doesn't count? Doesn't the person who is claiming on the last number called deserve more because the other one was too slow? And then imagine four people claiming two on ten, one on twenty and another on five the number before the number before ten, what are they going to do now???

No there has to be a rule governing this and that is the rule and it MUST be explained along with the other rules at the beginning of each and every session and most importantly The Entertainments Manager and 'coats have a responsibility to NEVER WAIVER FROM IT!!!

If you were one of those 'coats' you really wouldn't want to read any more would you? No and I didn't blame them when I laid all this out in 'Tales of Superblue' but the worst is over now and once they get the above in their head the rest is a doddle really. So let's move on with a spring in our step and a chirpy grin on our faces shall we? As I take you into the scary world of the by-daily event in a 'coat's' life that has caused ignominy of so many. Allow me to disclose my musings about........

HOW TO CALL BINGO
Straight that's the most valuable piece of advice I can give them here, call it straight.
No messing about
No using confusing phrases or sayings such as Kelly's eye
No changing speed because they are getting bored
No trying to be flash to impress someone
Just call it straight

Once the figures and rules have been covered the lead into every game will be the same. They will tell you the colour of the ticket you should be on for that game. They tell you what you are playing i.e. either a line or a full house. They remind you to give a nice loud shout so THE CALLER can hear. Then just call the numbers as they appear before them.

I will include the historically humorous bingo sayings on the website so that they have them and can use them when playing a 'non cash' fun game of bingo but when calling for a 'cash game' they should follow these simple guidelines and they will be watertight if a complaint is made. We stopped using these because those that went to bingo regularly knew most of them although there were some geographical variations they were for the most part the same all over. However many guests never play the game except for that one time of the year when they are on holiday. This meant that the caller could start to say Two little.....the game is stopped by a seasoned player we pay them out and move onto the next game. Later of course our once a year player realises that the caller was about to say two little ducks..twenty two, 'quack quack' and that they were waiting for that very number themselves. You can see what a mess it could all become so now we just do it straight and get it done in a professional manner.

The caller should go at a nice steady pace trying to gauge the speed of the slowest players in the room. Say every number at least twice if not three times for example:

The number one

"On its own the number one….number one" "six and eight…..sixty eight"

This will make the caller call the games melodically and allow the slowest of players to find that number on their books and mark it off. It also helps to stop confusion as to which number they called and importantly it stops them starting the next number too quickly. Once a claim has been made they must stop the game immediately unless the caller has just started to say the next number or are half way through etc. Announce there has been a claim for a full house or a line on the number ??? And ask if there are any other claims on that number. For instance:

"We have a claim for a single line on the number six, over in the lounge area, are there any other claims in the room on the number six?"

This does two things it ensures no one is missed on that claim and also gives the claimant a chance to realise that they are either claiming for the wrong thing, a line instead of a full house say. And crucially they may realise they have missed the chance and don't in fact have the last number. Thus they can quickly back out of the claim without too much fuss and embarrassment and the caller can carry on. I give them a serious word of warning here though in that...if this does happen the caller should not begin to call another number until they have completely checked that there no other's for that claim.

Something like;

"Ladies and gentlemen that was a void claim we are playing for a line on the orange ticket the last number called was the number six are there any claims for a line on the number six?"

Yes? Then obviously check that claim

No?

"Ok ladies and gents there are no more claims so we shall be carrying on with the same game and that is for a single line on the orange ticket in your books the last number was on its own the number six... the number six and the next number is.....all the fours forty four....forty four"

I know it all seems over the top but every Entertainments Manager and 'coat' that heeds this will so thank me for it one day, it has come about within the industry because of years of learning the best way to avoid that grief and ensuring your holiday happiness.

CHECKING THE CLAIM

As I have already said they will have placed a number of 'coats' around the venue to act as checkers for the claims. Although when they are doing this role they will keep their eyes and ears peeled for that quiet or non verbal claim....yes it is the players responsibility to make sure the caller hears them but its oh so much less grief if one of the 'costs' sees or hears a claim and shouts or blows their whistle and avoids that missed claim.

So let's look at checking that claim then. As the checker they will collect the winning ticket get that person to show them their room key, wrist band, club card etc etc and confirm over the mic that they can see this. Take the claim to an independent table and let someone on that table watch as they check the numbers and confirm that the ticket is the right colour for the game being played the last number is on the ticket and read out the serial number on that ticket. This will be checked on the board by the caller who will confirm, again on the mic, that it's within the start and end numbers and then they can just read the numbers on the ticket in numerical order and the caller will repeat each number back to them while checking that it has been called and is on the machine. While doing this once again highlighting the last number called when they get to it. So it should go like this:

Checker - "Just the one claim, I have seen the ladies room key, I'm going to ask this person to help me check the claim"

Shows the book to the independent person (never from same family, group or staff)

"The last number called number six is on the claim"

"It's on the orange ticket, serial number 12345"

Caller -"check" (or similar)

Checker – "Checking for one line on that ticket and the numbers are…last number called six"

Caller - "check six"

Checker - "fifteen"

Caller - "check fifteen"

Checker - "thirty three"

Caller - "check thirty three"

And so on until all numbers have been called.

If correct the caller will say so and begin the next game

If not the team will go through the motions, I laid out before, re a void claim.

I do ask Entertainments Manager and 'Coats' to please remember NAAFA throughout bingo!

If they have a machine than shows the numbers called and is visible to the entire audience that are playing that is fine you can check along with the caller. However if they are playing bingo in any other way shape or form they must get someone in fact I would say a couple of independent people to come and sit with the caller. So that they can observe that the caller is a) calling the correct numbers and b) check the winning claim has the correct numbers.

And that's it really, not much to it in the end, if they just stick to those rules I have set out for them they will be fine.

If working abroad I tell them to check what they are or are not allowed to do in that country and of course you can do the same if you have a grievance. But reputable holiday company's should be aware of all these facts and train their staff accordingly. For the UK if you're not sure about any aspect of gaming or gambling don't take someone's word for it check out the 'Gambling Commission' online or call for advice.

As promised the bingo slogans for fun bingo sessions *are on the website* <u>www. SUPERBLUE HAPPY HOLIDAYS.com</u>. If you know of any other humorous, intelligent or otherwise bingo sayings I would be grateful to receive them.

Kelly's Eye number 1, Two little ducks 22, Legs 11, Brighton line 59, Top of the shop 90...oh the fun

You can of course make up your own but 'coats' must remember what I said about people missing claims because others know them....making it not so much fun bingo.

If an Entertainments Manager or 'coat' does use them for 'cash bingo' on their own head be it!!!

HORSE OR DOG RACING ON FILM

In its simplistic form there really is not a great difference between the way Entertainments Managers and 'coats' will run these sessions and bingo.

They must be upfront transparent and open with how many tickets they have sold and how much they are going to pay out. This again should be displayed so all can see as well as being read out before each race begins so you know exactly how much you should receive if your dog or horse wins. The amount of tax and participation fee should be shown if it is applicable in just the same way. The big difference is that once they have sorted out all of the money and worked out the odds, there is only one way they can affect the outcome and that is to cheat. I am not even going to insult you by alluding to how that is possible but all Entertainments Managers should be alert to who is doing what during these events. Then they can have a lot of fun with this activity and make it a really special experience for you.

The premise is straightforward all they do is sell a number of tickets for each race to correspond to the number of runners. So if there are seven runners they will have seven sellers each with a numbered and coloured ticket. The first and last serial numbers sold are recorded so that only tickets with serial numbers between those will be paid out.

They will work out and announce the odds and ALWAYS get someone to randomly pick a film, video or DVD and run the race. The winning dog or horse paying out the price stated beforehand.

WORKING OUT THE ODDS

I would always try to get someone from the accounts dept or similar to join us for this event and let them do the sums. But basically it's just the amount of money taken less any tax or participation fee divided by the number of tickets sold. Oh and by the way the price of tickets is the same for each horse or dog and must be well advertised. You can buy as many of one number or a combination of numbers as you like, and if you are lucky enough to have more than one winning ticket you get paid out on each of the ones you do have. The horses and dogs can all have silly fun names on the day but for clarity I will just stick to boring old numbers for now.

So say for example:

They sold 100 tickets at £1 per ticket

Meaning £100 to pay out in prize money

Say there were seven runners (that's the usual number for horse races)

They would split the winning tote as follows:

#1 sold 5 tickets so if it wins it would pay £20

#2 sold 10 tickets so if it wins it would pay £10

#3 sold 30 tickets so if it wins it would pay £3.34

#4 sold 1 ticket so if it wins it would pay £100.00

#5 sold 4 tickets so if it wins it would pay £25

#6 sold 9 tickets so if it wins it would pay £11.12

#7 sold 41 tickets so if it wins it would pay £2.44

Now the more astute amongst you will have noticed that the camp will be out of pocket by a only a few pence from time to time because I have rounded the prize money up to the nearest whole figure. I recommend that Entertainments Managers seek advice on this from their centre, site, camp, village, park, hotel or resort manager who, in my humble opinion would be wise to advise giving up the odd pence here and there, but never should they just take it from the guests. (Of course there may be participation fee and / or tax to be deducted)

Before taking part in any 'Race Night' or 'Casino Night' type activity, Entertainments Managers and 'coats' must be sure they know what they are doing and that they are allowed to have such an activity where they are. I advocate they check the 'GC' website or call them for advice if in doubt.

PERFORMING RIGHTS SOCIETY

Not really sure why I put this here to be very honest but I think it was probably because there's not much to it really and again one of those things Entertainments Managers need to be aware of and know where to go for advice if they need to. The fact is that any kind of music, live or recorded, played for public consumption needs to be paid for. All venue owners or managers really should know this and have the correct licenses in place I would be amazed if this were not the case.

Main Contacts for the MCPS-PRS Alliance:

Postal address:

Copyright House, 29-33 Berners St, London W1T 3AB, Phone 020 7580 5544 - Fax: 020 7306 4455 or online.

And I think that's all we need to say about that.

CHAPTER TWENTY FIVE

HEALTH AND SAFETY

"It's not big and it's not clever"

How often have I heard those words over the years to describe my actions in an incident that resulted in an accident of one sort or another?

I've lost count of the times I have injured myself in ridiculous mishaps whilst trying to pull off some daft stunt or other.

So once more, in order to save your Entertainments Managers and 'coats' the pain and embarrassment that such activities court, I find myself opening that secret compartment, the crypt where my darkest secrets of silliness have been locked away for safekeeping, where tales of daring do and misadventure are hidden from prying eyes. Events where witnesses have been sworn to secrecy by uttering the sacred and haunting chant of:

"I don't believe you just did that"

I would love to say only a handful of souls ever observed this prankish behaviour, particularly when it all went very wrong, but alas my numerous feats of stupidity, foolhardiness, folly, madness, idiocy, inanity and downright craziness were more often than not performed with great gusto, bravado, showmanship, zest and passion at a holiday centre and to a capacity crowd. I would however like to say that all of these reckless exploits where executed as a foolish and carefree young man, I would like to say that!

So it is with trepidation that I undo the giant padlocks, remove the massive chains, daub the rusty old bolts with WD40 and strain with every sinew of muscular power as the hinges creak to liberate the colossal oak door from its cobweb enfolded frame. **CAREFULLY THOUGH!!!** Not too much now; just a crack, just enough to allow a meagre sampling two fables of disaster to escape the vault of calamity. That's it that one there! Quickly get it in the jar and close that lid really tight. Alright alright stop pushing, there is only room for one more of you in this book, now then which one will serve as evidence of my propensity to commit acts of unqualified hazardous lunacy? Mmm now let me see. Oh yes of course you'll be perfect, ok into the jar with you. Job done!

So two lucky little anecdotes have been chosen to serve as a warning for all, that not taking Health and Safety seriously can truly be hazardous to your health but which one to start with? Oh we might as well go back to where it all began indeed to the very incident that was to cement the legend that Superblue really was…..well…..super!

MUMMY I JUST SAW SUPERBLUE FLYING!

I know we talked about it earlier in the book but let me just to remind you for the purposes of this story that although I didn't realise it at first I had set myself quite a gruelling task when I asked Richard to let me run with my invention of a 'character' called Superblue. With him only agreeing to it if I was prepared to give it 100% full time commitment and make sure Superblue would appear whenever he called for him. And trust me the fabulous Mr Walsh put the resolve of this brand new bluecoat well and truly to the test.

This meant that whilst working my socks off, as we all did on his team, I would also have to wear the majority of my Superblue costume under my bluecoat uniform in readiness to slip away at a moment's notice and emerge as Superblue when he was summoned. That meant constantly having a pair of yellow tights, ridiculously coloured swimming trunks and Superblue t-shirt as undergarments while having the cape and funny bird mask to hand somewhere nearby in a bag that I carried everywhere. Despite the fact that this was very hot and uncomfortable it was enormously rewarding to see the faces of the children after Richard had made them yell at the tops of their voices for Superblue. Giving me only those few moments to disappear perform a quick change routine and miraculously materialise from all sorts of places thereby keeping everyone guessing and the mystery alive. One such place was very impressive………..I would actually appear from the sky.

The sky?

Well that's how we made it seem to the boys and girls anyway. In effect I actually came from a second story chalet, swung from a tug of war rope (so very strong) which was tied to one of the balcony struts outside that chalet and made my decent from there. But having rehearsed and rehearsed this manoeuvre over and over I had it down to slick perfection so that it would be a treat for the young ones.

This illusion took place during the donkey derby when the sports field was packed with lovely families having great fun. It went really well the first couple of weeks, it was great, a real show stopper, they always screamed with delight when Superblue dropped in from above, even though I don't like heights it was really worth putting myself through the fear for the spectacle it created. The kids, well the younger ones anyway, thought Superblue could fly and that's all that mattered. Well that was when I made the fatal error, I got a bit blasé about the stunt and took it for granted that others had taken certain steps to ensure my apparent defiance of gravity would go without a hitch as they had throughout all of those practice sessions and as they indeed had done prior to the live feat for the past couple of weeks. But this was to be the week the children would actually see Superblue fly……..for real!

I was goofing around with Lippy, a wonderful donkey with a hair lip, playing games like we used to do. He was an amazing creature, you could put a child of any age of any size on his back and he would be as gentle as a lamb, but let an adult try to mount him and all hell would let loose, even if the adult was smaller than the largest child he allowed onto his saddle. I will never know how and why he was that clever but it astounded me every time it happened. He would follow me around and nudge me from behind if I ignored him for too long and this would have mums, dad and kids alike in fits of laughter. The other boy bluecoats tried to get me to stand on his back once whilst wearing a ballerina's tutu. Well that was a health and safety story all of its own, Lippy turned his head around and looked me straight in the eye and I swear the look in his eyes said, "now you of all people know better than to be up there don't you?" and with that he flipped his back upwards throwing me into the air and catching me with a back-kick on the way down for good measure. He then strolled over to where I was laying in a crumpled heap and gave me a big wet lick across my face. I was in agony but it had been my own fault and he had forgiven me. So you see donkey derby's can be hazardous just like any other event that we would run especially if we took something for granted, which reminds me I was telling you about the day that

Superblue flew wasn't I?. Well there I was messing around with Lippy as usual when the call rang out over the speakers. It was Richard whipping the children into a frenzy wanting Superblue to come and see them at the donkey derby. I snuck away and climbed the metal staircase to the second floor chalet where I had pre-arranged to leave my little bag containing my cape and mask. I quickly removed my uniform and slipped these on ready for my big entrance, only waiting until Richard and the 'coats' had got the audience participation as about as mad and loud as it could get. Then I took a great big gulp tried to ignore my fear of heights once more and came running out of the chalet dived towards the rope hanging over the balcony and went over the side bracing myself to be suddenly stopped from my outward sky-bound journey as the rope ran out of slack and it took the strain where it had been tied to the balcony strut.

I braced myself and waited, waited, waited and waited…nothing, wow they must have left a lot of slack on the rope this week, this is going to be a close one. So I waited, waited and waited…still nothing.

When I opened my eyes I could not believe what I was seeing! I was passing over the heads of all those lovely children and to this day I can hear their cheers of delight as Superblue rushed through the air above them completely unaided. Even Lippy looked up with an expression on his face that would not be out of place on the donkey from Shrek that said "You really have gone too far this time mate"

What was going on?

Why was the rope not stopping me?

How did I get this far out from the balcony?

Why am I still so high up?

How much is this going to hurt?

What was going on was simple I had gone for the rope with such vigour that when I took off I really took off; it had to be that way for the illusion to work. The rope was not stopping me because unfortunately the person who was supposed to tie it to the balcony strut had forgotten to and putting those two factors together was the reason I had reached a great distance out from the balcony and was flying at a velocity that kept my trajectory level with the high second floor balcony.

How much would it hurt?

Guess!

Yep you got it. I landed in mangled mess of yellow tights, blue cape, yucky coloured trunks, the beak on the stupid birds mask sticking somewhere unpleasant and thinking "oh my god there must be loads of blood the kids can't see that", I also genuinely thought I had broken my back I was so winded I could not breath for what seemed a lifetime.

But amazingly something takes over when there are more important people than yourself to consider and I found myself once again thinking "blood oh dear this will look terrible, the children!" So I tried to get my breath as quickly as I could and checked to see if I could somehow hide all that nasty stuff from them.

Blood, what blood? I couldn't believe it, I was battered, bruised and winded but not a cut on me.

That's when it hit me!

Superblue had just flown through the air!

But that would only be the case if he then got up and carried on as if nothing had happened, nothing had gone wrong and he was not in pain.

So that's what happened, I got to my feet flung my arms in the air and shouted "did someone call for Superblue?"

The boys and girls went wild!

The mums and dads realising exactly what had just transpired applauded, whistled and cheered!

It had happened! It would go into the annals of Pontins history! A thousand or so guests, bluecoats, other staff and Lippy had just witnessed it.........

Superblue actually flew!

I ran around like a lunatic for the next hour before disappearing into a nearby chalet and collapsing onto their bed. The nurse did come and check me over and there was a chance of slight concussion but in those days we just stuck to our motto 'the show must go on' not that I am telling today's Entertainments Managers and 'coats' to ignore medical advice, in fact I insist on the opposite.

A strange thing happened after that day though. Every time Richard started the call for Superblue Lippy would head for the bottom of that balcony and wait until I was down safely. No one, try as they did, could budge him from there until I was on terra firma.

Why this story for health and safety? Well it was going to be to illustrate two good points to consider but as it turned out a third one snuck up on me and is just as worthwhile and valid as the first two. That's good old Lippy helping me out again.

1. This is a great example of where, had I carried out a quick dynamic risk assessment my brain should have asked the question what if the rope has not been tied or tied properly, what if it hasn't been done for some reason this time?

The answer would have been simple………..check it!

From that day onwards I always checked the rope myself before donkey derby and then had someone stay with it until I had used it when they would immediately untie it and remove it from the balcony.

This was for two reasons

a. No one can meddle with it or untie it before I used it

b. No one else could use it and possibly hurt themselves

Oh and I had a couple of mattresses placed at the bottom to……just in case.

2. Remember I have told your 'coats' they are a role model to the young ones in particular? Well I ask them to please bear this in mind when they are considering any stunt especially involving a character. Superblue flew that day all those years ago and we made it perfectly clear then in simple but firm language that only Superblue could do this, that it would be dangerous for anyone else to try and that it would upset him if little girls and boys tried to copy him. That may seem a little over cautious to you in these days of violent, flying characters, blood and guts video games that children can get hold of but you need to remember it's our duty of care to every guest to keep you safe and sound. So whatever children may or may not be allowed to do at home is of no consequence to a 'coat'…none whatsoever! They must do what is right and proper in all circumstances and more than ever where children's safety is involved. I tell them that if it's dangerous for anyone or may encourage anyone to do something dangerous….. DON'T DO IT!!!

3. Ah yes the one that snuck up on me. My old friend Lippy has reminded me about something I have yet to talk about. Peer pressure is not always easy to avoid and you may be tempted to do something or indeed worse still get someone else to do something that you know for a fact is dangerous or that your instant risk assessment is telling you, may well be dangerous. I knew Lippy would not let me stay on his back but was talked into trying it for a laugh by the other 'coats'. Well I will give most things a go to make people even smile but the reality of this situation is that I knew he would throw me off so that would have been dangerous enough right there. However Lippy decided to teach me a very good lesson and followed up with a back kick that left my spinal area bruised and very painful for a long time. I have often reflected on the fact that he could easily have broken my back with those strong hoofed back legs of his and all in the name of getting a laugh. It did undeniably bring the house down and was the talk of the guests for days afterwards but it could have been such a different story, and the moral? Well that should be very evident to you by now. If you know or even think something is dangerous don't let anyone talk you into it for any reason whatsoever and especially not for a laugh. It's stating the obvious I know but for the sake of clarity: Your Entertainment Managers and 'coats' must never, under any circumstances, ever let you or any guest take part in any such act!

Lippy? Oh I was very light in those days he just would not have an adult of any size ride him not even his old friend Superblue and he was indeed a lovely friend, a gentle soul, a character. The donkey owner that used to bring them was gobsmacked when he inadvertently left Lippy off the tether one day and he began to follow me everywhere. From that day on he just left him to his own devices at my centres and if he needed him the donkey man just had to look for me and there would be Lippy. He actually followed me into the bar one day, now that *was* hilarious.

THE SECOND CAUTIONARY TALE DIRECT FROM THE VOLT CARRIES A MUCH SIMPLER MESSAGE

Club Tropicana was such a vibrant lively place to work, with guests from all over Europe rubbing shoulders all day and night, that being in charge of an animation (entertainments) team also made up 'coats', lifeguards, sports organisers, bands etc etc from that vast

European mix really meant being constantly on the ball, being on top of it all, all day and all night. So getting away and relaxing when I could was quite important for my mental health and Nick, my best mate out there, would make sure that I took that time out. However the only chance we would get to do this was often at the end of a very long, hot, hard and emotional day. So after we shut down our disco at one or two in the morning and the last of our guests made their way back to their chalets he and I would head off across the rocks for our night out. Let me just explain that Tropicana was set on its own beach surrounded by high rock formations. On the other side of one of these was the 'local town' where Nick and I were well known as being part of the management team from Club Tropicana and of course working for the incomparable Signor Domingo. We would clamber across this rock formation by steadily following narrow goat tracks that had been established over a number of years. These were slow, winding and at times quite steep so it would take some time to reach the summit then negotiate the maze of thorny shrubs and impenetrable thickets across the top before making a careful decent down the other side and finally taking the short walk on that beach and enter the town to enjoy their hospitality and nightlife. This would, at times, see us making that trip in reverse as the sun came up, grabbing a couple of hours sleep before diving into a shower and being dressed and ready to face another great day with our guests. Now you are probably sitting there thinking that's a very good message to take on board re health and safety. Don't work all day, climb rock faces, stay out all night and only have a couple of hours rest before starting it all over again and of course you would be right on so many levels so do take everything you are thinking right now on board, because you are in fact doing your own dynamic risk assessment right there. You do need to let your hair down from time to time, maybe not as often or with as little sleep as we did but giving yourself a break is a health and safety must.

Now then, as I said, somewhat worryingly even though you should have taken a lot from it already I haven't even touched on the lesson this story is intended to give yet.

It had been a brilliant day of blistering hot sunshine, the guests had joined in the numerous events we had put on for them, an adventurous new number we had rehearsed between those events had gone very well in the show and they loved it. All in all the world was a good place for us to be that night as Nick and myself made one of our, now legendry, trips across the rocks. It had been a very tiring day though and after only few hours partying: I, unusually, felt myself flagging a bit and suggested to Nick that it might be just as well to get back a little earlier that morning. He readily agreed and so after the customary round or two of shots from the owner of whatever bar we happened to be in at that time we headed back on that long reciprocal route over the rocks. There is something that happens to us mere mortals when we have had a shandy or two where we believe we are invincible and anything we say or do is definitely right. It is also amazing how everything is so very simple and logical. Why can we not see things so clearly when we are sober? Well it maybe because things are rarely that simple and logical as they appear under the influence of several pints, a few sangrias and a shot or two. I had had a smattering of alcohol during the night and the idea of traversing those pesky mountainous hills after such a long and exhausting day wasn't sitting right on my clear and simple thinking monitor. So engaging my one remaining brain cell and putting it to work on the problem I was very quickly able to come up with an unmistakable and uncomplicated answer to the dilemma.

"We will take a short cut"

"I am sure that if there was a short cut someone would have told us about it by now" Nick had clearly and simply worked out.

"No not take someone else's, find our own….simple ah?"

"Where are we going to find this short cut then?" I think the fear of what I might do next was sobering Nick up at this point.

"It's simple just go straight through this lot, how hard can it be?" Translated into sober that would read it's no problem old chap we just have to do what no other stupid person has done and penetrate the impenetrable thickets in the pitch darkness.

Back in tipsy world it seemed very logical, as it would, "cut our journey in half and we could use our secret short cut every night after that". Interpreted into tee-total that would have sounded more like: "well if it was that easy someone would have done it a long time before now."

Unperturbed and fearless behind my shield of inebriation I ventured forth into the green beast that was, to my mind, now just a nice little coppice that we would be through and out the other side in no time at all.

"Nick just follow me mate I will lead the way"

Which he did but from us telling this story hundreds of times over the years I now know he only did this to stop me from doing anything daft and getting hurt.

So when after about an hour of battling these stupid plants and going around in circles half a dozen times it was a massive relief to eventually spy the opposite ridge that would take us back down to Club Tropicana and bed. The only thing that stood in our way was a dense clump of yet more thickets but wait…..look a lone little bush with a clear path to that ridge directly behind it.

"See I told you it would be easy" I said to a Nick whose patience with me had ran out a good fifty minutes earlier. A Nick that stood there in his dress suit cut to sheds by the forest of thorns that I had dragged him through. A sober Nick!

"Come on grumpy just this one more little bushy wooshy to get by and we will be home and dry" said a confident intoxicated Superblue.

And before Nick could say a word I was off…

Off on a path to victory…..

Off to face my destiny as the conqueror of the mountain…..

Off to Ahhhhhhhhhhhhhh…..

Off to the bottom of a 100 foot ravine!

What? Oh I've told you a Hundred Million Billion times I never exaggerate! Well it was at least 50 feet anyway.

That sweet little bush, the one that I was just going to brush past on my march to glory actually turned out to be the top of a huge tree that was poking out of a canyon, a very very very precipitous vertical almost sheer elevated hole! I bounced off just about every thick hefty branch on the way down before finally crashing to the ground all that way below. Nick was frantic with worry calling to see if I was even conscious so he could assess my injuries and begin to plan a way of getting a team there to get me out and administer the necessary first aid. I told you we have talked about it many times since didn't I?

"Wow I don't remember this being here before" I replied.

"What?"

"I don't remember this being here before"

"Of course you don't, no one is ever stupid enough to come this way, we have never been this way before, its madness to come this way"

"Why didn't you stop me then?"

I can't remember what his answer was to that exactly but I recall he was a little miffed with me at the time.

We laugh about it now of course that's what real friends do. Naturally being a true friend his emotional retort was partly due to the relief he felt on hearing my voice and receiving the echoed news from deep within that abyss that I was in fact unhurt. Yes it had happened again I had tumbled down a 100 foot chasm colliding hundreds of times with an enormous tree in the pitch blackness of night and was apparently coming out of it unscathed, only because I had landed on a bed of soft leaves that must have built up over who knows how many years. God love him, Nick sat at the top of that cliff talking into the dark void until daylight approached and we were able to work out a way up using that tree. It did take several attempts but I got there in the end and we stood silently in ore and wonder of one of the most beautiful sunrises I have ever seen.

Then I turned to him, now rather more abstemious (sober) and said "you look a mess" He was about to get cross with me again and tear me off a strip when he took a deep breath looked back at the sun that was just nipping up to its rightful place over our beach smiled at me and replied "I told you not to wear that suit to cross the rocks didn't I"
Suit?
Oh no my wonderful pure white suit, my pride and joy, the best every Entertainment Managers suit, a fabulous piece of summer clothing design...oh no not my white suit!

There we were Nick in his dress suit me in my lovely white suit, cut to pieces, completely stained in greens and browns from all that foliage and of course I did have a small cut or two from my modest tumble so red was a particularly vibrant colour on that once pristine cloth. There we were walking back up our beach, onto the club itself past the handful of staff that, were up and about at that early hour. They just stared at us, I would like to say in disbelief but I am afraid it was more that they were, shaking their heads and wearing a look that said "What have those crazy pair been up to now?"
We walked silently past all the bungalows containing our happily sleeping guests eventually reaching the entertainment staff compound where we just stopped for a second smiled at each other shook hands and said goodnight.

A couple of hours later we were up and at em!

Yes I know it all sounds like a wonderful adventure and in our lives it was, as I say we have and probably always will tell that and all our other stories, every time we have a new audience that will listen, just as I and my other best friend Phil do. You are sure to be bombarded with them if you meet any of us. They were fabulous for us they are part of what made us who we are today and I would not swap a single moment of my magical time with those two great men for anything in the world and am proud to say that even after all I put them through we are still the best of friends today.

But that's not to say that youngsters reading this should aspire to perform such calamitous exploits, on the contrary you should aspire to have your own wondrous times in safety, having gained knowledge of the pitfalls from us. Which again reminds me, I do digress a little don't I? Pitfalls? Oh yes of course I remember what I was going to say now. It's important to have a good time when you are out relaxing but drink does have different and strange affects on people. Always try to stay within sensible limits and not to put yourself or others in danger. On your well deserved holiday particularly in hot weather or abroad where you may not know the strength of drinks be especially careful take it easy and pace yourself. Never go anywhere alone in these situations for if you are going to drink for any period of time. You never know your buddy could just save your life!

Very often these days we see headlines in the newspapers about some local council or other making completely bonkers mad rulings in the name of health and safety and as my mate said the other day "it's like living in a nanny state". I have to agree with him, it does seem a bit like that at times and do I really need to be told how to keep myself safe? And what about you, the guests? We have always cared about your welfare haven't we? Of course we have never knowingly put you in any danger. So why the need for this chapter at all? Well the reality is those daft rulings aside, health and safety legislation has actually improved the working lives of many people. It's one of those elements of British law that's not one rule for one person and another for someone else it's generally fair across the board. Even a Commissioner of the Metropolitan Police Service appeared at court following the death of one of his officers in a recent case. So the Health and Safety Executive do have very strong powers to uphold this particular aspect of the law. However I don't want you getting all paranoid about this subject. There should be a person who is responsible for the corporate health and safety at your holiday centre and I would like to think all staff there will be taught various things that they will need to know in relation to that venue. So I only intend to cover a few basics that will help keep you safe and sound. In fact many of those bonkers mad, so called, health and safety stories are quite simply not true at all. We love a good gossip and a bit of folk law but the paranoia rumour mill can actually do more harm than good when it comes to health and safety rulings. For instance take a look at some of the myths that, if the HSE weren't there to put the record straight, could actually affect how we would perform our duty as 'coats' or Entertainments Managers.

Myth: Adults can't put plasters on children's cuts June 2008

THE REALITY

We've often heard of teachers, volunteers and carers being told to ask parents for permission, or even requiring parents to drive over and put the plaster on themselves. This persistent myth causes a lot of unnecessary hassle and worry.

There is no rule that says a responsible adult can't put a plaster on a child's minor cut. Some children do have an allergy to normal plasters. If you know a child is allergic you can use the Hypo-allergenic type of plaster. The important thing is to clean and cover the cut to stop it getting infected.

Myth: Toy 'weapons' in a play had to be locked-up and registered with the police
March 2008

THE REALITY

Reports said that the theatre company were just following HSE's guidance sheet.

HSE's guidance is clear; it deals with real weapons and the kind of accurate replicas that can cause serious injury or be used in robberies. Not plastic toys.

We trust the play did well with all the free publicity!

Myth: Every possible risk needs a safety sign

THE REALITY

Using too many signs just guarantees no one will read any of them.

Safety signs are useful when there's a significant risk which can't be avoided or controlled in any other way. But that doesn't mean you should add a sign for every possible risk, however trivial.

Where there are serious risks in your workplace, don't just rely on signs - take practical steps to deal with them. If you do need a sign, make sure it has the right symbol and is clearly visible.

Myth: Children were banned from riding at a donkey derby
October 2007

THE REALITY

We recently heard that HSE had banned children from riding donkeys in a donkey derby and so had to be replaced with inflatable sheep. This was news to us.

In reality the change appears to have been due to the cost of the insurance premium. HSE had no involvement at all. Other donkey derbies took place around the country without any problems. If you're organising a public event, it's wise to look for an insurer who specialises in this kind of policy, talk with them if the standard terms cause difficulty and plan properly so that the risks are responsibly – and sensibly managed.

Myth: Kids must wear goggles to play conkers
September 2007

THE REALITY

This is one of the oldest chestnuts around, a truly classic myth. A well-meaning head teacher decided children should wear safety goggles to play conkers. Subsequently some schools appear to have banned conkers on 'health & safety' grounds or made children wear goggles, or even padded gloves! Realistically the risk from playing conkers is incredibly low and just not worth bothering about. If kids deliberately hit each other over the head with conkers, that's a discipline issue, not health and safety.

Myth: Egg boxes are banned in craft lessons as they might cause salmonella
August 2007

THE REALITY

This story started after a school briefly banned children from using cardboard egg boxes to make things, threatening years of Blue Peter tradition. They were concerned that children might catch salmonella.

Within a few days the school realised there was guidance from the County Council and an organisation for teachers called CLEAPSS, making clear that as long as egg boxes and toilet roll centres look clean, there is no reason why they should not be used.

Just another storm in an egg cup...

Myth: All office equipment must be tested by a qualified electrician every year
July 2007

THE REALITY

No. The law requires employers to assess risks and take appropriate action.

HSE's advice is that for most office electrical equipment, visual checks for obvious signs of damage and perhaps simple tests by a competent member of staff are quite sufficient.

Check out their guidance shown below on their website www.hse.gov.uk.

- Office electrical safety / Maintaining other electrical equipment / Sensible risk principle

Myth: New regulations would require trapeze artists to wear hard hats
June 2007

THE REALITY

Despite being widely reported at the time and regularly repeated since, this story is utter nonsense. There never were any such regulations.

Hard hats do an excellent job of protecting building workers from falling debris - but they have no place on a trapeze.

Myth: Workers are banned from putting up Christmas decorations in the office
November 2007

THE REALITY

Bah Humbug! Each year we hear of companies banning their workers from putting up Christmas decorations in their offices for 'health and safety' reasons, or requiring the work to be done by a 'qualified' person.

Most organisations including HSE and local councils manage to put up their decorations, celebrating the spirit of Christmas without a fuss. They just sensibly provide their staff with suitable step ladders to put up decorations rather than expecting staff to balance on wheelie chairs.

Myth: Risk assessments must always be long and complex
May 2007

THE REALITY

On its own, paperwork never saved anyone. It is a means to an end, not an end in itself - action is what protects people. So risk assessments should be fit for purpose and acted upon.

OK, if you're running an oil refinery you're going to need a fair amount of paperwork. But for most, bullet points work very well indeed.

See what they mean – check out the example risk assessments on their website www.hse.gov.uk.

- Example risk assessments
- Sensible risk principles
- 5 steps to risk assessment

Myth: HSE has banned stepladders
April 2007

THE REALITY

We have not banned stepladders - nor have we banned ladders! Despite this, the allegation is regularly repeated and some firms have fallen for the myth and acted upon it.

For straightforward, short duration work stepladders and ladders can be a good option, but you wouldn't want to be wobbling about on them doing complex tasks for long periods. A large number of workers are seriously injured or killed using ladders and stepladders each year. So: Yes – HSE want people to use the right equipment for the job. Yes – there are some common-sense rules for using them safely. But no – HSE have not banned them!

See what they say about it on their website www.hse.gov.uk
- Sensible risk management
- Ladders
- Falls

As I said don't go getting all paranoid about this subject you are on holiday after all. There will most certainly be that person responsible for the corporate health and safety at your holiday centre. Also your entertainment's team and other staff really must have been taught the variety of things they will need to know relating to it. You can find in depth answers to any question you may have on the HSE website **www.hse.gov.uk**.

Source of above 'Myths' info is the Health and Safety Executive who kindly supplied a large amount of the material for research on this chapter.
PSI Licence C2008001625

HEALTH AND SAFETY IN THE ENTERTAINMENT AND LEISURE INDUSTRY

The website www.hse.gov.uk has numerous links and simple to follow advice for those of us in the industry and I allude too much of this in 'Tales of Superblue' but........

The message is clear and simple - IF IN DOUBT ASK!!!

The Health and Safety Executive are there to HELP not to HINDER!!!

The important message to get across really is that health and safety is every ones responsibility. So if you come across anything at any time that you feel could put you or anyone else in danger or harm, no matter how minor that may be, you must act to prevent it. It will come as no surprise to you that Entertainments and Stage Managers will have specific responsibilities regarding yourself and your fellow guests, their staff and visiting acts etc. Again I talk to them about this in 'Tales of Superblue and you can find it on Superblue's website www.SUPERBLUE HAPPY HOLIDAYS.com

One of the most significant aspects however does directly concern you and that is that they MUST conduct a risk assessment for each and every activity that they plan to run.

WHAT IS RISK ASSESSMENT?

The HSE says:

A risk assessment is simply a careful examination of what, in your work, could cause harm to people, so that you can weigh up whether you have taken enough precautions or should do more to prevent harm. Workers and others (That means you) have a right to be protected from harm caused by a failure to take reasonable control measures.

Again I delve into this, and the 5 steps to risk assessment, in great depth in 'Tales of Superblue' and on the website www.SUPERBLUE HAPPY HOLIDAYS.com. So you can check it out for yourself if you ever need to.......hopefully this will never be the case though.

As for Entertainments Managers and 'coats', when should they be thinking of carrying out a risk assessment?

- During the planning of a major event?
- When considering how many and the type of extinguishers to have by the stage knowing there is a fire eating act on that evening?
- When a colleague asks if they can strap you to a spinning board so that they can try out their brand new *blindfolded* knife throwing act for the first time?

Actually the answer is all of the above.

The fact is they will be carrying out 'dynamic' risk assessments as each day unfolds. Not that they will complete a form for every one that would just be silly, they would never get any work done if they did that. There may be events however where they are required to fill out a form or two or they might just feel that one is appropriate under the circumstances. We generally do this subconsciously in any case so I am just highlighting the obvious here really so that you are aware of the sort of decisions that they should be making in relation to the health and safety of yourself and colleagues. Generally speaking this will come into play when any of the aforementioned take part in any event or employment that comes under their jurisdiction for instance:

During competitions or shows -

Are props and costumes safe?

Is anything they're asking you to do too strenuous?

Can you fall, trip or otherwise hurt yourself in anyway?

Are special effects such as pyrotechnics or strobe lighting being used properly and have they warned their guests of such use?

Has the stage management been conducted professionally?

Trips, rambles, special events and excursions etc -

Are the venues or events suitable for the age and ability of their guests?

Do they have sufficient staff to ensure safety?

Do they have the right staff to ensure safety?

Do those staff, have appropriate qualifications?

This is by no means an exhaustive list merely an example of the sort things that must be taking into account particularly, but not solely by Entertainments Managers.

Their motto should be-

The RIGHT person doing the RIGHT job for the RIGHT people at the RIGHT place at the RIGHT time................

Er?...... I think that's right?.......Mr right....employed.....lovely guests.....nice bit of fish....cuckoo cuckoo cuckoo.........yep that's right!

The whole day and evening can be fraught with hazards and they are responsible for ensuring that they temper having to deliver copious amounts of fun and laughter with keeping everyone safe and sound. The general programme, shows and competitions may have been worked out by someone else but that does not mean they can just switch off and say "that makes it someone else's problem". If they see an obvious risk or hazard with any aspect, of not only their core business but anything anywhere on the centre, Entertainments Managers and 'coats' must bring it to the attention of the appropriate manager ASAP if there is time or even stop the event or otherwise prevent you guests and other staff from being where the danger may be if necessary.

I heartily recommend that Entertainments and Stage Managers in particular peruse the entertainment and leisure section of the HSE website where they will find some extremely useful information regarding our trade.

Many holiday centres now have costume characters as an integral part of their programme and these are hugely popular with our younger guests. The temptation can be to use these characters as much as possible even, as I have recently observed, taking the place of visiting children's cabarets and replacing any kind of live music, bands or duos etc. You will already know my feelings on this sort of, in my view, short changing their guests. However, apart from, at some centres, you wanting to throttle one of them when, for the tenth time that day, they tell your children to come and ask for yet more money to spend in the shop, these costumes do carry their own H & S risks and once more they can find out what I say about this in 'tales of Superblue' You of course can check out the website www.SUPERBLUE HAPPY HOLIDAYS.com

FIRST AID FOR THE PUBLIC

The Health and Safety (First-Aid) Regulations 1981 do not oblige employers to provide first aid for members of the public. However, many organisations provide a service for others, for example places of entertainment, fairgrounds and shops and HSE strongly recommends that employers include the public and others on their premises when making their assessment of first aid needs.

In the case of holiday centres the reality is that Entertainment Managers and 'coats' are with their guests for long periods of time and range from the very young to the elderly. It is inevitable that from time to time they are going to be present when someone unfortunately becomes ill or has an accident. It's all to the good if they are first aid trained, indeed in my opinion everyone in the industry should have at least some grounding in the basics. However if they're not it is imperative that they know who is and how to get hold of that person in an emergency. Many centres do have a resident nurse or even a doctor these days but the correct initial first aid is essential and can literally be a life saver. I make it clear that First aid equipment is NEVER EVER to be used in any other way other than what it was intended for……FIRST AID. It is not to be used for costumes, jokes, pranks or competitions etc. The day they do this you can guarantee that item will be needed in an emergency!!! So I pose the following question to them in 'Tales of Superblue': Do you want to be the one to explain to a family that the vital piece of first aid kit was missing when it was needed because you used it to dress up as an Egyptian mummy for a laugh? No? I thought not….

First aid kits will be placed in a variety of areas and be accessible for use by trained personnel. Not going to bore you now, it's the usual website to find out more www. SUPERBLUE HAPPY HOLIDAYS.com

I feel a bit like a nagging nanny myself at the moment but some things just need to be said for the sake of completeness in any chapter of a book such as this. The sentence normally begins with the statement 'It goes without saying' and then the author goes right ahead and says it anyway…….

Oh well there's no way around it I suppose……It goes without saying that neither they nor you should never mess with anything you don't understand or aren't qualified to handle or repair etc. Particularly electrics, chemicals, machinery…er…no actually I will take that back. Not particularly anything. Don't mess with ANYTHING you're not qualified to!!!

FIRE OR EVACUATION

One thing that I can say with some certainty is that they must have a procedure for evacuating any of the venues on your holiday centre. This is a critical part of the Entertainments Managers and 'coats' job and as I have alluded to elsewhere in the book people will be looking to them for guidance and leadership in any situation that will require this action. There ought to be a person designated as the fire officer at their centre so they should seek them out and make sure the very minimum they know 'off by heart' is………..

- The procedure in the event of fire or other reason to evacuate
- Where extinguishers are and what type of fire they are for
- Where all emergency exits are located

However it is also in your own interest to take note of any fire or evacuation notices within your rooms, chalets, caravans, clubhouses, theatres and programmes etc

Such events are thankfully very rare indeed but it never hurts to be prepared now does it?

And that's pretty much it for the corporate side of things.

PARTY ANIMAL

Please do bear in mind that your holiday will mean long days at times. It is important to keep yourself in good physical and mental condition. Most centres have gyms these days so why not take advantage of this, what should be free, amenity but ensure you are either familiar with the sports equipment or take an induction session. By their very nature holiday centres are located in some of the loveliest areas in the country making going for a walk or even jogging a real pleasure and of course there's always the pool to enjoy. If you are on an all inclusive or half board holiday enjoy the variety but try as much as possible to include your 5 a day fruit and veg and if you're on a self catering basis all I can say is shop well. Now I really am going to sound like your mum but it's a fact of life that a food or tummy bug can spread like wildfire through a population such as holiday centres and even the most salubrious cruise liners. Washing your hands before preparing a meal is an essential part of your health regime as is doing so after going to the bathroom. In many places you will now find they ask guests to use anti-bacterial sprays before entering dining areas. Please don't wait to be asked always use these if they are available. End of sermon!

MID SEASON BLUES

Is a generic term, but it is a little misleading in as much as these can strike any 'coat', Entertainments Manager or member of staff at any time. I am obviously not talking to you as a medical expert here so professional advice should always be sought. The simple fact is that all those hours of rushing about being the life and soul of the party, the constant smiling and being nice to everyone, the stress of show-time or putting on their own cabaret, the pressures of managing an exciting and full programme as well as dealing with the odd awkward customer or two and living in each other's pockets 24 hrs a day 7 days a week will take its toll on a person. And let's not forget, that what they are, a human being, and we humans can only do so much before we need a break from it all. Different people will have different points where they need this respite from those activities so while I ask them to please keep a watchful eye on each other for signs that someone is suffering from the 'blues' I also ask you to bring any signs of stress or fatigue to the attention of a manager. Again not talking from a medical standpoint but as a layman having witnessed it over the years it's basically a form of mental and or physical exhaustion. It would be very kind of you to assist Entertainments Managers and be on the lookout for telltale traits that one of the team may need a little help. So what should you be looking for? Anything out of the ordinary is the best way to answer that to be honest. I know that sounds a bit wishy washy but it's just about the truth of it. If someone wants to sleep all of the time or is irritable or starts to look thin, pale or generally run down these would be obvious signs that that person needs some sort of attention. But don't hinder your observations by narrowing your parameters to such obviousness. Anything out of the ordinary are the watchwords here, for example someone who is being over exuberant in their smiling and friendliness may well be overcompensating for the fact that they feel lousy inside or even, god forbid, taking something to 'keep them going'. Someone that starts to drink more than usual or is becoming unusually untidy or dirty can be signs. Anything out of the ordinary anything at all no matter how small. Entertainments managers should be prepared to rearrange schedules to allow this person some well deserved and needed time off. I would like to think 'coats' would rally around and assist the manager, in the short term at least, to give this person the time off without it affecting the programme too drastically. After all it may be their turn in the future and they will hopefully be there for them. I think it's important to stress, however, that any illness or suspected illness, mental or physical should receive the appropriate professional medical attention at the earliest opportunity.

ALCOHOL

You are in a holiday environment and while having fun and enjoying the odd alcoholic beverage it is very easy to get carried away with the lifestyle. I have forgotten many a party I was at during those heady 'superblue' days. The only message here is to try and be a bit sensible and drink in moderation. Department of Health guidelines state that men can drink between 3-4 units of alcohol per day without serious risk to health. This amount is reduced to between 2-3 units per day for women. These daily amounts apply whether you drink every day, once or twice a week, or occasionally. The NHS website states that alcohol affects different people in different ways. You can be affected a lot more quickly if you've got a small body frame, you haven't eaten or you're not used to drinking. Women can be affected by alcohol more quickly than men as they are often smaller and their bodies contain less water.

One unit is considered to be 10ml of pure alcohol. A unit of alcohol is equal to about half a pint of normal strength lager, cider or bitter, a pub measure (25ml) of spirits, or a 50ml pub measure of fortified wine (such as sherry or port). It's important to bear in mind that different drinks are different strengths so you can't always be sure how many units you've had. This is especially true if you're drinking export beers, high strength beers or pouring your own measures at home as they are usually far more generous than pub measures.

The NHS gives the following as a basic guide to units of alcohol:

- A pint of ordinary strength lager = 2 units
- A pint of strong lager = 3 units
- A pint of bitter = 2 units
- A pint of ordinary strength cider = 2 units
- A 175ml glass of red or white wine = 2 units (approximately)
- A pub measure of spirits = 1 unit
- An alcopop = 1.5 units (approximately)
- A can of beer or lager = 1.5 units

The NHS advice is to have a few days each week where you don't drink at all, but don't 'store up' your units and then binge drink. Binge drinking can affect your personal safety and put you at risk of serious health problems.

When it comes to smoking......don't! Well what did you expect me to say? The law has actually helped those that want to work in the industry with the introduction of the smoking ban in 2007. I dread to think how much smoke I inhaled over the years even though I have never had a single puff of a cigarette in my life...........and quickly moving on...**Do yourself a big favour and get lost!**

That's right you heard correctly....get lost. No not you my lovely guest. I tell Entertainment Managers and 'coats' to try and get away from the place altogether on their days off and even on their own at times. If they are doing the job properly they will always be invited to join guests on their day off and now and again that is fine. But I really recommend that they give themselves a complete break from it now and again if not once a week. Especially if they are the Entertainments Manager or in another specialised role because in my experience, once its known you are on site, you are never left alone and so don't actually get the mental rest bite that they deserve and need. In the short term this may not be too much of a problem but they need to be planning a sensible work – private life balance. You will recall what I said regarding so called mid-season blues and looking out for each other during these times. Well time off can often be an essential part of getting through this period. Again you can greatly assist by understanding if a Manager or 'Coat' politely declines to join you on their day off and generally not disturbing them on these days.

SEX

Of course I realise that you will be expecting all sorts of jovial innuendoes out of me on this subject but I'm afraid I am going to have to disappoint you on this occasion. The simple fact of the matter is that it's a serious subject in the context of your health and well being. I have no intention of either being judgmental or giving you the old 'birds and the bees' talk but to straightforwardly say 'play safe'. There are a number of sexually transmitted diseases out there meaning that not wearing protection with anyone but your regular partner is foolhardy to say the least. We all know about aids but sexually transmitted infections that are passed on through intimate sexual contact also include, amongst others, chlamydia, syphilis, and gonorrhoea. I would suggest the NHS Direct is a MUST visit website before you embark on your journey as a 'young holiday maker' or 'coat'. Part of the site is called the emergency contraception zone. This has a lot of the information you will need but also advice and where to get help and support if you need it including if you have forgotten to take precautions before intercourse.

Please Remember To Always Stay:

Safe sex

Assess risks

Fire, evacuation knowledge

Eat well, exercise and drink in moderation

RSPCA

Please don't forget the health and safety of our four legged, feathered or aquatic friends. If you have any issues or concerns regarding any animal or its welfare whether wild or tame contact your local vet or visit **www.rspca.org.uk** for advice and assistance. *Thank you*.

Visit SUPERBLUE HAPPY HOLIDAYS.com the home of honest holiday reviews

CHAPTER TWENTY SIX

NOW JUST IN CASE YOU MAY HAVE BEEN INSPIRED HERE IS......

How to become a holiday centre entertainer
'A COAT'

Take yourself all the way back to the very first page of the book. You know the one, a five year old little boy lost in a massive park, a frantic mother desperately trying to find him when suddenly.......................that voice, that tiny little voice booming out over the sand pit and paddling pool. A tiny little five year old, singing both the male and female parts of a pop song to a packed audience. A five year old that took himself up on stage and told the compere that he wanted to sing that song for those people! Was that little boy destined to be an entertainer? I think so don't you?

Surly that was too young to be making a start in the business wasn't it?

No actually many a star began treading the boards early in life maybe not all as early as five but early enough. The point is I am often asked at what age should someone start working towards becoming a 'coat'? And I think we just answered that one didn't we?

As you can imagine it is quite often a parent that is enquiring on behalf of their son or daughter which is quite handy really because the answer as you will now know is?....... Why it's as young as you like of course.

But that's not to say you will ever be too old either, oh no, my philosophy is if you have a dream or a goal in life.....go for it. I can tell you from personal experience that if you believe in yourself and are determined enough you can succeed and achieve things others only dream of at any age. But that is '*so*' for another book.

I have said many times in this book however, that the most important thing is of course a person's personality and I resolutely stand by that but you can hedge your bets and give yourself or your child, a good head start at any age. There are a myriad of things you can do to ensure you are eminently employable on a holiday centre entertainments team when the time comes.

- Taking dancing, singing or drama lessons is always a good move
- Some of you may even be lucky enough to go to a stage school but please don't lose your personality while there keep your feet well and truly on the ground. Remember if you're going for a job at a holiday centre you can't afford to be a precocious little so and so, you will be calling the bingo and sitting on the floor with the kids just like the rest of us!
- Taking part, learning the rules or gaining qualifications to any sport will undoubtedly prove to be an asset.
- In very much the same vein taking part in or running keep fit classes can only improve your resumé
- Any kind of child welfare, education or entertainment experience is good, qualifications are great
- Whether you just attend a local first aid course or go as far as joining the St John's Ambulance Brigade being trained to any level looks good on your curriculum vitae

- It doesn't hurt to visit places where you can watch, listen and learn about aspects of the job that may otherwise be a mystery to you. Bingo, a snooker hall, finding out when a local pub holds its darts and pool matches, even going along to a club when they hold a race or casino evening are all good examples of what could be a beneficial 'field trip' for you. Please note however that whilst these and many other venues are all brilliant news on your CV and allow you to discuss these subjects with some authority in an interview, the overriding factor when considering such ventures is personal safety. Make very sure you are happy that any venue you intend to visit is a reputable concern and frequented by legitimately decent customers. A simple phone call to the local police licensing officer will normally yield a response that will help you decide whether to go there or look for another establishment to further your education in that particular sphere. When dealing with venues that require membership to gain entry. I have found that a courtesy call or letter to the owner or manager is normally sufficient to facilitate a one off admission and can also go some way to ensuring your safety as those that are amicable enough to arrange a visit for you, tend to take care of you when you are there, nonetheless carry out the checks as I advocate.

- Start putting an act together and ensure you have a good strong audition piece
- Enter talent shows all around the country and get used to performing for and socialising with people from all walks of life and varied cultural backgrounds
- Attend as many auditions as you can for as diverse a number of roles or jobs that you can. Don't however necessarily take the first job you are offered if it's not quite right for you. Use it as good experience and keep trying until you get the one you want

- Agents? It's difficult to give blanket advice on this subject to be honest. I have met both great and bad agents over the years. The reality is that agents have their place in the entertainment industry and if you get a decent one they can be very good for your career. Do remember though that you don't need an agent to work at a holiday centre you can get there very easily under your own steam. Some companies won't accept you via an agent in fact as they prefer to directly recruit. Never pay an agent any fees up front, if they are a decent agent they can get you decent work, they will then be doing very nicely on the commission thank you very much! If you are tempted to work overseas via an agent be extremely careful and we will discuss that prospect shortly.

- By far and away one of the very best ways to prepare for the role of **Holiday Camp Entertainer** is to go on holiday as many times as you can to as many different centres as you can and observe those already in action. Remember what I have taught you in this book and see how they compare. Be inspired by those that excel and learn to avoid bad practice from those that don't. Make it known that you wish to enter the trade while you are at any parks, villages, centres, hotels, sites, resorts or camps you may be surprised at how much the 'coats' will allow you to join in and learn, dependent on your age and ability. It has even been known for guests to actually be offered a position on a team because they performed and fitted in so well whilst on holiday.

- You normally have to be 18 yrs old to be employed as a 'coat'
- Do remember that you don't necessarily have to have an actual talent as a stage performer to work on an entertainments team, a great personality is the key ingredient that a manager is looking for and the ability to communicate *fun fun fun* to the guests is a talent in itself. I have shown you many avenues to ensure you are a good candidate for the position the rest is up to you.

When you're ready it'll be time to apply for the best job in the world
Time you became a

CHAPTER TWENTY SEVEN

HOW TO CHOOSE YOUR CAMP AND WHO TO WORK FOR

As you have seen in chapter two there are many companies and independents to choose from. Pontins, Butlins, Warners, Potters, Haven & British Holidays, Park Resorts, Searles Holiday Resort, Parkdean holidays, South Devon Holidays, Hoeseasons, Cinque Ports Holidays to name but a few. But which one is right for you? Visit Visit Visit and then when you have had a good look visit again. I realise this is a very simplistic view on things but trust me, the reason it's so simplistic, is that it is simply the best way to find out which sort of holiday centre fits with your idea of what being a 'coat' is all about. You don't necessarily have to go for a whole week even. There are plenty of short mid week and weekend breaks just about everywhere now.

Many of you will have been going to the same centre for years, probably since you were small children and loyalty is a good attribute. But before you settle on that company never mind that actual holiday centre, do yourself the favour of looking at least one other type of venue and or company. There can be vast differences between centres. For instance learning your craft at a very large centre with state of the art equipment and stage management facilities, performing in front of thousands of people often in theatre like complexes. However at these centres you may well not get to spend much time with the guests and could just be a face in amongst many others on that stage, which is great if that suits you. Whereas you could be at a smaller centre, dashing around like the proverbial blue bottomed fly, running all sorts of activities during the day, constantly interacting with your guests and at night being the absolute star of the show where everyone knows your name. The disparity vis-à-vis where you could end up without any research into it at all is actually that stark a reality. It is particularly crucial that you allow yourself this kind of exploration before you embark on your very first season. Because choosing the wrong place or type of place to begin the lovely journey of adventure and wonderment, that is holiday centre entertainment, could have the catastrophic opposite effect and indeed in actual fact put you off it for life. And that would be a terrible shame and waste of a potentially brilliant 'coat'.

Visit Visit Visit

What?

Well you know by now, that when I feel something is important I keep on nagging you about it.....so anyway

Visit Visit Visit

When you do go to visit also look for several detailed points such as those below and make a note of them. They could help you decide which camp offers the best overall potential for your future and so determine where to go in the end.

- ♥ Is there a good team spirit
- ♥ Does there appear to be good leadership
- ♥ Is the programme good
- ♥ Look at the shows they are putting on
- ♥ Does everyone get a fair share or is the Entertainments Manager, for example, hogging the limelight
- ♥ Are the 'coats' allowed and or encouraged to perform their own cabarets
- ♥ What sort of amenities are there
- ♥ Talk to the 'coats' not necessarily divulging your interest in employment at first – get the true picture of how they feel about working there or at that type of centre
- ♥ Ask them about wages, working conditions, days off, accommodation and contracts etc
- ♥ If you can, talk to those 'coats' or ex 'coats' about where else they have worked and what they liked or disliked about those centres

It is never a good idea to base your decision on one person's opinions. People have good and bad experiences which can cloud their view of any on these points. It is far better to get a well rounded straw poll if you can and make your mind up from that. Even if there are differing viewpoints with that poll, you will still pick up on the aspects you need to concentrate on whether positive or negative. Watch out for constants such, as the same name cropping up time and again. Take heed of similar, positive or negative, impressions that person has left on a variety of people particularly if you are meeting them at different centres and that same name still pops up in conversation. Take note of the impact that person has made upon the lives of those commenting about them. Again be as alive to the encouragingly positive endorsements as you naturally will be to the vitriolic negative complaints.

The same theory applies to venue or company names that have a habit of slipping into the conversation. But remember to get a rounded view if you can.

As if there weren't enough variables for you to contend with another thing to bear in mind is that centres change from time to time. Why do they change? They change for any number of reasons to be honest such as new private ownership, being taken over by another company with a completely different ethos or even just cost cutting and whilst the introduction of a new Entertainments Manager will be your prime concern the replacement of any key manager can have a dramatic effect on life at that centre for example.

So once you have found your perfect place with your ideal company or independent owner, as much as you can, make a final check that things are as they were before committing yourself to it.

Of course we live in the real world and this is not always how things are going to go and you may find yourself being offered something at short notice and decide to take the chance. Well good luck to you is my overriding message and for the most part if it's a reputable company or decent independent your chances of being happy or at least not put off for life are quite good. If you should fall unluckily don't despair, it's not the end of the world try to keep your chin up and look for your next move. If it's a bullying or sexual harassment situation remember what I have told you about dealing with those.

If you are being brow beaten into staying by an agent that has sent you there remember he or she is only after their cut of your wages so if you walk out they lose it all and possibly the contract to supply other 'coats' in the future. So you see you're already a valuable commodity. Stay calm and negotiate with them and they will usually find a solution even if that is swapping you with another 'coat' from another centre. Remember to report any bullying or harassment of any kind so as to protect the incoming 'coat'. Because you are such a valuable asset to an agent don't be shy about negotiating a deal with them in the first place, you can often barter your services for better wages, hours and living conditions so be confident and don't sign anything until your happy with the deal being offered. If you are going to sign a contract with an agent in my opinion it's always worth talking to both a solicitor and Equity to have the contract and indeed the agent checked out.

And before taking up any contract consider some if not all of the following:

❖ Visit Visit Visit 'enough said'
❖ Talk to the centre owner and or general manager
❖ Talk to the Entertainments Manager
❖ Check what duties you are going to be expected to perform
❖ Are you going to be asked to 'run' the children's programme? for example
❖ Is the centre being given an accurate picture of your abilities by the agent
❖ If not make it clear that they are not
❖ Is this the right move for you!!!
❖ Always be suspicious of an agent or indeed anyone that will send you on any job, booking, season or anything else without at least meeting you in person if you are a 'personality coat' or actually seeing you perform if your an entertainer
❖ If abroad make very very very sure it's a non consummating gig

Once you have ensured all of the above is legal, above board, honest and straight, and you have decided to venture forth, you can be somewhat happy in the knowledge that you won't be alone. You will always have me there with you now and most of the answers are right here at your fingertips plus you can also check out the 'HOLIDAY STAFF' link on www.SUPERBLUE HAPPY HOLIDAYS.com.

CHAPTER TWENTY EIGHT
ABROAD AND CRUISING

CRUISE LINES

These are seen as the pinnacle of holiday centre entertainment and let's not forget that's what a cruise ship is after all, a floating holiday camp. Swish? Yes. Beautiful? Without a doubt. Flamboyant? Indubitably (well buoyant would be good wouldn't it). Ostentatious? Unquestionably. Convivial? Incontestably. They are certainly all of these things but at the end of the day still a floating holiday centre. They are much more affordable these days and just like the rest of the holiday sector there is something for everyone. Having recently appeared on the Sea Princess and The Balmoral myself, I am only too well aware of the fabulous feeling of appearing in a wonderful auditorium full of appreciative passengers used to top quality entertainment. But when you get down to basics pretty much everything I have laid out before you in this manuscript applies to this type of holiday entertainment in just the same manner as it does for all the others.

DISNEY 'MAGICAL' SHIPS

Yes they really do exist and what fabulous fun too.

I came across my first Disney ship when I was on the Sea Princess and we docked next to her on a Caribbean island. The music, the colour, the fun and laughter, wonderful! As the passengers left for shore and arrived back on board there was Mickey, Miney, Donald, Pluto and all the other marvellous characters larger than life to see them off and greet them back again.

The best bit of the day however, was just as dusk was setting in and it was very clear that the two crews were trying to beat each other to see who could get away first. Our Captain kept calling over the tannoy system for a particular couple, who were obviously late arriving back on board and stopping us from leaving.

Then suddenly it happened!!!…….The Disney ship lit up in all her Technicolor glory! Wow! All of her passengers came onto the decks and were waving to us. It was evident that they were having such a great party time of it! As if she hadn't put on enough of a show, as she gracefully slipped her mooring to head back out to sea all eyes were drawn to her proud captain stood in the wheelhouse. He slowly raised his arm in a deliberate and provocative manner reaching for the chain that would sound the enormous fog horns that a ship sounds off as it leaves port. He and our captain had eye to eye contact, a look of satisfaction was on the Disney Captains face as he developed a grin that said "avast me harties we won we beat you we are leaving port first, you can follow in my wake" he then ostentatiously took hold of the chain and as we all waited with baited breath to hear her loud victory fog horns sound off, he paused for one last smirk at our captain as much as to say "you ready for this matey?" and with a glint in his eye he pulled it …………….. "When you wish upon a star, makes no difference who you are"

Fog horn what fog horn? No fog horn just that wonderfully happy Disney tune ringing out in the warm still Caribbean night air.

What a moment! One I will cherish forever.

As their Captain smiled cheerfully at ours and gave him a friendly respectful salute the passengers on both ships went wild cheering and waving at each other. And then she was off, off into the darkness that was the Caribbean Sea only it wasn't so dark anymore there was this breathtaking beacon of brilliantly colourful sparkling light, an island of fun joyfully but majestically slipping through the moonlight waves reverberating to all of your, favourite Disney tunes. I swear the dolphins, that could clearly be seen all around her, were diving, spinning, flipping over and genuinely dancing and even singing with delight.

We sailed in her wake for some time but that magical moment seamed to transcend the distance between the two ships and pass into the hearts of both sets of passengers. I am sure all aboard her felt it for the entire fabulous time on their cruise but for one night at least the Disney spirit of fun, laughter, kindness, well being and let's face it……love, had spread infectiously over another.

For those of you that are considering children's entertainment I highly recommend that you take a look at working on a Disney Cruise ship. In fact whatever type of entertainer you are, except adult material obviously, you should look at this. Especially if you're a big kid like me and love the thought of working with Donald Duck and Co.

There are other great cruise lines to look at however and all offer something slightly different. You can try these directly but most of them use specialist agents so ask them which ones to contact also check out Superblue's website below..........................***Again never pay any agent up front.***

I have loved my Princess adventures and they are wonderfully beautiful ships as are, Royal Caribbean, Fred Olson and P&O etc. I did personally find Carnival cruises slightly more American orientated for passengers but they do employ British Cruise Staff.

Don't forget to give your honest cruise line reviews and read what others say at:
SUPERBLUE HAPPY HOLIDAYS.com

ABROAD

The very first thing that I am going to say on this subject is going to sound like a right cop out on my behalf but I would like to think that by now you will know very well that I would never short change you in anyway shape or form. So don't be despondent that this chapter is so small. As a matter of fact the only thing that has made it this small is that I have told you just about everything you will ever need to know throughout the rest of the book. I said it would sound like a right royal cop out didn't I? But honestly if you follow the general principals and guidelines I have given you thus far you won't be going far wrong and indeed will soon shine when working alongside others that haven't read this book. But let's just highlight some points that are worthy of extra attention when it comes to leaving these good old shores in search of adventures further afield.

Is it worth it? Well I can only speak for myself and an exceptionally good friend of mine but I had some of my best times abroad. At 'Club Tropicana' for example, for all the difficulties I endured to begin with, gave me one of the best and dearest friends a man could ever ask for, some of the funniest stories in my repertoire and turned out to be one of the most influential lessons in my education at the university of life and I personally think any new experience is good for the soul.

That being said personal safety is of paramount importance wherever you are but being in a foreign country can have its own dangers and pitfalls so.......

Never go anywhere without having a signed contract and before you even contemplate signing anything: *check the following*:

- If you're not sure about anything and, or, it's not a well known reputable company, have a copy of any contract looked at and checked over by a solicitor and, or, equity. If the agent is genuine, bona fide and truly above board they will have no problem with this.
- Be very wary of anyone who tries to talk you out of this!
- Remember what I said about anyone that offers you a job without even seeing you, never mind knowing what your talents are? Well this really does speak for itself. But you need to know that there are unfortunately some very unscrupulous characters out there that will purport to be agents or managements looking out for your best interest. When in fact all they want to do is ship you abroad as quickly as

possible grab their finder's fee and then leave you to fend for yourself, in all sorts of unsavoury places with sleazy people, doing things that are abhorrent to you.

Scared?
Good!!

- That was what I was after. But not for any literary effect, you see this is not a made up tale by any stretch of the imagination. This unfortunately is what happens in real life. I really really really want you to think about it very carefully before taking up any position, job or season abroad in any country.
- Obviously some are going to be inherently safer than others but if you treat them all with the same unyielding respect for yourself and your safety you will be doing the right thing.
- So make very sure that the agent you are talking to or the company whose advertisement you are answering is a reputable one
- Speak to Equity
- Ask 'The Stage' paper
- Ask the police
- Look up the Government websites
- Ask another agent that you may have worked for
- If no one knows of this agency, person or company WHY???
- If anything does not sit right my best advice would be to walk away from it let equity know and you may keep others from possibly making a terrible mistake too!
- Any decent agent reading this will welcome it because it keeps their trade clean and free from the predators

CONSUMMATION

This maybe something that you have not associated with entertainment contracts before but it is something that you need to be extremely aware of now. It does not necessarily have the same meaning that you would ordinarily give it. You absolutely categorically need to check any contract, particularly a dance contract, and be even more sceptical if you're not even a trained dancer, but to be completely sure ***any contract*** is a non-consummation contract. In other words you are being hired for your entertainment talents only. If it's anything but a pure and simple bona fide, authentic, genuine, legitimate, true, above board, real, valid and legal contract to perform at a reputable establishment through a reputable agent or work at a reputable holiday centre for a reputable company **DON'T TOUCH IT WITH A BARGE POLE!!!**

They come in all shapes, sizes and disguises but consummation contracts are more common than people might think, so just as an example, let me tell you that in some counties they are prevalent in nightclubs and lower class hotels. In some instances you may be one of the women who perform several short dance routines throughout the night. But then during the lengthy intervals of your 'show' you are required to sit with the guests and encourage them to buy you cocktails. For every cocktail a guest buys for you, you earn a percentage of the sale. You can see how easy it might be to be fooled into believing you were hired for a dance contract in a beautiful country only to find yourself actually acting as an escort in effect. I would hate to think you might get caught up in this, or heaven forbid anything worse, because I had not advised you of its existence. Unfortunately **some** of these venues remain successful because ladies from poorer countries are targeted and by and large they have no means to buy a return ticket home. While we are from a fairly affluent country, your circumstances could be such that you find yourself stuck in a nightmare scenario.

Consummation is an industry term that may be used in an advert or contract. But also watch out for other terms or mention of things such as 'guest contact' or 'interaction' out of, what would be normal context. It's not infallible but another indicator may well be the length of time you would be expected to be in a nightclub for example.

But apart from a few bits and bobs once you are there working for a safe reputable agent or company most things are much the same as in the book. Please remember all we said about health and safety, many countries that you will be going to will have a radically different view of this from ours, some are actually non-existent. But if you are with that reputable firm, I keep on about they should have covered all this with you before you left good old Blighty or certainly before you begin work out there. It is particularly important to Entertainments Managers because there are so many different aspects to consider, how many lifeguards to have for instance? You will be surprised at just how many countries the minimum number is.....none! Where have they got the local children's club staff from? Are they trained? Are they safe? How much do you and the guests have to pay the onsite doctor before they will treat you? Minefield or what? Well that's my point it can be, so stick to the reputable firms. 'Coats' however can still play their part in their own health and safety as well as that of their colleagues and guests by following the guidelines described in that chapter and fitting them around local laws.

Obvious differences in health and safety are going to be:

THE SUN

Ensure you have proper protection and use it wisely avoiding the hottest parts of the day if possible or covering up during them

SEX

A bit like the sun really, ensure you have proper protection and use it wisely. Nuff said

VISA OR WORK PERMIT

In many counties you will need a visa or work permit – Check with the Embassy or Consulate for that country again before you sign anything.

Did the agent or company tell you anything at all about it?

Was what they did tell you correct?

Have you got time to get what you need before they want you to go?

Do you meet the criteria needed to obtain one in the first place?

GAMBLING ETC

There are counties that take a very dim view of their laws being broken especially by foreign nationals. Again if you have paid attention you should have no need to worry because you will be working for a repu.........ok ok no need to shout at me.

If not and you are being asked to conduct any sort of gaming event or indeed anything that seems to you to be beyond 'ordinary straight forward' entertainment check it out. The internet is a wonderful thing and you can always phone the British Embassy or Consulate for the country that you are in.

IT'S ALWAYS BETTER TO BE SAFE THAN SORRY!!!

There are many places that you can go to check up on safe working abroad but I would suggest Equity for contractual enquiries and the official Foreign and Commonwealth Office Website as good starting points www.fco.gov.uk.

Check out the Holiday Staff link on **SUPERBLUE HAPPY HOLIDAYS.com.**

THE CURTAIN CALL

"AND FOR MY FINAL BOW"

<u>The BIGGEST rule of all</u>

Well that's just about it, I have said all I have to say for the time being and have thoroughly enjoyed writing this book for you. It does contain many aspects that are just my opinion of course, I don't have a string of letters after my name, indeed I have made many a mistake and had more than a few mishaps along the way but have been up front with you and highlighted many of them. However when you consider the book began with me on stage at the tender age of 5yrs old, takes you through my being part of and managing entertainment within the RAF and Holiday Centres for around twenty years and then you take into account that while life has taken me on some exciting excursions since then, I still perform stand up comedy to this very day, it could be said that they are opinions based on 50 years of experience. I do hope I have given you enough to encourage you to stand up for your rights because as I always say.........

"You've paid for it after all"

It has been necessary to illustrate the downside of some things covered in the book in order to emphasise the reasons why Entertainments Managers, "coats" and the holiday companies etc should be treating you correctly in the first place. Please don't get too hung up on those unpleasant consequences however, because you are now aware of their existence and are armed with the knowledge that prevents you putting up with these situations. All that is left for you to do is concentrate on fulfilling the BIGGEST rule of all.........
Enjoy yourself
Be Safe, Be Happy, Have FUN FUN FUN and ***ENJOY!!!***

I have so enjoyed talking to you, it has taken me four years to complete this little extravaganza but you're worth it. I am really looking forward to meeting many of you in person during my travels.

Happy Holidays!

Don't forget to check out what others say about their holiday experiences
At Home, Abroad and on Cruises
Before you book anything
Also *have your say* by adding your own review at:

www.SUPERBLUE HAPPY HOLIDAYS.com

You can also follow '*Superblue*' on
Facebook (Superblue Happy Holidays)
Twitter (I was Superblue)

'Superblue' and the 'Superblue' logo, Trade Mark (word mark) are patented patent number 2502776A & B

Visit SUPERBLUE HAPPY HOLIDAYS.com

With the young ones for their own pages and find out how they can become one of Superblue's Junior 'Super Agents'

Acknowledgements

There are so many people that I have to thank for making me who I am today
Some of them through kindness and others for teaching me how
to take care of myself the hard way

I have no intentions of dwelling on the latter so I would like to mention and thank those that have been so loving and kind to me along this journey

This whole thing began with a fantastic Mum as so many stories do, but there are tales that will never make this or any other book that make my Mum quite the most remarkable person I have ever met. Have I been a model son? No probably not even close but I hope this little effort makes her as proud of her little boy as she was the day she lost me to the stage at 5 years old. Mum you're simply the most courageous lady I know, I also know I would not be here now if it weren't for your strength, love and bravery..........Your simply the best Mother in the world and I love you very very much and dedicate this book to you.

It must be difficult to imagine someone taking 4 years to write a book having to completely restructure it after 2 years and, all but, begin again. It must seem like a nightmare for that person, going to work and rushing home to try and get another bit of a chapter done, locked away in a back room in all weathers tapping away at the keyboard, never getting a break or even a proper holiday because the holiday is always to gather even more material for the book, yes it must be really hard to imagine how much that writer has suffered. Well actually I enjoyed it most of the time but let me tell you right here and now, only when it was all over did I selfishly stop to think about the person who had to share all of that with me and did so without a complaint, quite the opposite in fact.....not only were they going through it with me but they were sacrificing so much more over this time, this can be a very lonely time for them, yet they heaped praise and compliments onto me for my efforts and gave me unconditional support and even massaged my ego at times when I began to doubt myself. They followed me on holidays that I now know they didn't really want to go on, but they went anyway because I needed to for the book. Trust me without the unconditional love, support and patience of my dear wife Linda there is no way on earth you would be reading this book today. I know she won't mind sharing the dedication of this book with my Mum because that's the type of lovely lady I am so fortunate enough to be married to....So my darling Mrs Superblue (as some of my mates call her now) after 4 long years this is dedicated to you with all my love......Thank you xxx

I talk about Phil and Nick and Nick and Phil (I love them both so dearly they are like brothers to me so I can't put one before the other) But I hope you won't mind me publicly thanking them both once more for all they have done for and meant to me over the years. A man could not ask for any better, more loyal or wonderful friends. Thank you is too small a statement for being the best mates in the world and for always being there but I can't think of a bigger one so **THANK YOU** my friends.

Superblue the character comes from photographs taken of me dressed as him at holiday centres in the 80's but it takes a special kind of artist to take a photograph of a subject and magically bring it to life. My friend Bob Cooke did more than just that he captured the very essence of who *Superblue* was, and indeed who I am. I will be always grateful to him for this and hope it inspires many more of you to contact him and let him work his incredible artistic talents on a book or project for you. Bob thank you so much for Superblue the Character long may he be enjoyed.

You can find Bob at: **Email** - cookygraphics@gmail.com **Office** - 01980 862 009 **Mobile** - 07866 280 237, **Write to** - Chalk Hill Cottage • Tytherley Road • Winterslow • Salisbury • SP5 1PZ

I want to express my never ending gratitude to someone who has become a very dear friend. He has managed me for some years now in situations that can be difficult to say the least. But he has been the greatest of men and supported and encouraged me over the four years that I have been writing this book, while we got on with the sometimes arduous, tasks before us. I would never have been able to juggle both and keep going while trying to do my best without his massive kindness, understanding and support. So Mr Chris Smart I humbly thank you from the bottom of my heart for all of the above but mostly for your friendship.

I dedicate the Junior **SUPER AGENTS** to my fabulous neighbours and friends Michelle and Keith who have made my life so much easier over the past few years, and to all of their wonderful children, including Ben, Ellie and Jamie who were the inspiration for the **SUPER AGENTS**

There are so many other terrific family and friends too numerous to mention but you know who you are and I send my love....Enzo get the Peroni's chilled mate!

Thank you all and God Bless

***

2229083R00255

Printed in Great Britain
by Amazon.co.uk, Ltd.,
Marston Gate.